CRITICAL CONVERSATIONS IN CANADIAN PUBLIC LAW

CRITICAL CONVERSATIONS IN CANADIAN PUBLIC LAW

Edited by Jena McGill, Karen Drake,
Kyle Kirkup, Anne Levesque, and
Joshua Sealy-Harrington

University of Ottawa Press

2025

Les Presses de l'Université d'Ottawa
University of Ottawa **Press**

Les Presses de l'Université d'Ottawa / University of Ottawa Press (PUO-UOP) is North America's flagship bilingual university press, affiliated to one of Canada's top research universities. PUO-UOP enriches the intellectual and cultural discourse of our increasingly knowledge-based and globalized world with peer-reviewed, award-winning books.

www.Press.uOttawa.ca

Library and Archives Canada Cataloguing in Publication

Title: Critical conversations in Canadian public law / edited by Jena McGill, Karen Drake, Kyle Kirkup, Anne Levesque, and Joshua Sealy-Harrington.
Names: McGill, Jena, editor. | Drake, Karen (Karen Anne), editor | Kirkup, Kyle, editor. | Levesque, Anne (Lawyer), editor. | Sealy-Harrington, Joshua, editor
Description: Includes bibliographical references. | Text chiefly in English; some text in French.
Identifiers: Canadiana (print) 20240439015 | Canadiana (ebook) 20240439058 | ISBN 9780776641898 (softcover) | ISBN 9780776641904 (hardcover) | ISBN 9780776641928 (EPUB) | ISBN 9780776641911 (Open access)
Subjects: LCSH: Public law—Canada.
Classification: LCC KE4120 .C75 2025 | LCC KF4482 .C75 2025 kfmod | DDC 342.71—dc23

Legal Deposit: Fourth Quarter 2025
Library and Archives Canada

Production Team

Copyediting	Valentina D'Aliesio and Jacques Côté
Proofreading	Michelle Fost and Cendrine Audet
Typesetting	Dany Lagueux
Cover design	Benoit Deneault

Cover Image
Denyse Thomasos. *Rally*, 1994. Acrylic on canvas, 274.32 x 426.72 cm. Courtesy of The Estate of Denyse Thomasos and Olga Korper Gallery. © Photo: Andre Beneteau.

uOttawa
PUO-UOP gratefully acknowledges the funding support of the University of Ottawa, the Government of Canada, the Canada Council for the Arts, the Ontario Arts Council and the Government of Ontario.

Canadä

Conseil des arts   Canada Council
du Canada   for the Arts

ONTARIO ARTS COUNCIL
CONSEIL DES ARTS DE L'ONTARIO
an Ontario government agency
un organisme du gouvernement de l'Ontario

Ontario

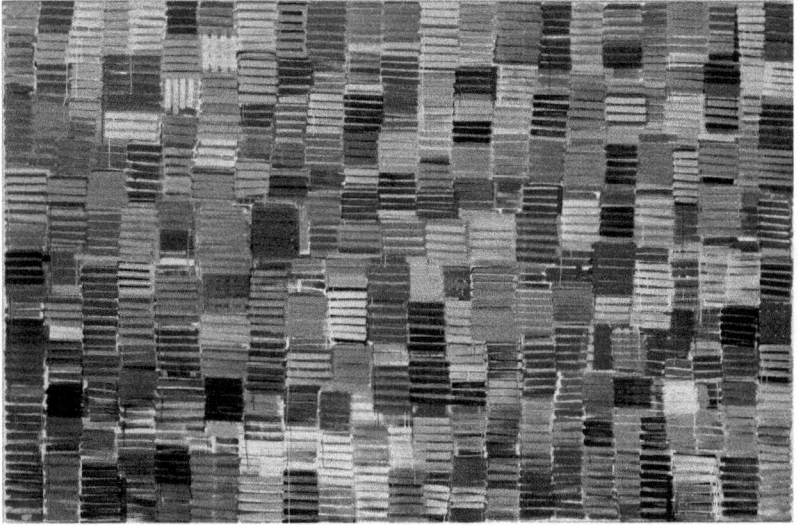

Denyse Thomasos. *Rally*, 1994. Acrylic on canvas, 274.32 x 426.72 cm. Courtesy of The Estate of Denyse Thomasos and Olga Korper Gallery. © Photo: Andre Beneteau.

Denyse Thomasos (October 10, 1964–July 19, 2012)

Born in Port-of-Spain, Trinidad, the acclaimed painter Denyse Thomasos was raised in Toronto and spent most of her professional career in Philadelphia and New York City. Thomasos earned a BA in Painting and Art History from the University of Toronto in 1987. She attended the Skowhegan School of Painting & Sculpture in 1988 and the following year completed her MFA in Painting and Sculpture at Yale School of Art, Yale University. Throughout her career she attended various residencies, such as the Ucross Foundation Artist Residency, in Ucross, Wyoming in 2000 and the Bogliasco Foundation Artist Residency in Genoa, Italy in 2003. She won numerous prestigious awards, including the Guggenheim Fellowship Prize in 1997; the Joan Mitchell Foundation award in 1998; and the New York Foundation for the Arts award in 2008; as well as grants from both the Canada Council and the National Endowment for the Arts. When Thomasos died in 2012, she was at the height of her career, with major museum shows, a full professorship, as well as New York and Toronto gallery representation. The Estate of Denyse Thomasos is represented by Olga Korper Gallery, Toronto.

Table of Contents

SECTION B: POLICING, CRIMINAL LAW, AND THE CARCERAL STATE

List of Figures

Acknowledgements

Thank you to our talented group of contributors, whose work in this collection and elsewhere continues to push the boundaries and assumptions of thinking about public law in all its forms.

This project would not have been possible without the contributions of several talented research assistants. Thank you to Clémentine Mattesco, Sarah-Claude L'Ecuyer, Nora Chahine, Ève Richard, Djoully Samentha Laube, Daniel Kim, Chloe Tessier, Bethanie Wilson, Dania Ahmed and Martin Kreiner. Additionally, we are grateful to the University of Ottawa Faculty of Law Research Office for its financial support of this project and to the staff at the University of Ottawa Press, especially Mireille Piché and Martin Llewellyn, for all of their efforts to bring this collection to life.

Finally, we are indebted to Professor Vanessa MacDonnell, Co-Director of the Public Law Centre at the University of Ottawa, who brought to us the original idea for a collection connecting critical approaches and public law topics and who continues to be an outstanding leader in Canadian public law.

Introduction

Joshua Sealy-Harrington, Karen Drake, Kyle Kirkup,
Anne Levesque, and Jena McGill*

This project began in the midst of some of the most significant social, economic, and political struggles of the past decade: the COVID-19 pandemic;[1] the enforced disappearances of the thousands of Indigenous children in unmarked burial sites linked to Indian Residential Schools, described by the Independent Special Interlocutor for Missing Children and Unmarked Graves and Burial Sites associated with Indian Residential Schools as constituting crimes against humanity;[2] unprecedented uprisings against police violence targeting Black and Indigenous communities and the ongoing harms of colonialism;[3] and, more recently, Israel's continuing

---

* Thank you to Professor Vanessa MacDonnell, Co-Director of the Public Law Centre at the University of Ottawa, who offered helpful feedback on this introduction.

[1] For insightful analyses of how members of equality-deserving groups in Canada were impacted by the pandemic, see e.g. Colleen M Flood et al, *Vulnerable: The Law, Policy and Ethics of COVID-19* (Ottawa: University of Ottawa Press, 2020).

[2] Kimberly Murray, Independent Special Interlocutor for Missing Children and Unmarked Graves and Burial Sites, *Upholding Sacred Obligations: Reparations for Missing and Disappeared Indigenous Children and Unmarked Burials in Canada* (Office of the Independent Special Interlocutor for Missing Children and Unmarked Graves and Burial Sites associated with Indian Residential Schools, 2024) at 79, online: </osi-bis.ca/report/final-report-october-2024-2/>. See also Canadian Geographic, "Unmarked Burial Sites Associated with Indian Residential Schools" (5 April 2024), online: <pathstoreconciliation.canadiangeographic.ca/>.

[3] See e.g. *Tracking (In)Justice: A Living Data Set Tracking Canadian Police-Involved Deaths,* (last visited 23 September 2025) online: <www.trackinginjustice.ca>.

horrors in Gaza, including catastrophic violence, forced displacement, and forced starvation, characterized by Human Rights Watch
and other leading human rights organizations as a genocide against
the Palestinian people.[4]

In their disproportionate impacts on racialized and economically
marginalized communities, Indigenous peoples, persons living with
disabilities, and vulnerable children and elders, these interrelated
events laid bare many of the entrenched inequities upon which so-
called Canada is built. Indeed, Canada began and persists in a state of
legally mediated political, economic, and social struggle. The starting
point for this collection is that it is necessary to understand these contemporary struggles in their continuity to see both how the law is, and
always has been, "bound up with domination and oppression."[5]

This collection seeks to reflect and ignite critical conversations
about the centrality of public law and its institutions, broadly defined
and deeply contested, to the (re)production of current inequities.[6] We
understand this project to be "critical" in two distinct, but interrelated
ways. First, this collection is critical because the various analytical
approaches taken by the authors can be described as falling under the
umbrella of, or engaging with, critical legal studies (CLS) or critical
approaches to law.[7] The CLS movement was born in the context of
Anglo-American law schools in the late 1970s and early 1980s, where

---

[4] Human Rights Watch, *Extermination and Acts of Genocide*, (19 December 2024), online:
<hrw.org/report/2024/12/19/extermination-and-acts-genocide/israel-deliberately-
depriving-palestinians-gaza>. See also Amnesty International, "'You Feel Like You are
Subhuman': Israel's Genocide Against Palestinians in Gaza" (London, UK: Amnesty
International, 2024), online: <amnesty.org/en/documents/mde15/8668/2024/en/>.

[5] Samuel Moyn, "Reconstructing Critical Legal Studies" (2023) 134:1 Yale LJ 77.

[6] According to colonial common law, the field of public law is concerned with the
relationship between government, or "the state," and society. However, Indigenous
legal traditions call into question the foundations of public law by disrupting the
idea of a singular, centralized state and legal system. See e.g. Val Napoleon,
"Thinking About Indigenous Legal Orders" in René Provost & Colleen Sheppard,
eds, *Dialogues on Human Rights and Legal Pluralism* (Dordrecht: Springer, 2013) 229.

[7] See Mari J Matsuda, "Public Response to Racist Speech: Considering the Victim's
Story" (1989) 87 Mich L Rev 2320 at 2323, who coined the term "outsider jurisprudence"
to describe the work of feminist and critical race scholars at American law schools.
In the context of Canadian legal education, see Natasha Bakht et al, "Counting
Outsiders: A Critical Exploration of Outsider Course Enrollment in Canadian Legal
Education" (2007) 45 Osgoode Hall LJ 668 at 672, who explain, "the term outsider [...]
describe[s] those who are members of groups that have historically lacked power in

it marked "the emergence of a new left intelligentsia committed at once to theory and to practise, and creating a radical left worldview in an area [i.e., law] where once there were only variations on the theme of legitimation of the status quo."[8]

The emergence of CLS posed new challenges and opportunities for other progressive legal movements of the 1980s with overlapping or similar commitments. For example, feminist legal theorist Carrie Menkel-Meadow noted that while both CLS and feminist legal theory are concerned with patterns of oppression and domination in law and legal institutions,

> [t]he main difference between the two ways of looking at the world is that the feminist critique starts from the experiential point of view of the oppressed, dominated and devalued, while the critical legal studies critique begins – and, some would argue, remains – in a male-constructed, privileged place in which domination and oppression can be described and imagined but not fully experienced.[9]

Similarly, Mari Matsuda, one of the founding scholars of critical race theory, acknowledged the "similar perspectives and goals of people of colour and critical legal scholars" but called for CLS to move away from abstract conceptualizing and look to the "distinct normative insights" of those who have experienced racial oppression to generate new ideas about justice.[10] These and other challenges to some of the

---

society or have traditionally been outside the realms of fashioning, teaching, and adjudicating the law."

8 Duncan Kennedy, "Critical Labour Law Theory: A Comment" (1981) 4:3 Indus Rel LJ 503 at 506. Key early writings of CLS include Duncan Kennedy, "Form and Substance in Private Law Adjudication" (1976) 89:8 Harv L Rev 1685 and Roberto Mangabeira Unger, "The Critical Legal Studies Movement" (1983) 96:3 Harv L Rev 561. In the Canadian context see e.g. J Stuart Russell, "The Critical Legal Studies Challenge to Contemporary Mainstream Legal Philosophy" (1983) 18:1 Ottawa L Rev 1. For a recent paper touching on the background and status of CLS theory in the American context, see Moyn, *supra* note 5.

9 Carrie Menkel-Meadow, "Feminist Legal Theory, Critical Legal Studies, and the Legal Education or 'The Fem-Crits Go to Law School'" (1988) 38 J Leg Educ 61 at 61. See also Robin West, "Feminism, Critical Social Theory and Law" (1989) 1:5 U Chicago Legal F 59.

10 Mari J Matsuda, "Looking to the Bottom: Critical Legal Studies and Reparations" (1987) 22 Harv CR-CLL Rev 323 at 323, 326.

core tenets of CLS resulted in the evolution of several distinct disciplines and critical approaches to law, many of which focused specifically on intersectional forms of oppression. For example, critical race theory was born from the work of Matsuda and other racialized and Indigenous legal scholars to "repai[r] the absence from critical legal studies of an analysis of how race and racialization are imbricated within legal doctrines and liberal legal frameworks."[11]

Contemporary critical scholars in Canada are diverse and include those employing critical race, feminist, decolonial, critical disability, queer, and other "outsider" theories and perspectives in approaching legal problems.[12] While each of these approaches offers unique, though often complementary and interconnected, insights to the study of law, critical scholars tend to share certain commitments and critical scholarship reflects some common themes. For example, starting points for most critical scholars include, though are not limited to:

- acknowledgment that law is deeply, inextricably intertwined with politics, economics, and social issues;
- an understanding that the law is never value neutral and tends to re-entrench existing power hierarchies in society by serving the interests of historically privileged communities while perpetuating the disadvantage of historically marginalized communities; and
- concern with the material effects of the law (i.e., what the law *does*) and normative questions about the law (i.e., what the law *should be*) instead of the purely descriptive accounts of law (i.e., what the law *is*) that tend to dominate legal scholarship and debate.[13]

---

[11] Brenna Bhandar, "Critical Race Theory" in Peter Cane & Joanne Conaghan, *The New Oxford Companion to Law* (Oxford: Oxford University Press, 2008).

[12] Because CLS did not produce a singular or monolithic body of scholarship, defining it precisely is a challenge. Trying to do so may be antithetical to the CLS project; indeed, some critical scholars, influenced by postmodernism, expressly resist attempts to systematize critical scholarship, instead emphasizing contingency, ambiguity, indeterminacy, and context as key insights of critical approaches.

[13] For a contemporary example of some of these commitments in action, see e.g. Jedediah Britton-Purdy et al, "Building a Law-and-Political-Economy Framework: Beyond the Twentieth-Century Synthesis" (2020) 129:6 Yale LJ 1784.

Ultimately, critical scholars are interested in the relationship between law and (in)justice and are oriented toward change. Indeed, while the contributors to this collection are a diverse group of scholars and legal workers hailing from many distinct intellectual traditions and practice contexts, they share a common political commitment to using scholarship to uncover the ways that law has been and continues to be a foundational site of inequity, violence, and oppression, and a shared belief in the value of critical theories and approaches to this important work.

Second, this collection is critical in terms of the importance, urgency, and necessity of deepening our understandings of the relationship between public law and contemporary inequities, including those exacerbated by the recent crises and struggles mentioned at the outset of this Introduction. As this collection demonstrates, critical approaches are not just relevant, but imperative to comprehensive understandings of the myriad ways that public law tools, mechanisms, and institutions both perpetuate, and might contribute to ameliorating, various kinds of intersectional subordination. Indeed, legal "[s]cholars and students today are newly interested in how legal regimes reflect and shape social and state power, and in intersecting subordination based on gender, race, sexual orientation, disability, or indigeneity. And inspiringly and rightly so."[14] It is, thus, an opportune moment to have the kinds of conversations included in this collection.

Reifying Hierarchy: Five Patterns in Law

Although the chapters in this collection could be organized in various ways—the groups they impact; the areas they inform; the methods they employ—we summarize them based on subject area, below. Before that summary, however, we briefly identify five cascading themes reflected across the chapters in this collection—and across our varied experiences with the law—that are pivotal to the law's consistent mobilization to reify extant power disparities in society. Those themes are: exceptionalism, capitalism, segmentation, incrementalism, and formalism. As the chapters in this collection show, careful

---

[14] Moyn, *supra* note 5 at 79.

interrogation by legal scholars and practitioners of these patterns is crucial to effective scholarly and organized resistance.

Canadian Exceptionalism

Across a diversity of contexts, Canada is routinely staged in comparison with the United States. This juxtaposition generates a fictional image of Canada from which a myth of virtue and progress is constructed. This illusion is apparent, for example, in the address of a former prime minister describing Canada as the "homeland of equality, justice and tolerance,"[15] and in the words of a former chief justice of the Supreme Court of Canada opining that Indigenous Peoples—as well as "peoples of diverse Asian and African stocks"— "live together in comparative, if not always absolute, harmony" in Canada.[16] The American comparison facilitates a particular imaginary of Canadian history and experience: "America had slavery, we had the underground railroad"; "America is assimilative, we are multicultural"; "America is imperial, we are peacekeepers."

Our point is not that Canada and America do not differ—they, of course, do. Rather, our point is that the ideological valence of their comparison is conservative. In other words, the comparison is not made to *explore* the distinct manifestations of hierarchy in Canada and America, but rather, to *deny or diminish* those manifestations in the former. In turn, these denials shape the social context in which law is not simply made, but interpreted—that is, this mythology of Canadian exceptionalism is *institutionalized* by law. Canadian patriotism purports to celebrate our justice in comparison with injustice abroad, and, especially, south of the border—but our national identity, instead, does the very same work that all national identities do: concealing the injustice inherent in the construction of national identity and the enforcement of national borders.[17]

---

[15] "Note for an address by Prime Minister Kim Campbell" (1 July 1993), online: <epe. lac-bac.gc.ca/100/200/301/ic/can_digital_collections/discourspm/anglais/kc/ 0107993e.html>.

[16] Beverley McLachlin, "Racism and the Law: The Canadian Experience" (2002) 1:1 JL & Equality 7 at 7.

[17] For an expansive analysis of some of these themes in the context of the "production of terrorist bodies against properly queer subjects" (at xxi) in post-9/11 America, see Jasbir K Puar, *Terrorist Assemblages: Homonationalism in Queer Times* (Durham: Duke University Press, 2007).

Capitalism

The assumption of a relatively benign social, political, and economic climate in Canada sets the stage for free market ideology. If the Canadian machine is not broken, so the logic proceeds, why fix it (in law, or otherwise)? In this way, the market forces that perniciously shape inequity in Canadian society are inseverable from the mythology of exceptionalism resulting from weaponized comparisons with the United States, above. These comparisons say, for example: private mental health care is acceptable because *everything* is private in America; private education is acceptable because debt loads are *greater* in America; private legal practice is acceptable because there is *less* access to justice in America.

To be clear, we understand that America is, in many ways, more privatized than Canada (and, in turn, less equal). But, again, that is not the point. As critical scholars in Canada, our concern is how such comparisons obscure undeniable oppression *within* the borders of the Canadian state—and, as some contributors to this collection explain, *by* our borders as well.

Segmentation

The intersecting systems within our society that create and maintain inequality cannot be tidily separated. And yet, that is precisely how our social order is routinely navigated—and, indeed, is precisely how legal education and practice are too often conceptualized. Law students are taught a narrow, compartmentalized vision of how law fits within the wider architecture of our social order, and relatedly, are, implicitly or explicitly, instructed against broader efforts at social change. In consequence, lawyers—positioned to wield a significant lever of political power in society—are limited in their understanding of where that lever fits in the political ecosystem.

Moreover, isolating law from other technologies of power obscures the ways in which law *in combination* with other technologies mediates our social order. A "right" to counsel in a private market where legal aid is chronically underfunded is, systemically, a right to inferior representation; a "right" not to be discriminated against in jury selection where criminal records, fluency in colonial languages, and income forbid or limit that right is, systemically, a qualified privilege;[18]

---

[18] On jury selection and representativeness, see e.g. Joshua Sealy-Harrington, "'Silly Anecdotes': From White Baselines to White Juries in *R v Chouhan*" (2023) 108 SCLR (2d) 109; Ebyan Abdigir et al, "How a broken jury list makes Ontario justice whiter,

and a "right" not to be deprived of life, liberty, and security of the person except in accordance with the principles of fundamental justice,[19] where mass incarceration, homelessness, and opioid epidemics are tolerated, is no right at all. The materiality of these "rights" is not defined in law alone. To adopt an exclusively legal lens, then, is to camouflage how law *and* politics shape our lives, especially the lives of those most exploited and oppressed.

Incrementalism

In our experience, one of the most dominant legal norms is incrementalism—that is, the presumed virtue of gradual social and legal change.[20] But how can this norm continue to be justified in the face of widespread, worsening inequities? When prisons overflow with Indian Residential School survivors, when the impacts of the climate crisis destroy and displace entire communities, when Black men are killed and harassed by police at egregious rates, when 2SLGBTQ+ youth die by suicide at alarming rates after experiencing harassment and discrimination in schools, when boil water advisories in First Nations communities persist for decades, when billions of dollars in child support are left unpaid across the country—by what moral framework is glacial resistance to such inequities defensible?

We acknowledge the limitations—indeed, the routine elitism—of courts in strategies of social change, and how such concerns can support progressive calls for judicial restraint. But the norm of incrementalism is not articulated solely—or, we would argue, even primarily—with the view that radical change must be advanced elsewhere. Rather, it is most often described as virtuous because justice is already largely thought to be secured (think back to how the Canadian political and legal leaders, above, describe this "great nation"). Our systems, our

---

richer and less like your community", *Toronto Star* (16 February 2018), online: <thestar.com/news/investigations/how-a-broken-jury-list-makes-ontario-justice-whiter-richer-and-less-like-your-community/article_f8b4ed4c-bea4-5e52-b435-cb6df1e4ccc6.html>.

[19] This right is enshrined in the *Canadian Charter of Rights and Freedoms*, s 7, Part I of the *Constitution Act, 1982*, being Schedule B to the *Canada Act 1982* (UK), 1982, c 11 [*Charter*].

[20] For a discussion of incrementalism in constitutional contexts, see e.g. Jula Hughes, Vanessa MacDonnell & Karen Pearlston, "Equality & Incrementalism: The Role of Common Law Reasoning in Constitutional Rights Cases" (2013) 44:3 Ottawa L Rev 467 at 472–474.

procedures, some argue, are the envy of the world. But this is, again, the segmentation—and exceptionalism—just explored. No matter how ostensibly fair our laws may appear (and, of course, we question that ostensible fairness as well), those laws cannot make justice when the social, economic, and political landscape translates the operation of those laws into demonstrable injustice.

Formalism

Although only a small minority of legal theorists subscribe to a formalist account of the law—that is, that the law *in reality* simply reflects the application of uncontroversial principles to facts—everyday discussions of law among both non-lawyers and lawyers alike tend to reinforce formalist accounts. Formalism asks, for example, what *is* the law? What does the law *require*? A silent ideology of formalism animates these innocuous questions and conceals law's political operation. As such, lawyers are foundational to maintaining the fiction of scientific legal reasoning that, at the first layer, reassures the public of a neutral order, but at the second layer, ensures that the existing unequal order remains undisturbed—at least, undisturbed by law.

Worse, this false neutrality not only limits the law's promotion of justice, but further, permits the weaponization of "law" against such promotion in other segments of society. With every passing reference to the Supreme Court "correcting" a court of appeal, or the quality of a judge turning on their academic credentials, we mystify a simple yet crucial truth: that the law is an active site of political resistance, not a passive site of apolitical reasoning.

All five of these themes are, in our view, quintessential to highlighting law's political operation: *exceptionalism* manufactures a false social context of equality and progress; *capitalism* maintains and/or exacerbates that social context by disregarding myriad imbricated legacies of oppression; *segmentation* conceals that persisting oppression which is mediated not through law alone, but through law's coordinate operation; *incrementalism* ensures that elite interests have the time needed to reconfigure hierarchy so as to conceal its enduring character; and *formalism* ensures that the ways in which law is mobilized to sustain that hierarchy are hidden from view.

These themes are, of course, phrased in abstract terms. But holding them front of mind as we approach concrete legal issues facilitates the recognition of inequality's (re)construction in law. The critical contributions contained within this volume elucidate the ways that these themes function in discrete settings of law and society. We encourage readers to not only engage with the words of our contributors, but further, to situate their analyses within broader settings of social, legal, economic, and political power—that is, we encourage readers to put these ideas *in conversation*. In our view, the tree of any one dispute will routinely mislead as to the forest of inequality's reconstitution.

The Chapters

Indigenous Peoples and Critical Approaches to Canadian Law
The collection opens with a series of chapters on Indigenous Peoples and critical approaches to Canadian law. Gordon Christie's chapter examines the possibility of developing an Indigenous version of critical theory or critical Indigenous theory. Christie begins by identifying two strands of critical theory commonly employed in the scholarship on Indigenous-Crown relations: the first strand draws from Marxist thought and tends to advocate for Indigenous nationalism in the form of a resurgence of distinctively Indigenous thought and law which would support separate Indigenous polities; the second strand includes interpretivists or post-structuralists who analyze Indigenous-Crown relations not in terms of the constraint of economic forces, but rather in the light of contingent human thought and action. Some contemporary interpretivists adopt a "politics of recognition" approach, according to which reconciliation involves recognition of Indigenous peoples as self-governing peoples by the Canadian state, as opposed to advocating for Indigenous separation.

Do either of these strands provide a useful basis for a critical Indigenous theory? Christie engages with the *capitalism* theme when he identifies value in using Marxist tools to explore the assault of economic forces, such as capitalist ideology on Indigenous peoples, provided the absolutist and deterministic elements of certain forms of Marxism are jettisoned. Turning to the interpretivist strand, Christie also sees value in recognizing the contingency of structures of oppression and dispossession. This approach is a vital move in exposing the patterns of *segmentation* and *formalism* within Canadian law. But some interpretivists presume the existence of a common discursive ground, which Christie argues does not yet exist, and may never exist if Indigenous and non-Indigenous systems of thought are incommensurable. A critical Indigenous theorist can avoid this outcome, according to Christie, by rejecting an all-encompassing model of truth that purports to be the right model for all social worlds, including Indigenous peoples. Instead, by turning its core insight on itself, critical interpretivist theory can recognize the contextual nature of its own theory of truth, and thereby make space for a critical Indigenous theorist to draw upon specifically Indigenous theories of truth.

In her chapter on Indigenous jurisdiction, Dayna Scott pushes back against the forces of *segmentation* and *formalism* by critiquing conventional means of teaching Canadian public law. Discussions of jurisdiction too often focus on the division of powers set out in the *Constitution Act, 1867*,[21] without interrogating the foundation of Canada's assertion of sovereignty and without exploring the continued operation of Indigenous jurisdiction. According to Scott, an exploration of alternative conceptions of jurisdiction—instead of a focus on the abstract notion of sovereignty—provides a more promising pathway for restoring Indigenous governing authority. Scott acknowledges the *incrementalism* of this approach but praises its practicality. While incrementalism and practicality are common features of a politics of recognition, Scott's thesis shares more in common with a resurgence approach. She uses Marxist scholarship to highlight the significance of jurisdiction as a site of struggle given the role of capitalism in the displacement and dispossession of Indigenous peoples not only from land, but from the authority to govern. Scott's strongest repudiation of *formalism* consists, perhaps, in the fact that the alternative conceptions of jurisdiction for which she advocates do not depend on the Canadian state extending or delegating jurisdiction to Indigenous peoples.

In each of their chapters, Harry LaForme and Lorena Fontaine expose the ways that *segmentation* and *formalism* operate within the Canadian state's exercise of authority over language requirements and rights. LaForme criticizes the federal government's recently introduced requirement that candidates for appointment to the Supreme Court of Canada must be functionally bilingual in English and French. Fontaine criticizes the federal government's *Indigenous Languages Act*[22] for falling short in its efforts to revitalize and protect

---

[21] *Constitution Act, 1867* (UK), 30 & 31 Vict, c 3, ss 91–92, reprinted in RSC 1985, Appendix II, No 5.
[22] SC 2019, c 23.

Indigenous languages. In so doing, they draw upon the history and current context of Indigenous-Crown relations, as well as Indigenous perspectives and worldviews.

LaForme argues that the functional bilingualism requirement has created a new barrier to Indigenous peoples being appointed as judges of the Supreme Court, and thus fails to advance reconciliation. His argument provides a counter against attempts to rely on the recent appointment of Justice Michelle O'Bonsawin—an Abenaki member of the Odanak First Nation who is fluently bilingual in English and French—to the Supreme Court to buttress Canada's supposed *exceptionalism* over the United States. LaForme explains that the functional bilingualism requirement severely narrows the pool of eligible Indigenous candidates for any future appointments because the rate of French-English bilingualism among Indigenous people is almost 50 percent less than that of non-Indigenous people in Canada. This fact is not surprising given that—as LaForme notes—the focus of residential schools was on annihilating Indigenous culture including Indigenous languages, rather than on providing education; French was not taught in residential schools outside of Quebec, and the last residential school operated until 1997.

In addition to the content taught, Fontaine documents other aspects of residential schools aimed at impeding Indigenous language transmission, such as intentionally locating schools far from Indigenous communities, restricting parental visits to the schools, and enforcing attendance at residential schools via fines and imprisonment. The damage caused by these measures is manifest when one understands the significance of language to Indigenous worldviews and value systems. Fontaine explains that according to at least some Indigenous legal traditions, language is a sacred responsibility and a gift from the Creator to be passed on. Thus, Fontaine argues, the failure of the *Indigenous Languages Act* to define an enforceable language right, to secure sufficient government funding for language transmission, and to implement the language provisions of the *United Nations Declaration on the Rights of Indigenous Peoples*,[23] results in ongoing cultural genocide. In terms of this collection's five themes, her argument rejects the *incrementalism* of the *Indigenous Languages Act* and maintains a vision that upholds Indigenous worldviews.

---

[23] GA Res 61/295, UNGAOR, 61st Sess, Sup No 53, UN Doc A/61/295 (2007) 1 [UNDRIP].

Finally, Kerry Sloan eschews *segmentation* when she lays the groundwork for a Metis constitutionalism that draws on Metis stories and philosophy, including Metis legal, spiritual, and political thought. Her critical engagement counters the popular discourse which creates caricatures of the Metis by ignoring Metis perspectives; in contrast, Sloan's exploration situates the Metis in wider Indigenous social and political contexts and proposes the following four elements of Metis constitutionalism: first, "Metis culture was created by and through pre-existing Indigenous social geographies" such as treaty protocols and kinship networks among Indigenous nations; second, the creation of the Nehiyaw Pwat—or Iron Alliance—between the Metis, Nehiyawak/Cree, prairie Anishinaabeg/Saulteaux, and Nakota/Assiniboine, likely in the early 1800s, was a key moment in the creation of the Metis nation; third, Metis culture borrows elements from European culture which are inextricably incorporated into Metis lifeways and thus do not diminish the Indigeneity of the Metis; and fourth, the principle of kinship/wahkotowin, which implies both interconnection and non-duality. Indeed, a commitment to non-duality infuses Sloan's chapter, as she aims to illustrate that seemingly contradictory elements of Metis constitutionalism might be not only equally true but also mutually constitutive. In so doing, Sloan uncovers and challenges the *segmentation* of the Canadian state's more static definition of Metis identity.

Policing, Criminal Law, and the Carceral State

The second group of chapters offer critical analyses of Policing, Criminal Law, and the Carceral State. In the first chapter, Lisa Kerr examines the sentencing of Indigenous people. Returning to the Supreme Court of Canada's foundational decision in *R v Gladue*,[24] she asks whether *Gladue* sentencing is exceptional. She argues that, at times, public commentary, academic accounts, and even judicial opinions have misstated the distinctiveness of *Gladue*. It is therefore imperative to clarify what *Gladue* does and does not do.

Step 1 of the *Gladue* framework requires sentencing judges to obtain and consider information about Indigenous offenders, including background and systemic factors. Kerr contends that there is nothing exceptional about this endeavour. In any sentencing matter,

---

[24] 1999 CanLII 679 (SCC).

contextual factors that may influence an offender's moral blameworthiness are central to applying the anchoring principle of proportionality. Where *Gladue* gives rise to more distinctive possibilities, she contends, is at Step 2, where trial judges are directed to consider "appropriate procedures and sanctions" in the sentencing of Indigenous offenders. While Step 1 is largely ordinary sentencing, Step 2 may provide a pathway to decarceral alternatives, including those rooted in Indigenous laws, institutions and practices. Kerr argues that *Gladue* has provided legal and political space within the state sentencing system for Indigenous-led justice initiatives.

Kerr's chapter engages questions of *segmentation*. By critically interrogating the contradictory legacy of *Gladue*, Kerr invites us to notice the importance of refusing to isolate this precedent from its underlying context and its relationship to different technologies of power. Her chapter also contributes to the theme of *formalism*. It would be difficult, if not impossible, to understand the diffuse legacy of *Gladue* by only looking at how sentencing judges have applied it over the past 25 years. By attending to a variety of sources describing *Gladue*, including those by politicians and commentators in public forums, Kerr invites us to notice the circuitous *Gladue* pathways that exist in both our legal and political orders.

Reakash Walters, similarly, examines the role of contradiction in progressive legal advocacy. She considers whether advocacy for prison abolition is possible within the confines of the carceral state. One of our themes is Canadian *exceptionalism*—Walters, however, critiques the exceptionalism in defensive legal work for "criminalized and illegalized" people. She acknowledges that such work provides a "crucial service." But she pushes us further: "To achieve critical gains towards prison abolition, lawyers committed to transformative change should develop a clear set of political commitments and practices: an abolitionist lawyering ethic." In this way, she de-exceptionalizes so-called "social justice" legal practice unmoored from a broader structural critique of the legal system.

Walters' analysis illustrates the intimate connection between this volume's themes and abolitionist politics in general: *capitalism* (i.e., how "[r]acialization, poverty, mental disabilities and substance use act as proxies for criminality in the Canadian criminal legal system"); *segmentation* (i.e., how "the criminal legal system is multi-faceted and carceral logics are too central to our culture for abolition to be independently realized in the courtroom"); and *formalism* (i.e., how the "Canadian legal order views Canada's 'justice' system as apolitical and just" when "we know the outcomes are unjust" and "state violence is doled out along racial and class lines"). Viewed in this way, abolition becomes *a*—perhaps *the*—case study of critical legal theory and practice.

In their chapter, Véronique Fortin and João Velloso examine the punitive nature of Canadian criminal law. The authors explore the gap between law on the books, as defined in legal doctrine, and its everyday realities. They examine the various systemic pressures that result in punishment arising before the adjudication of guilt and the plural forms of law that are brought to bear on the lives of people who use drugs, those with mental health issues, and people who are unhoused. Drawing on the insights of scholars of new penology, Fortin and Velloso expose the ways that regulatory criminal law (i.e., record of offences), administrative law (i.e., social assistance), and municipal law (i.e., zoning) shape the everyday lives of people situated at multiple axes of oppression. The authors provide a powerful rejection of the *segmentation* of law and, in doing so, reveal the many ways that punishment is allocated beyond the formal dimensions of the criminal legal system.

In his chapter, Vincent Wong tackles a topic that has become increasingly significant during the editorial process for this collection: "Racial McCarthyism," or systematic attacks on speech advocating for racial justice, which is cast as "divisive" and producing "discomfort," thereby warranting its censorship. Again, Wong's analysis is illustrative of several of the animating themes of this collection. He links this censorship to racial *capitalism* and how "simultaneous critiques of race and class serve as a major threat to white nationalism and the capitalist order in America." He also notes how critical legal analysis is specifically threatening in its lack of *segmentation*: "political economy analysis is something that legal academia has not done enough, in part due to the narrow search for universalized doctrinal precepts inherent in 'thinking like a lawyer.'" This, understandably, leads to Wong's critique of *formalism*. Indeed, one of the central McCarthyist critiques of critical race theory is "CRT's suspicion and critique of liberalism in the United States, particularly claims of legal objectivity [and] neutrality."

Wong begins his analysis with President Trump's Executive Order against "Race and Sex Stereotyping," i.e., against how schools of thought like critical race theory crucially examine the "legacies of systemic racism and sexism." Wong extends this case study to the

Canadian context, discussing the StopSOP campaign at the Law Society of Ontario, which sought to suppress critical race theory in legal theory and practice. Wong illustrates how Racial McCarthyism from America has migrated into the Canadian legal community, including by mobilizing near-identical rhetoric of "divisive" concepts. In discussing the suppression of speech in solidarity with Palestinian liberation, Wong demonstrates how Racial McCarthyism is present not only in the legal community, but also in academic, political, and media settings. The parallels in McCarthyist tactics are notable. By "drawing from the Trumpian playbook" censorship in Canada similarly distorts solidarity with Palestine as hateful. Wong does not mince words in terms of the gravity of the current situation: "At stake is our very ability as researchers, teachers, and students to interrogate and speak the truth about the role of law and legal institutions within the broader legacies of settler colonialism, white supremacy, and heteropatriarchy both at home in the Canadian nation-state and abroad."

In her chapter, Lisa Kelly tells a new story about the foundational police powers decision in *R v Grant*[25] where the Supreme Court developed a doctrinal framework to determine when unlawfully obtained evidence should be excluded under s. 24(2) of the *Canadian Charter of Rights and Freedoms*.[26] The decision also provided guidance about police powers, particularly the law of detention. Kelly contends that, despite being one of the most widely cited and analyzed Canadian criminal law cases in recent decades, little attention has been paid to the police patrol that led to Donnohue Grant's arrest in the first place. Abstracting *Grant* from the school surveillance context, she contends, obscures the racial, class, and generational hierarchies that produced it. While appellate courts ultimately concluded that police officers had psychologically detained Donnohue Grant, Kelly argues that they also instantiated so-called "neighbourhood policing" tactics that fall short of detention. In this way, Canadian courts played a key role in expanding—rather than contracting—the powers of the carceral state. Kelly's account urges us to notice how the rhetoric of protecting vulnerable young people in schools functions as a powerful tool within our legal and political orders.

---

[25] 2009 SCC 32.
[26] *Charter, supra* note 19, s 24(2).

By revealing the use of constitutional rights to expand police powers, Kelly's chapter illustrates the collection's theme of *segmentation*. Rather than imagining courts and Canadian constitutional law as a bulwark against coercive state power, Kelly's account underscores the experiences of people ensnared in the tentacular apparatuses of the criminal legal system. In this telling, Canadian constitutional law facilitates—rather than constrains—draconian powers of the state. Kelly's chapter also speaks to the theme of *formalism*: in underscoring the school surveillance context of the *Grant* decision, Kelly reveals law as an active site of political struggle. The decision to install police officers in schools to surveil students, usually under the guise of school safety, is simultaneously mediated by law and politics.

Finally, the second section concludes with a powerful "(love) letter" to legal workers from Meenakshi Mannoe. Like Walters, Mannoe wrestles with the idea of safety beyond the confines of carceral institutions, an analysis that confronts our themes repeatedly. For example, on *exceptionalism*, Mannoe points out how after the George Floyd uprising, "agencies such as the Canadian Association of Chiefs of Police quickly distinguished fundamental differences in North American policing models"—when, as Mannoe observes, Canadian policing, too, must be contextualized as "enforcing the violent [and] colonial" occupation of Canada.

Again, like Walters, Mannoe de-*exceptionalizes* legal workers, even those who understand their role as progressive. She explains how they "must also recognize that their education and skillset are designed for cooptation." This is, in part, premised on the belief that we simply lack "enough 'good' people" working within carceral institutions, in stark contrast with Mannoe's view: that "[t]here is no reforming this racist system!" In this respect, Mannoe situates many policing reforms within a logic of *incrementalism*: "Ultimately, police oversight agencies—civilian or government-controlled—simply legitimate policing narratives. None of these agencies is willing to acknowledge that police have no jurisdiction, and neither do the overseers that enable their violence. In reality, police violence against Indigenous people is part of the continued colonial occupation of Canada." Mannoe further illustrates the pernicious effect of *formalism* in police oversight mechanisms. For example, Mannoe notes that "B.C. prosecutors' charge assessment guidelines include consideration of whether or not prosecution is in the 'public interest.' The notion of a fair and objective assessment of public interest erases how

systemic racism and colonial ideologies define law, order, and justice." As such, each of these contributions strives to navigate the
dilemma of working within and without carceral institutions in the
broader pursuit of racial justice.

Boundaries and Borders of Public Law

The third section of the book gathers chapters on a diversity of subjects that push us to think more expansively about the boundaries
and borders—literal, disciplinary, and rhetorical—of public law. These
chapters examine seemingly disparate questions of citizenship and
migration, children's rights, religion, disability, and taxation; yet a
common theme across these chapters is the role that public law norms,
mechanisms, and institutions play in reinscribing and reenforcing
existing hierarchies of power.

The third section begins with a chapter by YY Brandon Chen,
who considers the ways that the section 15 equality guarantee of the
Charter of Rights and Freedoms has consistently failed to redress discrimination claims based on non-citizen status.[27] Chen identifies three doctrinal barriers from the Supreme Court's jurisprudence faced by
claimants alleging discrimination on the basis of non-citizenship: first,
reliance on the mobility rights clause of the *Charter* as precluding equality claims based on non-citizen status; second, the tendency of courts to
look for evidence that an impugned law or action treats *all* non-citizens
less favourably than citizens in order to ground an equality claim for
differential treatment based on lack of Canadian citizenship; and,
third, the refusal of courts to acknowledge "immigration status" as an
analogous ground that could better capture many of the claims brought
by non-citizens.

Chen's analysis is revelatory of the complex, often insidious
ways that Canadian *exceptionalism* operates. In demonstrating how
national identity and citizenship are closely guarded and carefully
policed by legal institutions, Chen's chapter disrupts the dominant
Canadian narrative of equality and progress for all. The analysis also
exemplifies the ways that *incrementalism* and *formalism*—broadly
accepted features of legal reasoning that, when relied upon by courts
and judges, tend to go unchallenged—make invisible the material
injustices at the heart of equality claims. Indeed, the profound

---

[27] *Charter, supra* note 19, s 15.

injustices experienced by the migrant and non-citizen claimants in the cases Chen recounts are frequently reduced to formal legal questions about what the law is and what it requires.

Next, looking to recent social, political, and legal debates about Muslim veiling as a case study, Ashleigh Keall queries the work that "choice talk" does in religious freedom jurisprudence in Canadian constitutional law.[28] Drawing upon feminist accounts of choice and agency, Keall begins by challenging the false binary between the "freely choosing" and "coerced" woman that animates popular and legal understandings of veiling. Her analysis demonstrates how the practice of veiling is often more varied, nuanced, and complicated than the choice/coercion binary allows. This part of her chapter contributes to our understanding of the contours of Canadian *exceptionalism*, inviting careful consideration of the ways that religious minorities— inseparable from racial and ethnic minorities—are situated as "other" within the dominant Canadian paradigm of egalitarianism.

Keall's analysis then highlights the foundational role that choice plays in religious freedom jurisprudence under section 2(a) of the *Charter* and asks: what happens when the choice-based doctrine of religious freedom is brought to bear on the complexities of veiling practice? Drawing attention to the *formalism* of section 2(a) doctrine, Keall's analysis reveals the ways that veiling women "are wildly underserved by the prevailing method and structure of religious freedom doctrine in Canadian law." More broadly, Keall's analysis, like Chen's, highlights the ways that resorting to law often requires or results in a "flattening of human experience" that obscures the diverse and complex realities of injustice.

Mona Paré's chapter examines children as subjects of law in Canada. Her chapter adds to the dialogue on the theme of *segmentation* in Canadian public law by illustrating how the fact that children do not neatly conform to traditional notions of "rights holders" poses a barrier to the full and meaningful realization of children's rights. Paré demonstrates the disconnect between, on the one hand, the recognition that children are protected under the *Canadian Charter of Rights and Freedoms*, and, on the other hand, the fact that their rights have not been fully, equally, and meaningfully recognized in Canadian law. Paré argues that the unique position of

---

[28] *Charter, supra* note 19, s 2(a).

children as individuals who are dependent on their parents or legal guardians requires a reimagining of the relationship between the child and the state.

In his chapter, Ravi Malhotra employs a critical disability perspective, which seeks to reimagine a world that is truly inclusive of disabled people, on the pattern of *incrementalism* in Canadian public law. Malhotra brings the foundational ideas of writers such as Michael Oliver and Colin Barnes into conversation with radical French philosopher Cornelius Castoriadis to examine the Ontario Court of Appeal decision in *Longueépée v University of Waterloo*.[29] While acknowledging that the decision will result in incremental gains for people with disabilities in post-secondary enrolment, Malhotra argues that critical disability theory requires going beyond an individualized approach of providing accommodation as an exception to the rule. He concludes by explaining how the theoretical insights gleaned from a reimagined critical disability theory might help us better understand human rights law in the context of post-secondary education.

The final chapter, by Samuel Singer and Allison Christians, most squarely engages the theme of *capitalism*. Drawing from feminist legal scholarship, critical race theory, Indigenous legal studies, queer legal studies, critical disability studies, and trans legal studies, their chapter illustrates how the Canadian tax system shapes and maintains socioeconomic inequities. Rejecting the impulse toward *segmentation*, Singer and Christians begin by identifying the range of interrelated factors that influence tax law decision-making, including not only law, but "economic theory, social and cultural dynamics, and perhaps most importantly, politics."

Then, laying the groundwork for future scholarship in this area, Singer and Christians highlight the importance of bringing critical perspectives to bear on a variety of tax law issues. First, using examples of two discrete domestic tax rules—tax relief for medical expenses and the tax treatment of menstrual products—the authors show how critical engagement reveals the myriad complex policy choices involved in tax law line drawing and surfaces the "disparate impacts of seemingly objective tax rules." Then, the authors look to the difference that critical perspectives make in analyzing and understanding

---

[29] 2020 ONCA 830 (CanLII).

two highly complex tax law regimes—those governing the relationships between Canada and Indigenous nations and between Canada and foreign states. The authors conclude by identifying the need for "broad and inclusive" engagement with tax law policy decisions to better leverage the insights of critical tax law theory.

Conclusion: Dialogue and Conversation

The chapters in this collection are best viewed *in dialogue*. In a broad sense, these scholars are aligned in their commitment toward social justice in the public law domain. But can each of their strategies, recommendations, or ideas be pursued simultaneously, or rather, do they fundamentally conflict? Is it possible to pursue a case-by-case approach, depending on context? Or does the scarcity of our resources—both emotional and financial—demand an overarching theory that rejects certain strategies outright while fully committing to others? Our hope is that, by grouping these voices, we can advance a critical conversation on the ideology and methodology of social change. While we are critical of Canada's "Conversation Industrial Complex"—of Canadian institutions often discussing but rarely doing social change—we nevertheless hope that the contributions in this collection and the conversations they promote can help shape what we do and inspire us to do more.

SECTION A

INDIGENOUS PEOPLES AND CRITICAL
APPROACHES TO CANADIAN LAW

Critical Theory and Crown-Indigenous Relations

*Gordon Christie**

Abstract

With attention turned to addressing historic injustices inflicted upon Indigenous peoples by the Canadian state, and on building a more just future, questions arise about the role critical theory (CT) might play in making sense of Crown-Indigenous relations. Here, strands of critical theory are explored, focus eventually falling on an influential variant propounded by James Tully, one which calls for "mutual recognition" as a starting point for meaningful reconciliation. From the perspective of a critical Indigenous theory (CIT), deep problems are identified in following those who champion this form of a "politics of recognition," as it rests, at the level of theory and purported fact, on the presumption that Indigenous ways of thinking have already been subsumed within non-Indigenous worlds of meaning.

* I would like to acknowledge the endless patience and kindness of one of the editors, Professor Karen Drake, as she guided me through the production of this chapter.

Résumé

Avec l'attention portée sur la rectification des injustices historiques infligées aux peuples autochtones par l'État canadien, et sur la création d'un avenir plus équitable, des questions émergent quant au rôle que pourrait jouer la théorie critique (TC) dans la compréhension des relations entre la Couronne et les Autochtones. Ici, diverses branches de la théorie critique sont explorées, avec un regard particulier porté sur une variante influente proposée par James Tully, qui prône la « reconnaissance mutuelle » comme point de départ pour une réconciliation significative. Cependant, du point de vue d'une théorie autochtone critique (TAC), des problèmes profonds sont identifiés dans l'approche des personnes qui défendent cette forme de « politique de la reconnaissance », car celle-ci repose, au niveau théorique et factuel, sur la présomption que les modes de pensée autochtones ont déjà été subsumés dans les cadres de signification non autochtones.

The Crown[1] has interacted with Indigenous peoples in what is now Canada for many generations. Today, Crown-Indigenous relations (CIR) are informed by this history, and by understandings of the nature of this history. One type of contemporary scholarship—critical theory (CT)—is particularly attentive to the ways that history, law, and politics interrelate with attempts at producing understandings. Fundamentally concerned with oppression, domination, and dispossession, focused on the subjects of oppression and domination, CT aims at producing more reflective, grounded models of CIR. Accounts of CIR that fall under CT, however, are themselves diverse in methodology, underlying theory, and outcome.

In this chapter I map out some of the dominant strands of CT, tracing out concerns that animate critical theorists as they go about theorizing CIR. The intent is to determine CT's utility to those trying to make sense of CIR, particularly as the business of addressing injustices and working toward a better future is increasingly vigorously taken up across Indigenous-Canada. In the middle of this work, we

---

[1] The term "Crown" here broadly refers to the Canadian state, manifest in the executive, legislative and judicial branches of the government.

get caught up in thinking about the place of a "politics of recognition" in relation to CT, as one of the most influential strands of CT—that propounded by James Tully—ultimately relies upon the purported need for the state to properly recognize Indigenous peoples (and for Indigenous peoples to recognize the state's legitimacy). The notion that one should be carried along by the general flow of CT toward a politics of recognition is challenged, particularly with focus on the question of whether a critical Indigenous theory (CIT) can be constructed, one that borrows aspects of CT while remaining decidedly Indigenous. Ultimately, aspects of some of the underlying threads that go into informing CT are deemed worthy of serious consideration, but any critical approach that leads the Indigenous scholar toward the necessity of recognition as a precondition for meaningful reconciliation (or justice) is argued to be potentially dangerously inappropriate.

It will be helpful, as we work our way through these analytical threads, to consider a particularly difficult type of situation unfolding in numerous Canadian areas as we move into the mid-twenty-first century. Consider an Indigenous people's territory. While over the last century and a half Canada has asserted absolute dominion over this territory, the Indigenous people tied to these lands and waters have tried to maintain and exercise the ability to make decisions about human/non-human interactions according to *their* sense of responsibilities to the territory's many dimensions. Today, across Canada, the assertion of Crown sovereignty increasingly runs into reinvigorated assertions of Indigenous authority.[2] How are CIR theorized in relation to this sort of contemporary fundamental territorial dispute?

---

[2] For example, highly visible instances in just one Canadian jurisdiction, British Columbia, include: the struggle over the Coastal Gaslink pipeline in Wet'suwet'en territory (for one side of the dispute see *Coastal GasLink Pipeline Ltd v Huson*, 2019 BCSC 2264), struggles over Haida Gwaii (note the structure of the *GayG̱ahlda "Changing Tide" Framework for Reconciliation*, online: <https://www2.gov.bc.ca/assets/gov/environment/natural-resource-stewardship/consulting-with-first-nations/agreements/gaygahlda_changing_tide_framework_agreement.pdf>), and controversies along the route of the TMX pipeline (for example, with Secwepemc resistance, see Boston Laferté, "Secwepemc set up new camp in hopes of halting TMX construction, leads to five arrests" (23 October 2020), online: <martlet.ca/news-secwepemc-new-camp-halts-tmx/>).

Critical Theory Sketched

To begin, what is critical theory? Besides its focus on explicating matters of oppression, dispossession, and domination, it is theory critical of other mainstream (or dominant) theories, not just in relation to *products* of mainstream theorizing but also *how* mainstream theorists approach the business of theorizing. A wedge can be driven between dominant and critical theories by thinking of the nature of their accounts and how theorists see themselves doing their work, but a deeper divergence lies in relation to very different thoughts at play about roles theory can and does play in our socio-political worlds.

By and large, mainstream theoretical accounts of CIR have already in hand *models of justice* put to the task of evaluating Crown-Indigenous relations, providing guidance to actions meant to respond to contemporary problems.[3] While historically these models either proclaimed or presumed universality of content and reach, contemporary mainstream theorists are often more circumspect, typically claiming for their models only a form of localized truth (or, they simply avoid getting caught up in arguments about the reach of their models). Just a generation or so ago, one could argue that mainstream theorists were quite ambitious and oblivious to possible limits of their work: by contrast critical theorists were then (as now) consciously enwrapped in concerns about context and perspective. Today, however, drawing such a clear line is not so easy.

What remains is a divide between those who pursue their work with a commitment to providing accounts that *purport* to do nothing but describe and, when appropriate, prescribe, and critical theorists who argue that much that passes for impartial, neutral theory is actually critically caught up in political struggle. Turning this argument on mainstream theories, the claim is that these purportedly impartial intellectual structures should be seen as facilitating attempts at justifying certain configurations of power, thereby assisting in the creation and re-cementing of certain oppressive and dispossessive elements of our society.

---

[3] How these models of justice are produced is intriguing, but we need not engage with such questions. Indeed, we need not worry about theoretic content—we focus on the critical take on mainstream theories, their presumption of some degree of universality, tied to notions of impartiality, objectivity, and neutrality.

CIR and Variants of CT

Within CT we come across, in the context of theorizing CIR, two general forms of theory. On the one hand, we locate those more aligned with contemporary forms of Marxist thought. On the other hand, we find those who disavow key Marxist principles and develop separate forms of critique adhering more fully to an underlying interpretivist account of theorizing. We can sketch out these camps and highlight their differences if we consider how they approach the history of CIR.

We begin with pre- and early contact periods between European arrivals and long-standing Indigenous societies. At these earliest points, ways of living in collectives and interacting with neighbours were very differently conceptualized and realized. Both sorts of worlds—those grounded in French and British political and intellectual histories and dozens of distinct social worlds grounded in Indigenous political and intellectual histories—were products of centuries of experimentation and construction. Each separate society was possessed of the means of giving meaning to their built socio-political worlds. After generations of interaction—substantially lived under frameworks of understanding that arose in the intersections of different social worlds—the power of European settlers and their governments ascended in the nineteenth century, and their understandings of how to live in the same space as Indigenous polities radically shifted.

Contemporary Marxists construct subsequent chapters of this narrative with insights about the early development of a capitalist economy in what became British North America and Canada. Generations of Indigenous dispossession and oppression are explained as falling under the logic of primitive accumulation and exploitation (in distinct and varied forms).[4] Later Marxist threads— responding to intriguing ways capitalism met collectivist challenges from those exploited, and developing accounts of how hegemonic instruments and techniques function—argue that the situation of contemporary Indigenous societies is particularly dire, as forces work to *naturalize* structures and ways of thinking that constrain Indigenous individuals.[5] Today, the Crown works in concert with economic

---

[4] Glen Coulthard, *Red Skins, White Masks: Rejecting the Colonial Politics of Recognition* (Minneapolis: University of Minnesota Press, 2014).

[5] Rajagopal, for example, argues that oppressed and dispossessed peoples around the world find themselves subject to the hegemonic force of international law,

powers to maintain and strengthen control over not just the lands and bodies of Indigenous peoples, but over their individual and collective thoughts and actions. The prescription is clear: Indigenous peoples cannot return to worlds they are bound to—those within which, for example, they hold sacred responsibilities to non-human kin—without removing the suffocating blanket of capitalism. Such a reality will require changes in both Crown law and policy, and how Indigenous people themselves now too commonly think about the world—a resurgence in distinctively Indigenous thought is demanded, alongside continuing efforts to rebuild separate authoritative Indigenous structures of law, economics, and politics.

Those in the interpretivist camp provide superficially similar accounts of past events, but they resile from the notion that *forces* structure events—in particular, that economic forces constrain and determine how human actors and entire societies think and act. An account grounded in classic Marxist doctrine imagines impersonal forces working through and on societies, while interpretivists (here we might switch labels and call them post-structuralists) hold that all such apparent forces are the products of human thought and action (which is essentially free and creative). While many people might *feel* trapped in economic and political realities, interpretivists argue they can struggle not just *for* freedom, but engage in struggles *of* freedom.[6] These latter forms of struggle engage the post-structuralist/interpretivist theoretical underpinnings of this approach, as it imagines that citizens living within a polity can challenge practices or techniques of governance, as all are *built*—none are themselves structural aspects of the world such that we actors and agents must accept that we are but impotent web-trapped flies.

While this might appear a relatively minor point of divergence between two critical camps, as we dig deeper into how they respectively theorize CIR we find connections to substantive and seemingly irreconcilable differences in theory and prescription. We begin with a simple query: why would the contemporary Marxist not just accept

---

gradually internalizing systems of oppression operating through international law: Balakrishnan Rajagopal, "Counter-Hegemonic International Law: Rethinking Human Rights and Development as A Third World Strategy" (2006) 27:5 Third World Q 767.

[6] James Tully, *Public Philosophy in a New Key*, vol 1 (Cambridge: Cambridge University Press, 2008) ch 8 at 257 [Tully, *PPNK*].

that the structures they imagine are built? After all, the classic Marxist sees things like law as components of the superstructure, as elements of society that serve simply to reflect and support economic structures of capitalism. It seems a short step to accepting that economic structures are themselves built and malleable. Indeed, contemporary Marxists now speak of the "relative autonomy" of the superstructure, envisioning a back-and-forth process of building and adjusting between economic structures and systems of thought which arise in superstructural settings.[7]

The contemporary Marxist can thereby create a layered view of "theory," not far removed from earlier, classic forms. *In the world*, the world around us, we find theory capable of this power to reflect and support economic structures, and to feed back into the base-structures of the world. But removed from all this we still find Marxist "grand theory," the account we are now sketching, a higher-level modelling of the world "below," meant to carry with it an element of *truth*. The world "down there" *is the way it is being described*, the contemporary Marxist holds, while *within* this world so described we see—from our higher vantage-point—"theories" that function to further economic interests.

Meanwhile, the interpretivist embraces "interpretation all the way down." All theory is on the same footing, the product of socio-historic times and places. On this view of theory and theorizing, it is a mistake to imagine any sort of "grand theory," purporting to provide a measure of objective truth. We work with *theories of our time and place* alongside our *interpretive abilities*—thus we develop models of understanding (*not* "truth" in any sort of objective sense). All this is laid out suggestively in Borrows' and Tully's Introduction to *Resurgence and Reconciliation*,[8] and developed in great detail in Tully's *Public Philosophy in a New Key* (PPNK).[9]

---

[7] See Raymond Williams, "Base and Superstructure in Marxist Cultural Theory" (1973) I:82 New Left Rev 3. Williams argues that rather than think in terms of a determining base and determined superstructure the better articulation of the starting point for Marxist analysis would be that "social being determines consciousness": *ibid* at 120. The nature of social being is such that, of course, it will not be cut off from the influence of consciousness.

[8] John Borrows & James Tully, "Introduction" in Michael Asch, John Borrows & James Tully, eds, *Resurgence and Reconciliation: Indigenous Settler Relations and Earth Teachings* (Toronto: University of Toronto Press, 2018) 3.

[9] Tully, *PPNK, supra* note 6.

Interpretivist CT and the Path Taken by Borrows and Tully

As we descend into the interpretivist approach, we need to disentangle the path Borrows and Tully follow from what a generic critical theorist in the interpretivist camp might consider doing to make sense of CIR. We find this separation where Tully envisions making sense of CIR.[10] It is at this point of divergence that we begin to encounter the roots of a problem for the Indigenous scholar as she looks to the value and utility of critical theory.

Tully characterizes crucial events of our collective past century-plus of history as the pulling of Indigenous peoples into a world governed by the state.[11] In the first few generations of this period, practices and techniques of governance were applied to Indigenous peoples conceptualized by the state as less-than-citizens, as wards of the state in need of lifting up via the varied gifts of civilization. By the late twentieth and early twenty-first centuries these practices have shifted, and—as we determine current CIR—their nature must be carefully unraveled. The aim of political science as applied to CIR is, then, to explore the nature of these practices and techniques of governance, particularly as they shift over time, being careful to theorize neither along lines adopted by dominant political theory nor, of course, along Marxist lines. These practices, the interpretivist holds, must be seen as activities in the world, where the world around us of thought and action is *all* that we can access and work with.[12] Thus, we find ways of making sense of practices of governance which *themselves* function variously in the world. None of these ways of making sense objectively

---

[10] In two chapters in volume 1 of Tully, *PPNK, ibid*, Tully's critical approach is applied to CIR, while in other chapters he elucidates the general nature of his approach to theorizing. Equally important in achieving a sense of how all this fits together are several sets of his responses to critics – especially those who reside in the other critical camp.

[11] Tully argues that the "relevant institutions of [...] Canada constitute structures of domination [...] because they are now relatively stable, immoveable and irreversible vis-à-vis any direct confrontation by the colonised population." These structures, he goes on to argue, "'incorporate' or 'domesticate' the subordinate Indigenous societies. These two concepts are widely used by Indigenous peoples to refer to the form domination takes: that is, as a matter of fact and of the coloniser's law, Indigenous peoples exist *within* the dominant societies": *ibid* at 259-260.

[12] Tully speaks of pulling theory down into the world in the Introduction to Tully, *PPNK, ibid*.

describe such practices, though some theorists might so claim as they simultaneously develop discourses that serve political purposes, such as justifying colonial law and policy.[13]

We find ourselves today, then, embedded in a complex social world, with various forms of discourse available—interpretations and understandings we can begin to put to use in our projects, such as efforts in struggles for and of freedom. As we think of CIR, we must be mindful of our time and place: what theories of practices of governance can we turn to with hopes of finding tools to manipulate to serve our ends (such as the dismantling of colonial law and policy and the creation of a world that can begin to satisfy our sense of justice)? Note that who constitutes "we" here is essentially important.

So, we come to Tully's take on how this approach plays out in the context of contemporary CIR. The current situation, he argues, is characterized by a specific outcome of Canada's colonial history: "The problematic, unresolved contradiction and constant provocation at the foundation of internal colonization [...] is that the dominant society coexists on and exercises exclusive jurisdiction over the territories and jurisdictions that the Indigenous peoples refuse to surrender."[14] Furthermore, "the system of internal colonisation remains in place and the two presumptions that reinforce it [the Crown presuming that the 'exercise of exclusive jurisdiction over territories of Indigenous peoples is not only effective but also legitimate', and the unspoken presumption that 'there is no viable alternative'] remain largely unquestioned in negotiation and litigation."[15] Recall the sort of situation introduced earlier—we find across Canada Indigenous territories where the Crown asserts absolute control over lands and waters, but where independent Indigenous legal and political authority remains manifest and exercised.

Tully argues, however, that finding themselves subject to internal colonization also means Indigenous peoples are subject to a "vast array of more mobile and changeable techniques of government by which Indigenous peoples and their territories are governed in a wide variety of ways within the [...] Canadian political system[]," a simple

---

[13] In the middle of "The struggle of Indigenous Peoples for and of freedom" (*ibid* at 266-276) Tully describes how political theory from the late nineteenth century up to today functions to carry out just this task.

[14] *Ibid* at 262.

[15] *Ibid* at 287. The two "hinge propositions" are presented at 276.

corollary of the fact that "Indigenous peoples exist *within* the dominant societies."[16] Here we encounter a common point of dispute
between two general camps of critical theorists (one we return to
later): on one hand, those aligned to some degree with contemporary
Marxist thought tend also to be Indigenous nationalists, arguing for
the continuing political independence of pre-existing and persisting
distinct polities,[17] while, on the other, Tully (and, seemingly, some
Indigenous scholars taking the interpretivist approach) move toward
a "politics of recognition" (a path fundamentally at odds with the idea
of Indigenous separation).

A CT adhering to an interpretivist approach need not, however,
descend to a grounding on the floor of recognition. The drive to
respond to the "unresolved contradiction" at the heart of contemporary Canada's problems through recognition and negotiation flows
from theoretical underpinnings of the general interpretivist approach
and specific notions developed by Tully. We begin by noting that
underlying the general interpretivist approach is a breathtaking
model of the state of human nature and the place of the human in the
larger world. We might label "transcendental" those grand theories
decried by interpretivists which detach from the messy lived worlds
of people in societies and aspire to provide "comprehensive and
exclusive theories of [...] contested concepts."[18] These theories claim
to provide tools to answer *all* questions about how humans ought to
organize themselves socially and politically. By contrast, the interpretivist puts humans squarely and solely within worlds of language
and discourse—all we can ever (meaningfully) aspire to do is work
with concepts and ideas at hand, studying how some forms of discourse function to guide and organize the governance practices of the
communities we find ourselves in, hoping that we can work out strategies that might shift what we take to be problematic aspects of these
forms of discourse.[19] All is politics—there are no such things as

---

[16] *Ibid* at 259–260.

[17] See e.g. Coulthard, *supra* note 4; Audra Simpson, *Mohawk Interruptus: Political Life Across the Borders of Settler States* (Durham: Duke University Press, 2014).

[18] Tully, *PPNK, supra* note 6 at 29.

[19] Tully provides something of a proviso—if citizens are trying to engage with an oppressive governing body that refuses to engage, citizens may, appropriately, entirely disengage. It would then be arguable these citizens are not truly under the governance authority of the governing body.

determinative or definitive answers to any of our questions, and all politics is contained within shifting and contingent built-worlds.

Tully's vision of an interpretivist CT is of a "species of 'practical philosophy'" that "seeks to characterise the conditions of possibility of the problematic form of governance in a redescription (often in a new vocabulary) that transforms the self-understanding of those subject to and struggling within it, enabling them to see its contingent conditions and the possibilities of governing themselves differently."[20] Indigenous peoples engaged in struggles "of" freedom, then, are enjoined to work out how to "transform [their] self-understanding" as they struggle with the problematic form of contemporary Canadian governance that maintains the two "hinge propositions" noted earlier.[21] Note, though, that for this to effect transformation in CIR, problematic forms of governance must be seen as such not just by Indigenous peoples governed by the state, but by *all* those subject to its governance, *and* by those whose practices and techniques constitute governance within the nation-state. The "them" and "themselves" whose eyes are opened to the contingent condition of forms of governance and the possibilities of different forms must include citizens of Canada and their governing bodies.

Tully's Shift to Recognition and Ensuing Tension with Indigenous Nationalism

As we move further into this picture of how to think and act under the interpretivist strand of CT, we find ourselves being guided toward a particular variant of the theoretical approach. Tully's shift to a focus on recognition begins to spin out a specific analytic thread, arguably removed from a general interpretivist stance one might adopt in making sense of CIR. We begin, innocuously enough, with his thoughts on barriers in the way of Indigenous peoples' struggles "of" freedom, noting it will take some effort at tracing out and following Tully's

---

[20] Tully, *PPNK, supra* note 6 at 16.

[21] Namely: the Crown presumption that the "exercise of exclusive jurisdiction over territories of Indigenous peoples is not only effective but also legitimate," and the unspoken presumption that "there is no viable alternative": see text accompanying note 15.

path until we arrive at the grounding for a stance marked as a politics of recognition.

Tully argues that in the way of transforming understandings in the context of contemporary CIR is the fact the Crown does not approach Indigenous peoples with the right principles in mind for there to be the possibility of respectful dialogue and negotiation which could lead to meaningful reconciliation. Tully's scheme proposes five principles, the central being that of "mutual recognition." A condition to a fair process of negotiating reconciliation is that "Aboriginal peoples and Canadians recognise and relate to each other as equal, coexisting and self-governing peoples throughout their many relations together."[22]

"Recognition," here a heavily loaded term, implies that the Crown would accept the legitimacy of attributes recognized as marking Indigenous polities. Leaving aside for the moment why one would think the Crown would come to this position, we need to see the initial connection between the path Tully lays out for responding to the fact of the continuing effects of colonialism and the underlying interpretivist approach to making sense of CIR. Within this underlying approach, the material we have to work with (as theoreticians, but also as those working to effect transformative change) are currently functioning ideas. None of these ideas are, the interpretivist holds, fixed or immutable. The way forward, then, is through a deep understanding of the current spectrum of contingent ideas and involves finding ways to shift ideas away from those that currently dictate how the Crown sees and treats Indigenous peoples to ideas that make it possible to address the "fundamental contradiction" at the heart of the contemporary situation.

Given generations of hard work already put to the unsuccessful task of trying to have the Crown accept Indigenous peoples as "equal, coexisting and self-governing peoples," one might think this path unpromising. What, then, of the obvious alternative, direct action (particularly revolutionary or radical)? Such action, however, must also be animated by theory, and so we wonder which ideas could drive us to (or at the very least, facilitate) forms of radical action.

---

[22] Tully, *PPNK, supra* note 6 at 229.

Tully argues that any such ideas—most commonly held together and given energy by contemporary Marxist ideology—lack nuance, are over-broad, lead to self-absorption, marginalization and disempowerment, and encompass "essentializing, a priori, absolutist, universalizing terms of separatist resurgence."[23] Furthermore, the "polarizing" "binary world view" underlying all this (of friends/enemies, bourgeois/proletariat, Indigenous/non-Indigenous) does not fit with "many traditional ways of knowing and being."[24] Along with arguments about the impracticality of overturning capitalism and re-invigorating independent Indigenous polities and economies,[25] we here *seem* to encounter fundamental disagreement on the level of deep theory animating different forms of CT. Borrows and Tully argue that the Marxist approach is wrong-headed, for all these reasons, which leaves, then, the search for a proper way to come to make sense of CIR (supplied by this account). As we press on, though, note that this constitutes an evaluation of the Marxist/nationalist approach *from the perspective of* an interpretivist form of CT.

The Indigenous scholar (or polity) looking for ways to make sense of contemporary CIR need not, however, agree with this characterization of the nature and strength of Marxist-inspired quasi-nationalist accounts. In particular, the Indigenous scholar could look to Marxist thought for insight into *how* our current world has been structured—*why* do we find ourselves constrained in these ways (regardless of how contingent the systems that constrain us might be)? Shorn of notions of economic forces and material determinism, Marxist accounts of the rise of capitalism offer intriguing and plausible narratives about changes in economic structures and relationships (themselves grounded and made possible by changes in how people come to think of themselves and their relationships to others and the world around) that sweep over Indigenous peoples and their territories. While it is true that the commonly envisioned endpoint for the grand version of this narrative is a communist utopia, an imagined world far removed from the lives and concerns of

---

[23] Borrows & Tully, *supra* note 8 at 7.

[24] *Ibid* at 6–7.

[25] These arguments emerge most clearly in Tully's response to critics, in Robert Nichols & Jakeet Singh, eds, *Freedom and Democracy in an Imperial Context: Dialogues with James Tully* (London, UK: Routledge, 2014), though they also appear (more as statements than arguments) in Borrows & Tully, *supra* note 8.

(most) Indigenous peoples, this does not detract from the fact that capitalism has been a core driver behind devastation and loss Indigenous collectives have endured (and *continue* to endure). Indeed, the Indigenous scholar could strip ideas and insights from Marxist analysis and treat them as Tully proposes—as ways of thinking with a time-and-place grounding. Why, when we think of options for "transforming understandings," would we not turn to ways of thinking that respond to the fundamental role capitalism has played in Canada's colonial history?

Here we detect a particular strain of "impracticality" Borrows and Tully implicitly evoke through deployment of *their* underlying approach: they hold that a Marxism-inspired "transformation of understandings" is doomed to failure, as the mechanism for transformation is limited to shifts along axes that already *make sense within given forms of thought animating practices of governance.* And Canadian society—that larger body that ultimately must transform its self-understandings—simply does not see the world in any way that challenges capitalism. A puzzle concerning the Borrows and Tully approach—its deep conservatism—clears up once one digs deeply enough into their theoretical underpinning.

Tully responds to criticism that he gives short shrift to concerns about the forces of capitalism by arguing that *PPNK* is fundamentally *about* "informal imperialism," those "'processes' that spread and reshape [capitalism and the modern state] and relations around the world and protect them against insurrection" where "[i]nformal imperialism carries on the project of colonial imperialism of spreading the module of institutions of capitalism and the modern state by violent means, yet in a non-colonial manner."[26] He is, he argues, entirely alive to the ways colonialism/imperialism and capitalism intertwine in Canada's history, but nevertheless he has reason to think that directly challenging capitalism—particularly through Marxist-informed prescriptions—is not an acceptable path to follow.

This might appear, once again, to fundamentally shift the debate we have been examining—focused on *forms of theory* in relation to CIR—to a separate ground, about the base-practicality of one approach over another. But as we just noted, underlying theoretical commitments remain, playing key roles in structuring even a debate

---

[26] Robert & Singh, *supra* note 25 at 236 (Tully responding to Antonio Y Vázquez-Arroyo).

ostensibly about which approach would be practically reasonable. When we tease out these deeper theoretical commitments, we circle back to the fact that Tully uses a specific interpretivist variant of CT to push a particular take on how to understand CIR, one that might perhaps not actually embrace critical doctrine.

Before we dig more deeply into the morass lying at the level of theorizing this variant of CT, we can extract more cause for concern on the level of "practicality" if we look to how Tully supports the argument that the modern Marxist/nationalist approach to understanding CIR, and acting in response to its account, is unacceptable. Here, we narrow focus to a core argument Borrows and Tully advance about the undesirability of a Marxist approach to addressing CIR. Such an approach, they argue, dismisses the interdependence that already exists between Indigenous and non-Indigenous societies. It advocates, they claim, a (violent?) turning away from non-Indigenous peoples.[27] The sort of interdependence or interweaving the pair must ultimately rely upon at the level of underlying interpretivist theory is *not*, however, some amorphous web of societal interrelations between Indigenous and non-Indigenous peoples (where, after living in one geographic space for many generations, interdependence is impossible to deny), but rather the interpenetration of previously distinct *ways of thinking* in Indigenous and non-Indigenous societies.[28] Furthermore, when we turn to theorizing CIR we are not thinking about intercultural

---

[27] As something of an aside, elsewhere Tully labels an alternate critical approach "the violent critical tradition" (*ibid* at 235), though it must be noted that the violence almost always comes from the state in response to attempts to "turn away" or remain independent, and not from Indigenous peoples who try to pursue inherent forms of authority.

[28] One might also question the purported interdependence and interweaving Borrows and Tully do discuss and ask just how visible and viable it is in the most important areas—in, for example, how Indigenous and non-Indigenous peoples think of how humans relate to non-humans and the rest of the world they inhabit. Consider this passage from *PPNK*:

Respect has a somewhat different significance in Aboriginal and non-Aboriginal cultures. [...] [Within many Aboriginal groups respect] is bestowed on all members of the circle of life because they are members of the circle of life: to animals, plants, waters, spirits, as well as to human beings. [...] [Within non-Aboriginal culture there is a sense of respect] similar to the circle of life sense in Aboriginal culture. Here, human beings are said to warrant a certain respect in virtue of being human, as being of equal dignity and thus treated as ends rather than means. This general sense of respect is often extended beyond

dialogue, but are focused on relations between the Canadian state and dispossessed and oppressed Indigenous collectives. Practices of governance Tully focuses our attention on are those of the larger state, the notion being that Indigenous peoples and their systems of thought are capable of interacting with forms of thought animating state practices. *In the context of CIR* Borrows and Tully must—within their theoretical approach—reach for forms of interdependence and intermixing on the level of ways of thinking about practices and techniques of governance that simply do not yet exist. More troublingly, these forms of interdependence may never exist.

We see the problem starkly if we return to the type of situation introduced earlier, the sort erupting across Canada as we continue into the twenty-first century. Choose any one of those situations and contemplate how practices of state governance play out (as the Crown continues to assert absolute dominion over lands and waters). One can, and likely *should*, agree that all this is contingent, that no forces, immutable structures, or ways of thinking *dictate* that things function this way. Yet one finds little reason to think that struggles "of" freedom in this context hold out any chance of success. Again, while we easily slip into debates over practicality (where no path forward, frankly, looks particularly promising), this is also—and more fundamentally—a debate over *how* to *think* properly about the world around us and how we should approach problems.

A key query is whether we are driven to conceive of Indigenous peoples as already *inside* the world governed by the state, or whether we can sensibly think of some Indigenous collectives as yet to be respectfully invited in. And key to this is the realization this is *not*

---

the human species, to all living things, to God's creatures and to nature [Tully, *PPNK, supra* note 6 at 242–243].

Ecological devastation wrought upon the world the last few centuries is difficult to overstate. The looming extension of inter-related forms of environmental catastrophe as the planet warms and weather patterns dramatically shift looks to be one of the very few truly existential threats humanity has faced. Do we actually see, in the face of all this, something in non-Aboriginal society that is similar to the Aboriginal sense of respect for life that Tully hints at in this passage? The grounding of the notion of respect in Western systems of thought he points to (in Kantian ethics!) is arguably a core causal force driving us inexorably closer to the existential threat, so far as it is rooted in an entirely human-focused way of thinking of life and meaning. The idea that this personhood-rooted notion is "often extended beyond the human species" is dangerously delusional.

about day-to-day life within a society, but about being "within" common forms of discourse. Conversations about acknowledgement of the contingency of practices of governance and resultant work toward negotiated forms of interaction involve a dialogic encounter between *bodies that exercise authority* (and decidedly not about social relations between members of societies these bodies represent). For this struggle "of" freedom there must already be a common discursive ground constituted by a web of systems of ideas that exists in-between *these* bodies. Such ground does not exist, and, indeed, arguably may be impossible in principle—at least not without the state fundamentally changing how it understands itself and how it acts in the world.

It might seem this has not slipped Tully's attention. At several places he notes a hard limit to dialogue aimed at reconciling deep differences—no matter how hard the oppressed and dispossessed wish the discussion to move forward, it may go nowhere.[29] Here, we need to keep track of the precondition Tully sets for meaningful dialogue: recognition by the state of Indigenous peoples as "equal, co-existing and self-governing."[30] Several times we have passed by a natural question: why might the state accede to this? Why would one think the state—which grounds its current interactions with Indigenous peoples on the presumption that its absolute sovereign power is *legitimate*—shift its thinking about how it fundamentally conceives of Indigenous peoples? Fact is, acknowledgement of a hard limit misses the deeper problem with theory, as within Tully's system the only possibility one can consider is that one side of a dialogic encounter may refuse to shift its understandings. What we notice missing in CIR, however, is a *common discursive ground* making possible meaningful dialogue.

At least as troubling is the fact that even if we acknowledge this pressing problem, issues may run deeper than the absence of a common ground. Indeed, in this context a common ground may be inconceivable. One might think that what discussions lead to is up to the discussants, but it is open to wonder beforehand what possible common ground (within which we would locate possible resolutions) might look like. Consider, yet again, the type of situation introduced earlier—two bodies assume legitimate authority not just over their respective

---

29 Tully, *PPNK, supra* note 6 at 24.
30 *Ibid* at 229.

membership but over a single territory. One might think some sort of arrangement—a new form of federalism?—could be worked out to accommodate this difficult problem of multiple-authorities. But problems lie beneath this issue. First, Indigenous and non-Indigenous discussants may well come to the initial stage of working out how to interact armed with incommensurable systems of thought and action. Second, on the deepest level of the interpretivist approach, we note a troubling presumption: that Indigenous peoples must already live in a world *dominated* by the interpretivist theory of theorizing.

Deep Tensions on the Level of Theory and the Possibility of a Critical Indigenous Theory

These problems can be linked by thinking about how the notion of "truth" is variably understood between interpretivist CT camps. As we do so we also locate a site for—and rough parameters of—a critical Indigenous theory (CIT). We begin by looking at the debate between the camps of interpretivist critical theorists from a high vantage point. On the one hand, we find an approach that eschews "transcendental" theories, that attempts to locate theory at the level of citizenry and politics. Under this approach, truth is placed *in* the world: to the extent we can talk of truth, it is an attribute that only makes sense *within* a socio-cultural setting: i.e., *these* people *here* at *this* point in time have a specific notion of truth they use in *this* way (revealed in the ways they work with their built concept). Alternatively, we have those who work under a "grand theory" which provides definitive answers as to how to think about CIR. This may seem paradoxical—how could an interpretivist CT spin out a variant that seems to provide a "transcendent" theory of truth?—but to see this possibility one need only adopt the same two-level model of theory-construction we encountered earlier when we thought of the contemporary Marxist. This theorist, recall, might accept that in the concrete worlds we all inhabit, social structures are indeed all built by societies (and so are contingent and malleable), but want to adhere to a "higher" view of human-social-economic-legal structures which posits certain truths about what is going on in the built-world. Switching to the interpretivist umbrella, we find a camp of interpretivist CTs who want to press the notion that all theory is embedded in time and place, that all theorizing is socio-culturally-bound, yet present this account from "on high"—this, they argue (or, more commonly it seems, presume) is the truth about "truth." Of course, to make this sensible, they do need some grand theory (even if it only lies in the background).

The transcendental form of interpretivist CT engages a concept of truth the critical Indigenous theorist might want to avoid. Why, after all, would one (regardless of cultural grounding) think there is some oddly fixed way things are such that, once it is captured in our model, we have (potentially at least) magically arrived at answers to all our questions about what we should think and how we should act? Universalized, a priori, essentialist models (built on a foundation of "truth" understood in a transcendental form) are viewed suspiciously by most in the current, larger intellectual world.[31] But, for very different reasons, CIT should also view with suspicion the grounding of the interpretivist model, whether of the transcendental or non-transcendental variety (though particularly of the transcendent form).

The general interpretivist approach is, after all, the product of a very specific Western intellectual history. One can see the myopia of the model of truth the interpretivist works with if one traces out threads of the intellectual history leading to this particular socio-cultural model. We could begin before the Middle Ages in Europe, but starting at a point just before the Enlightenment unfolds keeps our historical sketch manageable. Truth at that time was, for most European intellectuals, understood to attach to beliefs humans could hold that weakly reflect the pure divine state of the contents of the mind of an all-knowing, all-seeing God. Achieving a gods-eye point of view was the ideal—a statement is true if it reflects or captures what is held or known in the mind of the infallible, all-knowing creator of all. By the early stages of the Enlightenment this model was beginning to shift, as early explorers in the slowly-opening world of scientific inquiry asked pressing questions about the status of what one might uncritically take to be truths about the natural world. Note, though, that questions asked in this process only make sense against the backdrop of the pre-Enlightenment model of "perfect" truth to which humans aspire.

---

[31] While this has been true in the humanities, and to some extent in the social sciences, for quite some time, it is noteworthy that this understanding of truth and knowledge in the sciences more generally (at least that is, in the philosophy of science) has, over the last few decades, become relatively mainstream. See e.g., Peter Godfrey-Smith, *Theory and Reality: An Introduction to the Philosophy of Science* (Chicago: University of Chicago Press, 2003).

Skeptical arguments from Descartes, for example, have their sting to the extent the end sought in quests for truth is an incorrigible, absolute piece of unshakeable knowledge.[32] The *cogito* being the only piece of knowledge Descartes can originally find that meets conditions set by such a background model, all the rest of human knowledge is purportedly to be built on the basis of this singular point. Shortly after, we see "secular" forms of these skeptical arguments. For example, Hume assumes a necessary backdrop for there to be real force behind certain arguments: how do we know *for certain* that event B will always follow event A, no matter how many times we have seen B follow A (with what we presume to be a causal link between them)?[33]

We can skip the next few centuries, as by the late eighteenth century the pattern has been firmly established—with truth characterized by what can be *certainly* known, it is devilishly difficult to defeat easily-constructed skeptical arguments. In reaction to centuries of failure in constructing arguments defeating these all-too-powerful skeptical arguments an anti-thesis emerges—the model of "truth" as *entirely* context-bound. The impossibility of achieving the god's-eye point of view—the sensibility of which, note, is entirely contained within a very specific religious history—drove the development of notions of context-dependent truth that, in beginning from *inside* language and discourse, preserve the centrality of the human (itself a core position of a very specific religious worldview), and preserve the position of the human as a unique instrument of reason and will. A very particular religious intellectual history has thereby been carried on into a new—but still deeply myopic—chapter.

Might one, gazing at this intellectual history from a point outside it, reconsider the underlying model that provides criteria for something being "true" (or, known to be true)? There are numerous pre-Christianized Indigenous worlds of thought that do not follow a parallel path, that do not embrace the notion of truth emergent out of the model of the perfect being animating Judeo-Christian spheres. In these worlds of thought humans are not made in the image of this perfect being, blessed

---

[32] René Descartes, *Meditations on First Philosophy: With Selections from the Objections and Replies,* 2nd ed, translated by John Cottingham (Cambridge: Cambridge University Press, 2017).

[33] David Hume, *Enquiries Concerning Human Understanding and Concerning the Principles of Morals,* 3rd ed by Selby-Bigge (Oxford: Clarendon Press, 1902).

with capacities (reason being primary) that make it possible (and desirable) to seek something like the thought that exists in the mind of an all-powerful, omniscient being. In many Indigenous intellectual histories humans are simply *here*, part of the natural world, forming societies just as do the beaver and the bear, with truths about how to live in the world that developed by living in the world and thinking about the world as experienced. Indeed, non-human kin live in the same world and have come to know—in their own ways—how best to do so.

It might seem a path can lead the interpretivist out of the narrowness of their socio-culturally-grounded position—indeed, a path demanded if internal consistency is to be maintained within this grand theory. Why can the interpretivist not simply fully accept the deep position on truth it has built up? That is, given that social worlds are treated as constructed, and so truth-claims that arise within a given social context are treated as aspects of those webs of belief that everything is wrapped up in, why not transpose this position to a higher level, to the level of *theories about truth*? From this position all theories—*including theories developed as interpretivist*—are similarly entirely context-dependent. This position—encompassing a high degree of internal consistency—might then seem to allow for full embrace of the notion that Indigenous peoples can each have their own theories of truth.

Such internal consistency, however, comes at a high cost given the topic at hand, making sense of CIR. The interpretivist has to acknowledge that at this time and in this place (where place is not so much geographic as it is about the location of a specific meaning-generating environment) a particular theory of truth has emerged, one that is the product of engagement with a long, complex and ultimately religiously-grounded intellectual history. This theory of truth is very much non-Indigenous at its roots, and the only way we can begin with the approach Borrows and Tully advocate to making sense of CIR is if we *first* place Indigenous peoples into *this* location (that is, *inside* a world thoroughly dominated by a non-Indigenous intellectual history).

We return to a fundamental point of disagreement. Are Indigenous peoples already captured within a world of meaning that has all its dominant roots in non-Indigenous ways of thinking, or is the task ahead to determine how Indigenous peoples can work out an arrangement such that their independent conceptual-realities can co-exist with those that have tried to destroy them over the last seven-plus generations? A deep problem for the interpretivist approach is that it rests upon the presumption that this sort of question is moot, as the business of negotiating the meaning of reconciliation is premised on the presumed interdependence of Indigenous and non-Indigenous forms of thought, right down to the point where non-Indigenous theorizing about theory subsumes possible alternate Indigenous worlds.

In a sense, it all comes down to whether or not the interpretivist is willing to (or must) accept that they embrace a grand theory in the transcendental sense. It would seem they have a choice. On the one hand, they could cling to an embedded view of context-dependency, so that a grand transcendent theory of truth (an all-encompassing model of truth the way they conceive of it) is held to be the *right* model for *all* social worlds, while *under* this model of truth, within specific social worlds, one finds embedded specific context-dependent models of truth, some of which may not accept the higher-view. On the other hand, the interpretivist critical theorist could attempt to be more fully internally-consistent, accepting that their seemingly-transcendent model is *itself* just a time-and-place instantiation (one with a decidedly non-Indigenous pedigree, the product of a felt-need to address failings of the absolute-certainty model of truth of the early Enlightenment), in which case they would have to accept that when they turn to making sense of CIR their approach is parochial (that, for example, an Indigenous model of truth may simply not agree with their approaches to how to theorize about and make pronouncements on that matter).

Borrows and Tully seem to work under a grand theory, and presume Indigenous peoples find themselves inhabiting a social world governed by the state, a social world wherein they have no more than the ability to engage in struggles over how the governing political bodies understand the nature of their practices of governance. An Indigenous critical theorist need not agree with either position, as they may come from a people with their own theory of truth, one that continues to inform today's struggles, and they can disagree with the notion that their community is already embedded within a socio-discursive world governed by the state.[34]

---

[34] Ambiguity is possible here. In a sense, all Indigenous communities in Canada find themselves *governed by the state*, if by that is meant that they all have little real choice in obeying laws of the state. But in another sense—tied directly to notions of legitimacy, *particularly* as this notion finds meaning from within an Indigenous community purportedly falling under state governance—an Indigenous people may be truly self-governing.

Lessons Learned: Framework for a Critical Indigenous Theory

What does the Indigenous scholar and activist take away from thinking about the possible utility of CT in making sense of CIR?

There are several basic elements of CT the Indigenous scholar may find acceptable as starting points. First, the suspicion—ultimately leading to deep critique—of mainstream theory and theorizing. Second, the focus on matters of oppression and domination (cast as concern with freedom and non-domination). And third, focus on the lived experiences of those oppressed and dominated (as material out of which is built the scaffolding for thoughts about how to make sense of the world of oppression and domination). If we fix our attention just on these three elements, we find within CT both contemporary Marxist and interpretivist strands.

Furthermore, both camps—along with the Indigenous critical theorist—would likely find little fault with Tully's articulation of the current problematic at the heart of CIR, that "dominant society coexists on and exercises exclusive jurisdiction over the territories and jurisdictions that the Indigenous peoples refuse to surrender," as well as the fact the situation persists due to adherence by the Crown to two basic presumptions: that the "exercise of exclusive jurisdiction over territories of Indigenous peoples is not only effective but also legitimate," and that "there is no viable alternative."[35]

Beyond this, though, there is fundamental disagreement between the two critical camps, as the one group searches for (and finds) a theory of social and political philosophy that serves to explain the nature of this problematic situation and to prescribe appropriate responses to it, while the other holds that no such theory—in an objective or absolute sense—exists. Suitably adjusted—problematic components stripped away and the remainder tuned for the task of assisting the Indigenous scholar striving to make sense of CIR—the Indigenous critical theorist can find helpful aspects of positions and arguments from within both strands.

Further deep insights, however, must emerge from the intellectual history of whatever specific Indigenous community to which the theorist is connected. Some Indigenous people today are deeply embedded within worlds constructed by latecomers to North America,

---

[35] See the text accompanying notes 14 and 15.

and understandably have little interest in anything other than finding a respectful position therein.[36] Some Indigenous nations, however, have taken on the language of nationhood—transposed to the context of internal colonialism—and continue work within intellectual traditions reaching back many generations. While in such cases ideas currently worked with are inextricably interwoven with European forms of discourse, there remains a self-determining core, a sense in which these people persist as the same people from generations ago, building on truths developed over eons. The latter sort of community will more naturally ground an Indigenous scholar intent on developing CIT, though the contours and content of the developed theory will largely depend on this person's position within their particular Indigenous socio-cultural world.

What, of a general nature, can we say of a framework for CIT? Clearly, cruder (typically older) forms of Marxism need to be shorn of some of the deepest Marxist positions, as it is almost certainly not the case that an Indigenous scholar would find much value in the larger, absolutist, deterministic theory on offer. That said, exploring how economic forces have battered Indigenous collectives, especially how capitalist ideology has both supported and been supported by state governance structures and systems of belief, explaining much of the movement of the state over the last few centuries, would surely have value. What about Marxist prescriptions and the leaning of Indigenous-Marxist scholars toward Indigenous nationalism? Here we can swing around to issues of practicality, removed from deeper theoretical commitments that we noted the interpretivist illicitly casts on the matter, and seriously consider the possibility of removing global forces of capitalism (as these work through and with the support of state institutions) from the lives of Indigenous polities.

We have as well seen that some strands of interpretivist critical theory can be an inappropriate springboard for CIT, particularly when it leads the theorist toward the dead-end of a politics of recognition. That said, it is invaluable to work through how contingent the seemingly-immutable worlds of oppression and dispossession are, as their roots in theory and forms of justification are all shown to be

---

[36] This is a claim made about communities or peoples, and so in a number of ways is problematic. No "people," Indigenous or otherwise, are so homogenous that such absolute claims can possibly be true, and even identifying the Indigenous "people" about which such a claim might be made is a complex matter in colonial Canada.

built and malleable. Through such work ways of struggling free of these webs can be suggested. Their built-nature, however, does not in itself reveal these structural constraints to be moveable or transformable *from within*—as we traced out the Borrows and Tully approach to CIR we came up to the wall of Crown sensibility, to the approach's allegiance to both the legitimacy of Crown authority over Indigenous peoples and to Crown understandings of Indigenous peoples and their place within Canadian society. Clearly, moving beyond wishful thinking—the interpretivist pollyannish-approach to effecting meaningful change in CIR—must be an objective of CIT.

We noted earlier a choice facing those following the interpretivist approach: either accept an absolutist model of truth and theorizing, proclaiming that all truth is entirely context-dependent and all theory is time, place, and people bound, or adopt a more reflexive stance, and from this stance note that interpretivist critical theory is itself time, place and people bound.

An Indigenous critical theorist could note how the first choice is imperialistic to the extent it presumes the applicability of its grand theory of truth to worlds built by Indigenous peoples. Tully's approach shows how taking this path plays out, eventually leading to the status quo of a hopelessly inadequate politics of recognition. The second path, besides being more aligned with general critical theoretic commitments, makes space for a CIT. The Indigenous critical theorist acknowledges the grounding of interpretivist models of truth and theorizing in the development of centuries of Western intellectual thought, places all this "over there" (*they* think *this* way—it underscores *their* way of doing things), and continues to build on truths and on understandings of how truths have been and can be arrived at that their community has in hand (*this* is how *we* think and act in the world).

Indigenous Rights and Responsibilities to Language Transmission: Implementing Article 14 of UNDRIP

*Lorena Sekwan Fontaine**

Abstract

This chapter explores the historical practices and legislation that have harmed Indigenous language transmission, followed by an analysis of the rights and responsibilities outlined in the *Indigenous Languages Act, 2019* and the implications of the *United Nations Declaration on the Rights of Indigenous Peoples Act, 2021*. The chapter concludes that governments within Canada must address the historical injustice inflicted upon Indigenous languages. The lack of government support and funding for Indigenous language education continues to perpetuate cultural genocide.

---

* I would like to express my gratitude to five dedicated individuals with whom I have had the privilege of advocating for Aboriginal language rights in education in Canada for nearly a decade: Andrea Bear Nicholas, Maliseet from Nekotkok (Tobique First Nation), Professor Emeritus at St. Thomas University; Amos Key Jr., a member of the Mohawk Nation, conferred to the Sacred Circle of Faith Keepers of the Longhouse at Six Nations of the Grand River Territory; Karihwakeron Tim Thompson, Mohawk Nation at Wáhta Mohawk Territory; David Leitch, constitutional lawyer; Ian Martin, Associate Professor, Department of English at Glendon College.

Résumé

Ce chapitre explore les pratiques historiques et la législation qui ont nui à la transmission des langues autochtones, suivies d'une analyse des droits et responsabilités énoncés dans la *Loi sur les langues autochtones* de 2019 et des implications de la *Loi sur la Déclaration des Nations Unies sur les droits des peuples autochtones* de 2021. Il conclut que les gouvernements au Canada doivent s'attaquer à l'injustice historique infligée aux langues autochtones. Le manque de soutien et de financement gouvernementaux pour l'éducation en langues autochtones continue de perpétrer le génocide culturel.

> *The language has power. We believe that. When the children leave our school [...] I want them to have a strong sense of who they are—the land and the language. Because they are going to run into a lot of challenges. But if they have this inner cultural identity, this inner strength, they will be able to put up with any of it.*[1]

Indigenous language transmission is the vital process of passing down ancestral languages to the next generation, crucial for maintaining the distinctiveness and resilience of Indigenous peoples.[2] This transmission involves not only linguistic knowledge but also the values that play a central role in shaping cultural identity, worldview, value systems, and ceremonial practices. Language also holds a crucial role in informing Indigenous peoples' relationships with the land, animals, plants, and water.[3] Effective language transmission engages the entire community, including parents, grandparents, family, Elders, and community members. Educational institutions, particularly in the face of language endangerment, now play an even more significant

---

[1] Robert Matthew, Principal of T'selcéwtqen Clleq'mel'ten/Chief Atahm School, Presentation (delivered to the Standing Committee on Aboriginal Peoples at the 42nd Parliament 1st Session, Issue 51, 3 April 2019) online: <sencanada.ca/en/committees/appa/42-1>.

[2] Task Force on Aboriginal Languages and Cultures, *Towards a New Beginning: A Foundational Report for a Strategy to Revitalize First Nation, Inuit and Métis Languages and Cultures* (Winnipeg: Aboriginal Language Task Force, 2005) at 22.

[3] *Ibid.*

role. The government bears a responsibility to ensure adequate support and funding for language transmission, given past policies that targeted the destruction of Indigenous languages. Concurrently, Indigenous peoples have the responsibility of ensuring that children learn and understand their cultural identity and connections to their community and land through language transmission. Within Indigenous legal traditions, language is considered a sacred responsibility, as it is viewed as a gift from the Creator that must be safeguarded and passed on to the next generation.[4]

This chapter provides a brief overview of historical legislative and government practices that resulted in the harm to Indigenous language transmission. An analysis of the rights and responsibilities to language transmission in the *Indigenous Languages Act, 2019* and the implications of the recent *United Nations Declaration on the Rights of Indigenous Peoples Act, 2021* will also be explored.

Historical Harms

Between 1850 and 1867, there were several pieces of legislation that were passed under a policy of assimilation that impacted Indigenous linguistic sovereignty. The premise of the legislation was to deal with the "Indian Problem." Under the 1850 *Indian Protection Act* and the 1857 *Gradual Civilization Act*, the legislative objective was to gradually remove all cultural and legal distinctions between Indians and non-Indians through the process of enfranchisement. The policy from this period contradicted the numbered treaties that were negotiated between 1871 and 1921, particularly in the area of education.

In 1883, Canada's first prime minister, Sir John A. Macdonald, set the stage and rationale for genocidal policies in the House of Commons:

> When the school is on the reserve the child lives with its parents, who are savages; he is surrounded by savages, and though he may learn to read and write his habits, and training and mode of thought are Indian. He is simply a savage who can read and write. It has

---

[4] Harold Cardinal & Walter Hildebrand, *Treaty Elders of Saskatchewan: Our Dream Is That Our Peoples Will One Day Be Clearly Recognized as Nations* (Calgary: University of Calgary Press, 2000).

been strongly pressed on myself, as the head of the Department, that Indian children should be withdrawn as much as possible from the parental influence, and the only way to do that would be to put them in central training industrial schools where they will acquire the habits and modes of thought of white men.[5]

The objective as stated by Macdonald was to remove Indigenous children from their language and cultural influences and immerse them into an educational system that would teach them a new language and a Euro-male centred worldview. Then, in 1920, Deputy Minister of Indian Affairs Duncan Campbell Scott outlined the goals of cultural genocide when he informed a parliamentary committee that the government's objective was "to continue until there is not a single Indian in Canada that has not been absorbed into the body politic."[6] In this case, the goals were not only to eliminate the cultural identity of Indigenous children but also the nationhood of Indigenous peoples. It was mandatory that all "Indian children" attend residential schools. Historian John Milloy asserts that the fundamental purpose of Canadian residential school education from 1879 onwards was to "'kill the Indian' in the child for the sake of Christian civilization."[7]

The schools were intentionally located at substantial distances from Indigenous communities in order to minimize Indigenous children's contact with their culture and language. Hayter Reed, Indian Commissioner, advocated that Indigenous children be sent to residential schools a great distance away from the community. The rationale was to reduce the opportunities for parental visits to counteract assimilation of Indigenous children. In the 1880s, without any legal foundation or authority, parents were required to obtain a pass from the Indian agent in order to visit their children in residential schools.[8]

---

[5] *House of Commons Debates*, 5-1 (9 May 1883) at 1107–1108.

[6] Evidence of DC Scott to the Special Committee of the House of Commons Investigating the *Indian Act* amendments of 1920 (1920), Library and Archives Canada, (RG 10, vol 6810, file 470-2-3, vol 7) (L-2) (N-3).

[7] John S Milloy, *A National Crime: The Canadian Government and the Residential School System, 1879 to 1986* (Winnipeg: University of Manitoba Press, 1999) at xv.

[8] Laurie F Barron, "The Indian Pass System in the Canadian West, 1882–1935" (1988) 13:1 Prairie Forum 25 at 35.

If parents refused to send their children to residential schools, they could be imprisoned, fined, or both.

The government's hostile approach to Indigenous languages and cultures was reiterated in government directives. Reed stressed the importance of banning the use of Indigenous languages. In 1890 he was instructed to develop a draft of school regulations. Reed proposed that: "'[t]he vernacular is not to be taught in any schools. At the most the native language is only to be used as a vehicle of teaching and should be discontinued as such as soon as practicable.' English was to be the primary language of instruction, 'even where French is taught.'"[9] Although these recommendations were never incorporated into a formal regulation, a few years later, the department published its "Programme of Studies for Indian Schools" indicating that "[e]very effort must be made to induce pupils to speak English, and to teach them to understand it; unless they do the whole work of the teacher is likely to be wasted."[10] In 1895, Reed argued that without English, Indigenous children would be,

> permanently disabled, and from what Indians have said to me and from requests made by them, it is evident that they are beginning to recognize the force of this themselves. With this end in view, the children in all the industrial and boarding schools are taught in the English language exclusively.[11]

In keeping with this policy approach, the 1910 contract between the federal government and the churches required that schools were

> not to employ, except for a period not exceeding six months, any teacher or instructor until evidence satisfactory to the Superintendent General has been submitted to him that such teacher or instructor is able to converse with the pupils under his charge in English and is able to speak and write the English

---

[9] Truth and Reconciliation Commission of Canada, *The Final Report of the Truth and Reconciliation Commission of Canada. Volume 1, the History Part 1, Origins to 1939* (Winnipeg: Truth and Reconciliation Commission of Canada, 2015) at 616.

[10] *Ibid* at 165.

[11] *Ibid* at 616 citing Canada, *Annual Report of the Department of Indian Affairs, 1895,* xxii–xxiii.

language fluently and correctly and possess such other quali-fications as in the opinion of the Superintendent General may be necessary.[12]

When Indigenous parents complained or expressed concern that their children returned home uneducated, unable or unwilling to speak their language, the government turned their back and did nothing. The policy remained unchanged into the 1930s, when the "Programme of Studies for Indian Schools" advised teachers that "[e]very effort must be made to induce pupils to speak English and to teach them to under-stand it. Insist on English even during the supervised play. Failure in this means wasted efforts."[13] The Truth and Reconciliation Commission (TRC) concluded in their final report that:

> One of the few issues on which federal residential school policy was crystal clear was that of language. First, students were to be taught to speak English (or, in certain, limited cases, French). Second, to ensure the rapid adoption of English, Aboriginal lan-guages were to be suppressed. Although the use of Aboriginal languages was not completely banned at all times and in all places, it is clear that it was seen as a sign of progress if a princi-pal could report that Aboriginal languages were not spoken in the school, or, even better, that children had forgotten how to speak them.[14]

In 2015, the TRC released its final report that documented historical harms to Indigenous languages and its lasting traumatic impacts today.[15] In order to address these harms, the TRC called for language rights to be included in section 35 of Canada's *Constitution Act, 1982*.[16] Two years after the release of the final TRC report, Indigenous leaders reached an agreement of principles for co-development that would be based on the legislative and policy needs of the Metis, First Nations,

---

[12] *Ibid*, citing TRC, NRA, Anglican Church of Canada, General Synod Archives, ACC-MSCC-GS 75-103, series 3:1, box 48, file 3, Assistant-Deputy to S. P. Matheson, 25 November 1910.

[13] *Ibid*.

[14] *Ibid* at 615.

[15] *Ibid*.

[16] *Constitution Act, 1982*, being Schedule B to the *Canada Act 1982* (UK), 1982, c 11.

and Inuit peoples.[17] During the consultations several references were made to rights and omission to language transmission in Bill C-91, *An Act respecting Indigenous languages* (hereinafter referred to as Bill C-91).

In February 2018 there were a number of Indigenous leaders and expert witnesses that appeared before the Standing Committee on Heritage regarding Bill C-91. The Assembly of First Nations insisted on the need for the legislation to recognize language rights to education on and off reserve. It was stressed that immersion schools are required beginning with school-aged children.[18] The Chiefs of Ontario recognized that Bill C-91 fails to identify a specific language right.[19] The Canadian Bar Association agreed, indicating that Bill C-91 required a clause defining a justiciable right and that allowed "Indigenous peoples to seek out court remedies for violations of the rights it recognizes. Without this important amendment, the *ILA* (Indigenous Languages Act) risks being little more than another hollow promise."[20]

Then in March 2019, there were public presentations made before Senate on Bill C-91. Ellen Gabriel, Kontinónhstats, the Mohawk Language Custodian Association from Kanehsatà:ke, emphasized the need for rights to core funding for language transmission:

> [T]hose institutions in which the religious doctrines of superiority and racism have brought us to the point where we are looking at Canada to say, "Please help us with our languages because you

---

[17] Assembly of First Nations, "Co-Developing an Indigenous *Languages Act*" (Presentation delivered at a Special Chiefs Assembly, 4–6 December 2018), online: <afn. ca/uploads/sca-2018/Documents/Dialogue%20Sessions/Day%201%20-%20 December%204%2C%202018/01%20Languages/01%29%20Languages%20 Powerpoint.pdf>. The guiding principles for the legislation are as follows: 1) the importance of distinction-based legislation, 2) will address core spiritual beliefs, worldview, and relationship to land, 3) acknowledgement of government harms, 4) acknowledge Indigenous language rights are part of Aboriginal and Treaty Rights, 5) recognize the right to adequate funding for regional infrastructure, 6) recognize the right to Indigenous language educational systems off and on reserve.

[18] Assembly of First Nations, National Chief Perry Bellegarde, *Presentation to Standing Committee on Canadian Heritage on an Act Respecting Indigenous Languages* (Ottawa: Assembly of First Nations, 2018). The Brief was presented to the House on April 1, 2019.

[19] The Chiefs of Ontario, Bill C-91, *An Act Respecting Indigenous Languages for Consideration to the House of Commons Standing Committee on Canadian Heritage*. The Brief was presented to the House on April 1, 2019.

[20] The Canadian Bar Association, "Aboriginal Law Section" (March 2019), online: <cba. org/sections/aboriginal-law>. The Brief was presented to the House on April 1, 2019.

hold the purse strings"—if we had the money to be able to pay, as we do post-secondary students, the youth or even adults to go to school, then let's do it, because that's what is needed. We are not going to be successful in revitalization and maintenance if we don't have adult speakers to teach the children, if we don't have those first-language speakers to teach the second-language speakers exactly the meaning of what they are saying [...]. We need core, long-term, sustainable funding for experienced Indigenous languages organizations that have led the way in Indigenous languages preservation and revitalization [...] can't emphasize enough that this is an urgent situation. Language must be given priority and a special place because, without our languages, we have lost who we are as Indigenous people.[21]

Robert Matthew, Principal, T'selcéwtqen Clleq'mel'ten/Chief Atahm School also focused on the importance of rights to resources:

So money is very important, but they've managed to raise it for 25 years [...]. The problem is you spend so much time raising the money. Where should my energy be going? It should be going into the educational plan of the school and it should be going into the research [...]. I spend six months finding money and another six months accounting for it and only a month to spend it. My point is the legislation, to show real commitment to our language, it should be expressed in adequate and sustainable long-term funding.[22]

Natan Obed, president of Inuit Tapiriit Kanatami, revealed discrimination in funding allocation for language in Nunavut.[23] After two years of consultation, discussion and negotiation, the *Indigenous*

---

[21] Standing Senate Committee on Indigenous Peoples 42-1, No 51 (2 April 2019) (Ellen Gabriel, Kontinónhstats) online: <sencanada.ca/en/committees/appa/42-1>.

[22] Standing Senate Committee on Indigenous Peoples 42-1, No 51 (3 April 2019) (Robert Matthew) online: <sencanada.ca/en/committees/appa/42-1>.

[23] Inuit Tapiriit Kanatami, "ITK Submission to the House of Commons Standing Committee on Canadian Heritage. Bill C-91: *An Act respecting Indigenous Languages*" (21 February 2019), online: <ourcommons.ca/Content/Committee/421/CHPC/Brief/BR10362377/br-external/InuitTapiriitKanatami-e.pdf>. "Under the terms of the 2017–2020 Canada-Nunavut Agreement on French Services and Inuktut Language, for example, approximately $8,189 is allocated for each French speaker compared to $186 per Inuktut speaker per year": *ibid* at 3.

Languages Act received royal assent in June 2019 with much criticism by Indigenous leaders on the co-development process.[24]

Indigenous Languages Act

The objective of the *Indigenous Language Act*[25] is to support the revitalization of Indigenous languages. It also recognizes language rights as an Aboriginal right under section 35(1) of the *Constitution Act, 1982*. The legislation, however, does not recognize any specific enforceable language rights. The legislation is also absent on specific rights related to language education and linguistic sovereignty that are identified in *United Nations Declaration on the Rights of Indigenous Peoples* (UNDRIP). These rights are explicitly recognized in Articles 13, 14, 15 and 16 and they are implicitly recognized in Articles 2 (anti-discrimination), 11 (cultural traditions) and 12 (spiritual traditions). The right to language transmission is defined in Article 14:

1. Indigenous peoples have the right to establish and control their educational systems and institutions providing education in their own languages, in a manner appropriate to their cultural methods of teaching and learning.
2. Indigenous individuals, particularly children, have the right to all levels and forms of education of the State without discrimination.
3. States shall, in conjunction with Indigenous peoples, take effective measures, in order for Indigenous individuals, particularly children, including those living outside their communities, to have access, when possible, to an education in their own culture and provided in their own language.

---

[24] *Ibid*. "Inuit were led to believe that this was a co-development initiative, whereby our ideas, feedback, and submissions to the Department of Canadian Heritage would be respected and would contribute to a back-and-forth exchange of views and ideas. However, ITK was unaware that the Department of Canadian Heritage had developed materials and sponsored a Cabinet discussion which severely restricted the federal Crown's ability to engage in any back-and-forth regarding our positions. This led to a series of engagements in which Inuit communicated ideas which the federal government was either unwilling or unable to provide responses to": *ibid* at 5.

[25] Bill C-91, *An Act respecting Indigenous languages*, 1st Sess, 42nd Parl, SC 2019, c 23.

Article 14 of UNDRIP recognizes the right to language transmission, emphasizing that the revitalization of Indigenous languages in Canada depends on intergenerational continuity. It recognizes that, in today's context, this requires state-supported educational systems and institutions that teach Indigenous children their ancestral languages in the required subjects both on and off reserve.

There are several obligations and mechanisms to implement UNDRIP. The TRC Calls to Action recognize UNDRIP as the framework for reconciliation.[26] The *Indigenous Languages Act* also identifies Indigenous language revitalization as a contributor to the implementation of UNDRIP.[27] There is also the recent *United Nations Declaration on the Rights of Indigenous Peoples Act*, 2021, which requires Canada to support the implementation of UNDRIP by taking "effective measures."[28] Without amendments to the *Indigenous Languages Act*, it will remain inconsistent with UNDRIP and, therefore, in conflict with the *United Nations Declaration on the Rights of Indigenous Peoples Act*.

Conclusion

Language transmission is not only a government responsibility for addressing past harms in current contexts, but also a constitutional right that is recognized by Indigenous and international law. The closing of residential schools has done nothing to achieve intergenerational transmission of Indigenous languages. Almost all Indigenous children are still required by law to attend schools in French or English, where they primarily learn the dominant language at the expense of

---

[26] Truth and Reconciliation Commission of Canada, *Calls to Action* (Winnipeg: Truth and Reconciliation Commission of Canada, 2012) at s 48: "We call upon the church parties to the Settlement Agreement, and all other faith groups and interfaith social justice groups in Canada who have not already done so, to formally adopt and comply with the principles, norms, and standards of the *United Nations Declaration on the Rights of Indigenous Peoples* as a framework for reconciliation. This would include, but not be limited to, the following commitments: i) Ensuring that their institutions, policies, programs, and practices comply with the *United Nations Declaration on the Rights of Indigenous Peoples*."

[27] One of the main purposes of the *Indigenous Languages Act* is identified in section 5(g): to "contribute to the implementation of the United Nations Declaration on the Rights of Indigenous Peoples as it relates to Indigenous languages."

[28] *United Nations Declaration on the Rights of Indigenous Peoples Act*, SC 2021, c 14, Preamble.

their own ancestral language. In the majority of cases, they not only fail to acquire fluency in their Indigenous language but also learn to interact with others primarily in English or French. The absence of a guaranteed obligation to fund and adequately support the development of Indigenous language education, such as immersion programs on or off reserve, constitutes ongoing cultural genocide. The lack of appropriate government funding for language education institutions, on or off reserve, is contrary to Article 14 of UNDRIP and Indigenous law, which recognize language transmission as both a right and a responsibility.

CHAPTER A-3

Critical Approaches to Jurisdiction: The Struggle for Control of Indigenous Lands and Resources

Dayna Nadine Scott[*]

Abstract

This chapter questions the starting assumptions in thinking through questions of "jurisdiction" in public law, specifically in relation to assertions of inherent Indigenous territorial governing authority. It reviews the common conceptual images of jurisdiction we employ in law schools and offers resources from critical interdisciplinary theory for new conceptions. In highlighting examples of the present exercise of Indigenous territorial jurisdiction, such as the Kunst'aa guu— Kunst'aayah Reconciliation Protocol and the Tsleil-Waututh Sacred Trust Assessment of the Trans Mountain Expansion (TMX) project,

[*] I owe a debt of gratitude to my generous colleagues Professors Karen Drake and Sonia Lawrence for workshopping this chapter with me in 2022. Their insights, suggestions and reactions improved the work immeasurably. I would also like to thank Osgoode JD student Lo Stevenson for fantastic research assistance. The ideas expressed here have emerged from years of collaboration with leaders and organizers in Treaty No. 9 communities, and from valued conversations with brilliant interlocutors including Donna Ashamock, Wayne Moonias, David Peerla, Adrian Smith, Shiri Pasternak, Deb Cowen, Heidi Stark, Rob Clifford, Amar Bhatia, and Andrée Boisselle among many others.

the chapter urges public law scholars to adopt an orientation of pre-figuration in order to bring into being conceptualizations of jurisdiction that can enliven a decolonial legal future and a new constitutional order.

Résumé

Ce chapitre remet en question les hypothèses de départ concernant les questions de « compétence » en droit public, en particulier en ce qui concerne les affirmations relatives à l'autorité gouvernementale territoriale autochtone inhérente. Il examine les représentations conceptuelles courantes en ce qui a trait à la compétence véhiculée dans les facultés de droit et propose des notions issues de la théorie critique interdisciplinaire pour envisager de nouvelles conceptions. En mettant en lumière des exemples actuels de l'exercice de la compétence territoriale autochtone, tels que le Protocole de réconciliation Kunst'aa guu—Kunst'aayah et l'Évaluation sacrée du projet d'expansion Trans Mountain (TMX) par les Tsleil-Waututh, le chapitre invite les spécialistes en droit public à adopter une orientation de préfiguration. Cela vise à concevoir des conceptualisations de compétence pouvant donner lieu à un avenir juridique décolonial et un nouvel ordre constitutionnel.

The conventional starting point for students of Canadian public law in thinking through questions of "jurisdiction"—who can make decisions about what—is inevitably the "division of powers" stretching back to Confederation and the *Constitution Act, 1867*. If the topic in question is related to Indigenous lands and resources, from there the analysis typically progresses to consider the power vested in the federal Parliament over "Indians and lands reserved for Indians," and the resulting tensions related to the perceived overlaps or gaps in relation to heads of provincial legislative authority. But the whole framing is increasingly thrown into question as Indigenous leaders assert the "inherent rights" of Indigenous peoples to govern themselves as a result of their historic occupation and continued stewardship of the land. Those leaders reference systems of law and governance that preceded contact (and the Constitution) and remain in powerful effect today. It is slowly dawning on the settler legal establishment that Canada may assume sovereignty over all of the lands within its claimed borders, but Indigenous peoples' jurisdiction survives. What does this mean for public law understandings moving forward?

In this chapter, I draw insights from critical interdisciplinary scholarship on the concept of "jurisdiction" to offer resources for building a decolonial legal future, focusing specifically on governing authority in relation to lands, waters and resources. Nishinaabeg scholar Leanne Betasamosake Simpson says this about the Dish with One Spoon Wampum: it is an *"ancient template for realizing separate jurisdictions within a shared territory."*[1] My aim in this work is to demonstrate that making conceptual space for achieving "separate jurisdictions within a shared territory" is a pressing task for critical public law scholars: it is necessary for a decolonial legal future in the place we call Canada. The argument is that there are spheres of jurisdiction in relation to which the Crown should simply "step aside" (to borrow Gordon Christie's framing) so that Indigenous authorities can govern their lands and waters without interference.[2]

The story we tell about "jurisdiction" in Canadian law schools often skips over the part where the very assertion of Canadian sovereignty somehow erases Indigenous governing authority and bestows the settler state with exclusive control.[3] My purpose here is not to inquire into the "mystical foundation of colonial sovereignty,"[4] although critical scholars have for years wondered precisely how the

---

[1] Leanne Betasamosake Simpson, "Looking After Gdoo-Naaganinaa: Precolonial Nishnaabeg Diplomatic and Treaty Relationships" (2008) 23:2 Wicazo Sa R 29 at 38 [emphasis added]. The Dish with One Spoon Wampum Belt Covenant is said to represent a treaty made between Anishinaabe and Haudenosaunee peoples to peaceably share the territory surrounding the Great Lakes prior to European contact.

[2] Gordon Christie, "'Obligations', Decolonization and Indigenous Rights to Governance" (2014) 27:1 Can JL & Jur 259 at 278.

[3] Kent McNeil, "Indigenous Land Rights and Self-Government: Inseparable Entitlements" in Lisa Ford & Tim Rowse, eds, *Between Indigenous and Settler Governance* (New York: Routledge, 2013) 147 [McNeil, "Indigenous Land Rights"]; Shiri Pasternak, "Jurisdiction and Settler Colonialism: Where Do Laws Meet?" (2014) 29:2 CJLS 145 [Pasternak, "Settler Colonialism"].

[4] Brenna Bhandar, *Colonial Lives of Property: Law, Land, and Racial Regimes of Ownership* (Durham: Duke University Press, 2018) at 74. See also Karen Drake, "The Impact of St Catherine's Milling" in *Special Lectures 2017: Canada at 150: The Charter and the Constitution* (Toronto: Irwin Law and the Law Society of Upper Canada, 2017) 618; John Borrows, "Sovereignty's Alchemy: An Analysis of *Delgamuukw v. British Columbia*" (1999) 37:3 Osgoode Hall LJ 537.

Crown obtained sovereignty across all of its claimed territory.[5] Instead, accepting these "contending sovereignties of Canadian constitutionalism," my focus here is on how we might move forward practically now, working the "machinery of jurisdiction," to restore and enable Indigenous nations' governing authority in relation to the lands and waters they exist in reciprocity with.[6]

The move—taking a cue from the drafters of British Columbia's *Haida Gwaii Reconciliation Act* of 2010, as Heidi Kiiwetinepinesiik Stark has explained—is to conceptually "bracket" the abstract notion of sovereignty from the effective exercise of territorial jurisdiction.[7] Despite the settler state's posturing, Indigenous peoples' legal and political orders remain vital and intact.[8] And, as Renisa Mawani demonstrates powerfully, "Unlike sovereignty, which assumes a coherent and homogeneous unity of legal and political authority, jurisdiction points to the multiplicity and heterogeneity of law."[9] This chapter argues that alternative conceptualizations of jurisdiction can energize contemporary political projects to restore and enable Indigenous

---

[5] Kent McNeil, "Indigenous and Crown Sovereignty in Canada" in Michael Asch, John Borrows & James Tully, eds, *Resurgence and Reconciliation: Indigenous-Settler Relations and Earth Teachings* (Toronto: University of Toronto Press, 2018) 293. See also McNeil, "Indigenous Land Rights", *supra* note 3. Others make the argument that a "right of law-making jurisdiction" exists over a narrower subset of territories designated as Aboriginal title lands; see for example Douglas Sanderson & Amitpal C Singh, "Why Is Aboriginal Title Property if It Looks Like Sovereignty?" (2021) 34:2 Can JL & Jur 417 at 417.

[6] I note here that the language "jurisdiction *over*" is ubiquitous in settler framings. I am purposely avoiding that framing to force a reckoning with the way in which colonial understandings position humans as not only separate and apart from all non-human life and matter, but as having dominion "over" it in a hierarchical relation. I use the phrase "jurisdiction *in relation to*" instead.

[7] Not just on title lands, but everywhere Indigenous nations wish to exercise it. As Shiri Pasternak says, "Canadian assertions of sovereignty did not obliterate Indigenous governance authority, and as such, encounters between settler and Indigenous law reveal the unfinished project of perfecting settler colonial sovereignty claims": Pasternak, "Settler Colonialism", *supra* note 3 at 147.

[8] For a review of thinking about sovereignty by Indigenous scholars see Heidi Kiiwetinepinesiik Stark, "Nenabozho's Smart Berries: Rethinking Tribal Sovereignty and Accountability" (2013) 2013:2 Mich St L Rev 339 [Stark, "Smart Berries"]; Shiri Pasternak, "Jurisdiction" in Mariana Valverde et al, eds, *Routledge Handbook of Law and Society* (London, UK: Routledge, 2021) 178 at 180 [Pasternak, "Jurisdiction"].

[9] Renisa Mawani, *Across Oceans of Law: The Komagata Maru and Jurisdiction in the Time of Empire* (Durham: Duke University Press, 2018) at 24.

governing authority in relation to lands and resources, perhaps incrementally, but beginning today.

The chapter proceeds in three parts. The first part considers the story we typically tell about jurisdiction within Canadian public law and explains what is at stake on the ground in challenging the narrative and remaking the constitutional order. The second part introduces the common conceptual images of jurisdiction we employ and offers resources from critical interdisciplinary theory for new conceptions. The third part outlines the present exercise of Indigenous territorial jurisdiction, highlighting the *Kunst'aa guu—Kunst'aayah Reconciliation Protocol*, a "pocket" of separate, concurrent jurisdictions in Haida Gwaii,[10] and the Tsleil Waututh Sacred Trust Assessment of the Trans Mountain Expansion (TMX) project, an exercise of the inherent Indigenous jurisdiction to evaluate, deliberate on, and make decisions regarding proposed uses of the territory. And finally, I conclude by urging public law scholars to adopt an orientation of prefiguration in order to bring into being conceptualizations of jurisdiction that can enliven a decolonial legal future and a new constitutional order.

Part I: What is Jurisdiction?

Jurisdiction is central to how we understand and teach law. As a concept, jurisdiction forms part of our narrative foundation; the story we tell about law.[11] It is where we often begin.[12] Who can make laws? Where do they derive the authority to do so? In fact, I often start the new semester of a variety of law courses with an exercise to get students into the habit of thinking about where authority to make a rule comes from. The point of the exercise is to guide students through a "tracing back" of a rule, inevitably leading all the way to the *Constitution Act, 1867*, where the students can ultimately identify an

---

10 Deborah Curran, Eugene Kung & Ǧáǧvi Marilyn Slett, "Ǧviḷ́ás and Snəwayəɬ: Indigenous Laws, Economies, and Relationships with Place Speaking to State Extractions" (2020) 119:2 South Atlantic Q 215 at 221.

11 Pasternak, "Jurisdiction", *supra* note 8 at 178.

12 Adrian A Smith, "Toward a Critique of Political Economy of 'Sociolegality' in Settler Capitalist Canada" in Mark P Thomas et al, eds, *Change and Continuity: Canadian Political Economy in the New Millennium* (Kingston and Montreal: McGill-Queen's University Press, 2019) 167 at 167.

applicable head of legislative power in one or another of two possible "orders of government": the federal Parliament or a provincial Legislature.[13] As Kerry Wilkins says, "In Canada, each order of government, the federal and the provincial, has a catalogue of subjects about which only it may make laws. The Supreme Court has assured us that this distribution is rational and appropriate."[14]

The Constitution forms the legal basis of all authority, as the story goes.[15] Sections 91 and 92 "enumerate" the legislative powers of the respective orders of government: this is understood to form the basis for the legitimate *exercise* of jurisdiction over the listed subject matters.[16] The *authority* to make laws in relation to various matters or to address various mischiefs is either firmly established in practice through a straightforward reference to one of these listed subject matters (or its interpretation in jurisprudence, which becomes an accepted convention) or it becomes perennially contested and eventually established (or not) through one of the "residual powers." "The Environment" is notorious for being not listed (understandably, as a modern construct that emerged in the 1970s) in ss. 91 or 92 and has come to be

---

[13] As a federal nation, Canada's sovereignty is said to be divided between the two orders of government, although secondary authority can be delegated to municipal or other authorities. The territories present a somewhat different analysis, with devolution and modern treaties putting their inclusion beyond the scope of this chapter. The "division of powers" in Canada is often characterized as a "tug of war" even as it is more commonly about vacating or abdicating responsibilities to pay: Benjamin L Berger, Sonia Lawrence & Spiros Vavougios, "Constitutional Cases 2016: An Overview" (2017) 81:1 SCLR xli at l. In this framing, we often avoid the political implications of extending jurisdiction understood as the right to decide and the ability to fulfill responsibilities to steward, as they may apply under Indigenous legal orders.

[14] Kerry Wilkins, "Life Among the Ruins: Section 91(24) After *Tsilhqot'in* and *Grassy Narrows*" (2017) 55:1 Alta L Rev 91 at 94.

[15] But see Williamson J in *Campbell v British Columbia (Attorney General)*, 2000 BCSC 1123 [*Campbell*]. Outside of this case, the "continued existence of Aboriginal sovereignty" has been "effectively ignored": See Joshua Nichols, "A Reconciliation Without Recollection? *Chief Mountain* and the Sources of Sovereignty" (2015) 48:2 UBC L Rev 515 at 530.

[16] *Constitution Act, 1867*, 30 & 31 Vict, c 3 at ss 91, 92 (UK), reprinted in RSC 1985, Appendix II, No 5. The provincial and federal orders of government can pass laws that incidentally touch on matters outside of their jurisdictions as long as the "dominant purpose," of course, falls within. For example, see *Quebec (Attorney General) v Lacombe*, 2010 SCC 38.

understood as a matter of "shared jurisdiction."[17] It is known to be "always already contested – legally, socially, and politically."[18]

Jurisdiction over lands and resources, in contrast, has been considered to be relatively settled and uncontested, as far as subject matters go.[19] The authority to regulate lands and resources has been squarely allocated to the provincial legislatures.[20] The notion that "ownership" of lands and resources rests with the provinces is also, by now, considered a settled strand of the story.[21] As Nigel Bankes explains, "from a very early period in Canadian history, the courts confirmed that the

---

[17] Dayna Nadine Scott, "The Environment, Federalism, and the Charter" in Peter Oliver, Patrick Macklem & Nathalie Des Rosiers, eds, *The Oxford Handbook of the Canadian Constitution* (Oxford: Oxford University Press, 2017) 493 at 495.

[18] *Ibid.*

[19] As between federal and provincial orders of government, that is, and at least for some time. Section 92(a) was added to the *Constitution Act, 1867, supra* note 16, in the 1982 amendments, in an effort to settle the resource conflicts between the federal and Western provincial governments in the 1970s and early 1980s. Section 92(a) confirmed and entrenched provincial legislative authority over natural resource exploitation: Robert D Cairns, Marsha A Chandler & William D Moull, "The Resource Amendment (Section 92A) and the Political Economy of Canadian Federalism" (1985) 23:2 Osgoode Hall LJ 253; Luanne A Walton, "The Exploitation of Natural Resources in the Federation" in Peter Oliver, Patrick Macklem & Nathalie Des Rosiers, eds, *The Oxford Handbook of the Canadian Constitution* (Oxford: Oxford University Press, 2017) 533 at 534. Very recently, provincial contestation of federal authority to regulate in relation to climate change in a way that impacts resource extraction, and to assess the social and environmental impacts of major projects in a way that could affect permitting or approvals is also subject to fierce legal and political battles: *Reference Re Greenhouse Gas Pollution Pricing Act,* 2021 SCC 11 and *Reference re Impact Assessment Act,* 2023 SCC 23.

[20] Except, of course, in relation to disputes on the margins: see note 15.

[21] *Constitution Act, 1867, supra* note 16. "Jurisdiction over resources was distinguished from ownership of those resources at a very early point in Canada's history": Walton, *supra* note 19; see also Bhandar, *supra* note 4. This racial regime of ownership based on an ideology of improvement continues today. For a discussion of the contestation around the "public trust doctrine," through which the argument is made that governments have never "owned" public lands and resources such as forests, and merely hold them in trust for the benefit of the public, or sometimes "future generations," see Joseph L Sax, "Takings, Private Property and Public Rights" (1971) 81:2 Yale LJ 149 at 163; Anna Lund, "Canadian Approaches to America's Public Trust Doctrine: Classic Trusts, Fiduciary Duties & Substantive Review" (2012) 23:2 J Envtl L & Prac 135; Lynda Collins, *The Ecological Constitution: Reframing Environmental Law* (London, UK: Routledge, 2021).

numbered treaties provide a secure basis from which industry might obtain *resource rights from the Crown.*"[22]

Finally, in this narrative, the authority to legislate in the area of "Indians and lands reserved for Indians" is allocated in s. 91(24) to the federal Parliament, but Indigenous peoples themselves are not recognized as an order of government. In 1982, the constitutional protection of Indigenous rights was provided in s. 35, which states that the "aboriginal and treaty rights of the aboriginal peoples of Canada are hereby recognized and affirmed." It is worth noting that the content of the protected rights does not derive from the Constitution; the section "recognizes" rights already presumed to exist.[23]

The Royal Commission on Aboriginal Peoples in 1996 recommended that Indigenous governments be treated as one of three "orders of government," explaining that each order would "operat[e] within its own distinct sovereign sphere, as defined by the Canadian Constitution, and exercise[e] authority within spheres of jurisdiction having both overlapping and exclusive components."[24] And although some Indigenous nations have achieved some limited self-government rights through modern treaty agreements,[25] there does not appear to

---

[22] Nigel Bankes, "The Implications of the *Tsilhqot'in* (*William*) and *Grassy Narrows* (*Keewatin*) Decisions of the Supreme Court of Canada for the Natural Resources Industries" (2015) 33:3 J Energy Nat Resources L 188 at 209.

[23] Jeremy Webber, "Contending Sovereignties" in Peter Oliver, Patrick Macklem & Nathalie Des Rosiers, eds *The Oxford Handbook of the Canadian Constitution* (Oxford: Oxford University Press, 2017) 281.

[24] The failed Charlottetown Accord, 1992, had contemplated Indigenous governments as "one of three orders of government in Canada," and clearly contemplated that Indigenous governments should have a status equivalent to the federal and provincial levels, which, in Canadian constitutional law, are considered sovereign in their spheres: *Report of the Royal Commission on Aboriginal Peoples: Restructuring the Relationship*, vol 2 (Ottawa: Supply and Services Canada, 1996) at 232.

[25] Also, as Heidi Kiiwetinepinesiik Stark has explained, Indigenous nations have retained jurisdiction over various subject matters: "Child and family wellbeing, for example, has largely been an area of jurisdiction that communities have retained much longer than criminal jurisdiction. Historically, Indigenous nations maintained jurisdiction over marriage and adoption long after Crown assertions of sovereignty. These are often also the areas of jurisdiction the state is willing to recognize in Indigenous self-government agreements, though often on a conditional basis that measures aptitude and success through colonial standards," in Shiri Pasternak et al, "Infrastructure, Jurisdiction, Extractivism: Keywords for Decolonizing Geographies" (2023) 101 Polit Geogr 1 at 4.

be mainstream interest in comprehensive reform of the Canadian Constitution in the current political moment.

But the story is not settled. Where we actually *should* begin the narrative about "jurisdiction" in relation to lands and resources in Canada is somewhere else entirely: with an "unsettling" of these conventions brought on by an honest reckoning with the Canadian state's legitimacy—and with a questioning of the logic that provides that the Constitution somehow neatly divided all governing authority, across all territory, and allocated it among these specific orders of government, to the exclusion of all other pre-existing political and legal orders.[26] Fierce critiques of the "politics of recognition" have exposed how the avenues for justice for Indigenous peoples that have been opened up through the accepted channels—for "affirming aboriginal and treaty rights" through s. 35, for example—have led ultimately to disappointment. Critical scholars argue that the jurisprudence "has, in actuality, further provided federal and provincial governments with greater license to *invade* Indigenous territories through the violent judicial elimination of alternate legal orders and Indigenous jurisdictions."[27] As Corey Snelgrove says, leaning on the scholarship of both Heidi Kiiwetinepinesiik Stark and Gina Starblanket, this jurisprudence has furthered the "containment and circumscription of Indigenous treaty visions by legal and cultural rights discourses."[28] The present Canadian context is one that "includes a

---

[26] There has been some judicial consideration of these questions in Canada: in *Campbell, supra* note 15, Williamson J ruled that there was not an exhaustive division of powers between the provinces and the federal government in 1867. *Reference to the Court of Appeal of Quebec in relation with the Act respecting First Nations, Inuit and Métis children, youth and families*, 2022 QCCA 185, affirms the same point. This argument was also raised in *House of Sga'nisim v Canada (AG)*, 2013 BCCA 49, but the BCCA did not address it. The author acknowledges Professor Karen Drake for alerting me to these rulings.

[27] Michael McCrossan & Kiera L Ladner, "Eliminating Indigenous Jurisdictions: Federalism, the Supreme Court of Canada, and Territorial Rationalities of Power" (2016) 49:3 Can J Pol Sci 411 at 412. See also John Borrows, *Freedom and Indigenous Constitutionalism* (Toronto: University of Toronto Press, 2016); Glen Sean Coulthard, *Red Skin, White Masks: Rejecting the Colonial Politics of Recognition* (Minneapolis: University of Minnesota Press, 2014).

[28] Corey Snelgrove, *Bound by Reconciliation? Social Criticism, Treaty, and Decolonization* (PhD Dissertation, University of British Columbia, 2021) [unpublished] at 211 [Snelgrove, *Bound by Reconciliation?*], citing Heidi Kiiwetinepinesiik Stark, "Changing the Treaty Question: Remedying the Right(s) Relationship" in John Borrows & Michael Coyle, eds, *The Right Relationship: Reimagining the Implementation of Historical Treaties* (Toronto:

judiciary that both diminishes and subordinates Indigenous political authority to settler federalism, while translating Indigenous treaty visions into redistributive claims on portions of resource extraction."[29] Scholars rejecting a politics of recognition often embrace notions of Indigenous resurgence and "refusal,"[30] and emphasize movements to reclaim and restore the multitude of pre-existing and still-existing— *still-governing*—Indigenous legal orders, practices, and protocols that span across the borders and boundaries of what we call "jurisdictions."[31]

What Is at Stake?

Influential theorizations of settler colonialism, most notably by Patrick Wolfe, emphasize a distinction between colonial and settler colonial formations. Wolfe's account characterizes settler colonial invasion as "a structure not an event"[32] and argues that its "eliminatory logic" is oriented towards "displacing" Indigenous peoples and "replacing them on" the land.[33] In contrast to colonialism's aim to benefit from stolen labour in the invaded territories, settler colonialism's aim is territory.

University of Toronto Press, 2017) 248 [Stark, "Treaty Question"]; Gina Starblanket, "The Numbered Treaties and the Politics of Incoherency" (2019) 52:3 Can J Pol Sci 443.

[29] Snelgrove, *Bound by Reconciliation?*, *supra* note 28 at 117–118. Namely, redistribution or "sharing in the wealth" comes in the form of impact-benefit agreements (IBAs) or resource revenue sharing (RRS) deals. For critiques of these tools, see Dayna N Scott, "Extraction Contracting: The Struggle for Control of Indigenous Lands" (2020) 119:2 South Atl Q 269; Yellowhead Institute, "Land Back: A Yellowhead Institute Red Paper" (Yellowhead Institute Red Paper, 2019), online: <redpaper. yellowheadinstitute.org>.

[30] Coulthard, *supra* note 27; Audra Simpson, *Mohawk Interruptus: Political Life Across the Borders of Settler States* (Durham: Duke University Press, 2014); Taiaiake Alfred & Jeff Corntassel, "Being Indigenous: Resurgences against Contemporary Colonialism" (2005) 40:4 Gov Oppos 597; Robert YELḰÁTTE Clifford, "Saanich Law and the Transmountain Pipeline Expansion" (2019) Environmental Challenges on Indigenous Lands, Center for International Governance Innovation, online: <cigionline.org/ articles/saanich-law-and-trans-mountain-pipeline-expansion/>.

[31] John Borrows, *Canada's Indigenous Constitution* (Toronto: University of Toronto Press, 2010); John Borrows, *Drawing Out Law: A Spirit's Guide* (Toronto: University of Toronto Press, 2010); Hadley Friedland & Val Napoleon, "Gathering the Threads: Developing A Methodology for Researching and Rebuilding Indigenous Legal Traditions" (2015–2016) 1:1 Lakehead LJ 17; University of Victoria Faculty of Law, "Indigenous Law Research Unit", online: <ilru.ca>.

[32] Patrick Wolfe, *Settler Colonialism and the Transformation of Anthropology: The Politics and Poetics of an Ethnographic Event* (London: Cassell, 1999) at 2.

[33] *Ibid* at 1.

"Territoriality," according to Wolfe, is "settler colonialism's specific, irreducible element."[34]

This is what makes "jurisdiction" a site of *struggle* for Indigenous lands and resources today. The settler state is "a nationally-inscribed territorial ordering authority."[35] As Adrian Smith, relying on Ellen Meiksins Wood, makes clear, "the continuing if not deepening need of global capital is for 'a closely regulated and predictable social, political and legal order.'"[36] Because of this, as Glen Sean Coulthard has deftly shown, the ongoing displacement and dispossession of Indigenous peoples is the necessary basis for capitalist accumulation today. But it is not simple dispossession and displacement *from land* as we might ordinarily envision; it is dispossession from the *authority to decide*—to govern—that is also continuing.[37] The singular driving imperative of the settler colonial state is to provide access to Indigenous lands for extractive capital.[38]

It is for this reason that "[l]and, territory, and the forms of life attached to, or embedded within them are a permanent site of contestation and struggle between settler state authorities and First Nations."[39] The way that the settler state maintains control has "transmute[d] into different modalities, discourses and institutional formations" over time.[40] What I attempt to demonstrate here is that the present jurisdictional divisions in the existing constitutional

---

[34] Patrick Wolfe, "Settler Colonialism and the Elimination of the Native" (2006) 8:4 J Genocide Res 387 at 388 [Wolfe, "Settler Colonialism"].

[35] Adrian A Smith, "Seeing Like a Clinic" (2022) 59:1 Osgoode Hall LJ 37 at 37.

[36] *Ibid* at 43, citing Ellen Meiksins Wood, *Empire of Capital* (London, UK: Verso, 2003) at xi.

[37] Michael Asch, reviewing speeches by Indigenous leaders reacting to the prospect of including Aboriginal rights in the *Constitution Act, 1982* concluded that what Indigenous nations are struggling for is "political jurisdiction that includes a land base": Michael Asch, *Home and Native Land: Aboriginal Rights and the Canadian Constitution* (Toronto: Methuen, 1984) at 30. See for example, litigation launched recently against Canada and Ontario by ten Treaty No. 9 nations claiming that they never surrendered governance authority and seeking a "co-jurisdiction arrangement": Logan Turner, "Can the Crown make land decisions without First Nations consent? Treaty 9 lawsuit argues no", CBC (26 April 2023), online: <cbc.ca/news/canada/thunder-bay/treaty-nine-lawsuit-1.6822266>.

[38] Coulthard, *supra* note 27. See also Dayna Nadine Scott, "Extractivism: Socio-Legal Approaches to Relations with Lands and Resources" in Mariana Valverde et al, eds, *The Routledge Handbook of Law and Society* (Abingdon: Routledge, 2021) 124.

[39] Bhandar, *supra* note 4 at 25.

[40] Wolfe, "Settler Colonialism", *supra* note 34 at 402.

structure "conceptually exclude and undercut Indigenous legal orders and territorial responsibilities"[41] and that they need not do so. Because Indigenous jurisdiction is still being exercised on the land, the project of settler colonialism is unfinished and the space is more properly characterized as "interlegal."[42] Somehow, however, "[t]he picture that holds us captive is that sovereignty is a singular, exclusive absolute authority."[43] This is despite ample evidence of a multiplicity of vital Indigenous governance systems each structured within their own unique territories and place-based political orders.

As we repeat the simple story of jurisdiction in law schools, it is true that we often also acknowledge and lament (as Jodi Byrd has observed in relation to multicultural liberal settler society more generally) the "originary violence of colonial settlement."[44] But then, in failing to understand *how to* challenge the orthodox locating of all governing authority as falling naturally to the settler state, we simply "move beyond it, as if it could be surpassed," in Brenna Bhandar's words.[45] In the next section, I review some interventions from critical theory that provide resources to assist those seeking to mount a challenge.

Part II: Critical Scholarship on Jurisdiction

Emerging scholarly approaches across several disciplines including sociolegal studies, critical geography and settler colonial studies, see jurisdiction as a concept that can reveal (and question) "how authority is established, exercised, and contested [...]."[46] At its most basic, jurisdiction means, as Benton and Ross explain, the exercise of legal authority, "the power to regulate and administer sanctions over particular actions

---

41 McCrossan & Ladner, *supra* note 27 at 412.

42 de Sousa Santos introduced the idea of "interlegality" in the late 1980s: Boaventura de Sousa Santos, "Law: A Map of Misreading. Toward a Postmodern Conception of Law" (1987) 14:3 J L & Soc 279.

43 Pasternak, "Settler Colonialism", *supra* note 3 at 160.

44 Jodi A Byrd, *The Transit of Empire: Indigenous Critiques of Colonialism* (Minneapolis: University of Minnesota Press, 2011) at 39.

45 Bhandar, *supra* note 4 at 26.

46 Shiri Pasternak, *Grounded Authority: The Algonquins of Barriere Lake Against the State* (Minneapolis: University of Minnesota Press, 2017) at 3 [Pasternak, *Grounded Authority*].

or people."[47] But as Pasternak argues, the significance of jurisdiction is found in the "work" that it does: "it is through jurisdiction that settler sovereignty organizes and manages authority."[48] It is "the authority to have authority."[49]

Shiri Pasternak's masterful 2017 book, *Grounded Authority*, builds on the work of Lauren Benton, a scholar of colonial histories, who examined the "shift from the multicentric law of early modern empires to the state-centred law of high colonialism."[50] Benton demonstrated that empires did not achieve a uniform coverage of governing authority across space within the invaded territories, but those territories were instead characterized by "imperfect geographies."[51] The location of political authority was complex and multiple, and gave rise to "differentiated legal zones" across landscapes.[52]

Critical sociolegal scholar Mariana Valverde has explored how jurisdiction has been primarily understood through geographic concepts of scale and hierarchy. Drawing on de Sousa Santos' notion of "interlegality," she reminds us of the "constant interactions among different legal orders – each of which has its own scope, its own logic, and its own criteria for what is to be governed, as well as its own rules for how to govern."[53] Sometimes, differences in legal *scale* are treated as "technical matters on a par with a mapmaker's choice of cartographic scale," leading to the

---

[47] Lauren Benton & Richard J Ross, *Empires and Legal Pluralism: Jurisdiction, Sovereignty, and Political Imagination in the Early Modern World* (New York: New York University Press, 2013) at 6. Also it is about "the power to speak the law, bringing it into existence and defining who will be governed, as well as how and where": Pasternak, "Jurisdiction", *supra* note 8 at 178.

[48] Pasternak, *Grounded Authority*, *supra* note 46 at 4.

[49] *Ibid* at 1.

[50] Lauren Benton, *Law and Colonial Cultures: Legal Regimes in World History, 1400–1900* (Cambridge: Cambridge University Press, 2001) at i.

[51] Lauren Benton, *A Search for Sovereignty: Law and Geography in European Empires, 1400–1900* (West Nyack: Cambridge University Press, 2010) at 2 [Benton, *Sovereignty*]. Put differently, Taiaiake Alfred states that the "actual history of our plural existence has been erased by the narrow fictions of a single sovereignty": Taiaiake Alfred, "Sovereignty" in Philip J Deloria & Neal Salisbury, eds, *A Companion to American Indian History* (Malden, MA: Blackwell, 2002) 460 at 460.

[52] Pasternak, "Settler Colonialism", *supra* note 3 at 148.

[53] Mariana Valverde, "Jurisdiction and Scale: Legal 'Technicalities' as Resources for Theory" (2009) 18:2 Soc & Leg Stud 139 at 141.

sense that "quite heterogeneous modes of governance carried out by different legal assemblages appear to coexist without a great deal of overt conflict."[54] But Valverde's crucial insight is that the "everyday workings of jurisdiction" are exercises of *power*.[55] As she emphasizes, this is true "whether or not anyone is noticing it or challenging it," and these exercises of jurisdiction/power can tend to "naturalize the simultaneous operation of quite different, even contradictory, rationalities of legal governance."[56]

How Is Jurisdiction Imagined, Spatially?

Pasternak agrees that jurisdiction is a legal mechanism for "organizing how political power is exercised, spatialized, and contested."[57] But how jurisdiction is imagined, *spatially*, has a crucial influence on the juridical forms we expect it to take.[58] There are two images that dominate, and tend to be invoked together:

Lines On the Ground: Exclusive Authority, Evenly Filling Spaces Bounded by Hard Borders

If jurisdiction is "a fundamentally spatial concept," how do we imagine this?[59] Often, we conjure a hard boundary, a line drawn on a map.[60] This "illusion of neat boundaries containing internally coherent identities," as Paul Halliday notes, sustains us, even as we understand it to be failing. It "is as much a product of our geographical visions" as it is

---

[54] *Ibid.*

[55] In 1995, political scientist Radha Jhappan noted the structuring effects of federalism and called the division of powers under ss 91 and 92 a "power-grid" that limits possibilities for Indigenous self-governance: Radha Jhappan, "The Federal-Provincial Power-Grid and Aboriginal Self-Government" in François Rocher & Miriam Catherine Smith, eds, *New Trends in Canadian Federalism, 1st ed* (Peterborough, ON: Broadview Press, 1995).

[56] Valverde, *supra* note 53.

[57] Pasternak, "Jurisdiction", *supra* note 8 at 178.

[58] Renisa Mawani, in a remarkable study of oceans, "maritime worlds," and the role of moving ships in the making, spreading, and transforming ideas about jurisdiction, shows that "jurisdiction is much more than a territorial concept. In the British Empire, questions of jurisdiction often centred on the racial and legal status of people, populations, and territories, dividing Dominion/colony, native/foreigner, citizen/subject, and slave/free": Mawani, *supra* note 9 at 24.

[59] Pasternak, "Jurisdiction", *supra* note 8 at 178.

[60] Consider "European proprietary concepts such as exclusive possession that correspond so neatly to the visual geometry of conventional maps": Kirsten Anker, "Aboriginal Title and Alternative Cartographies" (2018) 11:1 Erasmus L Rev 14 at 19.

our political and legal ones.[61] Halliday writes that "[o]ur minds color in the whole of each space [...] with a single crayon. We don't use pastels, overlap tints, or paint outside the lines."[62]

In reality, scholars note that multiple authorities often govern in the same spaces, and these are more accurately characterized as having shifting and permeable boundaries.[63] Jurisdiction is more aptly conveyed by an image of multiple overlapping spheres of authority, like sheets of transparent paper overlaid each other, as described by Pasternak. She states that "[t]o visualize the dense jurisdictional overlap of legal pluralities," we can imagine that "as each transparent page is laid atop the other, the overlap of components" forms a complex jurisdictional picture of multiple kinds of governing authorities.[64] "To avoid misconstruing layers of jurisdiction as detached from one another," however, Pasternak also adds that "we need to be attentive to the nodes of connection where authorities meet."[65]

But familiar spatial representations have a stubborn persistence. In the settler tradition, the idea that dominates the legal imagination is territorial space as a "discrete, non-overlapping, absolute domain of space, despite how interpenetrated by capital and by competing jurisdictional claims its boundaries may be."[66] The failure to shade overlaps, paint in pastels and colour outside the lines "filters out the details of interlegality" and tells a misleading story.[67] In the true picture of jurisdiction that emerges, it is not territorial exclusivity that is operating. And to complicate things further, where Indigenous legal orders govern, it is not "rights to decide" so much as the *responsibility to steward* that is in play.

---

[61] Mawani, *supra* note 9.

[62] Paul D Halliday, "Laws' Histories: Pluralisms, Pluralities, Diversity" in Lauren Benton & Richard J Ross, eds, *Legal Pluralism and Empires, 1500–1850* (New York: New York University Press, 2013) 261 at 269. Here Halliday writes in relation to states, but the same image applies.

[63] See also McCrossan & Ladner, *supra* note 27 at 420.

[64] Pasternak, "Settler Colonialism", *supra* note 3 at 148.

[65] *Ibid.*

[66] *Ibid* at 153, citing Neil Brenner, "A Thousand Leaves: Notes on the Geographies of Uneven Spatial Development" in Roger Keil & Rianne Mahon, eds, *Leviathan Undone? Towards a Political Economy of Scale* (Vancouver: University of British Columbia Press, 2009) 26 at 38.

[67] Pasternak, *Grounded Authority*, *supra* note 46 at 18.

Pyramid: A Tiered Structure, a Nested Rank of Power

Despite the fact that the division of powers within Canadian federalism is explicitly organized around two parallel "orders" of government, with the federal Parliament and the provincial legislatures depicted as constitutional "equals" and not in dominant/subordinate relation, the notion of hierarchy still reigns in terms of how we conceptually organize "jurisdiction" *within* those orders of government.[68] Municipalities, as an example, are understood to exercise only the powers delegated to them by the provinces. Similarly, some extensions of jurisdiction to First Nations have been accomplished by federal statutory delegation.[69] As Joshua Nichols says, an act of delegation is "premised on an asymmetrical relationship: one party gives another party something they do not have (i.e., authority) and this transfer is a conditional one."[70] With the image of a pyramid, we imagine that power is ranked "from the highest to the lowest authority," or such that "certain issues are under the exclusive domain of particular authorities."[71] The notion of hierarchy is crucial to overcome in moving towards a decolonial legal order in Canada, because, as Pasternak has emphasized, and as I will explain in the next section, delegated forms of jurisdiction must be distinguished from exercises of inherent authority.

Re-Animating Static Diagrams of Governance

Neither of these images or conceptualizations of jurisdiction suffices, of course. As Valverde says, they are "somewhat static diagrams of governance."[72] They exist in dissonance with the "jurisdictional commotion on the land" that Pasternak describes.[73] In reality, there is a tangle of authorities; the overlay of multiple competing claims. "More often, when we really look at the spatial context of jurisdiction, we see a dense patchwork of institutional bodies crowding every place, often governing largely in isolation from each other despite overlaps and

---

[68] See also Benton, *Sovereignty*, *supra* note 51.

[69] The *First Nations Land Management Act*, SC 1999, c 24, as repealed by *Framework Agreement on First Nation Land Management Act*, SC 2022, c 19, s 121, is an obvious example.

[70] Nichols, *supra* note 15 at 517.

[71] Pasternak, "Jurisdiction", *supra* note 8 at 180.

[72] Valverde, *supra* note 53 at 139.

[73] Pasternak, *Grounded Authority*, *supra* note 46 at 18.

contradictions in mandate, authority, and geographic oversight."[74] And in fact, the settler jurisprudence betrays that we are quite comfortable with, even adept at, designing complex schemes for "determining the paramountcy of one set of laws over another."[75]

Further, the kind of mapping that is encouraged by the lines-on-the-ground and the pyramid conceptualizations of jurisdiction largely conforms to colonial logic and accepts colonial imaginaries of territory.[76] But it is not beyond our imaginative capacities to design "spheres of jurisdiction" as spaces where Indigenous law and governance systems freely function alongside a federal system like Canada's. In the section below, I explore experiments already being deployed.

Part III: The Present Exercise of Indigenous Territorial Jurisdiction

Indigenous peoples' decision-making is guided by comprehensive systems of law.[77] As Anishinaabe geographer Michelle Daigle notes, "prior to colonial settlement, Indigenous peoples on Turtle Island existed as diverse nations defined by their ancestral lands, kinship relations, governance structures, economic trading networks and well established yet fluid legal orders."[78] Increasingly, Indigenous communities are devising creative strategies for applying those laws and protocols in relation to lands and resources issues, and are simply *exercising* their jurisdiction, rather than seeking Crown recognition, cooperation, or acquiescence to do so.[79] These communities, as Gordon

---

[74] Pasternak, "Jurisdiction", *supra* note 8 at 181.

[75] *Ibid* at 178. For example, see *Multiple Access Ltd v McCutcheon*, [1982] 2 SCR 161.

[76] Anker, *supra* note 60.

[77] *Justice Within: Indigenous Legal Traditions* (Ottawa: Law Commission of Canada, 2006).

[78] Michelle Daigle, "Awawanenitakik: The Spatial Politics of Recognition and Relational Geographies of Indigenous Self-Determination" (2016) 60:2 Can Geographer 259 at 260.

[79] Robert YELḰÁTȺE Clifford's dissertation deals beautifully with the tensions caught up in these questions: Robert YELḰÁTȺE Clifford, *The old people are the song, and we are their echo: resurgence of w̱sáneć law and legal theory* (PhD Dissertation, Osgoode Hall Law School, York University, 2022) [unpublished]. For an example, see Batchewana First Nation's 2011 release of a "Notice of Assertions," which stated that the Band would begin issuing permits and demanding consent and full partnership in any resource developments across its traditional territory: Batchewana First

Christie explains, are making "fundamental *authoritative* decisions about what is acceptable use of their territory."[80]

The Tsleil-Waututh Assessment of the TMX

The Tsleil-Waututh Nation (TWN) in British Columbia conducted its own "independent assessment" of the proposed Trans Mountain Expansion (TMX) pipeline project in 2015.[81] The assessment was grounded in Tsleil-Waututh and Coast Salish legal principles of environmental conservation and stewardship. According to Curran, Kung, and Slett, the TWN Assessment, "is one of the most prominent contemporary applications of Indigenous law," notable for the fact that it also included "leading-edge scientific studies on oil spill probability and oil spill behavior."[82] The TWN concluded that leadership should continue to withhold support for the proposed pipeline expansion project.

Recent years have seen many Indigenous communities developing their own independent or "Indigenous-led" impact assessments in response to aggressive development and extractive pressures on their homelands, largely permissive state processes, and a dysfunctional "consultation" framework.[83] Indigenous assessments can be grounded in each nation's own social, political and legal orders—and crucially they can be placed along a spectrum to the extent they proceed under the authority of, parallel with, or completely independently of legislative processes under settler law.[84] A

Nation, "Notice of Assertions" (2011), online: <batchewana.ca/our-story/land/>. The Yinka Dene Alliance's interventions in respect of the proposed Northern Gateway project is another high-profile example. In respect of the idea that these assertions are increasing in incidence, Gordon Christie registers an important caveat: that "assertions of Indigenous authority were made throughout the overtly colonial era in Canada" and it may only be that their "visibility is enhanced in the contemporary setting": Christie, *supra* note 2 at 259.

[80] *Ibid* at 259. As Christie makes clear, "They are not asking for something from the state," but asserting powers they already believe themselves to possess.

[81] Tsleil-Waututh Nation, *Assessment of the Trans Mountain Pipeline and Tanker Expansion Proposal* (Treaty, Lands & Resources Department, 2015).

[82] Curran, Kung & Slett, *supra* note 10 at 230.

[83] Sarah Morales, "Indigenous-led Assessment Processes as a Way Forward" (2019) Environmental Challenges on Indigenous Lands, Center for International Governance Innovation, online: <https://www.cigionline.org/articles/indigenous-led-assessment-processes-way-forward/>.

[84] Donna Ashamock et al, "Exploring the Transformative Potential of Indigenous Impact Assessment" in Dayna Nadine Scott, Jennifer Sankey & Laura Tanguay, eds,

report prepared for the Gwiichin Council International states that Indigenous-led impact assessment processes "rely on and protect Indigenous culture, language, and way of life in ways existing government legislated systems have either never contemplated or are still not accommodating."[85]

The Tsleil-Waututh Assessment rejected the TMX project on the basis that it had the potential "to deprive past, current, and future generations of the Tsleil-Waututh community of control and benefit of the water, land, air, and resources in the territory."[86] TWN filed the Assessment with the state regulator, as evidence of TWN's lack of consent to the project. Perhaps predictably, however, the regulator, "ill-equipped to navigate questions of Indigenous rights and governance, treated the document as competing evidence on oil spills [but] failed to acknowledge TWN's jurisdiction."[87]

Experience with Indigenous impact assessments to date across the country demonstrates that motivations vary.[88] Sometimes, assessments are explicitly oriented *away* from the Crown and from proponents—intended primarily to serve the communities' own desire to understand the potential impacts of a proposed undertaking on the things that matter to them—for the purposes of coming to an informed position internally. In other cases, the assessments are oriented towards engaging with or "articulating with" Crown authorities—affecting the state issuance of permits or approvals. In still other cases, the assessments are explicitly aimed at binding the proponents—producing a decision that will have effect "on the ground."[89]

Operationalizing Indigenous Impact Assessment (2023), prepared for the Impact Assessment Agency of Canada's Policy Dialogue Program, online: <canada.ca/content/dam/iaac-acei/documents/research/operationalizing-indigenous-impact-assessment.pdf>.

[85] Ginger Gibson, Dawn Hoogeveen & Alistair MacDonald, *Impact Assessment in the Arctic: Emerging Practices of Indigenous-led Review* (Yellowknife: Gwich'in Council International, 2018) at 4.

[86] Tsleil-Waututh Nation, *supra* note 81 at 51.

[87] Curran, Kung & Slett, *supra* note 10 at 232. This is not to say the report did not have an impact.

[88] See e.g. Scott, Sankey & Tanguay, *supra* note 84.

[89] Jennifer Sankey, "The Stk'emlúpsemc te Secwepemc Nation Assessment of the Ajax-Abacus Copper and Gold Mine Project" in Scott, Sankey & Tanguay, *supra* note 84 at 25–42; Jennifer Sankey, *Using Indigenous Legal Processes to Strengthen Indigenous Jurisdiction: Squamish Nation Land Use Planning and the Squamish Nation Assessment of*

This makes impact assessment a crucial arena for experimentation with jurisdiction going forward.[90]

The Kunst'aa guu—Kunst'aayah Reconciliation Protocol

Engaging the Crown in exercises of inherent jurisdiction, of course, often encounters obstacles over the "competing sovereignties" point. Here, the *Haida Gwaii Reconciliation Act*[91] is instructive. In 2010, the British Columbia legislature established a co-management structure for the coastal archipelago that includes representation both from the Haida Nation and the province. The *Act* gives legislative effect to the *Kunst'aa guu—Kunst'aayah Reconciliation Protocol* negotiated between the provincial government and the Haida Nation. The Protocol places the Haida Nation representatives alongside Crown representatives at a common table to assess proposals for incursions onto the territory, determine allowable land uses, harvest intensities, etc. This type of co-management regime is not uncommon, nor would it be considered a radical expression of inherent jurisdiction. But what is instructive about this example, is the language in the *Act*'s preamble. It states:

> AND WHEREAS the Kunst'aa guu—Kunst'aayah Reconciliation Protocol provides that the Haida Nation and British Columbia hold differing views with regard to sovereignty, title, ownership and jurisdiction over Haida Gwaii, under the Kunst'aa guu–

---

the *Woodfibre Liquefied Natural Gas Projects* (PhD Dissertation, University of British Columbia, 2021) [unpublished].

[90] As Taiaiake Alfred notes in a 2021 report for the Impact Assessment Agency of Canada's Indigenous Advisory Committee, even though the new *Impact Assessment Act* does "allow for jurisdiction over impact assessments to be handed over to Indigenous groups," there is a "failure thus far to break the structural problem that consists in the fact that the entire impact assessment system up until now has been oriented to supporting proponents – even though the new legislation allows for movement towards a more just and equitable relationship in the decision-making process, previously established patterns of ingrained thinking limit the realization of the Act's potential": Taiaiake Alfred, "Indigenous Collaboration in Impact Assessment Challenges and Opportunities" (4 June 2021) at 11, online (pdf): <taiaiake. files.wordpress.com/2021/11/indigenous-collaboration-in-impact-assessment-challenges-and-opportunities-june-2021.pdf>.

[91] *Haida Gwaii Reconciliation Act*, SBC 2010, c 17 [*Act*]; Webber, *supra* note 23 at 291 calls it "an example of 'agonistic constitutionalism,' in which constitutional government acknowledges the pervasiveness of fundamental political disagreement."

> Kunst'aayah Reconciliation Protocol the Haida Nation and British Columbia will operate under their respective authorities and jurisdictions [...][92]

Remarkably, with this "sovereign act of the British Columbia legislature," as Jeremy Webber notes, the province "acknowledges the Haida's rival claims."[93] The *Act* registers the parties' fundamental disagreement with respect to sovereignty, title, ownership and jurisdiction, and yet moves past this to provide resources for the parties to implement the agreement, each "under their respective authorities and jurisdictions."[94] As Heidi Kiiwetinepinesiik Stark says, the Haida Nation agrees to both assert and then "bracket that question as a means of taking up *issues of jurisdiction* as a grounded and manageable question for the time being."[95]

What these examples demonstrate is that Indigenous assertions and *everyday exercises* of jurisdiction are presently disrupting settler claims to exclusive authority, if incrementally. Strategically, while it may not be possible to move the needle immediately to a position of "ultimate and unconstrained decision-making power,"[96] as Webber says, we can begin now to carve out "spheres in which Indigenous institutions and resources are able to be used, to be refined, and to flourish."[97] In this respect, the machinery of jurisdiction presents options for expressing and operationalizing multiple authorities acting concurrently in place: "[j]urisdictional thinking gives us a distinct way of representing authority."[98] The way Indigenous nations claim and conceive of jurisdiction differs from settler authorities: it is often expressed as a responsibility to steward, or take care of the homelands, rather than a "right to regulate." But these differences do not prevent their co-existence. We can carve out specific places, like Haida Gwaii, or specific processes, like impact assessment, where Indigenous

---

[92] *Act, supra* note 91, preamble.

[93] Webber, *supra* note 23 at 290.

[94] *Ibid.*

[95] Pasternak et al, *supra* note 25 at 4.

[96] Webber, *supra* note 23 at 298.

[97] *Ibid.*

[98] Shaunnagh Dorsett & Shaun McVeigh, *Jurisdiction* (Abingdon: Routledge, 2012) at 5; Sundhya Pahuja, "Laws of Encounter: A Jurisdictional Account of International Law" (2013) 1:1 Lond Rev of Int Law 63.

nations are eager to exercise effective jurisdiction in respect of the lands and waters they steward. These distinct spheres of jurisdiction demonstrate that Indigenous law and governance systems can exist alongside the other orders of government.

However, as explained in Part I, the struggle for jurisdiction is a high stakes struggle because "in the settler colony the colonial animus is driven by the need to control the land base for the continued growth of settler economies and for the security of settler populations."[99] In order to "reconcile" this driving imperative of the settler state with liberal desires of inclusion, the era we are living through is marked by the emergence of a plethora of creative state strategies to, as Pasternak argues, "replace the source of Indigenous law with a delegated authority of the Crown through the machinery of state jurisdiction."[100] Thus, as Curran, Kung, and Slett argue, while it is obvious that "Canada's claim to exclusive territorial authority across all the lands and waters is a failed project" the uncertainty and angst generated by this dawning reality "has only succeeded in more complex legal and political subterfuge as Canada has sought to mitigate this uncertainty with grander performances of recognition."[101] In other words, the louder the assertions of inherent jurisdiction become, or the more difficult they become to ignore, the more the settler state scrambles to "extend" jurisdiction to Indigenous peoples in its circumscribed, delegated forms. And yet, it is obvious that the legal source of Indigenous jurisdiction is not and cannot be the settler state.

Conclusion: Prefiguring Decolonial Legal Futures

> "jurisdictional assemblages have a strong
> path dependence [...]"[102]

The legislative powers flowing from existing jurisdictional divisions are "naturalized and taken as a given."[103] To not challenge or

---

99   Bhandar, *supra* note 4 at 25.

100 Pasternak, *Grounded Authority*, *supra* note 46 at 8.

101 Curran, Kung & Slett, *supra* note 10 at 205.

102 Valverde, *supra* note 53 at 144, says this in the context of her discussion of "the game of jurisdiction".

103 McCrossan & Ladner, *supra* note 27 at 422.

question this framework—this story about jurisdiction—in the teaching of public law in Canada, is to "perpetuate the myth that without settler-colonial governments, no one would be regulating or governing vast areas of the country."[104] However, instead of devising more convoluted settler state mechanisms for delegating authority, we must instead promote and affirm the actions of Indigenous communities reclaiming, simply *exercising*, and thus restoring their inherent governing authority. As public law scholars, we should be encouraging the withdrawal of state claims of jurisdiction rather than devising ways for the settler state to "extend" or delegate jurisdiction to Indigenous peoples.

Reconceptualizing jurisdiction inverts the habit of making Indigenous peoples "subjects of" (or "subject matters" of legislative authority under) settler law: it understands law's typical "subjects" also as its agents. Indigenous peoples are generating new legal forms, constituting legal orders, and exercising jurisdiction. They are actively making and re-making settler law and institutions through articulations of authority, implementation of their own practices and protocols, resistance, acquiescence, refusal, and strategic interventions. Similarly, settler institutions are reacting to, co-opting, incorporating into, and acquiescing to—in various doses, at various times—these experiments, demands and maneuvers. But this is, of course, not only a two-player game, especially in relation to lands and resources governance. Entrenched economic interests are crucially important to the dynamic, favouring certain configurations of legal obligations over others and using their considerable power and influence to achieve them.

The slow but inevitable disintegration of the settler state's claim to exclusive territorial authority means that intractable uncertainties, complexities, and pluralities are creating openings for new assertions, restorations, and reclamations of Indigenous jurisdiction. These are incrementally and inevitably shifting the terrain of struggle. Both Valverde and Pasternak have made the argument that working "in the register" of jurisdiction, to borrow Pasternak's phrase, may be

---

[104] *Ibid.* Recall that in *Tsilhqot'in Nation v British Columbia*, 2014 SCC 44, the Supreme Court of Canada abandons the doctrine of interjurisdictional immunity in the context of s 35 rights, with one rationale articulated by the Court being that if Parliament had not enacted legislation on a particular topic, then there would be no law governing the issue.

able to break the logjam of sovereignty: the contest of radical Crown title versus surviving inherent Indigenous jurisdiction. However, as Gordon Christie and others have pointed out, a focus on who governs what/where may distract us from asking pressing questions about *"how we might govern and be governed."*[105] Across Indigenous territories, it is obvious that the deep knowledge and respect for the land, and the authority to govern it, should go together.[106] As the work of many Indigenous scholars has powerfully brought forward, although diverse and distinct, many Indigenous legal orders include principles of deep relationality with lands, waters and other beings, an understanding that those elements exist in relation to each other, and not simple rights to take, but *obligations to protect and steward.*[107] Heidi Kiiwetinepinesiik Stark powerfully makes the point in her brilliant article "Nenabozho's Smart Berries: Rethinking Tribal Sovereignty and Accountability": "distracted by our struggle to prove and assert that we can, we have not paused long enough to ask if we want to. Are these the nations we want to be?"[108] Her reflection on how Indigenous nations and peoples want to relate to one another, and how they are going to be accountable to obligations to steward lands and waters for future generations, should prompt a broader reflection among settler legal scholars as well: how do we want settler orders to relate to Indigenous legal orders? What do we want our constitutional order to be?

This is where the element of prefiguration comes in: there is some promise in "getting free of the constrictors of the present" by "moving obliquely," as Rob Nichols advises.[109] Here, I take inspiration from land

---

[105] *Valverde, supra* note 53 at 145 [emphasis added].

[106] Pasternak, *Grounded Authority, supra* note 46. What "grounds" the various claims to authority? Different Indigenous leaders trace the source of legal authority to different sources, but many versions are consistent with Jeremy Webber's "Sovereignty 3": "that political power is, in a very real sense, self-authorized and self-determined—not dependent for its authority on the gift of any outside party": Webber, *supra* note 23 at 293. For some leaders, the source of the authority is "the Creator" or the natural world; for others, "self-preservation, political autonomy, and the collective rewards of territorial stewardship characterize the authority of Indigenous law": Pasternak, *Grounded Authority, supra* note 46 at 6.

[107] See for example, Stark, "Treaty Question", *supra* note 28; Starblanket, *supra* note 28.

[108] Stark, "Smart Berries", *supra* note 8 at 353.

[109] Robert Nichols, *Theft is Property! Dispossession and Critical Theory* (Durham: Duke University Press, 2020) at 146.

defenders, organizers, and scholars working towards "Jurisdiction Back" as a mode of moving into a decolonial legal future.[110] Jurisdiction Back can be characterized as moving obliquely from #LandBack, perhaps. #LandBack is a social movement, a political project of radical imagination that is bringing into being a profound shift in legal, social, and economic relationships to lands and waters.[111] Its goal is ultimately a return to Indigenous protocols organized around relationships and stewardship. Within Indigenous legal orders, the land is not "an object that is merely taken away, returned, and re-possessed,"[112] and thus, as Leanne Betasamosake Simpson powerfully puts it, "the opposite of dispossession is not possession."[113] The restitution must include, therefore, a return of governing authority, of jurisdiction.

Instead of "presum[ing] the forms that law will take,"[114] we can begin dreaming the legal and social geographies of the future, as Richard Ford states, "building the jurisdictions of the future today."[115] In this sense, a decolonial legal future is feasible, if propelled by a prefigurative politics. It is a future in which we develop skills and competencies in interlegality.[116] We must reject, as Sundhya Pahuja urges, the normative claims of settler state law to automatically and *"rightfully"* be law (in all places, for all purposes), and instead treat it as subject to "parochial (rather than universal) practice[s] of authorization,"[117]

---

[110] See for example, a successful collaborative team grant application employing this approach: Dayna Nadine Scott & Heidi Kiiwetinepinesiik Stark, "Jurisdiction Back: Material Approaches to Infrastructure Beyond Extractivism" (16 June 2024), online: <euc.yorku.ca/research-project/jurisdiction-back-infrastructure-beyond-extractivism/>.

[111] The 2019 Yellowhead Institute Red Paper brought Land Back, a very old idea, to renewed scholarly life, exposing the varied mechanisms of land theft and alienation that continue in Canada today: Yellowhead Institute, *supra* note 29.

[112] Gina Starblanket & Elaine Coburn, "'This Country has Another Story': Colonial Crisis, Treaty Relationships, and Indigenous Women's Futurities" in Heather Whiteside, ed, *Canadian Political Economy* (Toronto: University of Toronto Press, 2020) 86 at 87.

[113] Leanne Betasamosake Simpson, *As We Have Always Done: Indigenous Freedom Through Radical Resistance* (Minneapolis: University of Minnesota Press, 2017) at 43.

[114] Pasternak, "Settler Colonialism", *supra* note 3 at 148.

[115] Richard T Ford, "Law's Territory (A History of Jurisdiction)" (1999) 97:4 Mich L Rev 843 at 928.

[116] Andrée Boisselle, *Law's hidden canvas: Teasing out the threads of Coast Salish legal sensibility* (PhD Dissertation, University of Victoria, 2017) [unpublished].

[117] Sundhya Pahuja, "Public Debt, the Peace of Utrecht and the Rivalry between Company and State" in Alfred HA Soons, ed, *The 1713 Peace of Utrecht and its Enduring*

grounded in the specific geographies, as well as the legal, political, and cultural traditions of the territory. Within this space, we can leverage new conceptualizations of jurisdiction grounded in "overlapping, shared and competing legalities."[118] In the resulting constitutional order, we interrogate why and if it makes sense for settler authorities to continue to govern particular matters in particular places.[119] We rebuild, on the basis of an "ancient template," a new constitutional order for realizing Indigenous jurisdictions within shared territories.[120]

Effects (Leiden Boston: Brill Nijhoff, 2019) 156 at 171.

[118] Mawani, *supra* note 9 at 187.

[119] Jeremy Webber says that an element of "experimentation" is part of a functioning "intersocietal" legal order, "to determine what might serve as workable principles of co-existence in this land": Webber, *supra* note 23 at 281; Nichols, *supra* note 15.

[120] Simpson, *supra* note 1.

CHAPTER A-4

Four Views of Metis Constitutionalism

Kerry Sloan[*]

Abstract

While historical settler tropes emphasizing Metis hybridity are now dismissed as being unenlightened and even racist, modern ones focusing on Metis liminality and amorphousness continue to downplay Metis distinctiveness. Meanwhile, some commentators are concerned with Metis people only in terms of their supposed roles relative to the Canadian state mythos. Now, in the midst of a broader Indigenous resurgence, Metis people's own constitutional stories have begun to be more widely discussed. In contributing to this development, the author seeks to centre Metis constitutional narratives while tackling questions about Metis identities and governance, and while addressing Indigenous theorists' concerns that hybridity erases Indigenous particularity. This chapter posits that while Metis people cannot avoid contending with hybridity theory, Metis philosophy, including legal and political thought, is not merely hybrid. Rather, it is fundamentally Indigenous but incorporates European borrowings; these borrowings were and are considered congenial to Metis lifeways. Thus, living a

---

[*] Thank you to Karen Drake and the anonymous reviewers for helpful comments on earlier drafts. I would like to dedicate this chapter in memory of three recently departed friends: Dawne Burron, Christine Goodwin Sagassige, and Elder Lloyd "Buddy" Wesley.

good Metis life should not require dispensing with these non-Indigenous elements. The author elaborates on these claims by providing four views of Metis constitutionalism: Metis cultures were created by and through Indigenous social and political geographies; a defining moment for the Metis was their entering into the Iron Alliance with their relatives the Nehiyawak/Cree, prairie Anishinaabeg/Saulteaux and Nakota/Assiniboine in the late 1700s or early 1800s; European borrowings are inextricably part of Metis culture and philosophy and are connected to Metis wahkotowin/kinship practices; finally, wahkotowin implies interconnection and non-duality, suggesting multiplicity and dialogue rather than hybridity as characteristics of Metis constitutionalism.

Résumé

Si les tropes historiques des colons mettant l'accent sur l'hybridité des Métis sont désormais rejetés comme étant rétrogrades, voire racistes, les représentations modernes axées sur la liminalité et l'amorphisme des Métis continuent de minimiser leur spécificité. Par ailleurs, certaines voix ne considèrent les Métis qu'à travers leur rôle présumé dans le mythe fondateur de l'État canadien. Aujourd'hui, au cœur d'une résurgence autochtone plus large, les récits constitutionnels propres aux Métis commencent à être plus largement discutés. Contribuant à cette évolution, l'auteure cherche à recentrer les récits constitutionnels métis tout en abordant les questions d'identité et de gouvernance métisse, et en répondant aux préoccupations des théoricien·ne·s autochtones selon lesquelles l'hybridité efface la particularité autochtone. Ce chapitre soutient que, bien que les Métis ne puissent éviter de confronter la théorie de l'hybridité, la philosophie métisse, y compris la pensée juridique et politique, n'est pas uniquement hybride. Elle est fondamentalement autochtone tout en intégrant des emprunts européens jugés compatibles avec les modes de vie métis ; ces emprunts étaient et sont considérés comme cohérents avec les pratiques de vie métisses. Ainsi, vivre une bonne vie métisse ne devrait pas nécessiter d'abandonner ces éléments non autochtones. L'auteure développe ces idées en fournissant quatre perspectives sur le constitutionnalisme métis : les cultures métisses ont été créées au sein et à travers les géographies sociales et politiques autochtones ; un moment clé pour les Métis a été leur intégration dans l'Alliance de fer avec leurs parents, les Nehiyawak/Cris, Anishinaabeg des prairies/ Saulteaux et Nakota/Assiniboines à la fin du xviiie ou au début du xixe siècle ; les emprunts européens font partie intégrante de la culture et de la philosophie métisses et sont liés aux pratiques de wahkotowin (parenté) métisses ; enfin, le wahkotowin implique interconnexion et non-dualité, suggérant multiplicité et dialogue plutôt que l'hybridité comme caractéristiques du constitutionnalisme métis.

Telling Our Own Stories

There are many stories that have been told about Metis constitutionalism. We have our own stories, both oral and written,[1] about the way we constitute ourselves; in fact, these abound,[2] but most have

---

[1] Metis oral literature is vast, and contains stories about international, national and family histories. See a discussion of the Metis storytelling tradition in Maria Campbell, ed, *Achimoona* (Markham: Fifth House, 1985). Published collections of Metis stories include: Lawrence J Barkwell, Leah M Dorion & Audreen Hourie, eds, *Metis Legacy II: Michif Culture, Heritage and Folkways* (Saskatoon: Gabriel Dumont Institute; Winnipeg: Pemmican, 2006) [Barkwell, Dorion & Hourie, *Metis Legacy II*]; Maria Campbell, trans, *Stories of the Road Allowance People*, rev ed (Saskatoon: Gabriel Dumont Institute, 2010); Norman Fleury, Gilbert Pelletier, Joe Welsh & Norma Welsh, eds, *Stories of Our People/Lii zistwayyr di la naasyoon di Michif: A Métis Graphic Novel Anthology* (Saskatoon: Gabriel Dumont Institute, 2008); Henri Létourneau, *Henri Létourneau raconte* (Winnipeg: Éditions CFL, 1992); Bruce Sealey, ed, *Stories of the Metis* (Winnipeg: Manitoba Metis Federation, 1973); Bailey Oster & Marilyn Lizee, *Stories of Métis Women: Tales My Kookum Told Me* (Calgary: Durvile & UpRoute Books, 2021). Metis memoirs are also a source of constitutional stories. See e.g. Guillaume Charette, *Vanishing Spaces: Memoirs of a Prairie Métis* (Winnipeg: Éditions Bois-Brûlés, 1976) (memoirs of Louis Goulet); Norbert Welsh, as told to Mary Weekes, *The Last Buffalo Hunter* (New York: T Nelson & Sons, 1939), reprinted (Calgary: Fifth House, 1994).

[2] Popular and scholarly works from Metis perspectives touching on Metis constitutionalism include Maria Campbell, *Halfbreed* (Toronto: McClelland & Stewart, 1973), unabridged restored edition (Toronto: McClelland & Stewart, 2019); Howard Adams, *Prison of Grass: Canada from a Native Point of View*, rev ed (Saskatoon: Fifth House, 1989); Diane Payment, *The Free People – Li Gens Libres: A History of the Métis Community of Batoche, Saskatchewan* (Calgary: University of Calgary Press, 2009); Brenda Macdougall, *One of the Family: Metis Culture in Nineteenth-Century Northwestern Saskatchewan* (Vancouver: University of British Columbia Press, 2010) [Macdougall, *One of the Family*]; Adam James Patrick Gaudry, Kaa-tipeyimishoyaahk – "We are those who own ourselves": A Political History of Métis Self-Determination in the North-West, 1830–1870* (PhD Dissertation, University of Victoria, 2014) [unpublished] [Gaudry, *Métis Self-Determination*]; Michel Hogue, *Metis and the Medicine Line: Creating a Border and Dividing

been largely ignored in the wider public discourse. Canadians are more familiar with non-Metis stories about Metis nationhood, tales that fictionalize Metis history and political culture, creating caricatures of the Metis as, for example, the lazy,[3] lusty sons of the fur trade, breeding "bastards,"[4] who nevertheless inspire admiration for their strength and *joie de vivre*; portrayals of Metis women are often colonialist and condescending: *métisses* are simultaneously resourceful, skillful, yet slovenly,[5] but always sloe-eyed and enticing, the sirens of

---

a People (Durham: University of North Carolina Press, 2015). See also Lawrence J Barkwell, Leah Dorion & Darren R Préfontaine, eds, *Metis Legacy: A Métis Historiography and Annotated Bibliography* (Winnipeg: Pemmican, 2001). Campbell's *Halfbreed* and Adams' *Prison of Grass* were Canadian bestsellers and were among the first books to bring Metis perspectives to a wider audience.

3   Alexander Ross, *The Red River Settlement: Its Rise, Progress, and Present State* (London, UK: Smith, Elder, 1856), reprinted (Minneapolis: Ross & Haines, 1957). Note that Ross' wife Sarah ("Sally") was Syilx/Okanagan, and the couple are the ancestors of many Metis and mixed Indigenous people. Nevertheless, Ross was highly critical of Metis and "halfbreeds." See Sylvia Van Kirk, "What If Mama Is an Indian? The Cultural Ambivalence of the Alexander Ross Family" in Jacqueline Peterson & Jennifer SH Brown, eds, *The New Peoples: Being and Becoming Métis in North America* (Winnipeg: University of Manitoba Press, 1985) 207.

4   Other comments suggest Metis are untrustworthy, "polluting" the "white race," ignorant, ungovernable, and exhibiting the "worst of both worlds." See Renisa Mawani, *Colonial Proximities: Crossracial Encounters and Juridical Truths in British Columbia, 1871–1921* (Vancouver: University of British Columbia Press, 2009); Adele Perry, *On the Edge of Empire: Gender, Race, and the Making of British Columbia, 1849–1871* (Toronto: University of Toronto Press, 2001); John Lutz, "Making 'Indians' in British Columbia: Power, Race, and the Importance of Place" in Richard White & John M Findlay, eds, *Power and Place in the North American West* (Seattle: University of Washington Press, 1999). Historian Hubert Howe Bancroft, explaining what he called the "Fur Trader's Curse," opined, "I could never understand how such men as John McLoughlin, James Douglas, Ogden, Finlayson, Work and Tolmie and the rest could endure the thought of having their name and honors descend to a degenerate posterity. Surely they were possessed of sufficient intelligence to know that by giving their children Indian or half-breed mothers, their old Scotch, Irish or English blood would in them be greatly debased, and hence they were doing all concerned a great wrong": Hubert Howe Bancroft, *History of the Northwest Coast*, vol 2 (San Francisco: History Co, 1886) at 651.

5   For instance, one of my great-grandmothers, Marie-Rosalie Marion, and her family, were described with surprise by a Euro-descended dinner guest as being clean, neatly dressed and polite. This account by JW Radiger, Head Clerk of the HBC, was recorded in Lillian Beynon Thomas, "Some Manitoba Women Who Did First Things" online: (1947–1948) 3:4 Manitoba Historical Society Transactions <mhs. mb.ca/docs/transactions/3/firstwomen.shtml>. Others mused in astonishment that

bush and plains;[6] Metis, with their in-betweenness, or multiple identities, have been seen as shifty, not-to-be trusted operators, whose loy-
alties are suspect,[7] and—further—as traitors and agitators (e.g., Louis
Riel, Gabriel Dumont) standing in the way of "progress."[8] Even some
of the more positive, benign characterizations suggest stereotypes:
the Metis as go-betweens,[9] as ciphers, or translators between worlds,[10]
or as paragons of multiculturalism.[11]

Metis women had become "remarkably adapted" to Euro-Canadian culture. See
Sylvia Van Kirk, *Many Tender Ties: Women in Fur Trade Society, 1670–1870* (Winnipeg:
Watson & Dwyer, 1980).

[6] See Erica Smith, "'Gentlemen, This Is No Ordinary Trial': Sexual Narratives in the
Trial of Reverend Corbett, Red River, 1863" in Jennifer SH Brown & Elizabeth
Vibert, eds, *Reading beyond Words: Contexts for Native History* (Peterborough:
Broadview Press, 1996) 364 at 375.

[7] Note that it was not only colonial actors who questioned the motivations of the
Metis; some First Nations people during the time of the Riel Resistances suspected
Louis Riel and his allies of exploiting them for his own political purposes; others
today suggest that the idea of a great "Metis-Indian alliance" was a myth. See e.g.
Blair Stonechild & Bill Waiser, *Loyal till Death: Indians and the North-west Rebellion*
(Calgary: Fifth House, 1997). Robert Innes disputes aspects of these claims in Robert
Alexander Innes, *Elder Brother and the Law of the People: Contemporary Kinship and
Cowessess First Nation* (Winnipeg: University of Manitoba Press, 2013).

[8] See e.g. Donald Creighton, *John A Macdonald: The Old Chieftain* (Toronto: Macmillan, 1955).

[9] This is a common metaphor used to describe Metis people, including Louis Riel,
who occasionally used it to describe himself. See, for example, Albert Braz's chapter
on this topic in Albert Braz, *The False Traitor: Louis Riel in Canadian Culture* (Toronto:
University of Toronto Press, 2003) at 9 entitled "The Go-Between: Riel as Cultural
Mediator." Metis poet Gregory Scofield illustrates the cultural divide Riel must
negotiate in Gregory Scofield, "Le Porte-parole/The Spokesman" in *Louis: The
Heretic Poems* (Gibsons, BC: Nightwood, 2011) at 45.

[10] Minelle Mahtani points out that the metaphors of "interpreter" and "translator" are
often used by people of mixed ancestry to describe themselves: Minelle Mahtani,
"Mixed Metaphors: Positioning 'Mixed Race' Identity" in Jo-Anne Lee & John
Sutton Lutz, eds, *Situating "Race" and Racisms in Space, Time, and Theory: Critical
Essays for Activists and Scholars* (Montreal and Kingston: McGill-Queen's University
Press, 2005) 77.

[11] According to Nikos Papastergiadis, "[i]n early records of colonial encounters, the
ambiguity surrounding hybrids was wrapped in ambivalence. On the one hand,
hybridity was blamed for causing bad health. The symptoms included fatigue and
indolence. Economic inertia, moral decadence and even syphilis were also effects
that hybrids supposedly brought to the New World." Nevertheless, mixed people
were also seen as serving to enlighten society by being "[...] lubricants in the clashes
of culture; they were the negotiators who would secure a future free of xenophobia."
See Nikos Papastergiadis, "Tracing Hybridity in Theory" in Pnina Werbner & Tariq

While there may be elements of truth to some of these more favourable portrayals,[12] Metis culture, history, law, and politics are much more complex and multifaceted than these popular fables imagine, as I hope this chapter will illustrate.

With time, more realism has crept into public portraits of Metis people and issues, as Metis culture and rights have become more frequent subjects of government reports, litigation, and the popular press.[13] Nevertheless, news media have tended to exploit and sensationalize the divisions within Metis society and political organizations (and there are many), and to take a prurient interest in corruption and incompetence among Metis politicians.[14] Even among writers of

---

Modood, eds, *Debating Cultural Hybridity: Multi-Cultural Identities and the Politics of Anti-Racism* (London, UK: Zed, 1997) 257 at 260–261.

[12] For example, although not merely "go-betweens," the Metis negotiated political and trade relationships with all their "cousins," including treaties with Canada and with other Indigenous nations. Regarding Metis and mixed Indigenous women in such roles, see Lucy Eldersveld Murphy, "Public Mothers: Native American and Métis Women as Creole Mediators in the Nineteenth-century Midwest" (2003) 14:4 Journal of Women's History 142; Émilie Pigeon & Carolyn Podruchny, "Bannock Diplomacy: How Métis Women Fought Battles and Made Peace in North Dakota, 1850s–1870s" (2022) 69:1 Ethnohistory 29. See also Allyson Stevenson, *The Metis Cultural Brokers and the Western Numbered Treaties, 1869–1877* (Master's Thesis, University of Saskatchewan, 2004) [unpublished].

[13] The Metis were studied by the Royal Commission on Aboriginal Peoples (1996); Metis identity was the subject of a Senate Committee report (The Standing Senate Committee On Aboriginal Peoples, *"The People Who Own Themselves": Recognition of Métis Identity in Canada* (Ottawa: Senate of Canada, 2013)); the Supreme Court of Canada in *Manitoba Metis Federation Inc v Canada (Attorney General)*, 2013 SCC 14, held that the federal Crown did not properly uphold its obligations regarding Metis lands in Manitoba; and Metis rights were the subject of a federal report by Thomas Isaac (Thomas Isaac, *A Matter of National and Constitutional Import: Report of the Minister's Special Representative on Reconciliation with Métis: Section 35 Métis Rights and the Manitoba Metis Federation Decision* (Gatineau: Indigenous and Northern Affairs Canada, 2016)). Other key SCC cases are *R v Powley*, 2003 SCC 43 [*Powley*] and *Daniels v Canada (Indian Affairs and Northern Development)*, 2016 SCC 12 [*Daniels*]. Jean Teillet's *The North-West Is Our Mother: The Story of Louis Riel's People, the Metis Nation* (Toronto: HarperCollins, 2019) [Teillet, *The North-West Is Our Mother*] was a Canadian non-fiction bestseller.

[14] For instance, the Métis National Council recently took the Manitoba Metis Federation to court (January 2022, Ontario Superior Court): see "Métis National Council files lawsuit making shocking allegations of corruption against former officials", *Global News Hour at 6* (28 January 2022), online (video): <globalnews.ca/video/8579887/metis-national-council-files-lawsuit-making-shocking-allegations-of-corruption-

popular and scholarly accounts of Canadian constitutionalism, the Metis are used as signs to indicate something other than themselves, with Metis ideas employed as symbolic stand-ins for various claims. For instance, while I was frustrated, but not really surprised, that John Ralston Saul falls into the "Metis-as-mixed" trap/trope[15] in using the term "Metis" to describe the influence of Indigenous philosophy on Canadian culture and politics—he goes so far as to say that Canada is a Metis nation[16]—I was a little startled to read in the work of the venerable political and legal philosopher Jim Tully, an ally of Indigenous peoples, the idea that being "Metis" represents having a "non-identity." In his work on constitutionalism entitled *Strange Multiplicity*, Tully elaborates an extended metaphor in Haida artist Bill Reid's carving *The spirit of Haida Gwaii* of 13 sghanna (spirit

---

against-former-officials>; a few months later, the Manitoba Metis Federation sued the Metis Nation of British Columbia in the Manitoba Court of Queen's Bench (April 2022), alleging defamation, among other things, and asking for special, aggravated and punitive damages, as well as special costs. See Dylan Robertson, "Manitoba Métis leader sues B.C. group for libel", *Winnipeg Free Press* (updated 26 April 2022), online: <winnipegfreepress.com/breakingnews/2022/04/25/manitoba-metis-leader-sues-bc-group-for-libel>.

[15] For instance, Metis scholar Chris Andersen critiques the idea that Metis people are merely people of mixed Indigenous and non-Indigenous ancestry, and points out that the Metis people have, over time, become a distinct people. See Chris Andersen, *"Métis": Race, Recognition, and the Struggle for Indigenous Peoplehood* (Vancouver: University of British Columbia Press, 2014). Definitions of Metis people as merely mixed have been common in Canadian consciousness, exemplified by 1938 Alberta legislation defining a Metis person as "a person of mixed white and Indian blood" who was not "an Indian or a non-treaty Indian as defined in The Indian Act": *An Act Respecting the Métis Population of the Province*, SA 1938 (2nd Sess) c 6, s 2(a).

[16] John Ralston Saul, *A Fair Country: Telling Truths about Canada* (Toronto: Penguin Canada, 2009). Metis scholars Adam Gaudry & Rob LA Hancock point out that such narratives obscure the real harms of colonialism: see Adam Gaudry & Robert LA Hancock, "Decolonizing Metis Pedagogies in Post-Secondary Settings" (2012) 35:1 CJNE 7. In another critique of Saul's book, Andrew Potter is skeptical of Saul's claim "that all the great virtues of the Canadian personality are owed to the country's Métis character, and so our desire for harmony and balance, our preference for diversity, inclusion and complexity, our renewed interest in egalitarianism—all are emanations of our aboriginal soul." See Andrew Potter, "Are We a Metis Nation?", *Literary Review of Canada* (April 2009), online: <reviewcanada.ca/magazine/2009/04/are-we-a-mtis-nation/>. In the same article, Potter also provides this "zinger": "Almost alone among his contemporaries, John Ralston Saul continues to stalk the Snuffleupagus of nationalism known as the Canadian Identity."

or myth creatures), all of them crossing boundaries in some way (gender, lifeform, local/migrant), together in a canoe. Tully suggests this configuration represents something paradigmatic about the Canadian collectivity, and contends that a kind of continual "questioning, contestation and renegotiation of their cultural identities seems plain for all to see."[17] In describing the beings in the canoe, Tully continues, "Is this not the constitutional game they are playing as they vie and squabble for position[?] [...] All the passengers are Metis, exhibiting the non-identity of cultural identities."[18] While, as Metis, we "know who we are,"[19] to others we have become signs of the possibility that Indigenous and settler peoples can all get along—in one big, happy Metis (mixed) family—or symbols of Canada as foundationally amorphous (if that's not an oxymoron), resisting the creation of personal and collective characterizations.[20] Again, while there are elements of truth in both of these representations, non-Metis stories about Metis people tend to reduce us to being a plot line in the story of Canada.[21]

I would like to tell a different story, a story about the richness and complexity of being Metis, and a story about Metis interconnections with other peoples and beings—with all our relations. Of course, it would be impossible in such a short work to provide a fulsome account of Metis constitutionalism, and this is not my intent. There is so much to say, especially about the hard work of people in Metis local governance today, the "practical results"[22] that constantly flow

---

[17] James Tully, *Strange Multiplicity: Constitutionalism in an Age of Diversity* (Cambridge: Cambridge University Press, 1995) at 25.

[18] *Ibid.*

[19] Martha Harroun Foster, *We Know Who We Are: Métis Identity in a Montana Community* (Norman: University of Oklahoma Press, 2006).

[20] Justin Trudeau has said there is no "core identity, no mainstream" in Canada: see Charles Foran, "The Canada experiment: Is this the world's first post-national country?", *The Guardian* (4 January 2017), online: <theguardian.com/world/2017/jan/04/the-canada-experiment-is-this-the-worlds-first-postnational-country>.

[21] Adam Gaudry, "The Métis-ization of Canada: The Process of Claiming Louis Riel, Métissage, and the Métis People as Canada's Mythical Origin" (2013) 2:2 aboriginal policy studies 64.

[22] At Louis Riel's trial for treason at Regina, in his July 31, 1885, address to the jury, he states, "During my life I have aimed at practical results. I have writings, and after my death I hope that my spirit will bring practical results." Reproduced in Hans V Hansen, ed, *Riel's Defence: Perspectives on His Speeches* (Montreal and Kingston: McGill-Queen's University Press, 2014) at 28.

from living our culture and laws in community and on the land.[23] While that is perhaps a story for another time, the narrative I present here is this: as Metis, we are distinctive in part because we originate from and are grounded in the cultures and worldviews of our Indigenous relations; however, our distinctiveness also flows from our having borrowed congenial cultural elements from our non-Indigenous relations. Further, the vignettes I provide below suggest that Metis constitutionalisms encompass seeming polarities: Metis identities may be multiplicitous and overlapping,[24] yet concrete and distinctive;[25] diasporic, yet nationalist.[26]

While I will sketch an outline of my narrative in more detail below, I first take a short but necessary detour into the difficult (and seemingly unavoidable) subject of Metis identities.

Metis Identities: Various Viewpoints

Many Metis thinkers have objected to splitting elements of Metis identity. While non-Metis people often think of being Metis as being "part Native" and "part European," Metis people view themselves as

---

[23] In the words of Emma LaRocque, *When the Other Is Me: Native Resistance Discourse, 1850–1990* (Winnipeg: University of Manitoba Press, 2010) at 145, "Native peoples in real life are going about reconstructing their lives and communities, pushing paradigms long before we can write our novels and poems, or our dissertations. This process is infinitely more subtle and interesting than any caricatures, tropes, allegories, arguments, dogmas, or speculations we theorists may try to sort out."

[24] Sharron A Fitzgerald, "Hybrid Identities in Canada's Red River Colony" (2007) 51:2 Canadian Geographies 186.

[25] Brenda Macdougall, "The Myth of Metis Cultural Ambivalence" in Nicole St-Onge, Carolyn Podruchny & Brenda Macdougall, eds, *Contours of a People: Metis Family, Mobility, and History* (Norman: University of Oklahoma Press, 2012) [St-Onge, Podruchny & Macdougall, *Contours of a People*] 422.

[26] See Sophie McCall, "Diaspora and Nation in Métis Writing" in Christine Kim, Sophie McCall & Melinda Baum Singer, eds, *Cultural Grammars of Nation, Diaspora, and Indigeneity in Canada* (Waterloo: Wilfrid Laurier University Press, 2012) 21; Dylan AT Miner, "Halfbreed Theory: Maria Campbell's Storytelling as Indigenous Knowledge and *Une Petite Michin*" in Jolene Armstrong, ed, *Maria Campbell: Essays on Her Works* (Toronto: Guernica, 2012) 147. Note Chris Andersen critiques "halfbreed theory" as being racialized: Andersen, *supra* note 15 at 56. But I think Miner's point is that Metis thinking encompasses dualities.

being more than simply mixed.[27] Similarly, mestiza scholar Paula Gunn Allen says that mestiza/o/x people are not "half and half" but "all in all."[28]

At the same time, there are movements among some Metis people to deliberately concretize Metis individual and community identities, thus eroding complexity. This may be for reasons independent of external actors, but I contend that, many times, Metis identity formation has been influenced by state law, as in attempts by Metis to bring themselves within the *R v Powley*[29] criteria, the test that determines whether Metis rights claimants will succeed in having their rights constitutionally protected. In this leading Supreme Court of Canada (SCC) case, proof of the existence of Metis rights worthy of protection depends on whether claimants can establish they are part of a "historic Metis community." This is a difficult test to meet,[30] for reasons that may be deduced from what follows.

Meanwhile, state law assumes hard divisions between Indigenous groups, even in the wording of s. 35 of the *Constitution Act, 1982,*[31] which classifies Indigenous people as belonging to one of three categories: "Indian," Inuit, or Metis. In some cases, state law also assumes narrow categories of indigeneity. Through the *Indian Act,*[32] for instance, the federal government tried to limit who could be defined as an "Indian," thus reducing the numbers of people, especially women, who could claim Indian status. While this definition has been expanded over time to reinstate First Nations (and some Metis) women who lost their status when they married non-"Indian" men, and to permit registration of their children, sex-based inequities in

---

[27] For a comprehensive and trenchant exploration of the issues, see Chelsea Vowel, *Indigenous Writes: A Guide to First Nations, Métis & Inuit Issues in Canada* (Winnipeg: Highwater, 2016) at ch 4 ("You're Métis? Which of Your Parents Is an Indian?").

[28] Paula Gunn Allen, "She Is Us: Thought Woman and the Sustainability of Worship" in Melissa K Nelson, ed, *Original Instructions: Indigenous Teachings for a Sustainable Future* (Rochester: Bear, 2008) 138.

[29] *Powley, supra* note 13.

[30] See Karen L Sloan, *The Community Conundrum: Metis Critical Perspectives on the Application of* R v Powley *in British Columbia* (PhD Dissertation, University of Victoria, 2016) [unpublished] [Sloan, *Community Conundrum*].

[31] *Constitution Act, 1982,* being Schedule B to the *Canada Act 1982* (UK), 1982, c 11.

[32] *Indian Act,* RSC 1985, c I-5.

Indian Act status criteria existed until 2020, continuing to prevent registrations.[33]

Defining Indigenous people narrowly in legislation that provided benefits and rights was consistent with attempts by the Crown to avoid taking constitutional responsibility for Indigenous peoples more broadly. In 1930, a reference was brought before the SCC about whether Inuit people should be classified as "Indians" for the purposes of s. 91(24) of the *Constitution Act, 1867* (i.e., whether they should be considered to be under federal jurisdiction); after much wrangling, the answer was "yes."[34] The same question involving the Metis languished in the courts for 18 years, until in 2016 the SCC in *R v Daniels* affirmed that Metis (and "non-status" Indians) are also "Indians" under s. 91(24).[35] Nevertheless, Metis people living on Metis settlements in Alberta must decide whether they will identify as Metis or register for Indian status (some people may fit within both legal definitions[36]) for the purposes of accessing Metis settlement benefits. This is because, with some limited exceptions, Metis people who register as status Indians are not entitled to Metis settlement membership.[37]

Whatever the source of contestation about Metis identities, these are not rarified, academic problems; questions of Metis identity are dividing the Metis nation, or at least the political organizations that

---

[33] Government of Canada, "Bill S-3: Eliminating known sex-based inequities in registration" (last modified 13 September 2022), online: <sac-isc.gc.ca/eng/14672149 55663/1572460311596>.

[34] *Reference re Term "Indians"*, [1939] SCR 104 regarding interpretation of s 91(24) of the *Constitution Act, 1867* (UK), 30 & 31 Vict, c 3.

[35] *Daniels, supra* note 13. Note that in *R v Blais*, 2003 SCC 44, the court held that Metis were not "Indians" for the purposes of the *Manitoba Natural Resources Agreement (NRTA)*, SC 1930, c 29.

[36] See Bonita Lawrence, *"Real" Indians and Others: Mixed-Blood Urban Native Peoples and Indigenous Nationhood* (Vancouver: University of British Columbia Press, 2004).

[37] *Alberta (Aboriginal Affairs and Northern Development) v Cunningham*, 2011 SCC 37 *[Cunningham]*. There are some people who were "grandfathered in" as both "Indian" (or Inuk) and Metis under the *Metis Settlements Act*, RSA 2000, c M 14, s 75 *[MSA]*. Theoretically, a Metis Settlements General Council Policy could be created that would allow Metis who are also "Indians" or beneficiaries under Inuit land claims to be members; see *MSA*, s 75(3.1). However, as Metis scholar Brenda Gunn contends, the decision in *Cunningham* reveals that "Indian and Métis are thought to be dichotomous in Canadian law": see Brenda L Gunn, "Defining Métis People as a People: Moving Beyond the Indian/Métis Dichotomy" (2015) 38:2 Dalhousie LJ 413.

represent many Metis people in Canada. In January 2020, the Métis National Council (MNC) suspended the Métis Nation of Ontario (MNO) for granting citizenship to people from mixed Indigenous communities in western Ontario that the MNC says are not legitimately Metis; however, the MNC did not remove the MNO. Either as a direct or indirect result of these conflicts, the Manitoba Metis Federation, the Métis Nation of Saskatchewan and the Métis Nation of BC have all left the MNC.[38]

Claims about belonging—or not belonging—can cause emotional anguish and conflicts between families and friends, and may unfortunately dilute our ability to collaborate in defence of our rights. They may also mar our ability to enact our kinship obligations.

As painful and destructive as Metis (and other) identity politics can be, and as obvious as it is that the drive to categorize Indigenous people is a feature of colonialism, it seems to be an impulse of human (not just "western") thought to impose social boundaries, to create a sense of who's "in" and who's not. People who don't fit neatly within constructed categories create nervousness among self-imposed guardians of those categories,[39] leading, for example, to social rules about ethnic exclusion, and thus to prejudice, segregation and even genocide.

What is a Metis person to make of the sometimes seeming fetish for purity—racial, social or intellectual? Some Metis people celebrate multiple identities, or use them of necessity;[40] others—owing to racism and self-silencing[41]—have tried to "pass" for white,

---

38 For further background, see Kerry Sloan, "Reference re *R v Powley*" in Kent McNeil & Naiomi Metallic, eds, *Judicial Tales Retold: Reimagining Indigenous Rights Jurisprudence* (Saskatoon: Indigenous Law Centre, 2020), [2020] CNLR Special Edition 125 at 129–131. There are other Metis political associations that are not connected to the Métis National Council and its provincial subsidiaries.

39 For an interesting example of historic nervousness about how to categorize Metis people in the United States, see Lauren L Basson, "Savage Half-Breed, French Canadian or White US Citizen? Louis Riel and US Perceptions of Nation and Civilisation" (2005) 7:4 National Identities 369.

40 See, for example, Doris Jeanne MacKinnon, *The Identities of Rose Marie Delorme: Portrait of a Métis Woman, 1861–1960* (Regina: University of Regina Press, 2012); Van Kirk, *supra* note 3. If these were examples of ambivalence, this "ambivalence" was a response to colonialism and racism.

41 Laura Smyth Groening, *Listening to Old Woman Speak: Natives and AlterNatives in Canadian Literature* (Montreal and Kingston: McGill-Queen's University Press, 2004).

and still others situate themselves within their indigeneity.[42] That is, *we* know who we are, but we might not always want others to know. This doesn't change the fact that we are distinctive, not merely hybrid, but—for all the current theorizing about how Metis are more than just mixed—we still receive messages that we must ally with one "side" or the other. These suggestions may be made for perfectly supportable reasons. I have been told, in conversations with various people, that one either follows an Indigenous life path ... or one does not. There is no "middle ground" and, ultimately, one must choose. I can understand this, as non-Indigenous life paths (colonialism, capitalism, contractarianism) on Turtle Island have been catastrophically damaging for Indigenous people (and others), leading to unspeakable loss. I can also understand the necessity of reclaiming and revitalizing Indigenous lifeways, including philosophical traditions, of reminding ourselves who we really are, through our own ways of being. Yet what do we do, as Metis, with the reality that non-Indigenous peoples and cultures have contributed to making us who we are? If we "split the lark," as Emily Dickinson says, will we "find the music"?

While I ask this (rhetorical) question, I agree with those who caution against trying to understand Indigenous ways of being through drawing parallels with other traditions, or against assuming that Indigenous philosophical traditions of non-dualism can be equated with hybridity theory or deconstructionism. Anishinaabe scholar Aaron Mills asks us to be mindful that, while Indigenous and Euro-derived constitutionalisms can be in dialogue, and even connected organically in some ways, they are rooted in their own ontologies and lifeways.[43] Inuit/Inupiat scholar Gordon Christie warns about the

---

[42] For some discussions of these concerns, see Cathy Richardson, "Metis Identity Creation and Tactical Responses to Oppression and Racism" (2006) 2 Variegations 56; Gabrielle Monique Legault, *Changing in Place: A Generational Study of an Indigenous Family in the Okanagan* (MA Thesis, University of British Columbia, 2012) [unpublished]; Annette Chrétien, *"Mattawa, Where the Waters Meet": The Question of Identity in Métis Culture* (MMus Thesis, University of Ottawa, 1996) [unpublished]; Sylvia Rae Cottell, *My People Will Sleep for One Hundred Years: Story of a Métis Self* (Master's Thesis, University of Victoria, 2004) [unpublished].

[43] In his essay, Mills says that "every system of law – Indigenous or not – has a home": Aaron Mills, "The Lifeworlds of Law: Revitalizing Indigenous Legal Orders Today" (2016) 61:4 McGill LJ 847 at 858. At 862–863, he provides the metaphor of such homes (community-based and people-based) as being trees, although acknowledging that

pitfalls of critical legal theories that question objective reality, and celebrate hybridity, as obscuring what is distinctive about being Indigenous.[44] While I support these cautions, I question how to apply them when Metis ontologies and lifeways—and thus constitutionalisms—contain both Indigenous and non-Indigenous elements, and when wrestling with questions of hybridity and essentialism/non-essentialism seems inescapable.

While I claim here that Metis ontologies and lifeways are foundationally Indigenous, this does not erase the fact that they are not only Indigenous, and it does not erase Metis distinctiveness. For instance, land-based groundedness is seen as an essential element of Indigenous identity; however, where mobility is common and ideas of territory complex,[45] the Metis way of being grounded may look different from the groundedness of other Indigenous peoples. Thus, I assert that, where mixedness is bred in the bone, being "all-in-all" should not mean being seen as inauthentic or co-opted.

Mapping the Narrative: Four Views Illustrate Three Claims

The four views of Metis constitutionalism that I narrate below illustrate the following claims: 1) Metis philosophy, including legal, spiritual and political thought, is fundamentally Indigenous, with

---

these trees may be entangled with others, as all are rooted in the earth. In his dissertation at 240, Mills suggests that law/lifeworld trees might communicate with others, as via mycorrhizae (metaphorically, treaty-related practices). See Aaron James Mills (Waabishki Ma'iingan), *Miinigowiziwin: All That Has Been Given for Living Well Together – One Vision of Anishinaabe Constitutionalism* (PhD Dissertation, University of Victoria, 2019) [unpublished] [Mills, *Miinigowiziwin*]. Mills claims in his dissertation at 216, "[…] rooted and liberal constitutional logics may translate and subsume (i.e., capture) each other, but cannot combine. Any claim as to a hybridized state of settler-indigenous law is false in that it occludes logical-structural difference."

[44] See Gordon Christie, "Law, Theory and Aboriginal Peoples" (2003) 2 Indigenous LJ 67; Smyth Groening, *supra* note 41; Mills, *Miinigowiziwin, ibid.*

[45] Kerry Sloan, "Always Coming Home: Metis Legal Understandings of Community and Territory" (2017) 33:1 Windsor YB Access Just 125 [Sloan, *Always Coming Home*]; John Borrows, *Freedom and Indigenous Constitutionalism* (Toronto: University of Toronto Press, 2016). Joseph Bauerkemper & Heidi Kiiwetinepinesiik Stark, in "The Trans/National Terrain of Anishinaabe Law and Diplomacy" (2012) 4:1 Journal of Transnational American Studies 1, have discussed mobility in Anishinaabe history and constitutionalism.

European borrowings; nevertheless, 2) sometimes it may be impossible to distinguish foreground and background; and 3) in the Metis context, following *miyo-wicetowin* ("the good life/path") should not require dispensing with borrowed elements of European culture.

The four views of Metis constitutionalism are 1) Metis culture was created by and through pre-existing Indigenous social geographies; 2) from this perspective, an originating moment of the Metis nation was the creation of the Nehiyaw Pwat/Iron Alliance between the Metis, Nehiyawak/Cree, prairie Anishinaabeg/Saulteaux and Nakota/Assiniboine (and, later, their relatives the Dakota), collectively a central force (literally and figuratively) on the Plains; 3) European borrowings are inextricably part of Metis culture, were incorporated as elements congenial to Metis lifeways, and do not diminish Indigeneity; 4) kinship/wahkotowin implies interconnection, but also non-duality, an important tenet of many Indigenous philosophies, including those of the Metis. As an element of wahkotowin, non-duality implies not the absence or mere porosity of boundaries implied by hybridity theory, but a multiplicity of connections—connections that derive from the earth and enliven how we constitute ourselves.

Four Views of Metis Constitutionalism

1. Metis culture was created by and through pre-existing Indigenous social geographies

Long before the arrival of Europeans, Indigenous peoples disseminated their knowledge about how to resolve conflicts; they practised persuading others to awaken to the truth that all beings are interconnected,[46] woven together[47] physically, socially. These understandings were based on observations of the natural world, its

---

[46] Maria Campbell, "We Need to Return to the Principles of Wahkotowin" *Eagle Feather News* (November 2007) 5, reproduced online: <https://www.metismuseum.ca/media/document.php/11751.mariacolumnNovember2007.pdf> [Campbell, "Wahkotowin"]; Elmer Ghostkeeper, *Spirit Gifting: The Concept of Spiritual Exchange*, 2nd ed (Raymond, AB: Writing On Stone Press, 2007).

[47] Sylvia McAdam (Saysewahum), *Nationhood Interrupted: Revitalizing* nêhiyaw *Legal Systems* (Saskatoon: Purich, 2015).

intricacies and interdependencies, and were inscribed in law,[48] internalized from earliest days.[49] Both physical and spiritual consequences flowed from ruptures of kinship, from acting as if one were alone in the universe.[50]

The Great Law of Peace of the Haudenosaunee, enacted to end generations of warfare, and to heal from resulting griefs, created a confederacy of related nations that has endured for centuries,[51] and has influenced settler governments.[52] Other confederacies existed: the Wabanaki (Mi'kmaq, Wolastoqey/Maliseet, Pesomukhati/Passamaqoddy, Abenaki, Penobscot), the Three Fires ("Chippewa," Odawa, Pottawatomi); and other treaties were entered into, such as the Dish with One Spoon, which resolved harvesting conflicts between the Anishinaabeg and the Haudenosaunee.[53] All over Turtle Island there existed nested and/or overlapping confederacies: vast networks of kinship—wakhotowin—

---

[48] John Borrows, *Canada's Indigenous Constitution* (Toronto: University of Toronto Press, 2010).

[49] Elder Charlene Jones, teaching given at Anishinaabe Law Camp, Neyaashiinigmiing (Cape Croker, ON, 1 September 2017).

[50] Metis stories derived from Nehiyaw and Anishinaabeg traditions involving the trickster often illustrate this. See e.g. "Nanabush and the Geese" in Barkwell, Dorion & Hourie, *Metis Legacy II, supra* note 1 at 41, told by Cynthia Genaille, as told by her mother Elizabeth Genaille, who was told it by her father, Louis Genaille (translated from Saulteaux/Anishinabemowin by Cynthia Genaille); compare "Legends of Wēsākechā, Part I" told by Anne Anderson and told to her by her mother Āsinē-wuchēwiskwes (Mountain Girl), her great-grandfather Māchēsis (Little Hunter), and by her great-grandmother Mistahēskwew (Much Woman) (translated from Cree/Nehiyawewin by Anne Anderson), in Anne Anderson, *Legends of Wēsākechā* (self-published, 1976) at 28.

[51] Kayanesenh Paul Williams, *Kayanerenkó:wa: The Great Law of Peace* (Winnipeg: University of Manitoba Press, 2018); Robert A Williams Jr, "Linking Arms Together: Multicultural Constitutionalism in a North American Indigenous Vision of Law and Peace" (1994) 82:4 Cal L Review 981.

[52] The following resolutions of the United States Congress acknowledge the contribution of the Great Law of Peace, including the laws governing the Haudenosaunee (Iroquois) Confederacy, to the development of the US constitution: S Con Res 76, 100th Congress, 2nd Sess (1988); HR Con Res 331, 100th Congress, 2nd Sess (1988).

[53] Leanne Simpson, "Looking after Gdoo-naaganinaa: Precolonial Nishnaabeg Diplomatic and Treaty Relationships" (2008) 23:2 Wicazo Sa Review 29. Of course, this is not to suggest that there was no warfare among Indigenous nations; rather, confederacies and treaties existed because people recognized the need to prevent and mitigate conflict.

engendering cultural and economic exchange,[54] promoting diplomacy. These were like "islands," or nodes, of a continental geographic web,[55] with various nations, and conglomerations of nations, connected across the continent by trade trails,[56] by songs, by ideas, by families.

The territories of northeastern Turtle Island are home to some of the Indigenous ancestors of the Metis: the Haudenosaunee, the Innu, the Huron, the Algonquin—and became home to people of various European nations who crossed the ocean and settled in these Indigenous territories.

Into the complex, multiplicitous, yet loosely cohesive pre-contact Indigenous world, newcomers came: first, and for a span of time, the Norse; and, seasonally, people fishing from western Europe: Portuguese, Basques, Bretons, Normans, English, Irish.[57] Thus, even before permanent, extensive European settlements, it is likely Indigenous and non-Indigenous people were in contact, creating trade and family relationships, aligned with the prevailing local realities.[58] As European settlement

---

[54] See André Le Dressay, Normand Lavallee & Jason Reeves, "First Nations Trade, Specialization, and Market Institutions: A Historical Survey of First Nation Market Culture" (2010) 72 Aboriginal Policy Research Consortium International 109; Shalene Wuttunee Jobin, *Upholding Indigenous Economic Relationships: Nehiyawak Narratives* (Vancouver: University of British Columbia Press, 2023).

[55] Isabel Altamirano-Jiménez, "The Colonization and Decolonization of Indigenous Diversity" in Leanne Simpson, ed, *Lighting the Eighth Fire: The Liberation, Resurgence, and Protection of Indigenous Nations* (Winnipeg: Arbeiter Ring, 2008) [Simpson, *Eighth Fire*] 175.

[56] David G Mandelbaum, *The Plains Cree: An Ethnographic, Comparative, and Historical Study* (Regina: Canadian Plains Research Center, 1979). The late Stoney/Nakoda Elder and land claims researcher Lloyd "Buddy" Wesley taught me that the Nakoda were part of a trade network that stretched into South America. He said that there were words in the Stoney language for "jaguar," "monkey" and "emerald," for example—words that referred to animals and minerals that did not exist in Nakoda territory, but of which pre-contact Nakoda people were traditionally aware.

[57] Peter Pope, "Transformation of the Maritime Cultural Landscape of Atlantic Canada by Migratory European Fishermen, 1500–1800" in Louis Sicking & Darlene Abreu-Ferreira, eds, *Beyond the Catch: Fisheries of the North Atlantic, the North Sea and the Baltic, 900-1850* (Leiden: Brill, 2008) 123.

[58] Note the creation, for instance, of Basque-Algonquian Pidgin, spoken on the Atlantic Coast and the Gulf of St. Lawrence until at least 1711: see Peter Bakker, "Basque Pidgin Vocabulary in European Algonquian Trade Contacts" (1988) 19 Papers of the Algonquian Conference 7. See also Denys Delâge, who states that when Jacques Cartier encountered Mi'kmaq people in Baie-des-Chaleurs/Maoi Pôgtapei in about 1534, the latter brought 50 canoes laden with furs, indicating they were already

increased and became more entrenched, these connections flourished, even in the face of conflict, because settlers and colonial leaders followed Indigenous treaty protocols and ways of avoiding interference with others' lifeways. Treaty protocols created kinship[59] and resulting obligations to provide respect and mutual aid.[60]

Over time, in these northeastern territories, peoples and their ideas met—familial, cultural, linguistic, economic, artistic, legal; and there they learned to live with each other.[61] Perhaps some found "middle grounds," where new cultures began to emerge, for example, in *le pays en haut*;[62] in others, mutual understandings were reached (even if tenuous or incomplete), leading to the creation of trade and gifting relationships,[63]

---

accustomed to trading with Europeans: Denys Delâge, *Bitter Feast: Amerindians and Europeans in Northeastern North America, 1600–64*, translated by Jane Brierley (Vancouver: University of British Columbia Press, 2014) at 82. Hamar Foster refers to Indigenous/non-Indigenous intersocietal law as stemming from practical necessities: Hamar Foster, "Law and Necessity in Western Rupert's Land and Beyond, 1670–1870" in Louis A Knafla & Jonathan Swainger, eds, *Laws and Societies in the Canadian Prairie West, 1670–1940* (Vancouver: University of British Columbia Press, 2005) 57.

[59] Aimée Craft, *Breathing Life into the Stone Fort Treaty: An Anishinabe Understanding of Treaty One* (Saskatoon: Purich, 2013).

[60] Aaron Mills, "What Is a Treaty? On Contract and Mutual Aid" in John Borrows & Michael Coyle, eds, *The Right Relationship: Reimagining the Implementation of Historical Treaties* (Toronto: University of Toronto Press, 2017) 208.

[61] Despite the reality that violence occurred throughout this period, Jeremy Webber claims there were reasons why Indigenous/non-Indigenous intersocietal law developed: colonists' vulnerability (i.e., they were vastly outnumbered in the early colonial period); economic interdependence; the need to create predictability in interactions over time: Jeremy Webber, "Relations of Force and Relations of Justice: The Emergence of Normative Community between Colonists and Aboriginal Peoples" (1995) 33:4 Osgoode Hall LJ 623. At 655, Webber states, "[…] intercommunal norms to govern relations between Aboriginal and non-Aboriginal peoples in northeastern North America […] were not the product of a straightforward exercise of sovereign power, but rather a long history of interaction and experimentation. From a series of *ad hoc* and pragmatic accommodations, a structure emerged that the parties themselves recognized to be normative and that they customarily invoked to resolve intercommunal conflict. In large measure, fact made law."

[62] Richard White, *The Middle Ground: Indians, Empires, and Republics in the Great Lakes Region, 1650–1815* (Cambridge: Cambridge University Press, 1991).

[63] Janna Promislow, "'Thou Wilt Not Die of Hunger…for I Bring Thee Merchandise': Consent, Intersocietal Normativity, and the Exchange of Food at York Factory, 1683–1763" in Jeremy Webber & Colin M Macleod, eds, *Between Consenting Peoples: Political Community and the Meaning of Consent* (Vancouver: University of British Columbia Press, 2011) 77.

treaties,[64] spiritual understandings,[65] and legal non-interference in practice.[66]

Thus, early Indigenous/settler relations may have been a source of formative experience and knowledge that was passed down through family stories. While I cannot say what the connections were, if any, between Acadian mixed ancestry people, or Inuit/European people, for example, and the Metis of the Northwest, it is clear from professional[67] and family genealogies, including my own, that the modern Metis nation has roots, in part, in the peoples—ancient and recently arrived—of the St. Lawrence River Valley and environs. Kebec (literally, "the place where the waters open") became—and still is—a confluence of cultures. (This is not to argue for or against the existence of the "eastern Metis" in Quebec or the Maritimes, but to state a historical fact.) With the fur trade and the cartage trade, these relationships began to spread inland—westward to the Great Lakes and beyond, and northward to Hudson's Bay—along the rivers, lakes and tracks that were the Indigenous trade highways of the day.

Ideas and practices brought together by all family members began to create distinctive cultural groups, undoubtedly with their own forms of local governance, although there is little history on these phenomena.[68] However, we know through practical realities

---

[64] Gilles Havard, *The Great Peace of Montreal of 1701: French-Native Diplomacy in the Seventeenth Century*, 2nd ed, translated by Phyllis Aronoff & Howard Scott (Montreal and Kingston: McGill-Queen's University Press, 2001); KP Williams, *supra* note 51; RA Williams, *supra* note 51.

[65] James (Sákéj) Youngblood Henderson, *The Mi'kmaw Concordat* (Halifax: Fernwood, 1997).

[66] Robert Hamilton, *Legal Pluralism and Hybridity in Mi'kma'ki and Wulstukwik, 1604–1779: A Case Study in Legal Histories, Legal Geographies, and Common Law Aboriginal Rights* (PhD Dissertation, University of Victoria, 2021) [unpublished].

[67] See DN Sprague & RP Frye, *The Genealogy of the First Métis Nation: The Development and Dispersal of the Red River Settlement, 1820–1900* (Winnipeg: Pemmican, 1983), and the various volumes of Gail Morin's compendium of Metis genealogy. For an individual Metis family history illustrating this point, see Heather Devine, *The People Who Own Themselves: Aboriginal Ethnogenesis in a Canadian Family, 1660–1900* (Calgary: University of Calgary Press, 2004).

[68] In Nicole St-Onge, "Familial Foes? French-Sioux Families and Plains Métis Brigades in the Nineteenth Century" (2015) 29:3 American Indian Quarterly 302, St-Onge tries to understand why the French-Sioux groups of the Upper Mississippi never seemed to create for themselves an identity as a people, and why they tended not to associate with the Plains Metis, especially the buffalo hunting brigades, although there were obvious cultural and social connections between the two groups. She

how much Metis practices have been and are rooted in Indigenous understandings, with European borrowings. For instance, the Metis practice of using "Hunt Captains" to be in charge of how many/which animals can be taken and when, and how hunts are organized and tracked (pardon the pun) is clearly rooted in the Cree (and other Algonquian) practices of designating the Kaanoowapmaakin or "tallyman."[69] In the Metis hunting law I learned from Elders, Hunt Captains, and other practitioners about how to spiritually prepare for a hunt, how to act during and after a hunt, and how to distribute meat and other animal products fairly[70] are parallels with Nehiyaw and Anishinaabe ideas and practices. Stories remind us that the animals, fish, birds, plants, fungi, and other beings are our relatives. Animals must be treated with respect, since they have sacrificed themselves so that we might live. One should prepare spiritually and ask permission before picking plants or mushrooms. A Cree/Metis story entitled "How They Hunted the Moose"[71] even tells us of a treaty between people and moose: the moose smoked the peace pipe with humans, agreeing that they would allow themselves to be killed and eaten to a limited extent, as long as humans agreed to protect their habitats, not interfere with their reproduction, take only what was needed, and not

---

posits that such differences might be connected to cultural divergences based on the varied maternal Indigenous heritages of Red River Metis. St-Onge points out that in works on Franco-Québecois historic relations with Indigenous people, such as Gilles Havard, *Empire et Métissages : Indiens et Français dans le Pays d'en Haut, 1660–1715* (Montréal: Septentrion, 2003), scholars are not claiming such intercultural interactions resulted in the rise of a distinct Metis identity. At the same time, in another article, St-Onge asserts that some Plains Metis did not have identities always distinctive from those of their Saulteaux relations: Nicole St-Onge, "Uncertain Margins: Metis and Saulteaux Identities in St-Paul des Saulteaux, Red River 1821–1870" (2006) 53 Manitoba History 2.

69 Cree Trappers Association's Committee of Chisasibi, *Cree Trappers Speak* (Chisasibi: James Bay Cree Cultural Education Centre, 1989); see also Cree Trappers' Association, *Traditional Eeyou Hunting Law* (2009), online: <creetrappers.ca/images/SpecialProjects/CTA-2009-TraditionalEeyouHuntingLaw-En.pdf>. Note that Hunt Captains may be of any gender, despite the English term "tallyman."

70 Sloan, *Community Conundrum, supra* note 30. These laws were taught to me as part of my dissertation interviews with Elder Lottie McDougall Kozak, Elder Eldon Clairmont, and Hunt Captains Dan LaFrance, Ron Nunn, Dean Trumbley and Mark Carlson, along with other community members.

71 See Michael J Caduto & Joseph Bruchac, *Keepers of the Animals: Native American Stories and Wildlife Activities for Children*, 2nd ed (Golden: Fulcrum, 2013).

waste animal products.[72] Hearing such stories, and seeing the reality on the land, we become alive to our dependence on others for our survival, and the recognition that those others have thought, feeling and independent being that must be acknowledged and respected. And with this knowledge comes responsibility and an implied trust: as we rely on others, so others rely on us.

The exchange and reciprocity between beings, practised since time immemorial, was enacted along inter-human webs, creating the ancient social networks that were later traversed by scouts, Metis and otherwise, showing new traders where their success might lie, weaving Europeans and some of their descendants into the warp and weft of Indigenous life.

Along these routes, languages were learned, and created, arts were engendered, stories were "sampled" and adapted, ideas adopted. Land use patterns were morphing, people were migrating, and other ties were being made, with the Indigenous nations that formed the kin networks of the soon-to-be Metis.

Kinship networks mirror territorial networks, which have been described by various Metis thinkers as webs connected by nodes.[73] These webs traverse and interlink the territories of nations with whom the Metis have kin relationships, sometimes giving rise to local ethnogenesis.[74] Some strands in these webs might also be in the nature of passage rights through non-allied territory, such as through Siksika/ Blackfoot lands in southern Alberta.[75] Given the high degree of

---

[72] For examples of both oral and written Metis laws about harvesting, see Fred J Shore & Lawrence J Barkwell, *Past Reflects the Present: The Metis Elders' Conference* (Winnipeg: Manitoba Metis Federation, 1997).

[73] Maria Campbell, "Foreword: Charting the Way" in St-Onge, Podruchny & Macdougall, *Contours of a People, supra* note 25 at xiii; Nicole St-Onge & Carolyn Podruchny, "Scuttling Along a Spider's Web: Mobility and Kinship in Metis Ethnogenesis" [St-Onge & Podruchny, "Mobility and Kinship"] in St-Onge, Podruchny & Macdougall, *ibid* at 59; Signa AK Daum Shanks, *Searching for Sakitawak: Place and People in Northern Saskatchewan's Île-à-la-Crosse* (PhD Dissertation, University of Western Ontario, 2015) [unpublished]; Jean Teillet, *Métis Law in Canada* (Toronto: Pape Salter Teillet, 2013); Sloan, "Always Coming Home," *supra* note 45.

[74] See Macdougall, *One of the Family, supra* note 2; Daum Shanks, *ibid*; Mike Evans, Jean Barman & Gabrielle Legault, "Métis Networks in British Columbia: Examples from the Central Interior" in St-Onge, Podruchny & Macdougall, *Contours of a People, supra* note 25 at 331.

[75] See *R v Hirsekorn*, 2010 ABPC 385, aff'd in part 2011 ABQB 682, aff'd 2013 ABCA 242, and Karen Drake's critique of it: Karen Drake, "*R v Hirsekorn*: Are Métis Rights a

mobility of the Metis, these webs were/are literally rivers, cart trails, and, today, highways—Canadian highways that follow ancient trade routes. Along these webs, knowledge also travelled: knowledge passed down to Metis from their Indigenous relations and passed down from them to their non-Indigenous relations. Nodes might represent trading posts, fishing camps, meeting sites, sacred sites, and settlements. Many of these nodes were/are Indigenous sites, and some are now Canadian towns, especially the sites of former trading posts, such as Thunder Bay (Fort William), Winnipeg, Edmonton, and Fort St. John.[76]

Thus, Metis geographies were vast[77] and their patterns can be seen as distinctive, given Metis people's particular economic and social roles. At the same time, they are reflective of pre-existing Indigenous lifeways that involved trade and other connections even beyond Turtle Island.[78]

> 2. From an Indigenous perspective, an originating moment of the Metis nation was the creation of the Nehiyaw Pwat/ Iron Alliance between the Metis, Nehiyawak/Cree, prairie Anishinaabeg/Saulteaux and Nakota/Assiniboine

While some argue there may be a defining political moment, such as the Battle of Seven Oaks in 1816[79] or the Metis uprising at Red River in 1821, that is the "genesis" moment for Metis nationhood or the place where the Metis nation "crystallized," at least in a Westphalian sense, there are

---

Constitutional Myth?" (2013) 92:1 Can Bar Review 149.

[76] See Christine Schreyer, "Canadian Geography as National Identity: Hudson's Bay Company Place Names and their Aboriginal Counterparts" (2014) 49 International Journal of Canadian Studies 315.

[77] Étienne Rivard, "'Le Fond de l'Ouest': Territory, Oral Geographies, and the Métis in the Nineteenth-Century Northwest" in St-Onge, Podruchny & Macdougall, *Contours of a People, supra* note 25 at 143.

[78] M Max Hamon, argues that these networks were critical to Louis Riel's success in "networking" across Turtle Island to support Metis interests: M Max Hamon, *The Audacity of His Enterprise: Louis Riel and the Métis Nation That Canada Never Was, 1840–1875* (Montreal and Kingston: McGill-Queen's University Press, 2020) at 224.

[79] While this is a narrative that many Metis people find compelling, it seems to stem from non-Metis interpretations of the significance of this battle, particularly by historians AS Morton, Michel Giraud and Gerald Friesen. See the discussion in Gerhard J Ens, "The Battle of Seven Oaks and the Articulation of a Metis National Tradition, 1811–1849" in St-Onge, Podruchny & Macdougall, *Contours of a People, supra* note 25 at 93.

no sharp delineations between processes, only fractal borders that look like straight lines from a distance. That is, the actual people involved in this moment were also involved in the previous "pre-genesis" moments. Their family ties, their knowledge, stretched back, eastwards. It was grounded in what came before. As with many organic processes, the creation of Metis consciousness resulted from multiple converging realities, arising both within discrete communities, and along the webs that connected them, fanning out in all directions.

While in many Algonquian medicine wheel teachings it is the east that is the source of life, perhaps it is appropriate that the Siouxan/ Oceti Sakowin (Dakota/Lakota/Nakota/Nakoda) belief is that the south is the source of *spiritual* birth,[80] as it is in the south that the Metis, with the Nakota/Assiniboine, shared in the inauguration of the Nehiyaw Pwat, or "Iron Alliance."[81] This was another defining moment: the spiritual creation of the Metis nation among her kin.

In what was likely the early 1800s, at the largest Sun Dance (Thirst Dance) ever recorded, the Metis, and fellow westward/southward migrants the prairie Anishinaabeg/Saulteaux, were inaugurated into the spiritual life of the Plains by the Nehiyawak/Cree and the Nakota/Assiniboine.[82] The Sun Dance coincided with the treaty between the four nations, consolidating family, cultural, political, and

---

[80] Joseph Epes Brown, recorder and editor, *The Sacred Pipe: Black Elk's Account of the Seven Rites of the Oglala Sioux* (Norman: University of Oklahoma Press, 1953).

[81] *Pwatak* (plural form) in Nehiyawewin (Cree language) refers to Assiniboine people; thus, *Nehiyaw Pwat* literally means "Cree-Assiniboine." See Mandelbaum, *supra* note 56 at 9. Some authors equate the Assiniboine with the Nakota ("eastern" close relatives of the Nakoda of Alberta): see Douglas R Parks & Raymond J Demallie, "Sioux, Assiniboine, and Stoney Dialects: A Classification" (1992) 34:1/4 Anthropological Linguistics 233. The word *Nehiyaw* means "four-bodied," referring to the medicine wheel teachings that posit that humans have spiritual, emotional, physical and intellectual aspects and that we (and other beings) function best when these are balanced: see Cree Elder Mary Lee, "Cree (Nehiyawak) Teaching" (2006), online: Four Directions Teachings <fourdirectionsteachings.com/transcripts/cree. pdf>; Paulina R Johnson, *E-kawôtiniket 1876: Reclaiming Nêhiyaw Governance in the Territory of Maskwacîs through Wâhkôtowin (Kinship)* (PhD Dissertation, University of Western Ontario, 2017) [unpublished].

[82] Nicholas Vrooman, "Many Eagle Set Thirsty Dance (Sun Dance) Song: The Metis Receive Sun Dance Song" in Barkwell, Dorion & Hourie, *Metis Legacy II, supra* note 1 at 187; Teillet, *The North-West Is My Mother, supra* note 13. The Gros Ventre/A'aninin/ Atsina entered the confederacy in the 1860s, although they were earlier allied with the Blackfoot/Siksika Confederacy.

economic ties that influenced the history of the Plains and beyond.[83] This timing suggests the Metis were already recognized by the other three nations as a political entity, a group of already related bands.

With the rapid expansion of links to the south in the Iron Alliance, and in later harvesting rights treaties with the Dakota[84] that built on this alliance, family networks also expanded,[85] and economic networks prospered. Metis were active in the fur trade in multiple roles, in the cartage trade, but also in fishing, and, eventually, farming.[86] Metis wealth and power increased and was consolidated; society flourished, blooming like flower beadwork, bearing its own plentiful fruits of dance, music, visual arts, cuisine, medicine, law, storytelling, and language.[87] This is when distinct Metis territories also began to be established through relationships with the nations of the Nehiyaw Pwat, creating communities in Manitoba, North Dakota, Montana, Saskatchewan, Alberta, and British Columbia.

At the same time as the Iron Alliance grounded the Metis in the spiritual traditions of the Plains, it was created in the context of

---

[83] For an example of how these relationships matter today in Cree kinship practices, see Innes, *supra* note 7.

[84] See the centennial project of St. Ann's Catholic Church, Belcourt, North Dakota (1985), a history of the Turtle Mountain parish and area, which contains excerpts of contemporary accounts of these treaties: *St. Ann's Centennial: 100 Years of Faith, Turtle Mountain Indian Reservation, Belcourt, North Dakota, 1885–1985* (Belcourt, ND: St. Ann's Catholic Church, 1985), online: <digitalhorizonsonline.org/digital/collection/ndsl-books/id/132693/>.

[85] Various stories tell of intermarriage and adoption between Metis and Dakota families, particularly at Turtle Mountain; see e.g. "Massacre d'une famille siouse par les Chippewas" in Letourneau, *supra* note 1 at 63. Metis leader Jean-Baptiste Wilkie, a treaty negotiator, married into the Dakota Nation. According to Maria Campbell, Gabriel Dumont carried Dakota and Cree medicine bundles: see Lawrence Barkwell, Darren Préfontaine & Anne Carrière-Acco, "Metis Spirituality" in Barkwell, Dorion & Hourie, *Metis Legacy II, supra* note 1, 184 at 185. My own family married into the Turtle Mountain Chippewas and had Dakota in-laws. On the intercultural nature of Turtle Mountain and environs, see Nicholas CP Vrooman et al, *"The Whole Country Was…'One Robe'": The Little Shell Tribe's America* (Helena: Little Shell Tribe of Chippewa Indians of Montana; Drumlummon Institute, 2012).

[86] Gerhard J Ens, *Homeland to Hinterland: The Changing Worlds of the Red River Métis in the Nineteenth Century* (Toronto: University of Toronto Press, 1996); Nicole St-Onge, "Variations in Red River: The Traders and Freemen Métis of St-Laurent, Manitoba" (1992) 24:2 Can Ethn Stud 2.

[87] Barkwell, Dorion & Hourie, *Metis Legacy II, supra* note 1, is a source for many aspects of Metis culture.

shifting Indigenous military alliances; later, it responded to conflicts with colonial powers and, eventually, with the nascent state of Canada. In addition, smaller-scale "local" alliances aided resistance to colonial activities: family-based unions of francophone Metis with anglophone ("halfbreed") Metis, who have been viewed by some scholars—and by some self-identifying "halfbreeds"—as culturally distinct, then and now,[88] came together as Canadian confederation and westward settler expansion were being planned. Eventually, they linked arms during the first Resistance in 1869 and in the negotiation of Metis rights in the face of the creation of the province of Manitoba in 1870. Despite government promises upon the entry of Manitoba into confederation, many people lost their lands, and migrated to the west, north and south; people migrated to places on the Metis web where they already had family and other social connections. One of these migrations was to Cree territory in Saskatchewan, at Batoche, near the Cree sacred site now known as St Laurent. Following the second Resistance at Batoche in 1885, a fresh wave of migrations followed, again along the same pathways.

Because of the fur trade west of the Rockies, and up into Dene territories, and because of the Red River expeditions bringing Canadien.ne.s and Metis into the Oregon Territory, Metis geographical networks expanded further. With their skills retained over the years from interacting with all their relations in the Nehiyaw Pwat and eastwards, and with increasing ties to settler families, the Metis nation was continually transforming, continually "becoming."

3. European borrowings are inextricably part of Metis culture, were adopted as being congenial to Metis lifeways, and do not diminish indigeneity

---

[88] Sandy Campbell, "'I Shall Settle, Marry, and Trade Here': British Military Personnel and Their Mixed-Blood Descendants" in Ute Lischke & David T McNab, eds, *The Long Journey of a Forgotten People: Métis Identities and Family Histories* (Waterloo: Wilfrid Laurier University Press, 2007) 81 at 89–91; Irene M Spry, "The Métis and Mixed-bloods of Rupert's Land Before 1870" in Jacqueline Peterson & Jennifer SH Brown, eds, *The New Peoples: Being and Becoming Métis in North America* (Winnipeg: University of Manitoba Press, 1985) 95; Gregg Dahl, "A Half-breed's Perspective on Being Métis" in Christopher Adams, Gregg Dahl & Ian Peach, eds, *Métis in Canada: History, Identity, Law & Politics* (Edmonton: University of Alberta Press, 2013) 93. Some people view the term "halfbreed" as derogatory, while others have tried to reclaim it.

The Metis story "The Origin of the Grey Ducks" is an obvious—and poignant—tale of the origin of the Metis.[89] According to storyteller and interpreter Marie-Louise Perron, this story combines a Dene story about the Raven changing from white to black (part of a trilogy called "The Deluge") with a French/Québecois story of the guile of the devil and the dangers (from a Christian perspective) of dancing and fiddle music ("The Devil As a Handsome Dancer").[90] In this story, a beautiful white duck of marriageable age is seduced by a handsome bird of unknown origin, dressed in black, European-style clothes. They attend a fiddle dance. His good looks and courtly manners trick her upwardly mobile parents into thinking he is a good match for her. They are pleased when the marriage occurs, but then don't hear from their daughter for many years. Meanwhile, the duck daughter is mistreated by her husband. She eventually leaves him, taking their two children with her back to her parents. The daughter is accepted back into the community without recrimination, and her children become the ancestors of a line of grey ducks.

In this story, Indigenous and non-Indigenous elements are combined, both in content and in form; that is, the story is what it says.

As it was the mothers, mostly Indigenous, who passed down culture and language even in the womb, and from earliest days, the basis of transmitted knowledge in Metis culture was Indigenous. Yet, there were parallels that would have allowed Indigenous people to understand European stories through their own constitutional

---

[89] Story recorded in Marie-Louise Perron, "'L'Origine des canards gris': Conte folklorique Métis et/ou étude en sociologie populaire"/"'The Origin of the Grey Ducks': A Tale from Metis Folklore and/or a Study in Popular Sociology" (1987) 40:3 Saskatchewan History 99, translated by Crystal Boudreau & Marie-Louise Perron; reproduced in Barkwell, Dorion & Hourie, Metis Legacy II, supra note 1 at 46.

[90] I found while reading the introduction to "The Origin of the Grey Ducks" (in Barkwell, Dorion & Hourie, Metis Legacy II, ibid at 46) that this story was passed down to the teller through five generations of women – and then I saw the names of two of my own great-grandmothers in this list. I felt sad to think that this story was lost to our branch of the family. This story was passed down through: Mary Anne Josephine Perron (Perron's aunt), her mother Celina (Ladéroute) Perron, her mother Marguerite (St. Arnaud) Ladéroute, her mother Genevieve (Contre) St. Arnaud, and her mother Louise ("Montagnaise") Contre. Genevieve St. Arnaud and Louise Contre are my direct ancestors. "Montagnaise" may refer to either Dene or Innu ancestry (this term was used historically in Québec to refer to Innu people) but given the partial Dene content of the story and the birthplaces of Genevieve and Louise in the Northwest Territories, it likely indicates that Louise was Dene.

lenses. The story of a spiritual mother, Mary, who brought her son as a gift to the world, and who needed to rely on the hospitality of strangers, would not have been incongruent with the story of Skywoman, pregnant with twins, who chose to visit earth through a hole in the sky (in Nehiyaw cosmology, the constellation known as the Pleiades, or Seven Sisters), bringing gifts.[91] In many versions of this story—which is itself a constitutional origin story common to many Algonquian nations—Skywoman needed help ... she needed a place to give birth and raise her children. She came to an earth that was a water world. To flourish in human form, she needed land, a place where she and her babies could survive. The animals knew there was land below the ocean but they would have to dive for it. Finally, the littlest of all, the muskrat, succeeded after others had failed. In some versions of the story, the muskrat dies in the attempt; sometimes he is revived, in others, he survives, but barely. This is a constitutional story, because it illustrates ways in which animals would agree to help humans, and it also illustrates that kinship obligations can extend to newcomers, to the point of sacrifice. From a Metis perspective, the muskrat is a creature inhabiting multiple worlds—hence his success in a new, border-crossing venture. Thus were the human families of the earth/sky brought within the kinship network of all other life.

While Indigenous understandings were the roots of Metis thinking and practice, European borrowings were common; for instance, European-style military organization informed periodic large-scale buffalo hunts, and European-influenced embroidery decorated Metis hunting gear.[92] European folk stories ended up as part of Metis stories, with overlaps, for instance, in the characters of the trickster: Wiisakaychak (Nehiyaw/Cree); Nanabush (Anishinaabe/Saulteaux); Iktomini (Assiniboine/Nakota/Nakoda) and the French/Québecois Ti-Jean or Chi-Jean.[93]

---

[91] The version reproduced here is "Skywoman Falling" in Robin Wall Kimmerer, *Braiding Sweetgrass: Indigenous Wisdom, Scientific Knowledge and the Teachings of Plants* (Minneapolis: Milkweed, 2013) at 3-5.

[92] Sherry Farrell Racette, *Sewing Ourselves Together: Clothing, Decorative Arts, and the Expression of Métis and Half Breed Identity* (PhD Dissertation, University of Manitoba, 2004) [unpublished].

[93] Regarding Ti-Jean and his parallels and manifestations around the world, including in France, see Évelyne Voldeng, *Les Mémoires de Ti-Jean : Espace intercontinental du*

Cultural overlaps existed in the French and Breton practices of female landholding of seigneuries,[94] with Metis river lots, or *rangs*,[95] often held by sister family groups.[96] These forms of land-holdings spread out wherever Metis families migrated south, west and north. Note that the adaptation of river lots in North America—sans feudal trappings—was congenial to Metis (Indigenous-derived) ethics of women as water protectors[97] and of collective responsibilities to fish and water.[98]

Similarly, it has been argued that aspects of Scottish and Orkney customary law and governance were easily assimilated and adapted by Scottish "halfbreeds."[99] Nicole St-Onge and Carolyn Podruchny suggest that Scottish clan practices paralleled those of their Indigenous relatives, and influenced the development of Metis trade and family networks.[100] Susan Sleeper-Smith contends that European Christian godparenting practices were aligned with Indigenous ways of creating

---

héros des contes franco-ontariens (Vanier, ON: Éditions L'Interligne, 1994). Ti-Jean, rather than being a trickster figure, was often characterized as an "everyman" (compare Little John of Robin Hood fame). However, some authors associate him, at least in his Caribbean manifestations, as a cousin of the Akan god/trickster figure Anansi: see e.g. Derek Walcott's play *Ti-Jean and His Brothers* (1958).

94   Female landholding was especially common in Brittany. See Wendy Davies, *Small Worlds: The Village Community in Early Medieval Brittany* (London, UK: Duckworth, 1988).

95   James Michael Hébert, *Culture Built upon the Land: A Predictive Model of Nineteenth-Century Canadien/Métis Farmsteads* (Master's Thesis, Oregon State University, 2007) [unpublished].

96   Maria Campbell, teachings given at Metis Nation of Greater Victoria Knowledge Holders gathering, Lekwungen Territory (Victoria, BC), 3 March 2017. On Metis matrilocality, see also Macdougall, *One of the Family, supra* note 2; Hamon, *supra* note 78.

97   Aimée Craft, personal communication, 2018. On Anishinaabe women as water protectors, see Aimée Craft & Lucas King, "Building the Treaty #3 Nibi Declaration Using an Anishinaabe Methodology of Ceremony, Language and Engagement" (2021) 13 Water 532; Reneé Elizabeth Mzinegiizhigo-kwe Bédard, "Keepers of the Water: Nishnaabe-kwewag Speaking for the Water" in Simpson, *Eighth Fire, supra* note 55 at 89.

98   Zoe Todd, "Fish, Kin and Hope: Tending to Water Violations in amiskwaciwâskahikan and Treaty Six Territory" (2017) 43:1 Afterall: A Journal of Art, Context & Enquiry 102.

99   Lawrence J Barkwell, Anne Carrière-Acco & Amanda Rosyk, *The Origins of Metis Customary Law, With a Discussion of Metis Legal Traditions*, The Virtual Museum of Métis History and Culture (2007), online: <metismuseum.ca/resource.php/07232>.

100 St-Onge & Podruchny, "Mobility and Kinship," *supra* note 73. See also Irene Ternier Gordon, *The Laird of Fort William: William McGillivray and the North West Company* (Victoria: Heritage House, 2013).

"fictive" kinship, and were thus easily assimilated by Indigenous people intermarried with French descendants.[101] Although I have not been able to find any literature on this, I wonder whether the practice of sending children to live with their grandparents to learn knowledge and skills overlapped with the Irish Brehon laws of child fostering with artisans.

In his book on Michif—the Metis language(s) that contains European (usually French) nouns and Algonquian (usually Nehiyawewin/Cree and/or Anishinabemowin/Saulteaux) verbs,[102] Peter Bakker states, "Michif is an impossible language."[103] While this may sound hyperbolic, Bakker says that some linguists literally doubt the existence of Michif, because it doesn't fit into the model of how a mixed language should look. First, Michif is a problem for the "family tree" language model, which states that every language has one parent language. As Michif is neither Algonquian in its entirety or Indo-European in its entirety, it presents a classification problem. Second, Michif appears to invalidate theories of language contact, which purport to describe processes of contact-induced change. Third, Michif is a language with "separate sound systems, morphological endings, and syntactic rules"; thus it "challenges all theoretical models of language."[104]

Despite the claims of linguists and language theoreticians, Michif exists, though "impossible." Metis communities might be seen from a colonialist viewpoint as being impossible, but that does not make them any less real. The impossibility of Metis communities might suggest a

---

[101] Susan Sleeper-Smith, *Indian Women and French Men: Rethinking Cultural Encounter in the Western Great Lakes* (Amherst: University of Massachusetts Press, 2001).

[102] There are various dialects of Michif, including Michif-Cree, Michif-French, Turtle Mountain Michif, and Île-à-la-Crosse Michif. Michif might be more accurately described as a language complex. The (reportedly extinct) Metis language Bungee contains Saulteaux, Scots (a language in its own right, or a Scottish dialect of English, depending on who is consulted), and Scottish Gaelic. Barb Hulme, an Elder in my community (the Metis Nation of Greater Victoria), says she remembers hearing Bungee spoken by her grandparents (personal communication, 2017). The dialect of Michif spoken in the vicinity of St. Louis, Saskatchewan, near Batoche, also contains Scottish Gaelic words (Maria Campbell, personal communication, 2018).

[103] Peter Bakker, "A Language of Our Own" in Rita Flamand, *Michif Conversational Lessons for Beginners* (Winnipeg: Metis Resource Centre, 2002) i at ii.

[104] *Ibid* at i–ii.

Metis theory that is also "impossible," and yet it may be both as distinctive and multiplicitous as Michif.[105]

4. Kinship/wahkotowin implies interconnection, but also nonduality, an important tenet of many Indigenous philosophies, including those of the Metis

Kinship, the family, is the origin of Metis life—literally and figuratively—and it is the family that continues to be the centre of culture, law and governance.[106] Extended kinship networks, as we have seen, have also been critical to the development of the nation.

The Nehiyaw concept of kinship, or wahkotowin, is important to Metis philosophy and implies the interconnection and interdependence of all beings.[107] According to Metis scholar Brenda Macdougall, wahkotowin is an expression of Metis values that are

> [...] critical to family relationships – such as reciprocity, mutual support, decency and order – [these] in turn influenced the behaviours, actions, and decision-making processes that shaped all a community's economic and political actions. Wahkootowin contextualizes how relationships were intended to work within Metis society by defining and classifying relationships, prescribing patterns of behaviour between relatives and non-relatives, and linking people and communities in a large and complex web of relationships.[108]

---

[105] "Locke, in the seventeenth century, postulated (and rejected) an impossible language in which each individual thing, each stone, each bird and each branch, would have its own name; Funes once projected an analogous language, but discarded it because it seemed too general to him, too ambiguous": Jorge Luis Borges, "Funes the Memorious", translated by James E Irby, in *Labyrinths: Selected Stories and Other Writings*, rev ed (New York: New Directions, 1964) 65. Angela P Harris discusses "Funes" and the tension between acknowledging multiplicity and creating community and positive action in "Race and Essentialism in Feminist Legal Theory" (1990) 42 Stanford LR 581.

[106] Hamon, *supra* note 78. Hamon states at 21: "The family was the primary public institution for the Métis. It was the centre of social relations and the root of political sovereignty." See also Shore & Barkwell, *supra* note 72.

[107] Campbell, "Wahkotowin", *supra* note 46; Macdougall, *One of the Family*, *supra* note 2.

[108] Macdougall, *One of the Family*, *ibid* at 8.

Because wahkotowin encompasses interconnections and interdependence, it can also imply non-duality,[109] which busts oppositions
(Indigenous/non-Indigenous, other/non-other, inside/outside, tradi-
tional/modern, sovereign/colonized, assimilated/unassimilated, urban/
rural, authentic/inauthentic) that purport to be "true" about Metis
people. However, non-duality, and even the "third space"[110] do not
fully describe Metisness; perhaps "spectra" comes closest to representing the extent of Metis multiplicity.

Of course, symbols and metaphors are only used to assist understanding and are not meant to be cudgels in an arsenal of fundamen-
talism. According to various Cree and Anishinaabe teachers, a variety
of teachings might be equally true.[111] For instance, Cree Elder Wilfred
Buck talks about star constellations in Nehiyaw understandings as

---

109 Anishinaabe knowledge holder Ken Albert has said that one of the foundations of
Anishinaabe thinking is non-duality (teaching given at Anishinaabe Law Camp,
Neyaashiinigmiing (Cape Croker, ON, 2017). John Borrows elaborates: "Anishinaabe
law supports and even celebrates indirection, metaphor, ambiguity, and double
entendre": John Borrows, "Heroes, Tricksters, Monsters, and Caretakers: Indigenous
Law and Legal Education" (2016) 61:4 McGill LJ 795 at 844. Non-duality is also
important to other Indigenous philosophical traditions. For example, Umeek
(E Richard Atleo) states: "The Nuu-chah-nulth struggle towards wholeness meant a
deliberate exclusion of any form of reductionism": Umeek (E Richard Atleo),
Principles of Tsawalk: An Indigenous Approach to Global Crisis (Vancouver: University
of British Columbia Press, 2011) at 140. According to Cree Moshom (Elder) Michael
D Thrasher and co-author Jennifer S Dockstator, "the existence of a dualist binary
stance is not substantiated within Indigenous philosophies": see Jennifer S
Dockstator & Michael D Thrasher, "Take Care of 'the Land' and 'the Land' Will
Take Care of You: Relationship-Building through an Introduction to Indigenous
Holistic Thought" in M Hankard & John Charlton, eds, *We Still Live Here: First Nations,
Alberta Oil Sands, and Surviving Globalism* (Vernon: J Charlton, 2016) 51 at 61. See also
Tewa scholar Gregory Cajete, *Native Science: Natural Laws of Interdependence* (Santa Fe:
Clear Light, 2000).

110 Homi Bhabha, *The Location of Culture* (London, UK: Routledge, 1994). For a discussion
of the potential use by Metis of the "third space" as a tool for resisting colonialism,
see Richardson, *supra* note 42. I look at arguments for and against the appropriateness
of the "third space" in Metis contexts in my dissertation: Sloan, *Community Conundrum,
supra* note 30; in this work, I also provide some thoughts towards the elaboration of a
Metis Critical Legal Theory (while acknowledging cautions around doing so).

111 See e.g. Ogimaawigwanebiik (Nancy Jones), "Gakina Dibaajimowinan
Gwayakwaawan/All Teachings Are Correct" in H James St Arnold & Wesley
Ballinger, eds, *Dibaajimowinan: Anishinaabe Stories of Culture and Respect* (Odanah,
WI: Great Lakes Indian Fish & Wildlife Commission, 2013) 9. Ogimaa Francis
Kavanaugh, "Ogichidaa Teachings - Respecting Alternative Teachings (Treaty #3

not being static—each constellation is associated with many stories (although these are interconnected); thus, each constellation has over-lapping forms that explain the relationships between stars in a given constellation.[112]

And, of course, the importance of non-duality does not negate that duality is also part of Indigenous philosophies. The Nehiyaw/Cree medicine wheel methodology asks people to consider what is both inside and outside the wheel: inside there are the positive aspects of the self, including spiritual, intellectual, emotional, and physical aspects; outside are the negative aspects of the self, including those relating to one's internal thoughts, traits, qualities and behaviours; nevertheless, the self—at the centre of the circle—encompasses both positive and negative aspects.[113]

With the foregoing in mind, I will offer tentatively that the infinity symbol on the Metis flag represents to me the simultaneity of both duality and non-duality. It is said to represent the "lobes" of Indigenous and non-Indigenous inheritance, joined together in the centre (the "where-you-are" of the medicine wheel) and the pathway flows continually, along a kind of mobius strip, here emphasizing one aspect of Metisness, there another.[114] In this metaphor, there is no foreground and no background; there is only being and becoming.

Further "Impossibilities" … and Possibilities

One of my aims in this chapter has been to illustrate the Metis as being situated in wider Indigenous social and political contexts, to show how we are part of the history of both pre- and post-contact treaty-

---

Anishinaabe Nation)", Grand Council Treaty #3 (2020), online (video): <youtube. com/watch?v=akbww5XghyI&feature=youtu. be&t=1>.

[112] Wilfred Buck, *I Have Lived Four Lives…* (Winnipeg: Arbeiter Ring, 2021).

[113] Herb Nabigon & Anne-Marie Mawhiney, "Aboriginal Theory: A Cree Medicine Wheel Guide for Healing First Nations" in Francis J Turner, ed, *Social Work Treatment: Interlocking Theoretical Approaches*, 4th ed (New York: The Free Press, 1996) 18 at 21.

[114] The infinity symbol is also said to represent the need to take the past, present and future into account when making important decisions. These elements of time are also always present; their separation is also an illusion. See Leah Marie Dorion, *The Giving Tree: A Retelling of a Traditional Métis Story* (Saskatoon: Gabriel Dumont Institute, 2009).

making, as treaty-making post contact was based in older principles that governed diplomacy between Indigenous nations. As Metis people, we are woven into the histories of our Indigenous forebears, and I encourage Metis people, when considering how we should constitute ourselves, to consider this reality. In making this claim, and the resulting suggestion, I have been mostly speaking to Metis people.

My second aim has been not so much rhetorical, but exploratory, and is addressed to those interested in understanding Indigenous law and legal theory. My second aim has been to explore the possibility that ideas that might seem opposed, or claims that might seem mutually exclusive, can be explored in connection with each other, without the need to chuck out one or the other, or to synthesize them.[115] In this exploration, I have tried to illustrate that some apparently contradictory aspects of Metisness might be equally true, and could even be mutually constitutive. For instance, I suggest that, while Metis philosophy and lifeways are foundationally Indigenous, Indigenous and non-Indigenous elements are inextricably linked in Metis culture. The first suggestion does not counter the claim that suggests that hybridity in Indigenous constitutionalism is invalid; to use Mills' tree metaphor, Metis constitutionalism might resemble an Indigenous tree (roots, trunk) with European graftings (branches). This analogy seems to be in line with my claim that Metis people chose to incorporate European cultural elements because they seemed "congenial" to their Indigenous lifeways. However, the second suggestion seems to negate the first. Inextricable linkage implies mixed rootedness. In implying that both things could be true, I could be accused of coyly creating a "third space" that neatly disposes of cognitive dissonance. I am trying not to do that, in the same way that I claim Metis people and communities are not merely hybrid.[116]

---

[115] Another Metis writer who contends with apparently opposing ideas is political theorist Adam Gaudry, who looks at Metis political culture in the late 1800s. Gaudry talks about Metis constitutionalism as reflecting both independence (katipeyimishoyaahk) and interrelatedness (wahkohtowin). These are not seen as cancelling each other out, but form part of an inseparable whole. See Gaudry, *Métis Self-Determination, supra* note 2.

[116] See Gloria Anzaldúa, *Borderlands/La Frontera: The New Mestiza* (San Francisco: Aunt Lute Press, 1987) at 46 where Anzaldúa describes the mestiza (a "mixed" woman who also is a theorist and practitioner of mixedness) as the goddess Coatlicue who, like the Hindu goddess Kali, embodies creation and destruction, life and death, virgin and serpent. She embodies contradiction, "simultaneously, depending on

However, it may be impossible to completely avoid essentializing non-essentialism.[117]

Another impossibility that emerges from this discussion is the impossibility of certainty. If you are trained as a historian in the western tradition, it may be evident to you that I am not.[118] Further, I am interpreting matters that are contentious, and about which scholars—and Metis people—have been arguing for decades. This is deliberate, because my intent is to offer a perspective based in my own understanding, however limited, of Metis thought, (informed by both community knowledge and my limited experience as a scholar), and to invite dialogue. Dialogue is part of Metis pedagogies but it is also part of western philosophical methods.[119]

In advocating for earth-grounded dialogue between Indigenous and settler constitutionalisms, Aaron Mills suggests that such dialogue is not of the same kind as either liberal compromise or hybrid identity theory. He describes these latter two paths as leading to a

---

the person she represents: duality in life, a synthesis of duality, and a third perspective – something more than mere duality or synthesis of duality." In this and other earlier works, Anzaldúa developed "*mestiza* consciousness," in which the mestiza is a bridge between cultures and identities that literally and figuratively cross borders. Later, however, she develops the idea of the nepantlera, who destabilizes the identities themselves. As Martina Koegler-Abdi explains, "while a mestiza is constantly bridging differences and deconstructing the impact of identity and ethnic frames through multiplicity and synthesis, a nepantlera works to dissolve the categories that require the bridge in the first place": Martina Koegler-Abdi, "Shifting Subjectivities: Mestizas, Nepantleras, and Gloria Anzaldúa's Legacy" (2013) 38:2 Melus 71 at 81.

[117] These kinds of dualism-avoiding dilemmas have been questioned in a humorous way by Buddhist philosopher Peter Fenner in Peter Fenner, *The Edge of Certainty: Dilemmas on the Buddhist Path* (York Beach: Nicholas-Hays, 2002) at 109-110: "in rejecting a dualistic approach in favor of an integrated perspective, what we really have done is create a new dualistic structure [...] As soon as we distinguish a middle ground from the extremes, this becomes a new extreme, in the sense that the new options are that we are either in the middle or on the edge. We are either balanced or unbalanced, appropriate or inappropriate. To the extent that the middle ground is the place where we should be, therefore, it becomes a pole in another dualistic structure."

[118] My grandmother Helen Venne Sloan was the family historian (a traditional Metis role, passed down through generations of women), and she taught and entrusted this knowledge to me (although she was frustrated that I kept having to write things down!).

[119] Michael A Peters & Tina Besley, "Models of Dialogue" (2021) 53:7 Educational Philosophy and Theory 669.

dead end.[120] However, according to Anishinaabeg teachings made public concerning the Three Paths Prophecy Petroform (Tie Creek Site, Manito Api, Whiteshell Provincial Park, Treaty 3 Territory), it is possible that the separate paths of Indigenous peoples and settlers may one day "merge,"[121] according to people's choice. Mills hopes that this might mean that settlers will eventually accept Indigenous rooted lifeways (although he acknowledges it might mean the reverse).[122] My claim is that Metis constitutionalism, with its lifeways that are both rooted and mixed rooted, prefigures the possibility of an earth-based constitutional merging.

---

[120] Mills, *Miinigowiziwin, supra* note 43 at 200.

[121] The term "merge" reminds me of, but does not equate with, the exception Smith Groening makes in her critique of hybridity theory: *supra* note 41. She says, intriguingly, that perhaps hybridity could offer hope if it "is based on reciprocal merging": *ibid* at 143. However, she doesn't expand on what "reciprocal" might imply.

[122] Mills, *Miinigowiziwin, supra* note 43 at 17–20.

Wanted: Indigenous Representation on the Supreme Court of Canada (But the Indian in the Child Must Be Gone!)

*Harry S LaForme**

Abstract

This chapter critically examines the challenges and barriers to Indigenous representation on Canada's highest court. It highlights the historical and ongoing exclusion of Indigenous people from meaningful participation in the country's judicial system. While the 2022 appointment of Justice Michelle O'Bonsawin marked a significant milestone, the imposition of functional bilingualism as a requirement for Supreme Court justices presents a substantial obstacle for many Indigenous candidates. This chapter argues that this requirement disregards the colonial history that has systematically denied Indigenous people access to education in both of Canada's official languages, English and French. The chapter critiques the federal government's failure to meaningfully address this issue, despite its promises of a renewed nation-to-nation relationship with Indigenous peoples. The author underscores the importance of lived

* Thank you to Kyle Wyatt, Editor-in-Chief, "Literary Review of Canada" and Aideen Nibigon, "A. Nabigon Consulting Inc." for their support and valuable contributions to this chapter.

Indigenous experience in the judiciary and calls for the removal of unnecessary barriers that perpetuate colonial dominance.

Résumé

Ce chapitre examine de manière critique les défis et obstacles à la représentation autochtone au sein de la plus haute cour du Canada. Il met en lumière l'exclusion historique et continue des peuples autochtones d'une participation significative au système judiciaire du pays. Bien que la nomination en 2022 de la juge Michelle O'Bonsawin ait marqué une étape importante, l'imposition du bilinguisme fonctionnel comme exigence pour les juges de la Cour suprême constitue un obstacle majeur pour plusieurs candidat·e·s autochtones. LaForme soutient que cette exigence ne tient pas compte de l'histoire coloniale qui a systématiquement privé les peuples autochtones d'un accès à l'éducation dans les deux langues officielles du Canada, l'anglais et le français. Le chapitre critique l'échec du gouvernement fédéral à aborder de manière significative cette question, malgré ses promesses d'une relation renouvelée de nation à nation avec les peuples autochtones. Il souligne l'importance de l'expérience autochtone vécue au sein de la magistrature et appelle à la suppression des obstacles inutiles qui perpétuent la domination coloniale.

One fundamental pillar of our democracy is its judicial system for adjudicating conflicts. That's why, in 1875, an eight-year-old Canada created its highest court, which originally consisted of six judges, two of whom were from Quebec, in recognition of the province's unique civil law system. In 1949, the complement of judges on the Supreme Court of Canada was increased to nine. By law, three of those judges must be from Quebec; the remaining six are chosen through tradition or convention—three from Ontario, two from the Western provinces or Northern Canada, and one from the Atlantic provinces.[1] Neither law nor convention has historically required that justices are functionally bilingual.

Since 2015, former prime minister Justin Trudeau consistently promised a new nation-to-nation relationship with Indigenous people,

---

[1] *Supreme Court Act*, RSC 1985, c S-26, s 6.

one based on the recognition of rights, respect, cooperation, and part-nership. Indeed, in June 2017, on National Aboriginal Day, he doubled down on this promise and proclaimed that, "No relationship is more important to Canada than the relationship with Indigenous Peoples. Our Government is working together with Indigenous Peoples to build a nation-to-nation, Inuit-Crown, government-to-government relation-ship—one based on respect, partnership, and recognition of rights."[2]

Evidence of the prime minister's sincerity can be found in his mandate letters to Cabinet Ministers, including the Minister of Justice. Those letters include the responsibility to "help ensure that [...] Indigenous Peoples [...] are reflected in positions of leadership."[3] But there is also reason to doubt this sincerity.

Until 2022, there had never been an Indigenous judge of the Supreme Court of Canada. It was only then that this shameful over-sight was corrected with the appointment of Justice Michelle O'Bonsawin, an Abenaki member of the Odanak First Nation who is a fluently bilingual Franco-Ontarian. So, in September 2022 we finally were able to celebrate the appointment of an Indigenous person to sit on the Supreme Court of Canada. Trudeau finally took the opportu-nity to make a gesture on his nation-to-nation promise. But I fear that any future appointments—if there are to be any—will be faced with the very problem that confronted the government in appointing Justice O'Bonsawin—a very small and very limited candidate pool.

The prime minister thought about the Supreme Court often. In 2016, shortly after he took office, he announced the formation of a new independent, non-partisan advisory board, tasked with providing "non-binding, merit-based recommendations to the Prime Minister on judicial appointments to the Supreme Court of Canada."[4] As part of its mandate, the board is to seek gender balance and to reflect the diversity of Canadian society, "including Indigenous peoples."[5] And

---

[2] Canada, "Statement by the Prime Minister of Canada on National Aboriginal Day" (21 June 2017), online: <pm.gc.ca/en/news/statements/2017/06/21/statement-prime-minister-canada-national-aboriginal-day>.

[3] Minister of Justice and Attorney General of Canada Mandate Letter (13 December 2019), online: <pm.gc.ca/en/mandate-letters/2019/12/13/archived-minister-justice-and-attorney-general-canada-mandate-letter>.

[4] Office of the Commissioner for Federal Judicial Affairs Canada, "Terms of Reference of the Advisory Board" (2023), online: <fja.gc.ca/scc-csc/2023/mandate-mandat-eng.html>.

[5] *Ibid* at s 8(f).

in doing so, it is to identify three to five qualified and functionally bilingual candidates for each judicial vacancy.[6] That is, candidates who are conversant in the languages of Canada's "founding nations," English and French.

Recent amendments to the *Official Languages Act*,[7] which received royal assent on 20 June 2023, now make this mandate of the advisory board a legal requirement. Section 16(3) requires Canada to ensure that every federal court judge who hears proceedings in French can do so without an interpreter.[8]

Functional bilingualism means that a Supreme Court appointee can read materials and understand oral argument without the need for translation or interpretation. Ideally, a judge can also converse with other judges and with counsel during oral arguments in both French and English.[9]

Despite Trudeau's repeated lofty declarations and proclamations about Indigenous people and their future relationship with Canada, the new functional bilingualism requirement has created a largely unnecessary barrier to putting an Indigenous candidate on the Supreme Court. Unnecessary because reasonable alternatives to functional bilingualism are available.

The Toronto-based criminal lawyer David Butt, for instance, has suggested that French proficiency should be a competitive advantage, not an imperative. This would not be unlike gender parity—an important but not essential factor. Butt suggests that "this more nuanced approach would emphasize pan-Canadian bilingualism without excluding many worthy candidates in non-francophone communities who quite understandably declined to learn a language with no local utility for them."[10]

---

[6] *Ibid* at s 6(1).

[7] RSC 1985, c 31 (4th Supp).

[8] Previously, s 16 (1) of the *Official Languages Act* exempted Supreme Court of Canada judges from this requirement. This was changed on 20 June 2023, by removing that exemption.

[9] Canada, Independent Advisory Board for Supreme Court of Canada Judicial Appointments, *Report of the Independent Advisory Board for Supreme Court of Canada Judicial Appointments (August–September 2016)* (Ottawa: Independent Advisory Board for Supreme Court of Canada Judicial Appointments, 2016), online: <fja-cmf.gc.ca/scc-csc/2016-MalcolmRowe/mrowe-report-rapport-eng.html#bm17>.

[10] David Butt, "French Proficiency Shouldn't be Mandatory for Canada's Supreme Court Judges", *The Globe and Mail* (10 December 2018).

In establishing his advisory board and its mandate, the prime minister ignored or forgot that full English-French bilingualism amounts to an exclusionary test for most Indigenous candidates. He ought to have known that the English-French bilingualism rate has long been lower for the Indigenous population, which makes up about five percent of Canada, than for the non-Indigenous population. And he ought to have known that in 2016, only about 10 percent of Indigenous people, including Indian, Inuit, and Métis in Canada, were able to conduct a conversation in both of the country's official languages, compared with 18 percent of the non-Indigenous population. More to the point, he knew that only seven percent of First Nations people and six percent of Inuit were bilingual.[11]

That reality should have given Trudeau pause—so that he might appreciate how possible Indigenous candidates for Canada's highest court would be extremely limited, if not non-existent, especially when legislated or traditional regional representation is factored in.

Some Background

When I first entered law school in 1974, there were only four Indigenous lawyers in all Canada. Today, there's an estimated two thousand. Not all Indigenous law graduates self-identify as Indigenous, of course, and not all practice law. Many work in related fields. Nonetheless, Indigenous people now have decades' worth of legal education in colonial law.

As of August 2024, there are 946 federally appointed judges in Canada, along with roughly 50 vacancies. These numbers include appointments to the Supreme Court, Courts of Appeal, federal courts, and trial courts.[12] There are approximately 49 active Indigenous judges in Canada: 27 sit on the Provincial Courts, appointed by their respective provincial governments; 20 sit on the Superior Court or Queen's Bench, appointed by Ottawa; and 2 sit on Courts of Appeal in British Columbia and Ontario, and now one sits on the Supreme Court of Canada, also appointed by the federal government.

---

[11] Statistics Canada, *National Household Survey* (Ottawa: Statistics Canada, 2016).

[12] Office of the Commissioner for Federal Judicial Affairs (August 2024), online: <fja.gc.ca/home-accueil/index-eng.html>.

By effectively excluding all but one of these 49 judges from consideration for the Supreme Court, Trudeau ignored more than their qualifications. He also ignored salient facts of British colonization and its unilateral taking of total control over the lives of Indigenous people since long before Confederation. The prime minister knew full well that complete colonial control over the first inhabitants was passed along to Canada upon Confederation through the *British North America Act, 1867*.[13] While complex, the history of what happened next is fairly simple to recall.

In 1876, the Canadian government's position was that "our Indian legislation generally rests on the principle, that the aborigines are to be kept in a condition of tutelage and treated as wards or children of the State."[14] In 1939, in the case of *Reference re Term "Indians"*, a decision of the Supreme Court endorsed this position when it decided that "the English word 'Indians' was to be construed and translated as 'sauvages.'"[15] And 11 years later, in *St. Ann's Island Shooting & Fishing Club Ltd. v Canada*, the Court reinforced the nature of Canada's obligation and held that the *Indian Act* "embodie[d] the accepted view that these aborigines are [...] wards of the state, whose care and welfare are a political trust of the highest obligation."[16] That colonial interpretation of the federal government's responsibility for Indigenous peoples continues today, especially through legislation such as the *Indian Act*.[17]

In 1879, the federal government—now being constitutionally responsible for everything Indian—addressed the issue of educating its "state wards." In doing so, it delegated the administration of schools to the various churches that were already performing this task. As a result, schools were denominational and fashioned after the boarding school model. The curriculum was very basic; it did not include learning both official languages. The purpose was to assimilate Indigenous

---

[13] *Constitution Act, 1867* (UK), 30 & 31 Vict, c 3, s 91(24), reprinted in RSC 1985, Appendix II, No 5. The Parliament of Canada has the legislative authority to make laws in relation to "Indians, and lands reserved for the Indians".

[14] *Report of the Royal Commission on Aboriginal Peoples: Looking Forward, Looking Back*, vol 1 (Ottawa: Supply and Services Canada, 1996) at 255, citing Department of the Interior, *Annual Report for the year ended 30th June, 1876* (Parliament, Sessional Papers, No 11, 1877) at xiv.

[15] [1939] SCR 104 at 117.

[16] [1950] SCR 211 at 219.

[17] RSC 1985, c I-5.

students, or, as Canadians have subsequently learned, to annihilate and ultimately remove Indigenous culture.[18]

By 1910, the federal government—needing to address the high costs of Indigenous education and its failure at assimilating students into white society—shifted its policy. It would no longer rely exclusively on the churches. New facilities were to be built for day schools, and the curriculum—already far less advanced than what was taught in provincial schools—was simplified even further. Thus, Ottawa significantly saved on educating Indigenous students.[19]

Throughout the 1920s, the education received by most Indigenous students was minimal and basic; the teachers were usually not certified, and the principals were usually clergymen with little to no experience in education. The result was that only three percent of students progressed past grade six. Three-quarters of the student body attended grades one through three.[20] At this point, Indigenous students were now required by law to attend residential schools.[21] These schools paid scant attention to teaching the languages of Canada's "two founding nations." Outside of Quebec, French wasn't on the program. Indeed, for far too many Indigenous students, these were not places of education at all—but places of horror, filled with extreme emotional trauma as well as physical and sexual abuse.

The last residential school was closed in 1997.[22] Today, all of Canada is trying to understand this sordid and dark history, which amounts to a cultural genocide.[23] All of Canada is wondering how to address the corrosive effects of assimilating the "sauvages"—none more so than the suffering endured and the intergenerational impacts on, among other things, education. All of Canada should also be asking how is it that Indigenous people are now expected to be functionally bilingual in English and French in order to sit on the Supreme Court.

---

[18] Jerry P White & Julie Peters, "A Short History of Aboriginal Education in Canada" in Jerry P White et al, eds, *Aboriginal Education: Current Crisis and Future Alternatives* (Toronto: Thompson Educational Publishing, 2009) 13 at 17–18.

[19] *Ibid* at 18.

[20] *Ibid.*

[21] *Indian Act*, SC 1919-20, c 50, s 10.

[22] Kivalliq Hall in Rankin Inlet closed in 1997.

[23] Harry S LaForme, "Yes, Genocide: Overruling Tepid Language", *Literary Review of Canada* (October 2019), online: <reviewcanada.ca/magazine/2019/10/yes-genocide/>.

Trudeau and his government ought to have known this history, but he insisted that it be ignored when Indigenous people are given the opportunity to participate in government and legal structures at all levels. In the view of the prime minister, the ability of an Indigenous person who wishes to participate in national decision-making to speak French is more important than Canada's "most important relationship with Indigenous peoples." One would be excused if they were to wonder what happened to the nation-to-nation relationship "based on respect, partnership, and recognition of rights."

What Is Happening Today

In 1982, the *Constitution Act* was patriated from the United Kingdom with specific reference to Aboriginal rights.[24] At the time, many Indigenous people thought the newly added section 35 of the *Act* would bring about significant change to their relationship with Canada.[25] Indeed, the federal government of the day believed it provided the basis for self-government negotiations with First Nations.

Since 1995, there have been several self-government agreements with First Nations, as well as agreements-in-principle, that explicitly address jurisdiction over education. The result of this approach, sadly, has not moved the needle, and control of Indigenous education basically remains with the federal government. There has been an "absolute failure of the current education system in Canada for First Nations," one researcher has noted, after looking across the country.[26]

Little, it would seem, has changed regarding Canada's total control of Indigenous people, including their education, which continues to be geared toward assimilation. This reality is now visited upon Indigenous candidates who choose to participate in administrative Canada. Although education has always been in the control of the federal government, that same government holds Indigenous people

---

[24] *Constitution Act, 1982*, being Schedule B to the *Canada Act 1982* (UK), 1982, c 11.

[25] *Ibid* at s 35(1): "The existing aboriginal and treaty rights of the aboriginal peoples of Canada are hereby recognized and affirmed."

[26] Daphne Mai'Stoina-Eagle Speaker, "Current Administration of Indian Control of Indian Education in Alberta: Implications and Challenges" (Doctoral Thesis, University of Calgary, 2015) [unpublished] at 183–84.

responsible for its legacy of neglect and failure when it comes to official bilingualism. If Indigenous people can't speak French, that is their problem. They are unqualified to even apply.

When reasonably considered, the bilingual barrier that the prime minister and his government created in 2016 seems to have been invoked to keep Indigenous people off the Supreme Court—to keep the status quo that's been in place since 1875. This ensures that colonial beliefs and institutions will remain intact and well guarded.

Guardians of the Status Quo

Consider the views and opinions that some of the guardians of the status quo have publicly shared about an Indigenous candidate's chances.

A few years ago, in an interview with the *Toronto Star*, the retired Supreme Court Chief Justice Beverley McLachlin is reported to have said that "the best way to one day see an aboriginal person named to the Supreme Court of Canada is for governments to appoint more indigenous judges to lower courts" and that the "country's highest court requires high-level judging and 'considerable' judicial experience." While she "welcomes ethnic diversity and more aboriginal judges in the system", she suggested that would-be candidates "must work their way up."[27]

The challenge for Indigenous aspirants to the high court, the former Chief Justice said, is not unlike the one "that women faced three or four decades ago when there were 'virtually no women on the bench.'"[28] That has changed, she said, because the federal government started appointing women at the trial level: "But the difficulty we have with racial minorities, Indigenous people is that we're just beginning this process of getting the judges in place on the trial benches and so on."[29]

Former Chief Justice McLachlin casually fails to consider colonial history. And she unthinkingly disregards that some Indigenous judges have been performing their judicial duties since 1994. Indeed,

---

[27] Tonda MacCharles, "More Indigenous Judges Needed in Lower Courts to Develop Skills for Supreme Court: Beverley McLachlin", *Toronto Star* (10 August 2016).

[28] *Ibid.*

[29] *Ibid.*

there has been an Indigenous judge on a Court of Appeal since 2004. How long must Canada's first inhabitants "work their way up"? And what constitutes "considerable experience"?

These are certainly salient questions considering the many past appointments to the Supreme Court and courts of appeal of non-Indigenous people with no judicial experience whatsoever, including Supreme Court Justices John Sopinka and Ian Binnie. Far from having "considerable judicial experience," as the former Chief Justice insists is important for Indigenous candidates, these were people with zero experience. An even longer list could be compiled of non-Indigenous judges being appointed who are not functionally bilingual in English and French.

Former Prime Minister Kim Campbell has also shared thoughts on the issue. As the then chair of the Independent Advisory Board for Supreme Court Judicial Appointments, she appeared before a Commons Committee on the nomination of Sheila Martin to the Supreme Court on 4 December 2017. In a manner that could be viewed as patronizing—with a touch of arrogance and a colonial ring—Campbell told members of Parliament that she had "absolutely no doubt" that an Indigenous judge would one day be appointed to the Supreme Court of Canada. The idea might be possible—"maybe within the next couple of rounds."[30] But at the moment, she said, "the pool of qualified Indigenous jurists in Canada is still 'small'." In 2017, the pool of Indigenous candidates was hardly "small." They just were not functionally bilingual.

The former prime minister continued with some cringeworthy comments: "It just sort of depends on where we are [...] when the next appointments are [made]. [...] I see (an Indigenous candidate) coming [...] and speaking French. They will take their place with great dignity and respect." Then she concluded: "Indigenous lawyers will take their place like anybody else and there will be no doubt as to their excellence and ability to do everything [...]. Their value on the court is not whether they are knowledgeable about Indigenous law—some may be, some may not be. It's that they will bring the lived experience of being an Indigenous person to the court."[31]

---

[30] Beatrice Britneff, "SCC Will Get an Indigenous Judge ... Eventually: Campbell", *iPolitics* (4 December 2017), online: <ipolitics.ca/2017/12/04/scc-will-get-indigenous-judge-eventually-campbell/>.

[31] *Ibid.* See also Gary P Rodrigues, "Harry LaForme on Failure to Appoint Indigenous Judges", *Slaw* (9 March 2020), online: <slaw.ca/2020/03/09/harry-laforme-on-failure-to-appoint-indigenous-judges/>.

More recently, the current Chief Justice of the Supreme Court, Richard Wagner, was interviewed by the CBC. He was asked if it was time to appoint an Indigenous candidate to the Court. "I think the court should reflect the society, and that means diversity," he said, while adding that the absence of a First Nations member didn't prevent the Supreme Court from ruling fairly and correcting "things if they needed to be corrected according to the evidence that was put forward."[32] Even without an Indigenous judge, the Supreme Court has been "able to release significant judgments in favour of recognition and reconciliation in a way with the Indigenous people."[33]

With respect, the Chief Justice may well believe his comments, but they are not entirely shared by the Indigenous population of Canada. The Supreme Court has written many judgments that affirm the colonial right to assert sovereignty and ownership over the territory of the first inhabitants, leaving them with a mere right to occupy and use their ancestral lands.[34] The Chief Justice may think and believe that such decisions are fair rulings, but I can assure him that Indigenous people generally do not.

The attitudes and opinions of these privileged guardians of the status quo illustrate how little support there seems to be for the inclusion of Indigenous judges at the highest level. Their comments suggest that Indigenous candidates are seen differently than others; they are held to a different standard too.

Such commentary must have given comfort to the prime minister. It may even have emboldened him to proclaim that Indigenous candidates to the Supreme Court must be functionally bilingual. So how heartfelt was the Prime Minister when he claimed his government has a "renewed, nation-to-nation relationship with First Nations peoples [...] based on the understanding that the constitutionally-guaranteed rights of First Nations are a sacred obligation"?[35] We have the answer

---

[32] Aidan Cox, "Lack of Indigenous Judge Hasn't Hurt Fairness of High Court Rulings, Chief Justice Says", *CBC* (18 June 2022), online: <cbc.ca/news/canada/new-brunswick/supreme-court-canada-judge-justice-1.6413254>.

[33] *Ibid.*

[34] See *Tsilhqot'in Nation v British Columbia*, 2014 SCC 44 at paras 69–70.

[35] "Statement by the Prime Minister of Canada after delivering a speech to the Assembly of First Nations Special Chiefs Assembly" (8 December 2015), online: <pm.gc.ca/en/news/statements/2015/12/08/statement-prime-minister-canada-after-delivering-speech-assembly-first#:~:text=%E2%80%9CIt%20is%20time%20for%20a,obligation%20that%20we%20carry%20forward.>.

when he responded with barriers to reconciliation rather than steps toward it.

Parting Comments

First Nations people have grown up under the complete control of the *Indian Act* and the colonial bureaucracy that runs it. For generations, the intention was to "kill the Indian in the child," such that "there is not a single Indian in Canada that has not been absorbed into the body politic and there is no Indian question."[36] To this end, the government wanted to also kill our languages. In most cases, they attempted to substitute English for what was taken from us. French really wasn't on their mind.

Trudeau's policy regarding English-French bilingualism—a requirement to even apply for an appointment to the Supreme Court—amounts to a return of cultural annihilation. To join those who make some of the most important decisions in Canada, one must first lose who one is and become like those who have historically been in control. In other words, kill the Indian in the child!

Ottawa and the Advisory Board speak while ignoring the colonial control of Indigenous education. They speak condescendingly about the necessity of French for an Indigenous judicial candidate. They speak while disregarding the truth of Indigenous history and the horrors of residential schools.

Why can't Indigenous people who speak English just learn French? For most Indigenous people, life in off-reserve communities that offer French-immersion courses is prohibitively expensive. There are few spaces available, and the competition is fierce. The reality that is white privilege is palpable. For most Indigenous people, in other words, learning French as a second language is not a remote possibility or priority. None of this is appreciated or understood by Ottawa.

Indigenous people have lived through the fierce and determined attempts by the government and the churches to eliminate us. Contrary to what Chief Justice Wagner believes, we know how to interpret and change colonial law and colonial thought better than a

---

[36] Facing History & Ourselves, "Until There Is Not a Single Indian in Canada" (last modified 28 July 2020), online: <facinghistory.org/en-ca/resource-library/until-there-not-single-indian-canada>.

Supreme Court that does not reflect our lived experience.[37] That's what an Indigenous judge on the Supreme Court would rely upon—lived experience—to inform their decisions and to imagine what Canadian law could be if it were not directed toward the destruction of our nations, cultures, and laws. But each year, valuable lived experience is lost. The bilingualism requirement prioritizes the French language over the lived experience of upholding one's Indigenous legal responsibilities, participating in Indigenous governance, and modeling Indigenous laws. When the bilingualism requirement is imposed, the pool of "qualified" Indigenous candidates shrinks drastically, excluding those who did not have the opportunity to learn French because they grew up within their First Nation where French instruction was not available. Resources for French translation are readily available, and yet understanding French without assistance is privileged over the lived practices of Indigenous traditions, governance, and laws.

Despite Trudeau's comments on the importance of a new nation-to-nation relationship with Indigenous people, I'm sure of one thing: Indigenous people remain a long way from being appointed to the Supreme Court as a matter of course. Because whenever there is even a possibility of another Indigenous justice on the Supreme Court, the guardians of the status quo simply erect new barriers to keep the majority of us out.

---

[37] *Supra* note 32.

SECTION B

POLICING, CRIMINAL LAW, AND THE CARCERAL STATE

Is *Gladue* Sentencing Exceptional?

*Lisa Kerr**

Abstract

Is *Gladue* sentencing exceptional? Clarity on this question is essential, as public commentary, academic accounts and even judicial opinions sometimes misstate or overstate the distinctiveness of the *Gladue* framework. Step 1 of the *Gladue* approach requires sentencing judges to obtain and consider information that speaks to the circumstances of an offender, including background and systemic factors as an Indigenous person. While this may result in a different sentence than would otherwise be imposed, there is nothing exceptional about that outcome. In any sentencing matter, mitigating information that bears on moral blameworthiness is central to applying the principle of proportionality. Where *Gladue* gives rise to more distinctive possibilities is in the Step 2 direction to trial judges to consider "appropriate procedures and sanctions" in the sentencing of an Indigenous offender. While Step 1 is largely continuous with ordinary sentencing, Step 2 contains considerable distinctive potential for sentencing to engage with alternatives rooted in Indigenous laws, institutions and practices.

---

* I am grateful to Melvyn Green for reading an earlier draft and offering generous commentary. The quality of his feedback far exceeded what I was able to do justice to here. Thanks also to Benjamin Ewing for our valuable ongoing conversation about these issues.

More generally, *Gladue* opened legal and political space within the state sentencing system for Indigenous-led justice initiatives.

Résumé

Les principes de détermination de la peine issus de l'arrêt Gladue sont-ils exceptionnels ? Il est essentiel de clarifier cette question, car l'opinon publique, les comptes rendus universitaires et même les avis judiciaires déforment ou exagèrent parfois le caractère distinctif du cadre Gladue. La première étape de l'approche Gladue exige que les juges chargés de déterminer la peine obtiennent et examinent des informations relatives à la situation du délinquant, y compris le contexte et les facteurs systémiques liés à son appartenance à une communauté autochtone. Bien que cela puisse mener à une peine différente de celle qui aurait été prononcée autrement, ce résultat n'a rien d'exceptionnel. Dans toute affaire de détermination de la peine, les informations atténuantes qui ont une incidence sur la responsabilité morale sont essentielles à l'application du principe de proportionnalité. C'est à la seconde étape que l'arrêt Gladue offre des possibilités plus distinctives, en invitant les juges de première instance à envisager des « procédures et sanctions appropriées » lors de la détermination de la peine d'un délinquant autochtone. Alors que l'étape 1 s'inscrit dans la continuité de la détermination de la peine ordinaire, l'étape 2 offre un potentiel considérable pour que la détermination de la peine s'appuie sur des solutions de remplacement ancrées dans les lois, les institutions et les pratiques autochtones. Plus généralement, l'arrêt Gladue a ouvert un espace juridique et politique au sein du système pénal pour les initiatives judiciaires menées par les Autochtones.

The plain language of s. 718.2(e), enacted as part of comprehensive sentencing reforms to the *Criminal Code* in 1996, told sentencing judges two things. First, restraint should be exercised in the use of imprisonment in all cases. Second, this principle of restraint should be exercised "with particular attention to the circumstances of Aboriginal offenders."[1] Three years later, in *R v Gladue*, the Supreme

---

[1] *Criminal Code*, RSC 1985, c C-46, s 718.2(e). At that time, section 718.2(e) read: "A court that imposes a sentence shall also take into consideration the following principles [...] (e) all available sanctions other than imprisonment that are reasonable in the

Court read these few words as a provision underpinned by a clear legislative purpose: to reduce the overrepresentation of Indigenous people in Canadian prisons.[2] The provision was also read as a direction to expand the use of restorative justice principles in sentencing, and to engage in these objectives "with a sensitivity to aboriginal community justice initiatives when sentencing aboriginal offenders."[3]

In 2008, Jonathan Rudin described *Gladue* as "clearly the most significant development in the criminal law for Aboriginal people over the last 25 years."[4] Along with mandating sentencing judges to obtain and consider relevant information about Indigenous offenders, *Gladue* has extended well beyond sentencing and now requires recognition of background and systemic factors in other substantive law areas, including bail, parole, criminal procedure and the law of evidence.[5] The number of "Indigenous courts"—which Rudin defines as a "catch-all for initiatives that have developed to better address the needs of Indigenous people who find themselves before the courts"— has also "increased rapidly", especially in recent years.[6] Hadley Friedland documents the range of initiatives across Canada developed under the mantle of *Gladue* that "ameliorate the current issues the mainstream justice system poses" for Indigenous individuals and communities.[7] There is considerable variety, but Friedland notes some commonalities, including that: they are funded within the existing

---

circumstances should be considered for all offenders, with particular attention to the circumstances of aboriginal offenders." Today, the section reads, in full: "(e) all available sanctions, other than imprisonment, that are reasonable in the circumstances and consistent with the harm done to victims or to the community should be considered for all offenders, with particular attention to the circumstances of Aboriginal offenders."

[2] *R v Gladue*, 1999 CanLII 679 (SCC) at para 87 [*Gladue*]. Cory and Iacobucci J. J.: "the aim of s. 718.2(e) is to reduce the tragic overrepresentation of aboriginal people in prisons. It seeks to ameliorate the present situation [...]".

[3] *Ibid* at para 48.

[4] Jonathan Rudin, "Aboriginal Over-Representation and *R v Gladue*: Where we were, where we are and where we might be going" (2008) 40 SCLR 68, 677–713 at 677.

[5] On the many impacts *Gladue* has had beyond sentencing, see Jonathan Rudin, *Indigenous People and the Criminal Justice System*, 2nd ed (Toronto: Emond Publishing, 2022) 145-206 [Rudin, *Indigenous People*].

[6] *Ibid* at 236.

[7] Hadley Friedland, "Navigating Through Narratives of Despair: Making space for the Cree reasonable person in the Canadian Justice System." (2016) 67 UNBLJ 269 at 292-296 [Friedland, "Navigating Through Narratives"].

mainstream justice system and operate in conjunction with it, they do not deal with serious or violent crimes, they strive to treat individual offenders with empathy and respect and to take an active role in telling their story and finding solutions, and they try to connect offenders to resources to recover from and manage their underlying issues.[8]

This chapter will focus on how *Gladue* operates within mainstream sentencing courts, and on the curious reality that while the Supreme Court was clear that the purpose of s. 718.2(e) is to reduce Indigenous incarceration and respond to systemic social conditions, it simultaneously said that sentencing judges cannot pursue that purpose in a direct or systemic way. While the Court invited the development of restorative justice principles and community-led justice initiatives for dealing with Indigenous accused, it also told sentencing judges not to avoid or reduce custody solely on the basis that an offender is Indigenous.

This puzzle at the heart of *Gladue* might come as a surprise, given *Gladue*'s general reputation as an exceptional sentencing approach reserved for Indigenous offenders. But the law as it stands is clear: the ultimate task of the sentencing judge to impose a proportionate sentence does not change in cases involving Indigenous offenders. Fundamentally, the judge must impose a fit sentence. In Canadian law, that means a sentence that reflects both the gravity of the offence and the offenders' degree of responsibility. In analyzing the latter question of responsibility or blameworthiness, judges regularly consider information that speaks to the circumstances of an offender. In cases involving Indigenous people, Step 1 of the *Gladue* approach tells judges that they have a duty in all cases involving Indigenous people to consider the kinds of background and systemic factors that are often mitigating.[9] The effect of Step 1 is to mandate judges to obtain this information, whereas in cases involving non-Indigenous offenders, consideration of this information will flow from whether and how counsel opts to adduce it.

Attending to this information often leads a judge to impose less custodial time or a non-custodial sanction. But we cannot take from

---

[8] *Ibid* at 294.

[9] I will use the labels 'Step 1' and 'Step 2' to refer to what the Supreme Court distinguishes as parts (A) and (B) of applying section 718.2(e). See e.g. Marie-Andrée Denis-Boileau & Marie-Eve Sylvestre, "*Ipeelee* and the Duty to Resist" (2018) 51:2 *UBC L Rev* 548 [Denis-Boileau & Sylvestre, "*Ipeelee*"].

the fact that *Gladue* often results in a less severe penalty that Indigenous people benefit from a separate sentencing range. These outcomes simply reflect the distinct circumstances that many Indigenous people who are involved in the criminal justice system are in. The Supreme Court has said that, at the level of principle, the task of the sentencing judge does not vary in response to even a compelling *Gladue* report. The task is still to discern a fit sentence and to blend the other objectives of sentencing as appropriate for the particular case.

Crown counsel may habitually soften their sentencing positions for Indigenous accused, but again, this does not disclose a separate, Indigenous sentencing range. As repeat players in criminal matters, Crowns will be attuned to what is a common empirical situation at this point in our history: that the moral blameworthiness of an Indigenous accused is less than that of a non-Indigenous person who has committed similar crimes. This flows from the fact that many Indigenous people have experienced the systemic social conditions that can serve as mitigating for the purpose of sentencing. But Gladue and then Ipeelee tell us that nothing changes in cases involving offenders who happen to be Indigenous: the direction in s. 718.2(e) to consider their social context is so that judges can properly apply the fundamental—and universal—principle of proportionality.[10]

Step 2 of *Gladue*, which directs judges to consider the types of "procedures and sanctions" that might be appropriate in light of Indigenous heritage or connection, is where greater potential for a meaningfully distinctive approach to sentencing for Indigenous offenders resides. The *Gladue* decision contained a rich discussion of the fact that the criminal justice system relies on traditional sentencing ideals, like deterrence and denunciation, that are often far removed from the understanding of sentencing held by Indigenous people and communities. The discussion is nuanced and avoids stereotypes, noting: "we do not wish to imply that all aboriginal offenders, victims, and communities share an identical understanding of appropriate sentences for particular offences and offenders. Aboriginal communities stretch from coast to coast and from the border with the United States to the far north. Their customs and

---

[10] Benjamin Ralston, *The Gladue Principles: A Guide to the Jurisprudence*, (2021, BC First Nations Justice Council) at 121.

traditions and their concept of sentencing vary widely."[11] And while many Indigenous conceptions of sentencing emphasize ideals of restorative justice—a tradition that should be seen as "extremely important" to the analysis under s. 718.2(e)[12]—the court is careful to note that restorative approaches should not be equated with lenience. In fact, restorative approaches can demand greater levels of accountability from an offender. The Court told sentencing judges to develop the concepts and principles of a distinctive approach under Step 2 over time.

These developments have indeed taken time, and innovations on the ground are not yet very visible in Supreme Court jurisprudence. Indeed, the Supreme Court has yet to even specify whether and how judges are obliged to engage with Indigenous-led alternatives as part of sentencing.[13] Rather than moving the law forward, the Supreme Court has often been taken up with responding to judicial resistance to the more basic principles established in *Gladue*. There are many examples where the Court has had to remind lower courts not to exclude particular Indigenous offenders from the regime, and of the diverse contexts in which *Gladue* principles apply.[14] Provincial appellate courts have also dealt with lower court resistance on many aspects of *Gladue*, including having to convey repeatedly

---

[11] *Gladue supra* note 2 at para. 71.

[12] *Ibid.*

[13] In Ontario, one appellate case held that it is an error of law for a sentencing judge not to carefully consider the recommendations of a sentencing circle which has occurred alongside sentencing: *R v Jacko*, 2010 ONCA 452 at para 81. In Nova Scotia, *R v Cope*, 2024 NSCA 59 at para 72-73, the court said that "sentencing circle recommendations should be carefully considered and addressed in sentencing" and that "there may be a basis for appellate intervention where the sentencing judge has erred by giving either too much or too little weight to the recommendations and where that error has had an impact on the sentence." (Leave to appeal to the Supreme Court of Canada granted on March 13, 2025.)

[14] For example, the Court has had to explain that there is a "duty […] to consider the unique circumstances of Aboriginal offenders" even with respect to serious offences, *R v Ipeelee*, [2012] 1 SCR 433 at para 85 [*Ipeelee*]; that Indigenous offenders need not point to a causal connection between their Indigeneity and their offence to benefit from *Gladue* principles, *Ipeelee* at para 83; that Indigenous background is relevant to assessing the constitutionality of a punishment under section 12, *R v Bouldreault*, 2018 SCC 58 at para. 83; and that Indigenous background can be used when constructing reasonable hypotheticals under the section 12 rubric, *R v Hilbach*, 2023 SCC 3 at para. 43.

that a defendant's disconnect from their Indigenous heritage does not disqualify them from *Gladue*'s application, but can itself be a relevant background factor.[15] So while there have been significant developments on the ground within the ambit of *Gladue*, namely an array of local alternative justice initiatives, appellate courts have had to continually remind mainstream lower courts to embrace the basic facts of how Indigenous background and systemic factors are essential to considerations of moral blameworthiness for all Indigenous accused. The result is a complex picture in which the legal system is still being nudged toward acceptance of foundational parts of *Gladue* that are not particularly distinctive or controversial, even as it has seen profound institutional change and experimentation at the local level that the *Gladue* framework made possible. My goal in this chapter is to get clear on what is and is not distinctive about the *Gladue* regime as it stands today.

There are two parts to this chapter. In Part I, I start with the *Gladue* decision itself. I point to how two features of the original opinion made it seem as if *Gladue* sentencing would be a particularly distinctive approach. First, the Court makes clear that the purpose of s. 718.2(e) is to reduce Indigenous rates of incarceration. Second, the decision directs lower Courts to refer to Indigenous conceptions of justice at sentencing under Step 2 of the new methodology. Both of these aspects of the original *Gladue* decision held great promise, but the force of the discussion about legislative intent was tempered by other parts of the decision. The invitation to develop Indigenous-led alternatives remains meaningful, but change has taken time, and the topic is ripe for renewed and detailed Supreme Court attention.

Part II of the chapter uses this argument about the universal features of *Gladue* sentencing to better understand the discussion on whether *Gladue* should be extended to Black defendants. In *R v Morris*, the Ontario Court of Appeal confirmed that judicial attention should be paid to the background and systemic factors of Black offenders.[16] But the Court stopped short of extending the independent duty that applies under s. 718.2(e) and *Gladue* to inquire into those circumstances. To justify this refusal, the Court points to what it says are strongly exceptional aspects of *Gladue* sentencing—what it says are

---

[15] *R v Kehoe*, 2023 BCCA 2 at para 56; *R v Dichrow*, 2022 ABCA 282; *R v Mercier*, 2023 ONCA 98.

[16] *R v Morris*, 2021 ONCA 680 [*Morris*].

unique features that cannot easily be extended or transported. My argument about the ordinary or universal features of *Gladue* sentencing offers a critique of this part of *Morris*.

To date, judicial practice has often stuck with a "safely deflationary view" of *Gladue*.[17] I have argued elsewhere, with Benjamin Ewing, that *Gladue* can and should be read to require judges to do more than simply apply the general principles of sentencing.[18] A more distinctive, meaningful approach is possible and could be a better fit for serving the law's purpose of reducing Indigenous incarceration without amounting to illegitimate race-based discounts. Those arguments speak to the future. In this chapter, however, my goal is to get clear on the past: the ways in which *Gladue* sentencing has often been ordinary sentencing.

Before turning to Part I to provide an outline of major cases like *Gladue* and *Ipeelee*, I want to briefly identify the stakes of understanding the truth about how *Gladue* sentencing has operated so far. There are prevalent misreadings of s. 718.2(e) and *Gladue* that misunderstand the distinctiveness of the approach as it stands. We should be prepared to identify and guard against these kinds of claims.

Mapping Misreadings

Part of my motivation in emphasizing the universal character of much of *Gladue*-informed sentencing is to guard against reactionary backlash to the *Gladue* project. What we might call the *Reactionary View*

---

[17] Benjamin Ewing & Lisa Kerr, "Reconstructing Gladue" (2023) 74:2 UTLJ 156 at 158. Even under that safely deflationary reading, which requires only that judges take care to consider the circumstances of Indigenous offenders in fixing a sentence, lower court judges have often failed to follow the approach. See e.g. Denis-Boileau & Sylvestre, "*Ipeelee*", *supra* note 7; Rhea Murti, "The Sentencing of Indigenous People in Canada: Where We Are Two Decades After *Gladue*" (2023) 29:1 Indigenous LJ 17.

[18] *Ibid*. Ewing and Kerr argue that part of the problem is that we lack clear explanations of when and why it is morally legitimate to pursue the aggregate social goal of reducing Indigenous imprisonment in the context of individual sentencing decisions. They explain how *Gladue* requires judges to open their minds to the reasons that many Indigenous offenders should be afforded mitigation, restorative justice, and community-based accountability. Ewing and Kerr suggest that their arguments fit the law as it stands but concede that their proposals go beyond what has been expressly articulated in the case law.

says that *Gladue* is an illegitimate race-based sentencing discount.[19] The *Reactionary View* has impacted the law in that judges have worried about it and guarded against it. Most prominently, as I discuss below, the 2012 *Ipeelee* decision responds to the *Reactionary View* as it was voiced in various lower courts and by some legal scholars. *Ipeelee* is in some ways preoccupied with defending against this reading. The upshot is that *Ipeelee* can be read as overly keen to depict *Gladue* as largely indistinguishable from standard Canadian sentencing law.

Proponents of the *Reactionary View* are often willfully misleading in how they describe the *Gladue* approach, particularly those who suggest it is a discount based on race. But there are also good faith efforts that can misread what *Gladue* entails. Consider, for example, a BC trial judge who recently warned that "a Tsunami" is coming to sentencing courts of false claims of Indigenous ancestry.[20] The judge warned that these false claims would be advanced so as to gain the "benefits" of being "sentenced as an Indigenous

---

[19] Several examples of the *Reactionary View* can be found in the original legislative debates on Bill C-41. For example, Bloc Québécois M.P. Pierrette Venne said this at second reading: "it is deplorable that the bill tries to sneak through the back door the concept of a parallel system of justice for Aboriginals. It is so well hidden that it is almost necessary to read Clause 718.2(e) twice to discover this enormity hidden under nine sneaky words [...]. Why should an Aboriginal convicted of murder, rape, assault or of uttering threats not be liable to imprisonment like any other citizen of this country? Can we replace all this with a parallel justice, an ethnic justice, a cultural justice? Where would it stop? Where does this horror come from?" "Bill C-41, An Act to amend the Criminal Code (sentencing) and other acts in consequence thereof", 2nd reading, *House of Commons Debates*, 35-1, No 93 (20 September 1994) at 5876 (Ms. Venne). This discourse continued in the years following. See e.g. Matt Gurney, "Inuit Politician Right to Call for End to "Dangerous" Special Sentencing for Aboriginals," *National Post* (13 September 2012), online: <nationalpost.com/opinion/matt-gurney-inuit-politician-right-to-call-for-end-to-dangerous-special-sentencing-for-aboriginals>; Lorne Gunter, "The Two Colours of Canadian Justice," *National Post* (4 January 2012), online: <nationalpost.com/opinion/lorne-gunter-the-two-colours-of-canadian-justice>. There are many contemporary examples of this type of false reading, including from at least one law professor. See e.g. Bruce Pardy, "The social justice revolution has taken the law schools. This won't end well", *National Post* (27 February 2018), online: <nationalpost.com/opinion/the-social-justice-revolution-has-taken-the-law-schools-this-wont-end-well>. ("Courts may impose more lenient penalties on Indigenous accused pursuant to the Criminal Code and the Gladue principles [...] Everyone is not subject to the same rules.")

[20] *R v Legault*, 2024 BCPC 29 at para 93.

person."[21] On the one hand, perhaps this judge was sensibly worried that false claims to Indigeneity could corrupt the legitimacy of *Gladue* or divert resources from legitimate claimants. On the other, one can also trace two possible misconceptions at play here. The first is that *Gladue* is a departure from the ordinary principles of sentencing, and the second is that *Gladue* requires only proof of racial ancestry. But the law is clear that if an offender cannot articulate a tie of some kind between background factors and their offence, *Gladue* will have no impact on the sentence.[22] Indigenous background is necessary but not sufficient for *Gladue* factors to impact the sentence.[23] What matters is adducing information that is relevant to sentencing, just as it is for any other offender. To the extent the judge's warning suggests that *Gladue* is both favourable and illegitimate special treatment based on race—and that the legal system ought to tighten controls on access as a result—it misreads how *Gladue* actually works.

Part I: *Gladue* in Theory and Practice

S. 718.2(e): A Clear Legislative Purpose that Cannot Be Directly Pursued

The Court's language in *Gladue* suggests a robust commitment to meaningful pursuit of an ambitious legislative purpose. It is unequivocal about the intent behind s. 718.2(e), which is "to respond to the problem of over-incarceration in Canada" and to "the more acute problem of the disproportionate incarceration of Aboriginal peoples."[24] Sentencing judges must play a key role in "remedying injustice against

---

[21] *Ibid.*

[22] See e.g. *R v L (F.H.)*, 2018 ONCA 83 at para 38: For Indigenous background to influence sentence, systemic and background factors must have impacted the offender's life in a way that: (1) Bears on moral blameworthiness and (2) Indicates which types of sentencing objectives should be prioritized; *R v Monckton*, 2017 ONCA 450 at para 115: Although Aboriginal offenders are not required to "draw a straight line" between their Aboriginal roots and the offences for which they are being sentenced, more is required "than the bare assertion of an offender's Aboriginal status"; *R v T.A.P.*, 2013 ONSC 797 at para 40: The *Gladue* assessment "must go beyond a technical assessment of bloodline."

[23] *Ipeelee supra* note 14 at para 75: "The mere assertion of one's Indigenous heritage is insufficient because s. 718.2(e) does not create a "race-based discount on sentencing."

[24] *Gladue, supra* note 2 at para 50.

aboriginal peoples in Canada," as they are among those decision-makers who determine most directly whether an Indigenous person will go into custody or whether other sentencing options may be employed. It said judges have an independent legal duty to apply s. 718.2(e) in all cases involving Indigenous defendants, regardless of whether counsel raised it.

The *Gladue* decision cites a large body of commissioned reports that detail the disproportionate incarceration of Indigenous people, all of which "cry out" for recognition of the "magnitude and gravity of the problem."[25] The figures are "stark" and reflect what may fairly be termed a "crisis in the Canadian criminal justice system."[26] The "drastic overrepresentation" of Indigenous people in custody is a "sad and pressing social problem."[27] This is why Parliament drafted s. 718.2(e), which is "Parliament's direction to members of the judiciary to inquire into the causes of the problem and to endeavour to remedy it, to the extent that a remedy is possible through the sentencing process."[28]

Yet *Gladue* is simultaneously clear that it is not the job of sentencing judges to pursue that legislative purpose directly. While the Court confirms a "judicial duty" to give the remedial purpose of s. 718.2(e) "real force,"[29] the sentencing judge's "fundamental duty" to levy a sentence proportionate to the gravity of the offence and to the moral blameworthiness of the offender remains "unchanged" by s. 718.2(e).[30] The Court emphasizes that proportionality is the fundamental principle of sentencing and that this is the same for Indigenous and non-Indigenous offenders.

The *Gladue* analysis has two steps. Under Step 1, judges must consider the background and systemic factors that may have played a role in bringing an Indigenous person before the criminal courts. In order to access that information, judges must take judicial notice—which means suspending the ordinary standards of formal proof—of the broad, collective experiences of Indigenous people and the impacts of colonialism. To be sure, this is a muscular use of the doctrine of

---

[25] *Ibid* at para 60.
[26] *Ibid*.
[27] *Ibid*.
[28] *Ibid* at paras 64–65.
[29] *Ibid* at para 34.
[30] *Ibid* at para 33.

judicial notice. However, judicial notice alone is not enough to impact the sentence. The purpose is not to remedy the overrepresentation of Indigenous people in prison *en masse* but rather to consider information that will enable the judge to impose a fit sentence in a particular case. An individual Indigenous offender must provide case-specific information showing how the collective experience of Indigenous people impacted them in a way that is linked to their offence.

This last point is clear when you look at how *Gladue* works today. Over time, specialized sentencing reports known as "*Gladue* reports" served to provide the requisite individual information and to provide points of connection and reflection on the more structural background factors. As Rudin describes the role of the reports: "most judges and lawyers have little knowledge of the systemic factors that the Court remarked upon in *Gladue*. *Gladue* Reports are often the vehicle through which this information can be conveyed."[31] This approach served to ameliorate longstanding structural bias against Indigenous people at sentencing, which flowed from the lack of knowledge in an almost entirely non-Indigenous judiciary.[32] In this way, we can understand *Gladue* as partly an attempt to remove a built-in risk of bias: making a predominantly non-Indigenous judiciary more aware of the circumstances of Indigenous defendants.[33]

---

[31] Rudin, *Indigenous People*, *supra* note 5 at 112.

[32] *Gladue*, *supra* note 2 at para 67, relying on Tim Quigley for this point. See Tim Quigley, *Some Issues in Sentencing of Aboriginal Offenders*, in *Continuing Poundmaker and Riel's Quest: Presentations Made at a Conference on Aboriginal Peoples and Justice*, ed by Richard Gosse, James Youngblood Henderson & Roger Carter (Saskatoon: Purich Publishing, 1994) at 275–276: "Socioeconomic factors such as employment status, level of education, family situation, etc., appear on the surface as neutral criteria. They are considered as such by the legal system. Yet they can conceal an extremely strong bias in the sentencing process. Convicted persons with steady employment and stability in their lives, or at least prospects of the same, are much less likely to be sent to jail for offences that are borderline imprisonment offences. The unemployed, transients, the poorly educated are all better candidates for imprisonment. When the social, political and economic aspects of our society place Aboriginal people disproportionately within the ranks of the latter, our society literally sentences more of them to jail. This is systemic discrimination."

[33] Maria Dugas makes this kind of point about the need for specialized sentencing reports for African Canadians: the point is to address the discriminatory impact that flows from the status quo of *absent* judicial awareness. Where past experiences are not considered, "there is a risk that systemic factors may inadvertently lead to discrimination in sentencing." Maria Dugas, "Committing to Justice: The Case for

Gladue is careful to guard against claims of special treatment—a concern that would be taken up more fully in *Ipeelee*. The direction to pay "particular attention" does not mean paying "more" attention, *Gladue* says, because it would be "unreasonable to assume that Parliament intended sentencing judges to prefer certain categories of offenders over others."[34] Rather, the direction to "pay attention" is interpreted as Parliament's appreciation of the fact that the circumstances of Indigenous offenders are unique and "different from those of non-aboriginal offenders."[35] Under this reading, the direction in s. 718.2(e) amounts to telling judges to do what is already their job as judges: to notice when the facts in the case at bar are different from other cases.

The idea that the provision is meant to direct judicial attention to the distinct factual circumstances of Indigenous offenders is well captured in this part of *Gladue* on the text and structure of s. 718.2(e):

> [...] the logical meaning to be derived from the special reference to the circumstances of aboriginal offenders, juxtaposed as it is against a general direction to consider "the circumstances" for all offenders, is that sentencing judges should pay particular attention to the circumstances of aboriginal offenders because those circumstances are unique, and different from those of non-aboriginal offenders.[36]

Under this account, what judges are told to do in a *Gladue* sentencing is ensure that the actual circumstances of the offender before them are considered and to pause on the question of whether prison is required (and remember, that principle of restraint is universal, not particular to Indigenous offenders in the drafting of the section). It is a reminder for judges to do what they ought to be doing in any event: ensure that relevant information is adduced, take judicial notice of appropriate material, pay attention to the facts of the case when imposing sentence, and consider whether custody is necessary. While *Gladue* says sentencing judges should "undertake the process of

---

Impact of Race and Culture Assessment in Sentencing African Canadian Offenders" (2020) 43:1 Dal LJ 103 at 121.

[34] *Gladue, supra* note 2 at para 37.

[35] *Ibid.*

[36] *Ibid.*

sentencing Aboriginal offenders differently," the end goal is no different from all other sentencing cases: to achieve a "truly fit and proper
sentence in the particular case."[37] Step 1 of *Gladue* is required to
redress judicial ignorance and neglect as to the situation of Indigenous
people. It improves the epistemic quality of a sentencing hearing
involving Indigenous people, but the "different approach" is largely a
push in the direction of formal equality—ensuring that Indigenous
defendants are not *worse* off in sentencing courts in terms of how their
moral blameworthiness is understood.

Step 2 is the part of *Gladue* that gave rise to the potential for a
distinct approach. This step requires judges to consider "the types of
sentencing procedures and sanctions which may be appropriate in
the circumstances for the offender because of his or her particular
aboriginal heritage or connection."[38] The idea here is that, for many
Indigenous offenders, the principles and objectives of sentencing in
the *Criminal Code* do not represent Indigenous values. At times, Step 2
is understood as being about the "efficacy" of punishment for
Indigenous people—the idea being that deterrence and denunciation
might not work as well as restorative or "healing" approaches.[39] But
Step 2 carries a deeper dimension, namely its recognition of distinct
Indigenous conceptions and methods of criminal sanction. These will
not, of course, always be restorative or healing-based.[40]

This discussion of Step 2 is a remarkable part of the *Gladue* opinion. Over several paragraphs, the Court implores sentencing judges to
consider the question of a just sentence from the historical and cultural
vantage point of Indigenous laws and communities.[41] The Court calls
on lower courts to develop a jurisprudence that makes use of "innovative sentencing practices, such as healing and sentencing circles, and
aboriginal community council projects."[42] The Court manages to avoid

---

[37] *Ibid* at para 33.

[38] *Ibid* at para 66.

[39] *Ibid* at para 80.

[40] On the ways in which Indigenous justice is often equated with restorative justice,
see Marie-Andrée Denis-Boileau, "The *Gladue* Analysis: Shedding Light on
Appropriate Sentencing Procedures and Sanctions" (2021) 54:3 UBC L Rev 537 at
586; Val Napoleon & Hadley Friedland, "Indigenous Legal Traditions: Roots to
Renaissance" in Markus D Dubber & Tatjana Hörnle, eds, *The Oxford Handbook of
Criminal Law* (Oxford: Oxford University Press, 2014) 225 at 238–9.

[41] *Gladue, supra* note 2 at paras 70–74.

[42] *Ibid* at para 74.

pan-Indigenous stereotypes, noting that the customs and traditions of sentencing will "vary widely" across different First Nations, Métis and Inuit peoples.[43] For many, however, the current "concepts of sentencing" are inappropriate because they have "frequently not responded to the needs, experiences, and perspectives of aboriginal people or aboriginal communities."[44] Hadley Friedland confirms the significance of this direction to incorporate Indigenous ideals and understandings of just sentencing, which invites us to "imagine people actively engaging with Indigenous legal reasoning" in a way that "could conceivably begin to bridge the gap between legitimacy and enforcement that currently exists."[45]

However, as subsequent history makes clear, this distinctive branch of *Gladue* received limited uptake in lower courts. Part of this might be due to the 1999 decision in *R v Wells*, in which the Court stressed that for more violent offences, it was reasonable to assume that deterrence and denunciation *would* be "fundamentally relevant to the offender's community."[46] Other explanations for the limited uptake of Step 2 are offered by Marie Andrée Denis-Boileau and Marie-Eve Sylvestre, who point to judicial resistance to both legal pluralism and any challenge to the state monopoly on matters of punishment.[47] In any event, the limited uptake of Step 2 by 2012 does not get much attention in the *Ipeelee* decision.

Ipeelee: *Defending Against the Claim of Special Treatment*

The *Ipeelee* decision repeats the lofty legislative purpose of reducing Indigenous incarceration, but depicts *Gladue* as largely about the Step 1 application of universal sentencing principles. Judges are to hunt for a fit sanction in light of the gravity of an offence and the degree of moral blameworthiness of an offender. Judges must ensure they have the information necessary for sentencing, but they are not required or even authorized to avoid incarceration on the basis that the defendant is Indigenous.

Ipeelee is often read as a decision that affirms the commitments in *Gladue* and tells lower courts to engage in meaningful

---

[43] *Ibid* at para 73.

[44] *Ibid*.

[45] Friedland, "Navigating Through Narratives", *supra* note 6 at 311.

[46] *R v Wells*, [2000] 1 SCR 207 at para 42 [*Wells*].

[47] Denis-Boileau & Sylvestre, "*Ipeelee*", *supra* note 9 at 78 and 99–101.

implementation. And *Ipeelee* does clarify and affirm a number of key parts of *Gladue*. First, it offers more detail on the substance of judicial notice in this context, telling judges to take notice of the "history of colonialism, displacement, and residential schools and how that history continues to translate into lower educational attainment, lower incomes, higher unemployment, higher rates of substance abuse and suicide, and, of course, higher levels of incarceration for Aboriginal peoples."[48] Second, it clarifies that sentencing judges have a duty to consider *Gladue* factors in all cases, even where the charges are serious and custody will be imposed. Finally, in passages that show sophisticated sensitivity to the complex workings of intergenerational trauma, the decision is clear that Indigenous people are not required to show a tight causal nexus between background factors and their offence.[49] These were all consequential conclusions that responded to various forms of judicial resistance to *Gladue* which had emerged over the years.

However, it must be remembered that Canadian sentencing law is broadly open to considering how the background of *any* offender may have contributed to their offending. *Ipeelee* stresses this universality. In the following paragraph, for example, the Court simultaneously emphasizes the exceptional living conditions of Indigenous people while confirming that background and systemic factors may be relevant in the sentencing of *any* offender:

> The overwhelming message emanating from the various reports and commissions on Aboriginal people's involvement in the criminal justice system is that current levels of criminality are intimately tied to the legacy of colonialism (see, e.g., RCAP, at p. 309). As Professor Carter puts it, "poverty and other incidents of social marginalization may not be unique, but how people get there is. No one's history in this country compares to Aboriginal people's" (M. Carter, "Of Fairness and Faulkner" [2002], 65 *Sask. L. Rev.* 63, at p. 71). Furthermore, there is nothing in the *Gladue* decision which would indicate that background and systemic factors should not also be taken into account for other, non-Aboriginal offenders. Quite the opposite. Cory and Iacobucci J. J. Specifically

---

[48] *Ipeelee, supra* note 14 at para 60.
[49] *Ibid* at paras 82–84.

state, at para 69, in *Gladue*, that "background and systemic factors will also be of importance for a judge in sentencing a non-aboriginal offender."[50]

The Court went to great pains to emphasize that "section 718.2(e) does not create a race-based discount on sentencing." This is the Court in a somewhat defensive posture, as it repeats that the "fundamental duty of a sentencing judge" to impose a fit sentence is unchanged by *Gladue*.[51] It says that *Gladue* simply responds to the fact that Canadian Courts had long failed to consider the unique circumstances of Aboriginal offenders: "Section 718.2(e) is intended to remedy this failure."[52] The duty is to consider the relevant facts, but the overarching legal task remains the same:

> The section does not mandate better treatment for aboriginal offenders than non-aboriginal offenders. It is simply a recognition that the sentence must be individualized and that there are serious social problems with respect to aboriginals that require more creative and innovative solutions. This is not reverse discrimination. It is an acknowledgement that to achieve real equality, sometimes different people must be treated differently.[53]

This part of *Ipeelee* can be understood in the context of the criticism that the Court was responding to. The defensive aspect of *Ipeelee* is connected to how the decision is responding to claims in an article by Professors Stenning and Roberts, which features prominently in the decision.[54] These critics describe s. 718.2(e) as an "empty promise" to Indigenous people because it was unlikely to have any "significant impact on levels of overrepresentation."[55] These same critics allege that a distinct sentencing method for Indigenous

---

[50] *Ibid* at para 77.

[51] *Ibid* at paras 76–77.

[52] *Ibid.*

[53] *Ibid* at para 71.

[54] *Ibid* at paras 65 and 68, citing Philip Stenning & Julia V Roberts, "Empty Promises: Parliament, The Supreme Court, and the Sentencing of Aboriginal Offenders" (2001) 64 Sask L Rev 137 at 167 [Stenning & Roberts, "Empty Promises"]. For response, see Jonathan Rudin & Kent Roach, "Broken Promises: A Response to Stenning and Roberts' Empty Promises'" (2002) 65 Sask L Rev 3.

[55] *Ipeelee, supra* note 14 at para 165.

defendants amounted to "hijacking the sentencing process in pursuit of other goals."[56] They argue that *Gladue* is inherently unfair in
creating unjustified distinctions between offenders who are otherwise similarly situated.[57] In response, the Court emphasizes the
ordinary or universal features of *Gladue* sentencing, saying that systemic and background material is potentially relevant in all cases.[58]
There is nothing unique offered to Indigenous offenders; it is simply
that the evidence quite often differs in their cases.[59]

The irreconcilable critiques of Stenning and Roberts—critiques
that *Gladue* simultaneously does too little and too much—contained
within a single publication are an almost poetic representation of the
challenges the *Gladue* project has faced. *Gladue* is sometimes framed
as simultaneously radically inadequate, incapable of achieving its
stated goal, and radically interventionist, hijacking what individualized sentencing ought to be.

When it resists these allegations, *Ipeelee* minimizes parts of
Gladue that make the regime meaningfully distinct. The decision does
not press for sentencing judges to engage in greater uptake of
Indigenous procedures or conceptions of justice under Step 2.
Admittedly, this would be hard for the Court to direct as a top-down
reform. But the point is that, to address the concern that *Gladue* sentencing amounts to unwarranted special treatment, *Ipeelee* casts
Gladue as simply being about imposing "just sanctions" that accord
with the "fundamental principle of proportionality" that applies in
all cases.[60]

Rather than inviting alternative approaches for Indigenous people, *Ipeelee* narrates s. 718.2(e) as an enactment concerned largely with
addressing longstanding discrimination against Indigenous people at

---

[56] *Ibid* at para 68.
[57] Stenning and Roberts, "Empty Promises", *supra* note 54 write at 158: "If the kinds of
factors that place many Aboriginal people at a disadvantage vis-à-vis the criminal
justice system also affect many members of other minority or similarly marginalized
non-Aboriginal offender groups, how can it be fair to give such factors more
particular attention in sentencing Aboriginal offenders than in sentencing offenders
from those other groups who share a similar disadvantage?"
[58] *Ipeelee, supra* note 14 at para 77.
[59] *Ibid* at para 76, explaining that this argument from Stenning and Roberts is
"premised on the argument that the circumstances of Aboriginal offenders are not,
in fact, unique."
[60] *Ibid* at para 68.

sentencing. This makes enforcing the provision a matter of levelling up to formally equal treatment. The historical problem had been that judges "failed to take into account the unique circumstances of Aboriginal offenders that bear on the sentencing process."[61] Section 718.2(e) is intended to "remedy this failure."[62] The problem was entrenched, such that Parliament opted for a specific direction to pay particular attention to the circumstances of Aboriginal offenders. Only this would "suffice to ensure that judges undertook their duties properly."[63] Hence, in *Ipeelee*, the remedial purpose seems to contract—shifting from a robust and distinctive approach to Indigenous sentencing to the mere achievement of formally equal treatment.

Ipeelee goes further still in defending s. 718.2(e) against the charge of mandating a "race-based discount" in the sentencing of Indigenous offenders. In a passage that implies a "natural" level of Indigenous incarceration with which this policy does not interfere, the Court says that *Gladue* does not ask Courts to remedy the over-representation of Aboriginal people in prisons by "artificially reducing incarceration rates."[64] In having judges pay heed to the circumstances of Indigenous offenders, section 718.2(e) does not disrupt the sentencing process that applies to all offenders, which requires "sentencing judges [to] engage in an individualized assessment of all of the relevant factors and circumstances, including the status and life experiences, of the person standing before them."[65] Indigenous people are simply often in a different empirical situation, with personal and systemic circumstances that "bear on the culpability of the offender, to the extent that they shed light on his or her level of moral blameworthiness."[66] But judges should not "automatically"[67] or "artificially"[68] lower the sentencing of any Indigenous person.

And while *Ipeelee* is clear that "current levels of criminality are intimately tied to the legacy of colonialism,"[69] these systemic

---

[61] *Ibid* at para 75.
[62] *Ibid*.
[63] *Ibid* at para 68.
[64] *Ibid* at para 75.
[65] *Ibid*.
[66] *Ibid* at para 73.
[67] *Ibid* at para 93.
[68] *Ibid* at para 75.
[69] *Ibid* at para 77.

failures—of which sentencing Courts are to take judicial notice—will only bear upon a sentence where "case-specific" information is tied to the question of a fit sentence. While the social conditions that produce criminality are systemic, the solution can only be an individualized adjustment to the penalty.

In our system, any non-Indigenous person who asserts those same kinds of case-specific factors would be just as entitled to have the judge consider background factors that may "bear on the offender's moral culpability" at sentencing.[70] Of course, it is unlikely that a non-Indigenous person would be able to point to a similar, devastating collective experience in relation to the Canadian state. The situation of Indigenous people bears special attention from Parliament and the courts. Special attention, but not special principles.

It is telling that the Supreme Court's reflections in *Ipeelee* on proportionality in sentencing are regularly cited in cases that involve the sentencing of non-Indigenous offenders.[71] As Benjamin Berger explains, the *Gladue* jurisprudence is the main source of the robust mode of "individualized proportionality" that he says defines Canadian sentencing today.[72] As Berger illustrates, Canadian judges can take a close look at the offender's circumstances, including the collateral consequences of punishment, state misconduct vis-à-vis the offender, and the experience or impact of imprisonment. Berger suggests that *Gladue* has come to set the standard: the *Gladue* principles, which demand "searching engagement" with a full range of background and individual factors, seem to have radiated out. In many cases, a *Gladue* sentencing hearing is exemplary, but it is not exceptional.

Ipeelee gives minimal treatment to Step 2. Although Justice LeBel notes that "the *Gladue* principles direct sentencing judges to abandon the presumption that all offenders and all communities share the same values when it comes to sentencing,"[73] there is no discussion of

---

[70] *Ibid* at para 75.

[71] See e.g. *R v Siwicki*, 2019 MBCA 104; *R v Wolfe*, 2022 SKCA 132; *R v Mitsakis*, 2022 ONSC 5390; *R v Bissonnette*, 2022 SCC 23.

[72] Benjamin L Berger, "Proportionality and the Experience of Punishment" in David Cole & Julian Roberts, eds, *Sentencing in Canada: Essays in Law, Policy, and Practice* (Toronto: Irwin Law, 2020) 368 at 383.

[73] *Ipeelee, supra* note 14 at para 74.

the "innovative sentencing practices"[74] that the *Gladue* Court told sentencing judges to develop. Perhaps such a discussion would have taken the Court too far beyond the issues and record in the case at bar. Still, it is worth noting that, though *Ipeelee* is widely regarded as a strong endorsement of *Gladue*, its central thrust is to underscore how Step 1 remains continuous with the ordinary sentencing principles of Canadian law.[75]

Conclusion: Is Gladue Sentencing Exceptional?

The *Gladue* architecture allows for distinct features in the sentencing of Indigenous offenders. Regarding Step 1, the approach is distinct in a single, narrow sense: judges have an independent legal duty under s. 718.2(e) to pause and inquire into the possibility of relevant background and systemic factors in the sentencing of an Indigenous person. This does amount to an exception from the ordinary adversarial context, in which judges are not obliged to investigate issues that counsel does not raise. But this is only a legislative prompt to ensure that sentencing judges have adequate information upon which to impose sentence and that they make use of the same doctrine of judicial notice that trial judges employ every day in civil and criminal cases. As Efrat Arbel summarizes, both *Gladue* and *Ipeelee* outline a distinct sentencing methodology but they do not meaningfully "assign legal responsibility" for high rates of Indigenous incarceration and instead "disperse responsibility for its production."[76]

In some cases, this step required by s. 718.2(e) will lead judges to seek out a *Gladue* report, which is a specialized pre-sentence report

---

[74] *Gladue, supra* note 2 at para 72.

[75] Kent Roach explains that judges seem more comfortable with Step 1 of *Gladue*, which entails the application of background factors to the question of moral blameworthiness. Roach pushes for Step 2 to be better realized, showing how Indigenous background may also be brought to bear on the question of the procedures and principles of sentencing. On this front, Roach argues that Canadian judges may not appreciate that the application of Indigenous law may serve not only to rehabilitate Indigenous offenders—it can also potentially be used to denounce and deter improper behaviour and help offenders accept responsibility in a manner that is consistent with individualized proportionality. See: Kent Roach, "Plan B for Implementing *Gladue*: The Need to Apply Background Factors to the Punitive Sentencing Purposes" (6 May 2019), online: <ssrn.com/abstract=3367159>.

[76] Efrat Arbel, "Rethinking the 'Crisis' of Indigenous Mass Imprisonment" (2020) 34:3 CJLS 437 at 442.

meant to be authored by experts in Indigenous culture and history, ideally in collaboration with the accused and their family. These reports help judges understand the accused and their community. While important, this is simply a specialized variety of pre-sentence reporting. In many cases, dossiers about the circumstances of offenders are submitted to the court, including, of course, many cases involving non-Indigenous people. Add to this that the law does not require the production of a *Gladue* report.[77] The required information can simply be provided by counsel in order for the judge to discharge her *Gladue* duties. Indeed, there is extraordinary regional variation in terms of funding and access to the expert production of these reports. Some parts of the country continue to have limited or no access, with *Gladue* factors simply appended to ordinary pre-sentence reports prepared by probation officers or offered to the court through submissions from counsel.[78]

The common understanding of Step 1 of *Gladue*, which has received the bulk of the attention in the caselaw over Step 2, is rarely framed in such narrow terms: as a directive to judges to acquire relevant information to apply universal or ordinary sentencing principles, possibly through the production of a specialized report. But that is the appropriately modest depiction of much of the law and practice as it has developed in many regions to date. What the *Gladue* imperative has largely done is improved the epistemic quality of sentencing hearings. It has helped to shed better light on the facts that speak to moral blameworthiness for many Indigenous people in sentencing courts. But to describe Step 1 as an exceptional approach in substance is to overstate the law as it stands today. In the current mainstream legal landscape, in many parts of the country, *Gladue* functions as a directive to judges to ensure that they do what is already fundamental to their role: make decisions in light of facts.

The majority decision in *R v Sharma* confirms this reality about the *Gladue* regime: that it does not require particular non-custodial

---

[77] Notably, the *Gladue* decision did not come up with the idea of these reports. The Court did not explain how sentencing judges would obtain the required case-specific information about Indigenous offenders. In 2001, Aboriginal Legal Services began to provide that information through what came to be known as *Gladue* reports. See Rudin, *Indigenous People, supra* note 5 at 119.

[78] See e.g. *Ibid* at 120–123; Alexandra Hebert, "Change in Paradigm or Change in Paradox? *Gladue* Report Practices and Access to Justice" (2017) 43:1 Queen's LJ 149.

outcomes for Indigenous offenders, nor does it suggest a distinct Indigenous sentencing range.[79] This is how the majority in *Sharma* is able to conclude that 718.2(e) was given effect in the case. Ms. Sharma's sentence was far below the 6–8-year range that has long been the law in Ontario for a first offence of importing this amount of cocaine. Since *Gladue* does not mandate a specific outcome for Indigenous offenders, much less a non-custodial penalty, the majority was able to conclude that s. 718.2(e) was not impaired by the impugned law, which limited access to a conditional sentence order for Ms. Sharma's 18-month sentence.[80]

The great distinctive promise of *Gladue* resides in the Step 2 direction to consider "appropriate procedures and sanctions" in light of Indigenous background, as well as the direction to welcome innovative sentencing initiatives at the community level. Across the country, meaningful reform initiatives and alternatives were catalyzed by this feature of the *Gladue* architecture. But these developments have taken time to develop, and meaningful attention to this part of *Gladue* has been limited from within the judiciary. In the wake of the 2017 *Ipeelee* decision, Denis-Boileau and Sylvestre analyzed 635 trial and appellate decisions regarding the sentencing of Indigenous people. Among other findings, they showed that Step 2 has "barely garnered judicial attention."[81] Post-*Ipeelee* decisions that applied Indigenous culture and its various legal orders were "practically non-existent."[82] Things may be different or changing today in some jurisdictions. But the general record of judicial inattention to Step 2 helps to contextualize the significance of the question of whether *Gladue* should be extended to Black defendants.

Part II: How *Morris* Reads *Gladue* as Exceptional to Prohibit Extension

In *R v Morris* (2021), the Ontario Court of Appeal affirmed that anti-Black racism is pervasive across social institutions in Canada. Echoing Step 1 of *Gladue*, the Court held that sentencing judges should take

---

[79] *R v Sharma*, 2022 SCC 39 [*Sharma*].

[80] *Ibid* at paras 79–81.

[81] Denis-Boileau & Sylvestre, "*Ipeelee*", *supra* note 9 at 577.

[82] *Ibid* at 580.

judicial notice of that social context where appropriate and also welcome case-specific information about the impact on individual Black
offenders.

But it also held that s.718.2(e) and the mandatory nature of the
Gladue approach could not be formally extended to Black defendants,
reasoning that the Court could not "equate Indigenous offenders and
Black offenders for the purposes of s. 718.2(e)."[83] The Court rested its
conclusion partly on a claim that there is no distinctive Black culture
when it comes to conceptions of justice that may need to be accommodated at sentencing.[84] The idea here is, essentially, that it would be
impossible to bring Step 2 of *Gladue* to bear in cases involving Black
people, or to invite community justice initiatives premised around a
shared commitment to something like restorative justice.

In pointing to the absence of a "fundamentally different view of
justice" among Black people, the Court returned to the doctrinal
impediment first identified in its 2003 decision in *Borde*. There, the
Court observed that "traditional sentencing ideals of deterrence, separation, and denunciation are often far removed from the understanding of sentencing held by aboriginal offenders and their community."[85]
Morris repeats this view, saying that there is "no basis" for finding a
similar "common historical understanding or rejection of particular
sentencing ideals" when it comes to Black offenders.[86]

I have two critiques of this part of *Morris*, in which the court
says that s. 718.2(e) cannot be extended largely because of the difficulties of transporting Step 2 of *Gladue*. First, it is far from clear that Black
communities in Canada—an extraordinarily diverse category in
terms of national origin, religion, ancestry, geography, immigration
status, and more—lack distinct conceptions of justice or ideas about
sentencing. With the right information in hand, it may be possible to
reach the same conclusion found in *Gladue*: that the current "concepts

---

[83] *Morris, supra* note 14 at para 118.

[84] *Morris, ibid* at para 123. The Court says that the rationale offered in *Gladue* and *Ipeelee* for
applying the restraint principle differently in respect of Indigenous offenders "does
not apply to Black offenders." Here, the Court says that there is no basis to conclude
that Black offenders, or Black communities, share a cultural view of what constitutes a
"just" sentence in any given situation. The uniqueness of Indigenous culture explains
the "very specific and exclusive reference" to "Aboriginal offenders" in s 718.2(e).

[85] *R v Borde* (2003), 168 OAC 317 at para 32, 8 CR (6th) 203 (ONCA).

[86] Factum of the Appellant in *Morris* at para 56.

of sentencing" are inappropriate because they have "frequently not responded to the needs, experiences, and perspectives" of Black people and Black communities.[87]

The Urban Alliance on Race Relations, an intervener in *Morris*, argued that searching for a "common historical understanding of sentencing" only serves to exclude culturally and historically diverse Black communities in Canada.[88] Relying on the absence of a monolithic Black culture as a bar treats "diversity as an impediment."[89] And remember: there is no single or "common" Indigenous understanding of just punishment, which the *Gladue* decision recognized.[90]

Second, citing Step 2 as the reason *Gladue* cannot be extended seems to ignore the absence of meaningful attention or implementation of Step 2 in many cases involving Indigenous offenders. In this way, the *Morris* opinion may overstate *Gladue's* exceptionality. By understanding *Gladue* sentencing in criminal courts as more distinct than it often is, the Court needlessly raised the stakes of a decision to extend its reasoning to new contexts.

To be clear, my motivation with this critique is not to attempt to ensure that Black people have access to Step 2 at sentencing. Indeed, I accept that for many Black offenders this material may be difficult to know and adduce, in the same way that it has been for many Indigenous offenders. Rather, what I am tracking is the consequence of the *Morris* refusal to formally extend the *Gladue* requirements and find that judges have an independent legal duty to inquire into the background and systemic factors when sentencing a Black offender. By noting the difficulties associated with a transplant of Step 2, the decision blocks meaningful and consistent enforcement of Step 1.

Another intervener, the Black Legal Action Centre, was concerned about this issue. They called for a regime that would ensure background and systemic factors would be considered "each and every time" that a Black person is sentenced.[91] That procedural protection is no doubt important, especially given minimal Black representation in the ranks of the judiciary (and the bar). There is good

---

[87] *Gladue, supra* note 2 at para 73.
[88] Factum of the Intervener Urban Race Alliance in *Morris* at para 27.
[89] *Gladue, supra* note 2 at para 73.
[90] *Gladue, ibid.*
[91] Factum of the Intervener The Black Legal Action Centre and the Canadian Association of Black Lawyers in *Morris* at para 22.

reason to believe that judges dealing with Black accused would benefit from having the same obligation to pause and acquire relevant
information as they do when sentencing an Indigenous person.

   Morris confirms, in effect, that much of the rest of the *Gladue*
jurisprudence applies. Black defendants are entitled to the proper
application of judicial notice;[92] sentencing judges should take a flexi-
ble approach to the admissibility of specialized pre-sentence reports
that lay out background factors and individualized information;[93] the
principle of restraint suggests that courts should "bear in mind well-
established over-incarceration of Black offenders, particularly young
male offenders."[94] Finally, "as with Indigenous offenders" the discrimination suffered by Black people has effects on their background,
character, and circumstances. In many cases, this may properly "play
a role" in "fixing the offender's moral responsibility for the crime,
and/or blending the various objectives of sentencing to arrive at an
appropriate sanction in the circumstances."[95]

   In sum, a great deal of *Morris* directs judges to be open to considering how anti-Black racism may bear upon the circumstances of
Black offenders that are relevant to sentencing, and the court borrows
many important ideas from the *Gladue* jurisprudence. But the court
stops short of formal extension of the *Gladue* regime, partly for the
reasons I have described. In contrast, the Nova Scotia Court of Appeal
in *R v Anderson*, handed down shortly before *Morris*, concluded that
the Step 1 imperative to consider systemic and background factors
can be sensibly extended to African Nova Scotians, and that it may
amount to an error of law for a sentencing judge to ignore or fail to
inquire into these factors.[96] In *Anderson*, the duty of sentencing judges
is not merely to welcome such information when offered. It may be an
error to "fail to consider an offender's background and circumstances
in relation to the systemic factors of racism and marginalization."[97]

---

[92] Courts should take "judicial notice of the existence of anti-Black racism in Canada
   and its potential impact on individual offenders." *Morris, supra* note 16 at para 123.

[93] Courts should "admit evidence on sentencing directed at the existence of anti-Black
   racism in the offender's community, and the impact of that racism on the offender's
   background and circumstances." *Ibid* at para 123.

[94] *Ibid.*

[95] *Ibid.*

[96] *R v Anderson*, 2021 NSCA 62 at para 118.

[97] *Ibid.*

The extension of Step 1 in cases involving Black offenders is required in order to properly apply the universal principle of proportionality in Canadian sentencing law.

Conclusion

The *Gladue* approach distinguishes Canada in its willingness to grapple with a broad historical and cultural record in a sentencing proceeding, and in its invitation for the development of Indigenous alternatives to sentencing. Mugambi Jouet underscores the comparative significance of this willingness, arguing that Canada is unique in its concerted effort to tackle systemic racism in criminal punishment.[98] The law under s. 718.2(e) and *Gladue* recognizes that the moral blameworthiness of Indigenous people must be considered in light of the impacts of destructive, discriminatory state projects on the lives of those Indigenous people who wind up in criminal courts.

But Canadian judges pay attention to the social realities that shape criminal offending in the lives of non-Indigenous people, too. Section 718.2(e) and *Gladue* was required as an epistemic prompt to Canada's largely white and middle-class judiciary—particularly so in the 1990s—given a lack of awareness of the treatment of Indigenous people by the Canadian state. *Morris* confirms that sentencing judges should also be open to grappling with information about social context that discloses the experiences of Black people in a society marked by systemic racialized disadvantage, but the Court in *Morris* may have overstated the stakes when it declined to extend the mandatory nature of that inquiry to cases involving Black accused. It should be uncontroversial to require judges to check that they have adequate information about a person before imposing criminal punishment on them, particularly for those whose unequal circumstances are partly caused and sustained by state action.

The Court in *Ipeelee* reminded us that "uniformity hides inequity" when it comes to sentencing.[99] But it's important to understand how much uniformity the Court actually insisted upon when it comes

---

[98] Mugambi Jouet, "Humanity, Race, and Indigeneity in Criminal Sentencing: Social Change in America, Canada, Europe, Australia, and New Zealand" (20 September 2023), online: <ssrn.com/abstract=4562748>.

[99] *Ipeelee, supra* note 14 at para 79.

to the sentencing of Indigenous people. In mainstream sentencing courts today, *Gladue* is primarily about information. It is about the facts that judges must have access to and must consider. It is about ensuring that a judge has a wide enough lens so as to understand the blameworthiness of criminal conduct. As Rudin puts it, what *Gladue* reports do is "tell the story of the offender" and "provide the court with many voices and perspectives on the individual before the court."[100] The ability to marshal those narratives is why the provision has been important to improving the quality of sentencing decisions involving Indigenous people. But it is important to know that there is nothing exceptional about careful attention to the circumstances of offenders in a system anchored in individualized proportionality.

---

[100] Rudin, *Indigenous People, supra* note 5 at 111–112.

Abolitionist Lawyers: Making Prisons Obsolete

Reakash Walters

Abstract

This chapter describes the need to develop an abolitionist lawyering ethic to resist the most corrosive aspects of Canada's criminal legal system and advance transformative societal change. It critiques the inefficacy and harm of incarceration, which disproportionately impacts racialized and marginalized communities, perpetuates inequality, and fails to achieve public safety or rehabilitation. Drawing on historical movements, contemporary advocacy, and case studies, the chapter delineates an abolitionist approach to legal practice that emphasizes movement lawyering, aligns with non-reformist reforms, and resists carceral logics. Walters acknowledges the dialectical tensions inherent to the working lives of justice-oriented lawyers operating within oppressive systems. Abolitionist lawyers must grapple with these tensions and leverage their skills to challenge harmful institutions while fostering generative pathways to abolition.

Résumé

Ce chapitre met en lumière la nécessité de développer une éthique de pratique de droit abolitionniste pour résister aux aspects les plus corrosifs du système juridique pénal canadien et promouvoir un changement sociétal transformateur. Il critique l'inefficacité et les méfaits de l'incarcération, qui affecte de manière disproportionnée les communautés racialisées et marginalisées, perpétue les inégalités et ne parvient pas à assurer la sécurité publique ou la réhabilitation. En s'appuyant sur des mouvements historiques, des revendications contemporaines et des études de cas, le chapitre propose une approche abolitionniste qui met l'emphase sur la pratique du droit ancrée dans les mouvements sociaux (« movement lawyering »), qui s'aligne sur des réformes non réformistes et qui s'oppose aux logiques carcérales. Walters reconnaît les tensions dialectiques inhérentes au travail des avocat·e·s orienté·e·s vers la justice opérant au sein de systèmes oppressifs. Les avocat·e·s abolitionnistes doivent composer avec ces tensions et utiliser leurs compétences pour contester les institutions nuisibles tout en favorisant des voies génératives vers l'abolition.

> Where life is precious, life is precious.
> - Ruth Wilson Gilmore

There is little empirical evidence that the corrosive imprisonment and punishment project reduces crime or makes communities safer.[1] In fact, some studies suggest that incarceration may increase recidivism.[2] Meanwhile, incarceration concentrated in Indigenous and Black communities reduces employment rates and income levels, erodes social relationships, and places increased socioeconomic strain on already marginalized communities.[3] Rather than improving public safety, incarceration further exacerbates social problems and perpetuates inequality.[4] Inequality and poverty significantly increase the likelihood a person will face social challenges and criminalization.[5]

---

[1] Steven Raphael and Michael A Stoll, *Do Prisons Make us Safer?: The Benefits and Costs of the Prison Boom* (New York: Russell Sage Foundation, 2009) at 153.

[2] *Ibid*.

[3] Akwasi Owusu-Bempah and Camisha Sibblis, "Expert Report on Crime, Criminal Justice and the Experience of Black Canadians in Toronto, Ontario" (2018) at 12, online (PDF): <handbook.law.utoronto.ca> [perma.cc/D3NW-BCQU].

[4] *Ibid* at 12.

[5] John Howard Society of Ontario, "Reality Check: Poverty and the criminal justice system go hand-in-hand" (1 January 2013), online: <johnhoward.on.ca> [perma.cc/GAK5-BQG3].

In recent years, legal actors and advocates in North America have become more vocal about the inherent violence of policing and imprisonment. Campaigns like the "progressive prosecutor" movement in America[6] and Canadian efforts to decarcerate during the height of the COVID-19 pandemic[7] indicate this. An abolitionist lawyering ethic[8] is urgent because Canadian punishment systems often treat criminalized, illegalized, marginalized and vulnerable people as disposable. Lawyers who represent these criminalized and illegalized people engage in crucial service provision and often are the difference between their clients' deportation or incarceration. But I suggest rigorous representation without a clear ethic will not create systems change.

To achieve critical gains towards prison abolition, lawyers committed to transformative change should develop a clear set of political commitments and practices: an abolitionist lawyering ethic.[9] The Canadian legal order views Canada's "justice" system as apolitical and just, but we know the outcomes are unjust; state violence is doled out along racial and class lines. Lawyers oriented towards justice should cultivate a clear political analysis and concrete strategic goals if we hope to end human caging in our lifetime. While legal strategies can produce discrete wins for social movements, the courtroom is only one site of political struggle. The criminal legal system is a problem too large to be transformed exclusively through litigation. There is latent political opportunity among direct service providers waiting to be tapped. Lawyers, especially those working in the criminal legal system, can develop an explicit ethic to leverage their practice within and against systemic violence more effectively. This chapter proceeds in two parts. In the first section, I explain why abolition is an urgent project and why prisons are the wrong answer to the public safety question. In the second section, I outline suggested elements of an abolitionist ethic. I hope this discussion offers shape to the ethic I suggest lawyers need to help realize fundamental systems change.

---

[6] Angela J Davis, "Reimagining Prosecution: A Growing Progressive Movement" (2019) 3:1 UCLA CJLR.

[7] Sabrina Jones, "'They're petri dishes for COVID-19': Advocates call for decarceration, vaccination of inmates", *CBC News* (20 March 2021), online: <cbc.ca/news/canada/toronto/advocate-call-for-decarceration-more-vaccines-1.5957949>.

[8] Debra Parkes, "Solitary Confinement, Prisoner Litigation, and the Possibility of a Prison Abolitionist Lawyering Ethic" (2017) 32:2 CJLS 165 at 179-185.

[9] *Ibid.*

Abolitionist lawyers have the range to step outside their professional class and participate in community-based efforts for social change. Abolitionist lawyers work with grassroots movements to resist state violence, avoid reformist efforts that further entrench the carceral state, unlearn carceral logics and prioritize community care. Developing and fortifying an abolitionist lawyering ethic also requires the ability to hold myriad tensions as both an abolitionist and a criminal legal system participant. Though the master's tools are unlikely to dismantle the master's house, those tools may be employed to weaken its foundation and create space for transformative work to flourish.

Why Abolition

The Attica Liberation Faction was a group of incarcerated organizers who peacefully submitted upwards of 30 demands to prison administrators in July 1971 to improve their conditions of confinement as part of their revolutionary struggle to abolish prisons.[10] The list they produced included demands for improved living conditions, religious freedom, an end to mail censorship and improved access to phone calls to loved ones. Incarcerated people in Attica were overcrowded, abused, denied health care, and limited to one shower per week and one roll of toilet paper each month.[11] After months of peaceful resistance, on 9 September 1971, prisoners seized control of the institution. Four days later, state police raided the collective of politicized prisoners and killed 10 guards and 29 prisoners in the process. The Attica prison uprising was the largest prison rebellion in North America and one of the catalysts of North America's prison reform and prison abolition movement.[12] John "Dacajeweiah" Hill, one of the people incarcerated at Attica, wrote that the only true "antidote" to his conditions was "the complete abolition of prisons and the revolutionary

---

[10] See Heather Ann Thompson, *Blood in the Water: The Attica Prison Uprising of 1971 and its Legacy* (New York: Vintage Books, 2016); Orisanmi Burton, *Tip of the Spear: Black Radicalism, Prison Repression, and the Long Attica Revolt* (California: University of California Press, 2023) at 81.

[11] Thompson, *supra* note 10.

[12] Gerald Benjamin and Stephen P Rappaport, "Attica and Prison Reform" (1974) 31:3 Academy Political Science 200 at 210.

overthrow of the system that needs them—capitalism."[13] In his book, *Tip of the Spear: Black Radicalism, Prison Repression, and the Long Attica Revolt,* Dr. Orisanmi Burton writes that "when the captives rebelled, they ruptured an acute site of racial-colonial domination and sowed the seeds of something entirely new."[14] In this way, the long Attica Rebellion was "an epochal act of abolitionist worldmaking."[15]

Fifty years later, the issues that galvanized prisoners in Attica remain relevant today in prisons across Canada. The conditions of incarceration are not much better than the ones that led to the famous 1971 uprising. In August and September of 2018, prisoners in Burnside jail, a provincial jail in Nova Scotia, organized a strike to protest their conditions.[16] In some ways, their list of demands echoed that of the Attica Liberation Faction; they requested basic necessities like adequate clothing, meals, towels to shower with, and shoes that fit. Canadian prisoners regularly report substandard food quality and quantity. In 2018 the Office of the Correctional Investigator found that food quantity and quality issues were contributing factors to a deadly riot in Saskatchewan Penitentiary.[17] Prison guards use force against incarcerated people over 2,000 times per year.[18] Despite recent government legislation that purported to end the practice, prisoners are too often involuntarily placed in solitary confinement for days, weeks, or months.[19] There is no limit to the length of time someone can be placed in solitary.[20] These small dark cells often meet the United Nations

---

[13] Burton, *supra* note 10 at 81.

[14] *Ibid* at 82.

[15] *Ibid.*

[16] Michael Tutton, "Nova Scotia inmate protest rare and effective, national advocate says", CBC news (8 September 2018) online: <cbc.ca/news/canada/nova-scotia/nova-scotia-inmate-protest-burnside-jail-1.4815858>; See generally El Jones, *Abolitionist Intimacies* (Halifax: Fernwood Publishing, 2022).

[17] Office of the Correctional Investigator, *Office of the Correctional Investigator Annual Report 2017–2018,* online: <oci-bec.gc.ca/cnt/rpt/annrpt/annrpt20172018-eng.aspx>.

[18] Justin Ling, "Houses of hate: How Canada's prison system is broken", Maclean's (28 February 2021), online: <macleans.ca/news/canada/houses-of-hate-how-canadas-prison-system-is-broken/>.

[19] Jane B Sprott and Anthony N Doob, "Solitary Confinement, Torture and Canada's Structured Intervention Units" (2021) online: <https://www.crimsl.utoronto.ca/sites/www.crimsl.utoronto.ca/files/Torture%20Solitary%20SIUs%20%28Sprott%20Doob%2023%20Feb%202021%29.pdf>.

[20] Ling, *supra* note 18.

definition of torture and can erode the sanity of its inhabitants.[21] In 2017, 70 prisoners overdosed in Canadian penitentiaries.[22] Canadian prisons host "special handling units" where prisoners are encouraged, and potentially coerced, into undergoing chemical castration.[23] Prisons and jails are additional sites where systemic racism is borne out. Nearly one-third of prisoners in Canada are Indigenous and about nine per cent are Black. Black and Indigenous prisoners are twice as likely to be on the receiving end of use of force, are more likely to be classified as maximum security, are more likely to be classified as "gang" affiliated, are more likely to be forced into solitary confinement and are less likely to secure parole.[24]

For many, jails and prisons are sites of institutional violence and neglect. Decades of placing people in cages has yet to deliver a safer society. Criminalization and punishment do little to serve the overall purpose and principles of sentencing articulated in s. 718 of the *Criminal Code*.[25] Research has revealed that incarceration does not yield deterrence, and imprisonment does not reduce crime rates.[26] In 2002, the Canadian Solicitor General commissioned a study on the effects of prison sentences and intermediate sanctions on recidivism. The authors looked at 111 studies involving over 442,000 offenders and found some correlation between longer sentences and an increased recidivism rate.[27] In 2000, the Supreme Court of Canada acknowledged that there is little empirical evidence supporting the presumption that incarceration deters criminal behaviour.[28]

---

[21] The United Nations Standard Minimum Rules for the Treatment of Prisoners (the Nelson Mandela Rules), UNGA, 70th Sess, A/RES/70/175 (2015), annex at rules 43-44.

[22] Ling, *supra* note 18.

[23] *Ibid.*

[24] Office of the Correctional Investigator, *Office of the Correctional Investigator Annual Report 2021-2022*, online: <oci-bec.gc.ca/en/content/office-correctional-investigator-annual-report-2021-2022>.

[25] *Criminal Code*, RSC 1985, c C-46, s 718.

[26] Robyn Maynard, *Policing Black Lives: State Violence in Canada from Slavery to the Present* (Halifax: Fernwood Publishing, 2017) at 113.

[27] Paula Smith, Claire Goggin & Paul Gendreau, "The Effects of Prison Sentences and Intermediate Sanctions on Recidivism: General Effects and Individual Differences" (January 2002) Public Works and Government Services Canada, online (PDF): <publicsafety.gc.ca/cnt/rsrcs/pblctns/ffcts-prsn-sntncs/ffcts-prsn-sntncs-eng.pdf.>

[28] *R v Proulx*, 2000 SCC 5 at para 107; see also *R v Hills*, 2023 SCC 2 at para 137.

Why do we choose to treat people with cruelty and vengeance and hope that they will emerge rehabilitated? We are taught in school, through political narrative, and in our media, that policing and punishment protect us from violence. When the police arrest individual perpetrators of violence we should send those people away, to prison, where they can be punished and rehabilitated. We are taught that prisons and police keep us safe. In his book *The End of Policing* Alex Vitale describes this view of policing and punishment as "mythical."[29] Instead, he describes the criminal legal system as a "revenge factory" that is primarily concerned with retribution rather than with justice.[30]

In 2020 many Canadian residents were forced to consider, some for the first time, whether policing and prisons were in fact institutions that bring "safety" to our communities. On May 25, 2020, George Floyd was lynched by three men in uniform and the rest of the world had access to that moment on repeat.[31] In Canada, we mourned the death of Regis Korchinski-Paquet, a Black woman who fell from a high-rise in downtown Toronto moments after the police arrived on scene.[32] We were also shaken by the murder of Ejaz Choudry, a Muslim man who was shot and killed by police in his home.[33] This horrific police violence led to millions protesting in the streets in the midst of a global pandemic and a swift shift in public opinion on policing and punishment. Mere months before the COVID-19 pandemic, abolitionists and their political views were considered fringe, even extreme. In 2020, over half of Canadian residents (51 percent) supported the idea of defunding police and redirecting funds to alternative forms of social support.[34]

---

[29] Alex S Vitale, *The End of Policing* (London, UK: Verso Books, 2017) at 28.

[30] *Ibid.*

[31] See e.g. Evan Hill et al, "How George Floyd Was Killed in Police Custody" (24 January 2020) *The New York Times*, online: <nytimes.com/2020/05/31/us/george-floyd-investigation.html>.

[32] Wendy Gillis, "What happened the night Regis Korchinski-Paquet died, according to Ontario's police watchdog" (26 August 2020) *The Toronto Star*, online: <thestar.com/news/gta/what-happened-the-night-regis-korchinski-paquet-died-according-to-ontario-s-police-watchdog/article_0a1b0360-789f-5e9d-9602-0bfbd6a3cbf2.html>.

[33] Shanifa Nasser, "No charges in death of Ejaz Choudry, 62-year-old shot and killed by police while in crisis" (6 April 2021) CBC News, online: <cbc.ca/news/canada/toronto/ejaz-choudry-no-charges-siu-peel-police-1.5976266>.

[34] Ipsos, "Canadians Divided on Whether to Defund the Police: 51% Support the Idea, 49% Oppose It" (27 July 2020), online: <https://www.ipsos.com/en-ca/news-and-polls/Canadians-Divided-On-Whether-To-Defund-Police>.

Abolitionists recognize that although people of all races and socioeconomic classes engage in criminalized behaviour, most people who are monitored, investigated, charged, convicted and incarcerated are poor, racialized, undocumented, and marginalized.[35] Racialization, poverty, mental disabilities and substance use act as proxies for criminality in the Canadian criminal legal system.[36] Though these communities are not "more criminal" than the white and powerful, they are disproportionately pursued as targets of criminalization by law enforcement.[37]

Prisons offer the public a symbol of safety, but rather than protecting society from "dangerous" people, prisons engender hostility and anger towards punishment institutions and the systems that empower them. As articulated above, prisons are sites of institutional violence and abuse. The authors of *Instead of Prisons* ask, "Can a person be 'corrected' in a cage? Can humanization occur in a dehumanizing atmosphere?"[38] Rehabilitation and healing are phenomena less likely to take place while a person is behind bars and more likely to take place in communities of care in co-operation with people invested in the harm-doers' well-being.[39] Rampant economic inequity creates the conditions for criminalized behaviour, while Canada's social systems fail to offer adequate options for poor and marginalized people to live dignified lives. Proactive national projects like housing for all and instituting a guaranteed livable income should displace punitive, reactive responses to harm.[40]

Abolitionist Lawyering

The notion of practising prison abolition as a lawyer may be reasonably viewed as contradictory. In her 1984 essay Audre Lorde writes

---

[35] Mark Morris, ed, *Instead of Prisons: A Handbook for Abolitionists* (Brooklyn: Faculty Press, 1976) at c 2 online: <prisonpolicy.org/scans/instead_of_prisons/chapter2.shtml>.

[36] Maynard, *supra* note 26 at 112.

[37] *Ibid.*

[38] Morris, *supra* note 35.

[39] *Ibid*; Vitale, *supra* note 29.

[40] Office of Senator Kim Pate, "Why a Guaranteed Livable Income?" at 1 online (PDF): <sencanada.ca/media/366455/senpate_glibi-perspective-document_08-15-2020_e.pdf>.

that "the master's tools will never dismantle the master's house. They may allow us temporarily to beat him at his own game, but they will never enable us to bring about genuine change."[41] This now-popular refrain has been used often as a reference point for interrogating whether law can be a vehicle for social transformation.[42] Many scholars and activists have suggested the answer is no. Well-known radical labour lawyer Victor Rabinowitz explained what, in his view, were the law's limits in effecting broad systems change: "All systems of law are constructed to protect the State and its economic base. Conduct that seriously threatens the survival of the State or that would effectuate a basic change in the economic system is, ipso facto, 'illegal.' Those in whose interests the State exists will necessarily make laws to protect those interests and that state."[43] In this way, immigration and refugee lawyers work to prevent their clients from being deported or further criminalized, but they also help the immigration system run more smoothly. Criminal defence lawyers do everything in their power to prevent their client from being convicted, but they are also the bedrock of an "efficient" punishment system. While lawyers can offer a lifeline by helping their vulnerable clients navigate a complicated system, their role also implicates them in that same system.

Legal strategies are only one of many methods available for community organizers and advocates to challenge and reform existing systems. In Dean Spade's article, "For Those Considering Law School," he rightly questions whether individuals committed to substantive justice should necessarily pursue a legal education at all.[44] Movement history reveals that precedent-setting lawsuits do not often bring about lasting social change. Transformation most often comes from broad, participatory, mass-based community mobilization.[45] The structural role of lawyers is to sustain the social, political, and economic interests of the powerful—not challenge it. Because few

[41] Audre Lorde, "The Master's Tools Will Never Dismantle the Master's House" in *Sister Outsider: Essays and Speeches* (Berkeley: Crossing Press, 1984) 110 at 111.

[42] Paul Butler, "Progressive Prosecutors Are Not Trying to Dismantle the Master's House, and the Master Wouldn't Let Them Anyway" (2022) 90:5 Fordham L Rev 1983 at 1985.

[43] *Ibid* at 1986.

[44] Dean Spade, "For Those Considering Law School" (2010) 6 unbound: Unbound Harvard J Leg Left 111.

[45] *Ibid* at 113.

poor and marginalized people have access to legal representation when they need it, lawyers often act for the powerful to reinforce systems of inequity and enforce settler colonial law.

I acknowledge throughout this paper that navigating these tensions is not easy. But we are not the first or the last lawyers attempting to transform a system while operating within it. For lawyers who wish to use their legal education and training to transform the existing system, we can consider strategies employed by advocates from the past and the present. These examples demonstrate that movement law[46], a focus on strategies that undermine institutional power rather than reify it[47], resistance to carceral logics[48], and a personal commitment to building positive alternatives to punishment and control [49] are all strategies abolitionist lawyers might employ and are components of a critical legal practice.

Movement Lawyering

An abolitionist lawyering ethic necessarily includes a practice of movement law because the criminal legal system is multi-faceted and carceral logics are too central to our culture for abolition to be independently realized in the courtroom. The movement for prison abolition began in community as a necessary response to oppression, and ongoing strategies towards transformation are continually generated in community. Movement lawyers view themselves not as separate from communities of struggle, but rather as part of those communities and commit themselves to that struggle for transformative change.

In his study of abolitionist lawyers fighting the 1850 Fugitive Slave Law, Daniel Farbman found that while these lawyers employed every possible legal strategy to frustrate and dismantle the system within which they were practising, they also knew they would not end slavery in the courtroom.[50] They understood that abolishing slavery required a broad political effort and that courts were only one site of resistance. They saw the clients they represented as not only

---

[46] Amna A Akbar, Sameer M Ashar & Jocelyn Simonson, "Movement Law" (2021) 73:4 Stan L Rev 821.

[47] Parkes, *supra* note 8 at 183.

[48] *Ibid*.

[49] See Allegra M McLeod, "Prison Abolition and Grounded Justice" (2015) 62 UCLA L Rev 1156.

[50] Daniel Farbman, "Resistance Lawyering" (2019) 107 Cal L Rev 1877 at 1887–1899.

individual clients with needs, but also potential opportunities to wage strategic battles against slavery.[51] These abolitionist lawyers were reasonably successful in their efforts; about 40 percent of enslaved people caught in the Fugitive Slave Law accessed freedom.[52] They not only helped free their clients, they also built political opposition to slavery locally and nationally by broadcasting their anti-slavery message through the media.[53] They were positioned to help Black people escaping slavery because they were already part of powerful grassroots networks.[54] These abolitionist lawyers used legal strategies to frustrate and delay the execution of the 1850 Fugitive Slave law and their tactics created opportunities for organizers to develop plans for escape, flood courtrooms, and raise money to buy fugitives' freedom.[55] They worked in tandem with community organizers to achieve freedom for individual fugitives and dismantle the system of slavery. Both broad-based mobilization and individual trial success were central goals of the anti-slavery movement challenging the horrific 1850 laws.

Movement lawyering involves ongoing relationship building with poor, working class, migrant, criminalized, and marginalized communities. These lawyers show up in community spaces and develop relationships of trust with people they serve so that when their legal training is required, movement lawyers can engage with members of community as equals. They can take direction from community members rather than viewing themselves as separate and apart from community struggle. This is often what distinguishes movement lawyers from other legal service providers. Movement lawyering is different from discrete, individualized service provision because movement lawyers recognize most legal issues do not arise solely as a result of an individual's personal decision making or life conditions; legal issues often present as a symptom of broader societal issues of poverty, systemic racism, white supremacy, ableism, and cis-heteropatriarchy.

In 2020, Sima Atri and Leora Smith co-founded a non-profit committed to movement lawyering called the Community Justice

---

[51] *Ibid*.
[52] *Ibid* at 1901.
[53] *Ibid* at 1898.
[54] *Ibid* at 1943.
[55] *Ibid* at 1898.

Collective (CJC). Their goal was to support social movements by offering community-based legal assistance with the intent of effecting systemic change.[56] The Community Justice Collective has provided legal support to a range of collectives, including gig workers seeking collective-bargaining rights, Indigenous land defenders facing criminal charges for protest activity, and victims of police violence seeking accountability for state-sanctioned harm.

Traditional legal practice is individual, not community oriented. At the Landlord and Tenant Board, the CJC's pro bono practice resisted the bifurcation of individual vs collective wins. During the spring of 2020, two groups of tenants created tenant associations to fight evictions for individuals who fell behind on their rent. Rather than each individual tenant retaining lawyers or representing themselves before the tribunal, the CJC asked the Landlord and Tenant Board (LTB) to let them represent all members of the tenant associations at a single hearing. The LTB allowed it. The CJC argued landlords were targeting tenants for eviction in retaliation for tenants attempting to bargaining collectively. The LTB agreed that tenants were subject to "differential treatment" based on their involvement with the tenant association and ruled the landlord's behaviour unlawful. The CJC's collective approach to representation allowed them to launch cohesive, consistent legal arguments and secure a just result for all association members.

Movement lawyers view their work as building people power in myriad ways and understand that litigation can, at best, complement social change movements. For example, CJC lawyers defended criminalized unhoused people living in temporary and semi-permanent housing communities in city parks. Residents and protestors were charged with trespassing or resisting arrest when police violently dismantled these essential housing locations. Here, the lawyers' litigation contributions were not the centre of the movement to assert a fundamental right to housing; instead CJC lawyers offered legal services that helped facilitate the work encampment residents were already doing. With legal representation helping them navigate the

---

[56] Simon Lewsen, "The 2021 Precedent Innovation Awards: The Community Justice Collective" (7 December 2021), Precedent (blog), online: <lawandstyle.ca/innovation/the-2021-precedent-innovation-awards-the-community-justice-collective/>.

legal system, residents were better equipped to continue their advocacy campaign for safe housing.[57]

Abolitionist movements need more legally trained contributors who share the collective vision for a future without policing, punishment, or prisons. Traditional lawyers are often exclusively accountable to their client, their firm or legal organization, and their regulator. Movement lawyers also maintain a relationship of accountability with the communities they serve. These lawyers maintain trusting relationships with grassroots organizers and impacted community members. They use their training to execute advocacy strategies both inside and outside formal law-making spaces.[58]

Non-Reformist Reforms

Not all reforms are good reforms. Not all reforms are bad reforms either. Abolitionist lawyers must have the political clarity to know the difference.

Prisons are spaces where horrific harm and abuse takes place. Incarcerated people are regularly strip-searched, assaulted, verbally abused, and sexually exploited. Prisoners are provided inadequate physical and mental health care and are regularly deprived of their basic needs. Prisons are also sites of what might be termed "mundane" cruelty. Incarcerated people are isolated from their family, friends, and support system. They are under-stimulated and often prevented from accessing interesting books, quality clothing, good food, and sexual intimacy. Prisoners express feelings of being alone, forgotten, and erased; like being "buried alive."[59] In these ways, prisoners are denied their humanity and dignity. For those of us who care for those inside, the "mundane" nature of these small cruelties feel urgent. It is easy to focus on improving the conditions of confinement in an effort to preserve the dignity of our loved ones. Unfortunately, efforts to improve the material conditions of prisoners can be co-opted by the institution and used as justification to invest more public

---

[57] *Ibid*; The Canadian Press, "Toronto homeless, their supporters vow to fight charges in encampment clearings" (16 September 2021) *Toronto Star*, online: <thestar.com/news/gta/toronto-homeless-their-supporters-vow-to-fight-charges-in-encampment-clearings/article_d197328c-0db0-522f-a036-45e4a3910842.html>.

[58] Scott L Cummings, "Movement Lawyering" (2020) 27:1 Ind J of Global Legal Stud 87 at 97.

[59] Jones, *supra* note 16 at 31.

money into human caging and expand the carceral project. There is no easy answer to this inherent tension. Abolitionists struggle to be strategic in our efforts to avoid inadvertently positioning *better prisons* as the alternative to prisons. The allure of reform can distract us from our goal: no prisons at all.

Activists, scholars, lawyers and community members have created tools to help us navigate these hard questions. In his book *Usual Cruelty*, Alec Karakatsanis suggests that before deciding whether a policy or proposal is meaningful, we should ask this question, "Would this reform result in greater or fewer resources going to the punishment bureaucracy?"[60] Rather than orienting away from incarceration, some reforms can add legitimacy to the current system and retrench the status quo. For example, some community members advocate for better mental health provision inside prisons and jails, while others advocate for individuals with mental health needs to be decarcerated entirely and either transferred to an appropriate mental health institution or into community to be closer to networks of support and to access culturally relevant programming. While adequate mental health provision for incarcerated people is important, institutionally funded mental health care providers face a unique set of obstacles when providing adequate care inside prisons and jails. The John Howard Society points out the contradiction of prisons and jails providing health care to incarcerated people. They say that correctional facilities are "designed to punish" and this goal is in conflict "with the accessibility and well-being elements associated with health care."[61] The question of how best to improve the material conditions of prisoners while avoiding further entrenchment of prisons is a fraught, ongoing challenge.

Often there is no clear answer, and advocates must urgently push for both short-term and medium to long-term goals. When the COVID-19 pandemic swept the globe, prisoners were at high risk of transmission and death because jails and prisons are congregate settings with dubious sanitation practices. Prisoners and their advocates could not reasonably choose between advocating for adequate PPE

---

[60] Alec Karakatsanis, *Usual Cruelty: The Complicity of Lawyers in the Criminal Injustice System* (New York: The New Press, 2019) at 96.

[61] John Howard Society of Ontario, "Myth: People who are incarcerated receive the same health care as the rest of Ontarians" (21 March 2017) The Counter Point, online (PDF): <johnhoward.on.ca/> [perma.cc/5CTQ-LR2M].

and immediate release of prisoners, they had to demand both. When punishment bureaucrats implemented extended lockdowns and solitary confinement as the "safe" institutional response to the COVID-19 pandemic, prisoners and their advocates argued that decarceration was the only way to reduce transmission and keep prisoners, staff, and the outside community safer. This call for early parole and decarceration became a familiar overture in the media and public discourse. Like the abolitionist lawyers of the 1800s, prison advocates used the COVID-19 pandemic as an opportunity to indict the Correctional Service of Canada for the abhorrent conditions of confinement. Their efforts shifted the Overton window on decarceration and provided opportunities for lawyers, service providers and other bureaucrats to join the call. As a result, during the first wave of the pandemic, the number of prisoners in Canadian prisons and jails was reduced by 19 percent.[62]

In addition to offering legal services and advice to individuals, abolitionist lawyers should remain connected with community movements to help differentiate between reforms that retrench power within punishment bureaucracies and "a move towards non-reformist reforms" that can divert power from carceral systems and pave the way for transformation. While abolitionist lawyers may not always have the latitude to demand immediate decarceration for their clients, they can make strategic demands that, at minimum, do not undermine abolitionist movements. Austrian-French theorist André Gorz articulated a strategy for systems transformation that includes taking "long-term and conscious action" towards broader movement goals.[63] He suggests that smaller structural changes can form elements of longer-term strategies that help movements build power and advance grassroots struggles for equity and freedom. Non-reformist reforms do not accommodate the current system; they undermine it. He writes, "a non-reformist reform is determined not in terms of what can be, but what should be." In this way, non-reformist reforms should light the path to alternative futures. In Amna Akbar's reading of Gorz,

---

[62] Sarah Smellie, "Calls grow for inmate releases as COVID-19 caseloads climb in jails and prisons", CBC News (5 January 2022), online: <cbc.ca/news/politics/calls-grow-inmate-release-covid-outbreaks-1.6304878>.

[63] Mark Engler and Paul Engler, "André Gorz's Non-Reformist Reforms Show How We Can Transform the World Today", Jacobin Magazine (22 July 2021), online: <jacobinmag.com/2021/07/andre-gorz-non-reformist-reforms-revolution-political-theory>.

non-reformist reforms are just as much about the exercise of people power as they are about the result. In Gorz's view, community efforts to shift their conditions are also an "experiment in the possibility of their own emancipation."[64] Abolitionist lawyers view themselves as part of these struggles to build collective power, trust, and understanding. Whenever possible, they make decisions in their practice that build collective power rather than state power.

In response to short-sighted calls for liberal reforms in the wake of the endemic police killings of 2020, a collective of abolitionists created a resource called 8 to Abolition to help orient community organizers towards a transformative future beyond policing and prisons. I view these eight demands as a helpful example of a move towards non-reformist reforms. The authors of 8 to Abolition are a collective of Black, Latinx, Asian, Arab, Muslim, white, trans, queer, migrant, disabled, sex working, caregiving, and working-class abolitionists. The eight abolitionist demands include 1) defunding the police 2) demilitarizing communities 3) removing police from schools 4) freeing people from prisons and jails 5) repealing laws that criminalize survival 6) investing in community self-governance 7) providing safe, accessible housing for everyone and 8) fully investing in care, not cops.[65] The 8 to Abolition resource offers a helpful example of how some communities develop a set of abolitionist demands. It is also a resource for abolitionist lawyers to reflect on in their practice. Where can the work of lawyers fit within frameworks of community organizing for transformative change? Also, what additional skills might be worth developing as a member of a movement for freedom, safety, and peace?

Unlearning Carceral Logics, Towards an Ethic of Care

The criminal legal system has trained us to equate justice and accountability with criminalization and punishment. When Gerald Stanley was acquitted by an all-white jury for killing an Indigenous man named Colten Boushie, Boushie's family pointed out the gross injustice of the system.[66] But also, when off-duty officer Michael Theriault

---

[64] *Ibid.*

[65] Mon Mohapatra et al, "8 to Abolition: Abolitionist Policy Changes to Demand from your City Officials" (2020) online: <arks.princeton.edu/ark:/88435/dspo11r66j429x>.

[66] Angela Brown, "Boushie family still looking for justice", Battlefords Now (11 February 2022), online:<battlefordsnow.com/2022/02/11/boushie-family-still-looking-

blinded a young Dafonte Miller and was sentenced to nine months incarceration, some members of the Black community felt Theriault's sentence was little more than a slap on the wrist.[67]

Prison abolitionists seek accountability, healing, and reconciliation for all parties when violence or harm happens. These are outcomes the criminal legal system rarely offers. Carceral logics shape both interpersonal and institutional responses to harm. It presumes that removing a person's liberty necessarily leads to safer communities. Non-carceral solutions challenge assumptions about punishment through caging and pushes us to develop responses to harm that respect individuals' bodily autonomy. To effectively pursue non-reformist reforms and creative responses to harm, abolitionist lawyers will be in constant tension with criminal legal systems and its advocates who will default to carceral remedies. For example, a lawyer advocating for her client to receive adequate health care can choose to argue her client be placed in a community-based mental health facility rather than requesting health care needs to be met in custody. Debra Parkes terms the practice of expanding the range of legal remedies for incarcerated people "thinking outside the bars."[68]

In addition to thinking outside the bars in his legal practice, an abolitionist lawyer implicates himself in the process of creating alternatives to the punishment system. While mass protests and public campaigns calling for abolition are valuable tools to galvanize the public, they are only a precursor to the work of building lasting alternatives to policing and punishment. The modern prison abolitionist movement draws on ideas from early slavery abolitionists like W. E. B. Du Bois. Du Bois understood abolition not only as an effort to end the formal process of chattel slavery, but also as a positive project to create conditions for liberation.[69] In this way, the modern abolitionist

---

for-justice/>.

[67] See e.g. rania.writes, "before you come with all your foolish "meanwhile in Canada" shit remember that #BarbaraKentner's family sits in a court room hearing how she was killed as "a joke"." (4 November 2020), online: <instagram.com> [perma.cc/AV79-JYRL]; Notanotherblacklife, "Sending strength to Dafonte Miller & his family." (5 november 2020), online: <twitter.com> [perma.cc/EK7Z-YNLR].

[68] Parkes, *supra* note 8 at 31.

[69] W E Burghardt Du Bois, *Black Reconstruction in America*, 1st ed (New York: Harcourt, Brace and Company, 1935) at 189 ("The abolition of slavery meant not simply abolition of legal ownership of the slave; it meant the uplift of slaves and their eventual incorporation into the body civil, politic, and social, of the United States").

framework must include the creation of substitutive social projects and institutions that redesign our public lives and address shared social problems like affordable housing, food security, interpersonal conflict mediation, and mental health care.[70] We might conceive of abolition as both decarceral and substitutive, as we develop alternative systems for social regulation. Lawyers committed to social change are part of this learning because we are simply community members with the same challenges, needs, and tensions as others.

Most of us lack the tools to prevent and respond to violence. Our culture's ideological allegiance to policing and prisons is mostly rooted in fear of violence without protection; no one wants to see harm continue unchecked. Now that we know there is little evidence that policing and prisons reduce violence and abuse in our communities, we are responsible for helping to create alternative processes to prevent and respond to harm. In our lifetimes, each of us is implicated in harm or violence either as a perpetrator, survivor or bystander. In *Practicing New Worlds: Abolition and Emergent Strategies*, Andrea J. Ritchie mobilizes adrienne maree brown's principle of the fractal to help ground the everyday project of abolition. In *Emergent Strategy: Shaping Change, Changing Worlds* adrienne maree brown argues that complex systems are fractal: small or local structures are replicated to create larger structures. This is important because in brown's view, "until we have some sense of how to live our solutions locally, we won't be successful at implementing a just governance system regionally, nationally or globally."[71] Ritchie uses this reasoning to explain why the abolitionist project must be implemented on the interpersonal, human level. Abolitionist lawyers can and should commence the work of abolition by shifting the way they respond to conflict and harm in their families, communities, and institutions. By examining the ways we engage one another and shifting our responses to each other away from those of carcerality and disposability, abolition becomes an actionable, everyday practice.[72] The choice to divest from policing and punishment includes an obligation to begin reckoning with violence and harm in our personal

---

[70] McLeod, *supra* note 49 at 1163.

[71] adrienne maree brown, *Emergent Strategy: Shaping Change, Changing Worlds* (Chico, California: AK Press, 2017) at 54.

[72] Andrea J Ritchie, *Practicing New Worlds: Abolition and Emergent Strategies* (Chico, California: AK Press, 2023).

relationships. It also involves a commitment to build community power, knowledge, capacity, and interdependence until we render the current carceral system obsolete.

Conclusion

An abolitionist lawyering ethic is not fixed. Each legal advocate can and should define her lawyering ethic according to her own values and location. Abolitionists often disagree on degree, method, timeline—but we all agree that we cannot cage, abuse, and punish ourselves into a safe society. Lawyers have the potential to make substantial contributions to the abolitionist movement, but they must develop a critical and strategic lawyering ethic in service of their goals. Without an abolitionist lawyering ethic, even well-intentioned lawyers can be absorbed into the punishment bureaucracy and used to maintain institutional interests. Abolitionist lawyers are also movement lawyers. They develop trusting relationships with on-the-ground organizers so they are well positioned to provide legal services that align with community goals. They can differentiate between a strategy that will entrench the status quo from one that will divest power from the carceral state and advance transformation. They are careful not to succumb to carceral logics; instead they help build positive substitutive projects as alternatives to punishment. Through the tensions and the contradictions, abolitionist lawyers are disciplined cultivators of hope.[73]

---

[73] See generally Jeremy Scahill, "Hope is a discipline: Mariame Kaba on Dismantling the Carceral State" The Intercepted (17 March 2021) online (podcast with transcript): <theintercept.com/2021/03/17/intercepted-mariame-kaba-abolitionist-organizing/>.

Être puni·e sans nécessairement être condamné·e : la punitivité avant procès et au-delà de la matière criminelle en droit canadien

Véronique Fortin et João Velloso

Résumé

Ce chapitre aborde la question de la punitivité dans le droit canadien, en mettant en lumière l'écart entre le droit criminel tel que défini par la doctrine classique et sa réalité empirique. Il s'intéresse aux pressions systémiques qui entraînent une forme de punition avant l'adjudication de culpabilité. Trois aspects de la procédure criminelle sont explorés, illustrant cette punition sans condamnation : la négociation de plaidoyers, la détention provisoire et les conditions de mise en liberté avant procès. Ce chapitre met en évidence les différentes dimensions de la transformation du rôle répressif de l'État, en s'appuyant sur la notion de « justice managériale » développée entre autres par Issa Kohler-Hausmann. Il montre également que cette transformation déborde du cadre du droit criminel, rejoignant la critique de Beckett et Murakawa sur l'« état carcéral fantôme ». En conclusion, il souligne l'existence d'une punitivité qui échappe aux garanties procédurales du droit criminel et qui impacte particulièrement les populations marginalisées, tout en restant souvent dans l'angle mort des spécialistes du droit criminel.

Abstract

This chapter addresses the issue of punitiveness in Canadian law, high-lighting the gap between criminal law as defined by classical doctrine and its empirical reality. It focuses on the systemic pressures that lead to a form of punishment before the adjudication of guilt. Three aspects of criminal procedure are explored, illustrating this punishment with-out conviction: plea bargaining, pre-trial detention, and conditions of release before trial. The chapter highlights the various dimensions of the transformation of the repressive role of the state, relying on the notion of "managerial justice" developed by Issa Kohler-Hausmann among others. It also shows that this transformation extends beyond the framework of criminal law, joining Beckett and Murakawa's cri-tique of the "shadow carceral state." In conclusion, it underlines the existence of a punitiveness that escapes the procedural safeguards of criminal law, particularly affecting marginalized populations, while often remaining in the blind spot of criminal law specialists.

L e chapitre qui suit traite de la punitivité en droit canadien. Nous nous intéressons à l'écart entre le droit criminel canadien, tel qu'il est défini par la doctrine classique, et sa réalité empirique, et notamment aux différentes pressions systémiques qui font que la punition survient parfois avant l'adjudication de culpabilité. Nous nous concentrons donc sur trois exemples de procédure criminelle qui ont pour effet de punir sans condamner : la négociation de plaidoyers, la détention provisoire et les conditions de mise en liberté avant procès. Dans ce chapitre, nous exposons différentes dimensions de la transformation du rôle répressif de l'État. La justice managériale, pour reprendre l'expression d'Issa Kohler-Hausmann[1], transforme la prise en charge criminelle. Mais elle fait aussi déborder le contrôle social en dehors du droit criminel. Cet élargissement de la pénalité a aussi été dénoncé par Beckett et Murakawa sous l'expression « *shadow carceral state* » (État carcéral fantôme)[2]. Nous

---

[1] Issa Kohler-Hausmann, *Misdemeanorland: Criminal Courts and Social Control in an Age of Broken Windows Policing*, Princeton, Princeton University Press, 2019; Issa Kohler-Hausmann, « Managerial Justice and Mass Misdemeanors » (2014) 66:3 Stan L Rev 611 [*Kohler-Hausmann 2019*].

[2] Katherine Beckett et Naomi Murakawa, « Mapping the Shadow Carceral State: Toward an Institutionally Capacious Approach to Punishment » (2012) 16:2 Theoretical Criminology 221 [*Beckett et Murakawa*].

relevons donc en conclusion la punitivité qui dépasse les limites du droit criminel, celle qui ne bénéficie pas nécessairement des garanties procédurales développées dans le cadre du droit criminel, celle qui reste souvent dans l'angle mort des criminalistes et qui pourtant a des conséquences néfastes sur les populations marginalisées.

Justice managériale et punition avant adjudication : l'écart entre la doctrine et la réalité empirique du droit criminel

> Le droit criminel vise à réduire les conduites socialement préjudiciables en énonçant et en punissant ce qui est inacceptable. Ses objectifs concernent donc essentiellement la dénonciation, la dissuasion et la punition de comportements jugés incorrects et mauvais par nature. Les crimes constituent les infractions les plus graves et sont passibles des peines les plus lourdes, car ils enfreignent des valeurs sociales fondamentales[3].

Une infraction grave, une sanction lourde qui vise la dénonciation, la dissuasion et la punition parce que l'ordre public a été ébranlé. Voilà la définition classique du droit criminel, une branche du droit public canadien de compétence fédérale. En première année de droit, le cours d'introduction au droit criminel et pénal enseignera typiquement les grands principes de la responsabilité pénale : l'*actus reus*, la *mens rea*, la classification des infractions, les moyens de défense et, s'il reste assez de temps dans la session, quelques notions de détermination de la peine et de garanties procédurales protégées par la *Charte canadienne des droits et libertés*[4].

Comme l'écrivent les auteurs d'un manuel de droit criminel, les professeurs Don Stuart et Steve Coughlan,

> In our view the major focus for studying criminal law in first-year law school should be on the tools that lawyers and judges

---

[3] Jean Jean Turgeon, « Fascicule 1 : Introduction au droit pénal général » à la p 1/1–1/29 dans Marie-Pierre Robert et Simon Roy, dir, JCQ Droit pénal – Droit pénal générale (7 novembre 2024).

[4] *Charte canadienne des droits et libertés*, art 7, partie I de la *Loi constitutionnelle de 1982*, constituant l'annexe B de la *Loi de 1982 sur le Canada* (R-U), 1982, c 11 [*Charte*].

must know and use in the daily business of the conduct of a criminal trial. It is obvious that law students, teachers and lawyers can better understand criminal law if they seek help from the many disciplines that now offer insights into the criminal justice system. However, time and energy are limited and choices have to be made. [...] Our choice is to concentrate on substantive principles and the trial context: the adversary system, how the elements of crime are proved, defences and sentencing issues. We promote a full inquiry into the methods of determining legal guilt and the major legal justifications and excuses[5].

En première année de droit, on enseignera ainsi l'importance primordiale de la présomption d'innocence ; soulignant que le droit criminel canadien, dans la tradition de la common law anglaise, a choisi de préférer qu'il y ait neuf coupables en liberté plutôt qu'un innocent en prison[6]. On enseignera aussi que le droit « répugne généralement à punir celui qui est moralement innocent[7], » c'est-à-dire celui qui n'a pas choisi, par un acte autonome, libre et réfléchi, d'enfreindre la loi. Mais il faut faire des choix, comme l'énoncent Stuart et Coughlan, et souvent les approches externes au droit seront laissées de côté pour occuper les heures parascolaires.

Bien que les grands principes du droit pénal soient fondateurs et cruciaux à toute formation en droit, une perspective critique[8] nous force à remarquer les nombreux angles morts des enseignements doctrinaux. Le premier de ceux-ci touche la population criminalisée. Bien que le droit criminel ait une vocation universelle, tous et toutes ne sont pas puni·es également. Malgré un manque criant de données

---

[5] Don Stuart et Steve Coughlan, *Learning Canadian Criminal Law*, 13e éd, Toronto, Carswell, 2015 à la p 7.

[6] William Blackstone, tel que cité par David Paciocco, *Getting Away with Murder: The Canadian Criminal Justice System*, Toronto, Irwin Law, 1999 à la p 177–78.

[7] *R c Sault Ste Marie*, 1978 CanLII 11 (CSC) à la p 1310, [1978] 2 RCS 1299.

[8] À cet égard, voir notamment l'excellent ouvrage de Jennie Abell, Elizabeth Sheehy et Natasha Bakht, *Criminal Law and Procedure: Cases, Context, Critique*, 5e éd, Concord, (ON), Captus Press, 2013 à la p 2, qui ont fait des choix différents dans la matière à couvrir et qui cherchent à exposer les enjeux de biais systémiques, comme le racisme, auxquels seront inévitablement confronté·es les étudiant·es qui auront une pratique en droit criminel. Merci à Rebecca Johnson d'avoir porté ce manuel à notre attention.

fondées sur la race[9], des chercheurs et chercheuses ont réussi à montrer la surreprésentation importante des personnes racisées et autochtones au sein du système de justice criminelle. Par exemple, Owusu-Bempah et ses collègues, à partir de données ontariennes de 2010, ont conclu que les hommes noirs risquaient cinq fois plus l'incarcération que les hommes blancs[10]. Au niveau canadien, les personnes noires représentaient 7,2 % des personnes sous supervision du système correctionnel fédéral en 2016, alors qu'elles représentaient tout juste 3,5 % de la population canadienne âgée de 15 ans et plus[11]. Quant aux personnes autochtones, alors qu'elles représentaient 3,8 % de la population canadienne en 2006, elles constituaient 18,5 % de la population sous supervision du système correctionnel fédéral[12]. En décembre 2021, l'enquêteur correctionnel décriait que « [d]ans un avenir très proche, le Canada franchira un triste cap : la moitié des femmes détenues dans le système carcéral fédéral seront d'origine autochtone, alors qu'elles représentent moins de 5 % de la population entière des femmes au Canada.[13] » Bien que les données soient rares, on sait également que les personnes à bas revenu ou sans emploi sont largement surreprésentées dans le système de justice criminelle[14].

Les enjeux de discrimination systémique dans le système de justice criminelle, en raison de ses racines coloniales et racistes, constituent une première et importante constatation, qui reste trop souvent dans l'angle mort d'un programme trop chargé. Mais non seulement les populations autochtones, racisées et marginalisées sont plus

---

[9] « Whitewashing Criminal Justice in Canada: Preventing Research through Data Suppression » (2011) 26:3 RCDS 653. Voir aussi Akwasi Owusu-Bempah et coll., « Race and Incarceration: The Representation and Characteristics of Black People in Provincial Correctional Facilities in Ontario, Canada » (2021) 13:4 Race & Justice 530, DOI: <10.1177/21533687211006461> [*Owusu-Bempah et coll.*].

[10] *Owusu-Bempah et al, supra* note 9.

[11] *Ibid.*

[12] Akwasi Owusu-Bempah et Scot Wortley, « Race, Crime, and Criminal Justice in Canada » dans Sandra M Bucerius and Michael Tonry, dir., *The Oxford Handbook of Ethnicity, Crime, and Immigration*, New York, Oxford University Press, coll. Oxford Handbooks Online, 2014 à la p 281–320

[13] Ivan Zinger, « La proportion de femmes autochtones détenues par le gouvernement fédéral approche les 50 % : l'enquêteur correctionnel publie un communiqué », Bureau de l'enquêteur correctionnel (17 décembre 2021), en ligne : <oci-bec.gc.ca/fr/>.

[14] Marie-Ève Sylvestre, « Vers un système de justice minimaliste et transformateur » : essai sur les principes et objectifs de détermination de la peine, préparé pour le ministère de la Justice du Canada, 2016-07-05, en ligne : <justice.gc.ca>.

souvent criminalisées, elles sont également plus souvent punies sans être condamnées. Aux fins de ce chapitre sur la punitivité, adoptant une approche critique sociojuridique[15], on remarquera aussi que la réalité empirique du droit criminel pour le moins contraste avec la présomption d'innocence. Pour ce faire, nous nous appuierons sur trois exemples : la négociation de plaidoyers, la détention provisoire et les conditions de mise en liberté avant procès. Il va sans dire que ces exemples ne sont pas exhaustifs et qu'ils constituent des illustrations d'un phénomène complexe, décrit ici de façon plutôt impressionniste par souci de concision.

La négociation de plaidoyers

Bon an mal an, 90 % des causes en droit criminel se règlent par des négociations de plaidoyers, c'est-à-dire sans aller à procès, sans adjudication de culpabilité[16]. La négociation de plaidoyer est « toute entente en vertu de laquelle l'accusé consent à plaider coupable en échange de la promesse par la Couronne de faire ou de ne pas faire quelque chose[17]. » La négociation peut survenir à tout moment en droit canadien, que ce soit avant la première comparution ou en cours même de procès. Les personnes accusées sont toutefois incitées à plaider rapidement coupables, pour minimiser le stress et les frais liés au procès[18], mais aussi pour mettre fin aux conditions de mise en liberté ou sortir d'une détention provisoire, comme on le verra plus loin. La négociation peut porter tant sur les accusations, les procédures que l'énoncé des faits, mais le plus souvent elle concerne la peine. La peine est le cœur du droit criminel. L'encadrement du pouvoir de

---

[15] Voir par exemple Susan S. Silbey et Austin Sarat, « Critical Traditions in Law and Society Research » (1987) 21:1 Law & Soc'y Rev 165.

[16] Bob Runciman et George Baker, Justice différée, justice refusée : l'urgence de réduire les longs délais dans le système judiciaire au Canada, Rapport final du Comité sénatorial permanent des affaires juridiques et constitutionnelles, *Justice différée, justice refusée : l'urgence de réduire les longs délais dans le système judiciaire au Canada (rapport final)*, juin 2017, à la p 50. Voir aussi Elsa Euvrard et Chloé Leclerc, « Les avocats de la défense dans les négociations des plaidoyers de culpabilité : quelles pratiques ? » (2015) 12 Champ pénal/Penal Field, en ligne : <journals.openedition.org/champpenal/9071>.

[17] Commission de réforme du droit du Canada, « Les discussions et ententes sur le plaidoyer » (1989) Ministère de la Justice, Document de travail no 60.

[18] Voir *R c Anthony-Cook*, 2016 CSC 43 (CanLII) au para 36, [2016] 2 RCS 204 [*Anthony-Cook*].

punir de l'État – puissant et énorme, allant jusqu'à prendre la liberté de quelqu'un pour la vie – est la raison d'être des garanties procédurales et de tous les grands principes de droit criminel. Pourtant, le quotidien des criminalistes est davantage composé de négociation des peines que de théories de cause sophistiquées dans des procès de longue haleine.

La common law veut que le procès criminel soit contradictoire (*adversarial* en anglais) : c'est dans le débat contradictoire qu'émerge la vérité[19]. Pourtant, le droit criminel est un droit négocié dans la grande majorité des cas. Le système repose sur cette négociation, elle est encouragée et célébrée. À partir des données historiques britanniques et américaines, le professeur américain Malcolm Feeley argumentait à la fin des années 1990 que le procès criminel a évolué depuis le 19e siècle. En effet, le processus de complexification du droit criminel a donné lieu à des procès plus imposants et impliquant plusieurs garanties procédurales ; il a consolidé le plaidoyer de culpabilité comme la forme de règlement des litiges par excellence[20]. Ce n'est pas seulement que les délais judiciaires exploseraient si l'ensemble des affaires criminelles allait à procès[21], c'est aussi que la justice criminelle n'est pas systématiquement équipée pour gérer des cas résultant d'une police professionnelle et d'une pratique criminelle spécialisée et sophistiquée (tant à la poursuite qu'à la défense).

Malcolm Feeley soulignait aussi les pressions systémiques pesant sur les personnes accusées et visant à les faire plaider coupables : « *the process is the punishment* » (la procédure est la punition),

---

[19] Jennifer Earl, « "The Process Is the Punishment": Thirty Years Later [Recension de The Process Is the Punishment: Handling Cases in a Lower Criminal Court, de Malcolm M Feeley] » (2008) 33:3 Law & Soc Inquiry 737 [*Jennifer Earl*] Malcolm M Feeley, *The Process Is the Punishment: Handling Cases in a Lower Criminal Court*, New York, Russell Sage Foundation, 1979.

[20] Malcolm M Feeley, « Legal Complexity and the Transformation of the Criminal Process: The Origins of Plea Bargaining » (1997) 31 Israel LR 183. Voir aussi le numéro spécial sur la négociation de plaidoyer de (1979) 13 : 2 Law & Soc'y Rev dirigé par Feeley.

[21] « Dans la mesure où elles font éviter des procès, les recommandations conjointes relatives à la peine permettent à notre système de justice de fonctionner plus efficacement. Je dirais en fait qu'elles lui permettent de fonctionner. Sans elles, notre système de justice serait mis à genoux, et s'effondrerait finalement sous son propre poids. » *Anthony-Cook, supra* note 18 au para 40.

écrivait-il dans son désormais célèbre ouvrage du même intitulé, en faisant allusion aux coûts (humains et financiers) des procédures d'avant-procès qui sont si élevés qu'ils deviennent plus onéreux que la peine envisagée. Tout compte fait, il vaut alors mieux plaider coupable que de faire valoir ses droits et se soumettre à un long et laborieux procès. Comme Jennifer Earl le souligne, les recherches de Feeley ont permis d'identifier :

> the shift from punishment after adjudication to pretrial punishment, from judges being responsible for sanctions to police and prosecutors being largely responsible for meting out sanctions, and to allowing others – such as bail bondsmen and defense attorneys – to also participate in the sanctioning process by affecting how long defendants will be held in pretrial detention and how long court processes surrounding a case will go on[22].

Ainsi le mythe voulant que la peine soit imposée après que les personnes accusées eurent été trouvées coupables hors de tout doute raisonnable à la fin d'un procès juste et équitable où elles auraient eu droit à une défense pleine et entière[23] est ébranlé. La relative certitude quant à la peine procurée par la négociation vaut davantage que l'incertitude de l'issue d'un procès, et il s'en trouve pour dire que c'est davantage le cas pour les personnes accusées racisées ou autochtones, qui sont disproportionnément punies plus sévèrement[24]. Dans ce contexte, il est inévitable que des personnes innocentes, ou qui à tout le moins auraient une défense valide à faire valoir, plaident coupables. En outre, comme l'explique la section suivante, la détention provisoire est également une pression importante dans la négociation de plaidoyer.

La détention provisoire

Au Canada, le nombre d'adultes en détention provisoire, c'est-à-dire en détention avant procès, alors que l'accusé est toujours présumé innocent, est supérieur au nombre d'adultes en détention après

---

22 *Jennifer Earl, supra* note 19.

23 Droits garantis par les articles 7 et 11d) de la *Charte, supra* note 4, arts 7, 11d.

24 Voir notamment Angela Bressan et Kyle Coady, « Plaidoyers de culpabilité par des Autochtones au Canada », ministère de la Justice du Canada, (2017), en ligne : <justice.gc.ca/fra/pr-rp/jr/pc-gp/pc-gp.pdf>.

condamnation, donc purgeant une peine. En 2020-2021, 67 % des détenus dans les établissements provinciaux étaient en détention provisoire, alors que ce chiffre s'élevait à 77 % en Ontario[25]. Cette réalité mérite qu'on s'y attarde.

Les graphiques suivants (figures B.3.1 et B.3.2) illustrent une tendance, depuis 2004, à l'augmentation de l'écart entre la détention provisoire (mesure coercitive avant et pendant le procès) et la détention après condamnation (peine).

Tendances des comptes quotidiens moyens des adultes dans les établissements de détention provinciaux et territoriaux, selon le type de détention, certains secteurs de compétence, 2004-2005 à 2014-2015

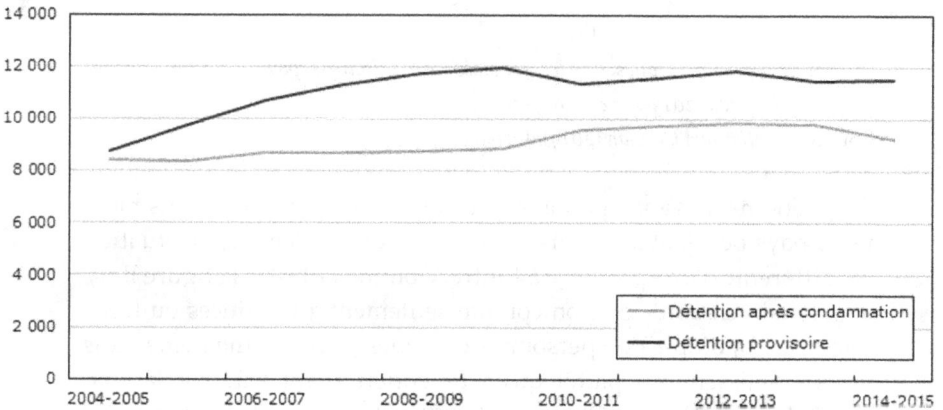

Figure B.3.1. *Tendances de l'utilisation de la détention provisoire au Canada, 2004-2005 à 2014-2015.*
Source : *Statistique Canada (2017), Juristat.*

---

[25] « Statistiques sur les programmes des services correctionnels : tableaux de bord interactifs », en ligne : <statcan.gc.ca>. Cette tendance à la hausse est confirmée par des données plus récentes obtenues par le *Globe and Mail*. Selon Sean Fine, pour l'année 2022-2023, ces chiffres sont plutôt de 80,4 % en Ontario, en plus de 3,7 % dans d'autres formes de détention administrative (immigration et garde à vue). Bref, la population carcérale des établissements correctionnels de l'Ontario qui purge effectivement une peine est de seulement 15,9 %. Sean Fine. « Vast Majority of Jail Inmates in Several Provinces are Still Awaiting Trial, Survey Finds », *The Globe and Mail* (30 octobre 2023), en ligne : <theglobeandmail.com>.

Taux quotidien moyen d'adultes en détention, dans un établissement provincial ou territorial, 2013-2014 à 2017-2018

taux pour 100 000 adultes

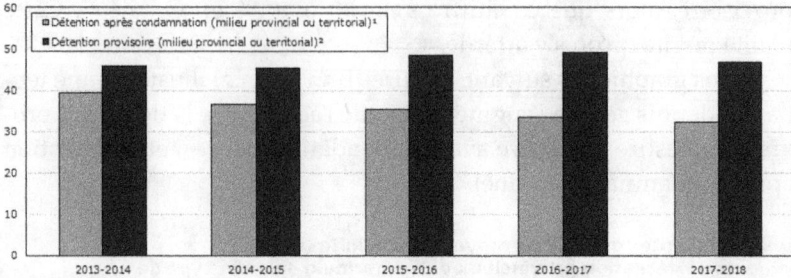

1. Désigne la détention dans un établissement provincial ou territorial (moins de deux ans) des contrevenants ayant été reconnus coupables d'un acte criminel. Les comptes d'adultes en détention après condamnation dans les provinces et les territoires comprennent les contrevenants purgeant des peines discontinues.
2. Désigne la détention des personnes en attente d'une nouvelle comparution devant le tribunal. La détention provisoire relève des systèmes correctionnels provinciaux et territoriaux.

Figure B.3.2. *Statistiques sur les services correctionnels pour les adultes et les jeunes au Canada, 2013-2014 à 2017-2018.*
Source : *Statistique Canada (2019), Juristat.*

Ce phénomène d'anticipation de la punitivité est présent dans plus-ieurs pays occidentaux, mais il faut noter qu'au Canada, la situation est différente d'une province à l'autre. Comme l'illustre la figure B.3.3, au Canada en 2018-2019, on compte seulement 3 provinces ou terri-toires sur 13 où plus de personnes détenues purgent une peine dans leurs établissements plutôt qu'en détention avant leur condamna-tion[26]. La situation en Ontario est particulièrement inquiétante, car plus de 70 % des personnes détenues sont en détention provisoire. C'est d'autant plus préoccupant qu'on sait que les chances de con-traindre un accusé à plaider coupable sont plus grandes s'il est en détention provisoire. En effet, une étude de Kellough et Wortley sur les audiences de mise en liberté sous caution a montré ceci :

---

[26] « Statistiques sur les programmes des services correctionnels : tableaux de bord interactifs », en ligne : <statcan.gc.ca/>. Cette tendance à la hausse est confirmée par des données plus récentes obtenues par le *Globe and Mail*. Selon Sean Fine, pour l'année 2022-2023, ces chiffres sont plutôt de 80,4 % en Ontario, en plus de 3,7 % dans d'autres formes de détention administrative (immigration et garde à vue). Bref, la population carcérale des établissements correctionnels de l'Ontario qui purge effectivement une peine est de seulement 15,9 %. Sean Fine, « Vast Majority of Jail Inmates in Several Provinces are Still Awaiting Trial, Survey Finds », *The Globe and Mail* (30 octobre 2023), en ligne : <theglobeandmail.com>.

The data from the regressions clearly indicate that the chance of coercing a guilty plea is greatly enhanced if the accused is held in pre-trial detention. By contrast, the Crown is more easily persuaded to drop all charges if the accused is released[27].

Proportion des comptes quotidiens moyens d'adultes en détention provisoire et en détention après condamnation, 2018-2019

pourcentage des comptes quotidiens moyens

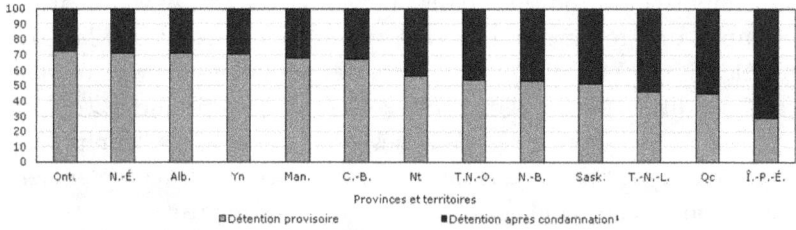

Provinces et territoires

□ Détention provisoire   ■ Détention après condamnation[1]

1. Les comptes d'adultes en détention après condamnation dans les provinces et les territoires comprennent les contrevenants purgeant des peines discontinues (lorsqu'ils sont dans l'établissement de détention) et les contrevenants purgeant des peines fédérales, le cas échéant.

Figure B.3.3. *Statistiques sur les services correctionnels pour les adultes et les jeunes au Canada, 2018-2019*[28].

Source: *Statistique Canada (2020), Juristat.*

En outre, il faut savoir qu'en Ontario, la durée des peines d'emprisonnement est relativement courte (58,7 % moins d'un mois et 10,8 % plus de six mois jusqu'à perpétuité)[29]. Dans ce contexte, la détention provisoire (donc avant l'adjudication de culpabilité) devient *de facto* la peine imposée la plus sévère et les plaidoyers de culpabilité deviennent pratiquement des formalités permettant aux contrevenant·es de sortir de prison. Peu importe si la personne accusée est coupable ou innocente, les données suggèrent que l'éventuelle peine d'emprisonnement sera déjà purgée au moment du procès ou au moment d'enregistrer un plaidoyer de culpabilité. Cela ne veut pas dire que le droit des peines ou plusieurs aspects du droit criminel

---

27 Gail Kellough et Scot Wortley, « Remand for Plea: Bail Decisions and Plea Bargaining as Commensurate Decisions », (2002) 42 : 1 Brit J Crim 186 à la p 198.

28 Jamil Malakieh, « Statistiques sur les services correctionnels pour les adultes et les jeunes au Canada, 2018-2019 », Centre canadien de la statistique juridique et de la sécurité des collectivités, Statistique Canada, 21 décembre 2020, en ligne : <statcan.gc.ca>.

29 Statistique Canada, Tribunaux de juridiction criminelle pour adultes, causes avec condamnation selon la peine la plus sévère, Tableau 35-10-0031-01, 2023-09-07 ; Tribunaux de juridiction criminelle pour adultes, causes avec condamnation selon la durée du placement sous garde, Tableau 35-10-0032-01, 2023-09-27.

n'existent plus au Canada, mais plutôt qu'ils sont utilisés en tant qu'outils de négociation des plaidoyers.

Les conditions de mise en liberté avant procès

Lorsque les personnes accusées réussissent à éviter la détention provisoire, et donc sont mises en liberté avant la tenue de leur procès, on leur impose des conditions dans la majorité des cas. À Montréal par exemple, une recherche a montré qu'entre 2002 et 2014 à la Cour municipale de Montréal, seules 4,7 % des personnes libérées l'étaient sans condition ou engagement[30]. « C'est donc dire que si l'on fait abstraction des personnes détenues dans l'attente de leur procès, 95,3 % des décisions judiciaires prises à ce stade comprenaient l'émission de conditions », même si « la forme de mise en liberté par défaut qui devrait être imposée à une personne prévenue inculpée d'une infraction, autre que les infractions très graves énumérées à l'art. 469, est la mise en liberté sur remise d'une promesse sans condition (paragr. 515(1))[31]. » De plus, les mesures de surveillance avant procès sont tellement privatives de liberté qu'elles sont vécues comme des peines. Pour reprendre les mots d'un participant à la recherche : « Moi, j'ai considéré que mes conditions étaient plus une punition que ma sentence [...] que mon procès[32]. » Comme l'écrivent Sylvestre, Blomley et Bellot,

> bail release conditions themselves [...] are a form of punishment, and, in some case, they are the only punishment. Yet their hybrid nature and the fact that they are not legally recognized or characterized as "punishment" *per se* means that they do not come with the safeguards and protections associated with formally punitive measures imposed after an adjudicative process, or even a negotiated plea[33].

---

[30] Marie-Ève Sylvestre, Alexandre Duchesne Blondin, Céline Bellot, Véronique Fortin et Nicholas Blomley, « Les conditions géographiques de mise en liberté et de probation et leur impact sur les personnes marginalisées à Montréal », mars 2018, p. 4. [*Sylvestre et coll.*].

[31] *R c Zora*, 2020 CSC 14 au para 21.

[32] *Sylvestre et coll.*, *supra* note 30 à la p 127.

[33] Marie-Ève Sylvestre, Nicholas Blomley et Céline Bellot, *Red Zones: Criminal Law and the Territorial Governance of Marginalized People*, Cambridge, Cambridge University Press, 2019 à la p 125–26.

Les conditions sont parfois excessivement difficiles à respecter, mais leur violation n'en constitue pas moins une nouvelle infraction criminelle, un « bris de conditions », une « infraction contre l'administration de la justice ». Ce type d'infraction est très fréquent et contribue aux portes tournantes entre les milieux défavorisés, les prisons et les cours de justice.

Pressions systémiques à plaider coupable et contrôle social

Tout compte fait, les pressions systémiques qui incitent les personnes accusées à plaider coupables rapidement sont nombreuses. Issa Kohler-Hausmann soulignait le même phénomène dans le contexte américain

> Defendants rarely have a short-term incentive to invoke formal adversarial procedures to challenge questionable police search-and-seizure practices because the process costs of doing so usually outweigh the formal sanctions being offered to dispose of a case early on[34].

La punition devient ainsi multiforme et s'étend dans le temps : elle ne survient plus qu'après l'adjudication de la culpabilité, mais se vit du moment de l'arrestation jusqu'à la sanction pénale. Elle prend la forme d'un contrôle social managérial, en ce sens que le système se préoccupe davantage de gérer de façon expéditive et efficace[35] des populations vues comme déviantes plutôt que de les punir après avoir jugé leur culpabilité sur la base du droit et des faits. « [R]ules of criminal procedure and criminal law are used as tools for the social regulation of populations over time, as opposed to punishing for individual instances of lawbreaking identified through factual adjudication[36]. » Ainsi, le juge n'est plus l'unique responsable de la punition ; en plusieurs circonstances, celle-ci arrive bien avant le procès et est distribuée et gérée aussi bien par des policiers et des procureurs de la Couronne que par des agents correctionnels. En ce sens, les auteurs Andrew Ashworth et Lucia Zedner se sont intéressés

---

[34] *Kohler-Hausmann 2019, supra* note 1 à la p 258.

[35] Voir notamment Richard-Alexandre Laniel et Max Silverman, « Justice néolibérale : quand la logique du marché intègre les institutions judiciaires » (2016) 16 Nouveaux Cahiers du Socialisme 43.

[36] *Kohler-Hausmann 2019, supra* note 1 à la p 98.

aux mesures coercitives imposées par l'État sur la base d'évaluation du risque et au nom de la prévention[37]. « Contemporary concerns about risk and the need for security have thus led to the proliferation of diverse practices of prevention. Together they significantly expand the state's exercise of coercive power over its citizens and thereby threaten core liberal values of individual liberty and autonomy[38]. » À l'ère de la justice managériale et préventive, et dans les suites de l'arrêt *Jordan*[39] sur les délais de justice[40], on punit aussi avant de condamner, pour mieux gérer de façon efficace et rapide des populations marginalisées[41].

Conclusion : la punitivité même au-delà de la matière criminelle

À partir de trois exemples de la réalité du droit criminel au Canada, soit les négociations de plaidoyer, la détention provisoire et les conditions de mise en liberté, nous avons vu que la justice managériale est au cœur même du droit criminel et qu'elle amène une *administrativisation* du champ de manière à gérer et punir promptement, et ce avant même l'adjudication de culpabilité[42]. Mais le caractère managérial de la justice se constate également dans sa tendance à sortir du champ criminel pour aller vers des régimes réglementaires et administratifs[43]

---

[37] Andrew Ashworth et Lucia Zedner, Preventive Justice, Oxford, Oxford University Press, coll. Oxford Monographs on Criminal Law and Justice, 2014, en ligne: <academia.edu>. Voir aussi Andrew Ashworth, Lucia Zedner et Patrick Tomlin, dir, *Prevention and the Limits of Criminal Law*, Oxford, Oxford University Press, coll. Oxford Scholarship Online, 2013.

[38] Lucia Zedner et Andrew Ashworth, « The Rise and Restraint of the Preventive State » (2019) 2 Annual Rev Criminology 429 à la p 437.

[39] *R c Jordan*, 2016 CSC 27 (CanLII), [2016] 1 RCS 631.

[40] Voir Stéphane Bernatchez, « L'arrêt *Jordan*, le management de la justice et le droit de la gouvernance : de la conversion des droits en nombres à la transformation de la culture juridique » (2016) 46 : 3 RDUS 451. Revue de droit de l'Université de Sherbrooke (RDUS) 451.

[41] Véronique Fortin, « The Control of Public Spaces in Montreal in Times of Managerial Justice » (2018) 15 Champ pénal/Penal Field, en ligne : <journals.openedition.org>.

[42] João Velloso, « Beyond Criminocentric Dogmatism: Mapping Institutional Forms of Punishment in Contemporary Societies » (2013) 15:2 Punishment & Society 166.

[43] Voir par ex Keramet Reiter et Susan Bibler Coutin, « Crossing Borders and Criminalizing Identity: The Disintegrated Subjects of Administrative Sanctions »

afin de disposer des atteintes à l'ordre et la paix publics. Ainsi, un autre angle mort de plusieurs criminalistes est l'existence de la punitivité en dehors des réponses à une accusation criminelle. Les systèmes de droit administratif ou de droit pénal réglementaire, par exemple, sont mobilisés pour gérer les comportements et punir. Ils deviennent ainsi une voie d'évitement des garanties procédurales[44], une voie expéditive qui permet de contrôler efficacement des populations jugées à risque[45]. Mais ce contrôle n'est pas moins punitif et limitatif de liberté. Pour le dire dans les mots de Beckett et Murakawa, qui avancent le concept de shadow carceral state[46], « the penal state increasingly encompasses both criminal and non-criminal institutions and illuminates new civil, administrative, and legally hybrid pathways to punishment. Some of these pathways are new; others are not new but have expanded so significantly in recent years that they must be addressed as expansions of carceral state power[47]. »

Nos recherches antérieures[48] ont montré que cet élément est particulièrement saillant dans le contexte de la décriminalisation et

---

(2017) 51:3 Law & Soc'y Rev 567.

[44] Pour une analyse du phénomène en contexte de droit de l'immigration aux États-Unis, voir notamment Stephen H Legomsky, « The New Path of Immigration Law: Asymmetric Incorporation of Criminal Justice Norms » (2007) 64:2 Wash & Lee L Rev 469, en ligne : <seattle.gov>.

[45] Voir notamment Malcolm M Feeley et Jonathan Simon, « The New Penology: Notes on the Emerging Strategy of Corrections and Its Implications » (1992) 30:4 Criminology 449, en ligne: <antoniocasella.eu>.

[46] L'option de Beckett et Murakawa pour le concept du shadow carceral state / de l'État carcéral fantôme n'est pas une opposition à l'idée de justice managériale, bien au contraire. La justice managériale apporte une nuance importante à l'idée d'État carcéral, traditionnellement liée au boom carcéral aux États-Unis sur la base de politiques pénales d'emprisonnement de masse avec un taux d'emprisonnement très élevé (culminant à ~750/100 000 hab. dans les années 2000) et associée aux longues peines d'emprisonnement. Beckett et Murakawa argumentent qu'un aspect fantôme de l'État carcéral n'est pas associé aux longues peines ni même aux peines d'emprisonnement : il s'agit d'un aspect administratif, managérial. C'est encore plus vrai dans le contexte canadien, où l'emprisonnement de masse s'opère à partir de taux d'emprisonnement plus modestes (~120/100 0000, avec de courtes, parfois même très courtes, peines d'emprisonnement et une haute circularité de la population carcérale). Au Canada, nos « longues peines » sont plutôt faites d'entrées et sorties de prison rapides et continuelles (phénomène des portes tournantes).

[47] Beckett et Murakawa, supra note 2 à la p 223.

[48] João Velloso et Véronique Fortin, « Governance of Recreational Cannabis Users in Canada: Jurisdictional Shifts, Punitive Decriminalization and Challenges for Harm

légalisation du cannabis. L'avènement de la *Loi sur le cannabis*[49] en 2018 a été célébré par bon nombre de personnes : enfin les stigmates et fâcheuses conséquences du droit criminel ne seraient plus associés aux consommateurs récréatifs d'une substance largement utilisée. Pourtant, une analyse minutieuse et centrée sur la punitivité de la gouvernance entourant le cannabis permet de constater que l'usage de ce stupéfiant, même licite, même prétendument décriminalisé[50], reste un comportement fréquemment puni au nom d'une panoplie de normes d'ordre criminel, pénal, administratif ou de droit privé. Par exemple, au Québec, il est interdit de fumer du cannabis sur la place publique en vertu de l'article 16 de la Loi encadrant le cannabis[51], sou peine de constat d'infraction et d'une amende variant entre 500$ et 1500$, et allant même jusqu'à 2250$ en certaines circonstances, et le double en cas de récidive. Et souvent, il est également interdit de fumer dans un logement locatif puisque, depuis le 15 janvier 2019, les propriétaires ont pu rajouter de façon unilatérale une disposition dans les baux interdisant de fumer du cannabis à l'intérieur de logements loués, incluant les balcons et terrasses[52]. Un manquement aux dispositions d'un tel bail pourrait éventuellement mener à sa résiliation et à l'expulsion du locataire. Et même avec l'autorisation de fumer du cannabis dans son logement, le locataire pourrait encourir une poursuite pour troubles de jouissance normale des lieux de la part des colocataires pour les odeurs résiduelles de fumée de cannabis[53]. Éventuellement son bail pourrait être résilié et il risque d'être condamné à payer des dommages-intérêts.

Comme on le constate, la consommation de cannabis est peut-être légale, mais elle est encore souvent punie. Le contrôle a simplement fait l'objet d'un transfert normatif. La juriste américaine Alexandra Natapoff soulignait d'ailleurs que la décriminalisation

---

Reduction » dans Vanessa Gruben et Chelsea Cox, dir, *First, Do Less Harm: Harm Reduction as a Principle of Law and Policy*, 2025, Les Presses de l'Université d'Ottawa, dans la coll. Health and Society, en 2024 ; voir aussi Véronique Fortin, João Velloso et Marie-Ève Sylvestre, « Vers une décriminalisation punitive du cannabis au Canada », 3ᵉ Biennale de droit criminel, mai 2019, Université de Montréal.

[49] *Loi sur le cannabis*, LC 2018, c 16[CT1].

[50] Voir *Velloso et Fortin*, *supra* note 48, pour une discussion sur la criminalisation continue du cannabis, malgré qu'on clame la décriminalisation et la légalisation.

[51] Chapitre C-5.3, Légis Québec RLRQ c C-5.3.

[52] *Ibid*, art 107.

[53] Voir notamment *Gurkan c Bertrand*, 2021 QCTAL 10152 (CanLII).

peut avoir un côté obscur : elle peut s'accompagner de dispositifs punitifs importants en dehors de la peine criminelle, qui prennent la forme d'interactions avec la police et de passage dans le système de justice pénale pour des infractions pénales réglementaires[54]. Robin Antony Duff, un des principaux experts en théories de la peine en common law, nous avertit d'ailleurs depuis longtemps des tentatives d'évitement des garanties procédurales associées aux procès criminels à partir de l'utilisation d'autres régimes[55].

Bien sûr, la décriminalisation du cannabis reste une avancée par rapport au *statu quo*, en dépit de ses côtés obscurs. Akwasi Owusu-Bempah souligne ainsi que les arrestations pour l'infraction criminelle de possession de cannabis avoisinaient le nombre de 50 000 par année entre 1998 et 2017 au Canada, alors que ce nombre a décliné jusqu'à 1378 en 2020, deux ans après la légalisation[56]. Ainsi, pour paraphraser Alexandra Natapoff, la critique de la décriminalisation du cannabis est moins un argument contre celle-ci qu'une mise en lumière de ses limites, et un appel à porter attention à la gouvernance punitive qui lui survit. Comme elle le souligne en contexte américain, mais la citation se transpose très bien en contexte canadien :

> For all its flaws, the ultimate value of decriminalization must be measured against the baseline of the status quo. [...] To put it another way, decriminalization can be thought of as a conservative response to a radical challenge. If we really wanted to shrink the criminal governance apparatus and meaningfully "decriminalize" our democracy, we would legalize minor conduct, constrain the police power of arrest, and roll back the entire petty offense process[57].

---

[54] Alexandra Natapoff, « Misdemeanor Decriminalization » (2015) 68:4 Vand L Rev 1055, en ligne : <scholarship.law.vanderbilt.edu>.

[55] Voir notamment Robin Antony Duff, « Crimes, Regulatory Offences and Criminal Trials », dans Heinz Müller-Dietz, dir, *Festschrift für Heike Jung*, Baden-Baden, Nomos, 2007, 87-98 ; Robin Antony Duff, « A Criminal Law for Citizens » (2010) 14 :3 Theoretical Criminology 293 ; et Robin Antony Duff, « Preserving Criminal Law? » dans Robin Antony Duff, Lindsay Farmer, Sandra E Marshall, Massimo Renzo et Victor Tadros, dir, *The Boundaries of the Criminal Law*, Oxford, Oxford University Press, coll. Criminalization, 2011.

[56] Akwasi Owusu-Bempah, « Canada's Legalization of Cannabis Is a Success Story, Despite a Shaky First Act », *The Globe and Mail* (15 janvier 2022), en ligne : <theglobeandmail.com>.

[57] *Natapoff, supra* note 54, à la p. 1109.

La décriminalisation et la légalisation du cannabis, en 2018, permettent de mettre en lumière comment le tournant managérial de la justice l'amène à sortir du champ criminel certains comportements sans pour autant cesser de les policer et de les punir, et ce avec toujours moins de garanties procédurales.

Ainsi, les juristes qui s'intéressent aux relations de pouvoir dans une perspective critique doivent s'intéresser au penchant du droit criminel pour la justice managériale, préventive et carcérale. De façon similaire, en mettant la punitivité au cœur de l'étude du droit public, en décloisonnant les différents domaines du droit pour accentuer leurs interrelations, on peut prendre la pleine mesure des effets délétères du contrôle punitif des populations marginalisées au sein, comme en dehors, du droit criminel. Ainsi, des recherches juridiques futures devraient s'intéresser à la punitivité sous toutes ces formes et non seulement à la peine telle qu'elle est étroitement définie en droit criminel[58].

---

[58] Voir à ce sujet la distinction laborieuse entre les sanctions administratives pécuniaires et les véritables conséquences pénales dans la décision *Guindon c Canada*, 2015 CSC 41. Voir aussi l'excellent texte d'Anne-Marie Boisvert, « Les dérives du droit administratif : les régimes de sanctions administratives pécuniaires comme "solution de rechange" au régime pénal », 2018 23:3 Can Crim L Rev 197.

The Hunt for Red October: Critical Race Theory and Racial McCarthyism

Vincent Wong

Abstract

After decades of academic debate, critical race theory (CRT) is now the primary target of a massive campaign of racial backlash, speech suppression, and historical revisionism in the United States. Beginning with Executive Order 13950, the anti-CRT movement continued to gain strength and expanded to a 50-state campaign. This chapter applies a law and political economy lens to these developments to argue that they are symptomatic of a recurring strategy of "racial McCarthyism." This strategy fuses two distinct but intertwining political anxieties: a domestic white racial anxiety that has been further exacerbated in response to the impacts of the protests against police brutality and racial injustice in the summer of 2020 combined with a geopolitical McCarthyist anxiety in response to a rising China. This discourse has also migrated outside the United States, including to Canada, where similar conditions of possibility exist for an anti-CRT racial McCarthyist campaign to take hold.

Résumé

Après des décennies de débats académiques, la théorie critique de la race (CRT) est désormais la cible principale d'une vaste campagne de réaction raciale, de suppression de la liberté d'expression et de révisionnisme historique aux États-Unis. Débutant avec le décret présidentiel 13950, le mouvement anti-CRT a continué de gagner en force, s'étendant à une campagne dans les 50 États. Cet article applique une perspective de droit et d'économie politique à ces développements pour soutenir qu'ils sont symptomatiques d'une stratégie récurrente de « maccarthysme racial ». Cette stratégie fusionne deux angoisses politiques distinctes, mais interdépendantes : une angoisse raciale blanche nationale, exacerbée par les impacts des manifestations contre la brutalité policière et l'injustice raciale à l'été 2020, et une angoisse géopolitique maccarthyste face à la montée en puissance de la Chine. Ce discours s'est également propagé en dehors des États-Unis, notamment au Canada, où des conditions similaires pourraient permettre l'émergence d'une campagne anti-CRT de maccarthysme racial.

In the 1990 blockbuster film, *The Hunt for Red October*[1], a state-of-the-art Soviet nuclear missile submarine goes renegade and the US government scrambles to find and intercept it. Set in 1984, *The Hunt for Red October* represents the existential fear of nuclear first strike through the symbolism of the shadowy submarine *Red October* as part of the broader cultural production of "Red Scare"—widespread hysteria and accompanying political suppression around the potential rise of communism and other leftist ideologies in the West.[2] Although the height of the Red Scare peaked with McCarthyism in the early 1950s, the collective linkages it forged between left-wing politics and subversion remains seared into the American national consciousness, primed for reactivation under favourable conditions.

A particular manifestation of McCarthyism—racial McCarthyism—would find fertile conditions to proliferate in the final months of

---

[1] John McTiernan, dir *The Hunt for Red October* (Paramount Pictures: 2 March 1990).

[2] There were two major instances of Red Scare in American history: the First Red Scare (1917–1920) which was a campaign of political suppression of suspected communists and anarchists after the October Revolution in Russia and the Second Red Scare (1947–1957) following Soviet occupation of Eastern Europe which was most well-known for political purges of alleged communists by Senator Joseph McCarthy. See Kenneth D Ackerman, *Young J. Edgar: Hoover and the Red Scare, 1919–1920* (New York: Viral History Press, 2008); Griffin Fariello, *Red Scare: Memories of the American Inquisition* (New York: W W Norton & Company, 1995).

Donald Trump's first presidency with the passing of *Executive Order 13950: Combating Race and Sex Stereotyping* (EO 13950).[3] The Order was passed in response to a well-funded[4] disinformation[5] campaign targeting critical race theory (CRT) beginning in early September 2020. Despite popular rhetoric, the Order itself never explicitly mentions CRT, but rather frames discussions around racial and gendered oppressions as "scapegoating"[6] and purges the Federal government, armed forces, contractors, and grant recipients of any training or activities that might run afoul of a list of nine vaguely defined "divisive concepts."[7] These include ideas that the U.S. might be fundamentally racist or sexist,[8] collective responsibility for legacies of systemic racism and sexism,[9] and any sort of discussion around racism and sexism that may cause individuals to "feel discomfort, guilt, anguish, or any other form of psychological distress on account of his or her race or sex."[10] The Order also enabled federal contracts to be terminated or suspended for violations,[11] required new contracts to include "divisive concepts" prohibitions, empowered the Secretary of Labor[12] and the Attorney General[13] to impose sanctions or sue for non-compliance, and created a hotline through the Office of Federal Contract Compliance Programs (OFCCP) to receive and investigate complaints.[14]

The direct and indirect censorship of racial and gender justice speech, programs, and policies from EO 13950 spread like wildfire. This included, *inter alia*:

---

3 *Executive Order on Combating Race and Sex Stereotyping*, EO 13950, 85 Fed Reg 60683 (22 September 2020), online: <https://trumpwhitehouse.archives.gov/presidential-actions/executive-order-combating-race-sex-stereotyping/> [*EO 13950*].

4 Judd Legum and Tesnim Zekeria, "The Obscure Foundation Funding 'Critical Race Theory' hysteria", Popular Information (13 July 2021) online: <popular.info/p/the-obscure-foundation-funding-critical>.

5 Brandi Collins-Dexter and Joan Donovan, "How a Racialized Disinformation Campaign Ties Itself to The 1619 Project" Columbia Journalism Review (11 March 2021) online: <cjr.org/opinion/1776-keyword-squatting-right-wing-media.php>.

6 *EO 13950, supra* note 3 at s 2(c).

7 *Ibid* at s 2(a).

8 *Ibid* at s 2(a)(2).

9 *Ibid* at s 2(a)(7).

10 *Ibid* at s 2(a)(8).

11 *Ibid* at s 4.3.

12 *Ibid* at s 4.4.

13 *Ibid* at s 8.

14 *Ibid* at s 4.4(b).

- Cancellations of equity trainings and workshops;[15]
- Cancellations of LGBTQ pride programming within government;[16]
- Class action lawsuits against government branches implementing racial equity policies;[17]
- Refusals of research funding for employing terms that interrogate systemic racism;[18]
- Administrative censorship of discussions around reparations and systemic racism at universities such as Stanford;[19]
- Firings of K-12 teachers;[20] and
- A state-level copycat legislation campaign that, as of 31 December 2022, has seen over 560 instances of government anti-CRT measures including legislation, executive orders, state attorney general opinion letters, state and local school board policies, resolutions, agency guidance, and high-level law and policymaker statements across 49 states.[21]

The political suppression of racial and gender justice work stemming from EO 13950 has permeated all areas of American society including education, healthcare, military, history, housing, social work,

---

[15] Hailey Fuchs, "Trump Attack on Diversity Training Has a Quick and Chilling Effect" New York Times (13 October 2020) online: <nytimes. com/2020/10/13/us/politics/trump-diversity-training-race.html>.

[16] The African American Policy Forum, "#TruthBeTold: Resist Trump's Equity Gag Order" (November 2020) at 10–12, online (PDF): <aapf.org/_files/ugd/62e126_903752833b384684a2e699327eafo5ca.pdf> [TruthBeTold Report].

[17] The Pivtorak Law Firm, "Critical Race Theory at the Center of Racial Discrimination Class Action Filed Against California State Agency" (19 October 2020), online: <piv4law.com/new-blog/2020/10/14/critical-race-theory-at-the-center-of-racial-discrimination-lawsuit-filed-against-california-agencies>.

[18] TruthBeTold Report, *supra* note 16 at 12.

[19] Khari Johnson, "Stanford Rushes to Comply with Trump Executive Order Limiting Diversity Training" VentureBeat (17 November 2020), online: <venturebeat.com/2020/11/17/stanford-rushes-to-comply-with-trump-executive-order-limiting-diversity-training/>.

[20] Emma Green, "He Taught a Ta-Nehisi Coates Essay. Then He Was Fired" The Atlantic (17 August 2021) online: <theatlantic.com/politics/archive/2021/08/matt-hawn-tennessee-teacher-fired-white-privilege/619770/>.

[21] Taifha Alexander et al, "CRT Forward: Tracking the Attack on Critical Race Theory" (April 2023), UCLA Law, at 4, online (PDF): <crtforward.law.ucla.edu/wp-content/uploads/2023/04/UCLA-Law_CRT-Report_Final.pdf>.

environmental protection, arts, and science.[22] However, this chapter is not a comprehensive narration of the origins and impacts of the anti-CRT campaign, nor is it a doctrinal legal analysis of EO 13950 and its copycat state-level relatives—as useful and timely as both of those projects would be. Rather, this chapter is primarily a law and political economy intervention that excavates the histories of McCarthyist political repression to show how anti-socialist panic in America has followed discursive patterns that are influenced by geopolitics, anti-Blackness, and inextricable from backlash against material claims for racial equality.

Such an analysis matters for lawyers, legal scholars, and the broader public because understanding these simultaneous racial, class, and geopolitical dynamics are essential for making sense of the incredible success of the anti-CRT campaign. Further, political economy analysis is something that legal academia has not done enough, in part due to the narrow search for universalized doctrinal precepts inherent in "thinking like a lawyer."[23]

The concept of racial McCarthyism draws attention to the entanglements between (1) backlash to racial justice mobilizations; (2) backlash to economic justice mobilizations; and (3) the national security dimensions engendered by both. Whereas McCarthyism originally developed in the civil rights struggle against Jim Crow and the rise of a post-war, nuclear-armed Soviet Union, there are significant differences in this contemporary moment. The political anxieties fomented by the racial reckoning of the George Floyd protests alongside the waning geopolitical hegemony of the U.S. in the face of a rising, facially socialist China has supplied fertile conditions for a revitalized twenty-first century racial McCarthyism to take hold. Further, racial McCarthyism, in a similar vein to the historical interventions of racial capitalism,[24] serves to reveal how McCarthyism has *always* been co-constitutive of anti-Blackness and racial backlash politics more broadly.

---

[22] *TruthBeTold Report, supra* note 16 at 11–13.

[23] Patricia J Williams, *The Alchemy of Race and Rights* (Cambridge: Harvard University Press, 1992) at 1–14.

[24] Perry Bacon Jr, "Why Attacking 'Cancel Culture' And 'Woke' People Is Becoming The GOP's New Political Strategy" FiveThirtyEight (17 March 2021) online: <fivethirtyeight.com/features/why-attacking-cancel-culture-and-woke-people-is-becoming-the-gops-new-political-strategy/>

Without excavating the historical antecedents of racial McCarthyism and its continued legacy, it can be perplexing to understand how the contemporary anti-CRT campaign could so quickly gain purchase as a cornerstone of American conservatism in the post-Trump era.[25] This historical analysis is urgent given the effectiveness of modern forms of racial McCarthyism (especially when they are not identified and interrogated as such) in legitimizing the censorship, demonization, and persecution of individuals and organizations fighting for social justice. It is also important to note that these historical anti-equality antecedents and their underlying search for a political boogeyman evolve and transform with the ruling political anxieties of the times to survive.[26]

This chapter proceeds by tracing the development of the anti-CRT campaign in the United States. and its travel to other jurisdictions, including Canada. It examines the historical antecedents of racial McCarthyism and why CRT was selected as the target for an anti-equality disinformation campaign and uses Derrick Bell's concept of interest-convergence to explain how both domestic and foreign white nationalist anxieties influenced the development of contemporary racial McCarthyism. Finally, it surveys some of the ways that organizations and activists are pushing back against the retrenchment of racial McCarthyism under the form of anti-CRT censorship.

Origins and Development of the Anti-CRT Campaign

Several weeks after the police killing of George Floyd in May 2020 triggered staggering protests globally against police brutality and racism, the Trump administration was reeling, attempting to find a vehicle to re-establish control of the political narrative. To do so, it was clear that it would have to excavate old ghosts, beginning with forays into a foreign Red Scare. President Trump's July 4, 2020 speech at Mount Rushmore framed Black Lives Matter protesters as "angry

---

[25] Perry Bacon Jr, "Why Attacking 'Cancel Culture' And 'Woke' People Is Becoming The GOP's New Political Strategy" (17 March 2021), FiveThirtyEight, online: <fivethirtyeight.com/features/why-attacking-cancel-culture-and-woke-people-is-becoming-the-gops-new-political-strategy/>.

[26] Reva B Siegel, "The Rule of Love: Wife Beating as Prerogative and Privacy" (1996) 105 Yale LJ 2117 at 2178–2187.

mobs trying to tear down statues of our Founders."[27] Trump specifically connected those uprisings to a Mao-era "left-wing cultural revolution [...] designed to overthrow the American Revolution."[28] But its hunt for Red October—a political boogeyman which could house a variety of racial and economic anxieties—ended on 1 September 2020, when Trump stumbled upon a Tucker Carlson interview on Fox News of conservative activist Christopher Rufo. Rufo asserted that CRT was "neo-Marxist rhetoric" that had "pervaded every institution in the Federal government" and had become "the default ideology of the federal bureaucracy [...] now being weaponized against the American people."[29] Three days later, the Office of Management and Budget (OMB) immediately issued a memo informing federal agencies that any training related to CRT or white privilege would be enjoined and defunded.[30]

On Constitution Day, 17 September 2020, Trump announced that he would sign an executive order to establish the President's Advisory 1776 Commission:[31] a national commission entrusted to "promote patriotic education" and ensure that "our sons and daughters [...] know that they are the citizens of the most exceptional nation in the history of the world."[32] According to the President's speech, the impetus for this heavy-handed ideological intervention was the threat of CRT, which he described as a "Marxist doctrine" that holds America as a "wicked and racist nation."[33] He further decried CRT "being forced into our children's schools," "imposed into workplace trainings," and

---

[27] "Remarks by President Trump at South Dakota's 2020 Mount Rushmore Fireworks Celebration | Keystone, South Dakota" (4 July 2020), online: <trumpwhitehouse. archives.gov/briefings-statements/remarks-president-trump-south-dakotas-2020-mount-rushmore-fireworks-celebration-keystone-south-dakota/>.

[28] *Ibid.*

[29] Sam Dorman, "Chris Rufo Calls on Trump to End Critical Race Theory 'Cult Indoctrination' in Federal Government" Fox News (1 September 2020) online: <foxnews.com/politics/chris-rufo-race-theory-cult-federal-government>.

[30] Russell Vought, "Memorandum for the Heads of Executive Departments and Agencies" (4 September 2020), The White House, online (PDF): <whitehouse.gov/wp-content/uploads/2020/09/M-20-34.pdf>.

[31] Establishing the President's Advisory 1776 Commission, EO 13958, 85 FR 70951 (2 November 2020).

[32] "Remarks by President Trump at the White House Conference on American History" (17 September 2020) online: <trumpwhitehouse.archives.gov/briefings statements/remarks-president-trump-white-house-conference-american-history/>.

[33] *Ibid.*

"deployed to rip apart friends, neighbours, and families" in order to "impose a new segregation."[34] Connecting the dots between CRT and the need for a patriotic rewrite of American history, Trump painted a picture of traitorous conspiracy against the American national project: "critical race theory, the 1619 Project, and the crusade against American history is toxic propaganda. Ideological poison, that if not removed will dissolve the civic bonds that tie us together, will destroy our country."[35] EO 13950 was promulgated several days later.

The political salience of the anti-CRT campaign has also crossed borders, resonating with global currents of white grievance in the face of mass movements for racial justice. The U.K. Tory government followed Trump's Executive Order by stating in the House of Commons that it was "unequivocally against" CRT and the teaching of "white privilege" to "white pupils"—despite the fact that the words "critical race theory" had never been uttered once in the U.K. legislature until that moment.[36] In Australia, the Senate passed a motion calling on the federal government to reject CRT from the national curriculum—despite no evidence that CRT played any role in K-12 curriculums or is taught with any regularity in Australia legal academies—pointing to aspects of the national curriculum that taught the histories and legacies of colonialism on First Nations peoples.[37]

In Canada, the mantle against CRT was taken up by the StopSOP campaign—a movement at the Law Society of Ontario dedicated to reversing a "Statement of Principles" (SOP) recommendation which required lawyers to acknowledge an "obligation to promote equality, diversity and inclusion" in the profession.[38] In April 2021, StopSOP

---

[34] *Ibid.*

[35] *Ibid.*

[36] UK, HC, Deb (20 October 2020), vol 682, cols 1011-1012 (The Minister for Equalities, Kemi Badenoch); Daniel Trilling, "Why is the UK Government Suddenly Targeting 'Critical Race Theory'?" *The Guardian* (23 October 2020) online: <theguardian.com/ commentisfree/2020/oct/23/uk-critical-race-theory-trump-conservatives structural-inequality>.

[37] Leticia Anderson and Kathomi Gatwiri, "The Senate Has Voted to Reject Critical Race Theory from the National Curriculum. What Is it, and Why Does it Matter?" The Conversation (22 June 2021) online: <theconversation.com/the-senate-has-voted-to-reject-critical-race-theory-from-the-national-curriculum-what-is-it-and-why-does-it-matter-163102>.

[38] Law Society of Upper Canada, "Working Together For Change: Strategies to Address Issues of Systemic Racism in the Legal Profession" (November 2016) at 2,

spokesperson Lisa Bildy sent an email to supporters informing them that their revamped campaign (named #FullStop) would focus on directly opposing CRT. Drawing from the Trumpian playbook, the email alleged that equity, diversity, and inclusion "dogma" was animated by CRT; that the teaching of CRT classes in Canada amounted to ideological "infiltration" (citing two young recently tenure-tracked Black law professors); and that analyzing institutions and interactions through the lens of race and power was "divisive."[39] A number of racialized lawyers' associations swiftly condemned the statement as grossly mischaracterizing CRT and implicitly denying the existence of systemic racism within the legal profession.[40]

Predictions that the anti-CRT hysteria would lose momentum with the inauguration of President Biden proved overly optimistic. Biden's repeal of EO 13950 coincided with the launch of the anti-CRT coalition[41] and the beginning of a 50-state anti-CRT legislative strategy. Some of the proposed legislation, such as Missouri's House Bill 952, explicitly makes the racial McCarthyist connection clear by banning use in school history curricula of materials that teach American history from the perspective of racially and economically marginalized groups, such as the *New York Times'* 1619 Project, BLM at School, and the Zinn Education Project.[42] A Legal Insurrection Foundation-funded website, Critical Race Training in Education, tracks public and private schools across America that embrace any sort of racial or gender equity programming for "parents and students concerned about [...] critical race theory."[43] A number of teachers have

---

online (PDF): <lawsocietyontario.azureedge.net/media/lso/media/legacy/pdf/w/wo/working-together-for-change-strategies-to-address-issues-of-systemic-racism-in-the-legal-professions-final-report.pdf>.

[39] Joshua Sealy-Harrington (@JoshuaSealy), Tweet, (18 April 2021), online: <x.com/JoshuaSealy/status/1383902400377810948

[40] Bernise Carolino, "Organizations Issue Joint Statement on FullStop Movement at Law Society of Ontario" Law Times (5 May 2021) online: <lawtimesnews.com/resources/professional-regulation/organizations-issue-joint-statement-on-fullstop-movement-at-law-society-of-ontario/355688>.

[41] Sam Dorman, "Legal Coalition Forming to Stop Critical Race Theory Training Around the Country" Fox News (20 January 2021) online: <foxnews.com/politics/legal-coalition-critical-race-theory>.

[42] US, HB 952, Prohibits the Use of the 1619 Project Initiative of the New York Times in the Public Schools of the State, 101 Gen Assem, Reg Sess, Mis, 2021 (enacted).

[43] Critical Race Training in Education, "About This Website" (last visited 22 August 2025), online: <criticalrace.org/critical-race-theory-today/>.

been fired as a result of these anti-CRT purges in education, including Tennessee High School teacher Matt Hawn, who taught his students materials elucidating the link between white grievances and racial violence in America.[44]

Racial McCarthyism: Past and Present

Ironically, the term "racial McCarthyism" has been deployed in the twenty-first century primarily by conservative pundits to decry what they perceive to be unfounded allegations of racism. For instance, in 2001, Republican House Majority Leader Dick Armey accused NAACP leaders of "racial McCarthyism" or "reverse race-baiting" for remarks that insinuated certain members of President Bush's cabinet appointees were sympathetic to Confederate political ideology and therefore racist.[45] A month later, the Wall Street Journal published an editorial condemning protests against an article published in a campus newspaper that argued against slavery reparations as "[m]oral intimidation through a species of racial McCarthyism."[46] Like with the anti-CRT campaign, these articles centre the injury and discomfort of being accused of racism over the actual racialized harms of practices of racial violence and subordination, while simultaneously uplifting the "divisive" and "polarizing" nature of these discussions. This framing of racial McCarthyism is remarkably ahistoric given that Red Scare has historically been used to vilify and suppress racial justice activists in the United States, particularly prominent African Americans.

The connection between Black liberation struggles and the Red Scare during the years of the American Civil Rights Movement has only recently been given detailed treatment by historians.[47] After the landmark 1954 school desegregation case of *Brown v Board of*

---

[44] Green, *supra* note 20.

[45] Laurie Willis, "NAACP Leaders Accused of 'Racial McCarthyism'" The Baltimore Sun (25 February 2001) online: <baltimoresun.com/news/bs-xpm- 2001-02-25- 0102240178-story.html>.

[46] Wall Street Journal, "Racial McCarthyism" (20 March 2011) Editorial, online: <wsj. com/articles/SB9850344486371404957>.

[47] See Yasuhiro Katagiri, *Black Freedom, White Resistance, and Red Menace: Civil Rights and Anticommunism in the Jim Crow South* (Baton Rouge: Louisiana State University Press, 2014); Jeff Woods, *Black Struggle, Red Scare: Segregation and Anti-Communism in the South, 1948–1968* (Baton Rouge: Louisiana State University Press, 2004); George

Education,[48] Southern segregationists "sought to conceptualize the civil rights movement as communist-tainted in order to recase a peculiarly southern problem as one of national concern"[49]—what historian Yasuhiro Katagiri describes as a "politics of insecurity" to maintain Jim Crow racial oppression.[50] What resulted was a toxic combination which melded the strategy of white massive resistance in the South with U.S. Cold War nationalist anxieties.

Southern segregationist McCarthyism began to gain momentum after the House Un-American Activities Committee (HUAC) published a report entitled *The American Negro in the Communist Party* in late 1954.[51] As the influence of the HUAC and Joseph McCarthy himself began to wane at the Federal level, Northern "professional anti-Communists" looked for work to do. Some crossed the Mason-Dixon line to connect national security concerns to white Southern backlash movements opposing efforts to end Jim Crow.[52] The regional character of racial McCarthyism also traces a historical through line: the six states that established their own statewide anti-Communist committees during the 1950s and 1960s to discredit civil rights activists—Louisiana, Georgia, Arkansas, Tennessee, Florida, and Mississippi—were all the very same states that passed anti-CRT legislation and/or administrative bans in 2021.[53] Revisiting these connections allows us to better understand how racial McCarthyism has evolved over time in the American South—a dynamic that Reva Siegel describes as "preservation-through-transformation."[54]

Of course, racial McCarthyism was not confined only to the Jim Crow South. For African American leftists during the McCarthy era, "to be Black was to be Red."[55] Politically active Black artists and

Lewis, *The White South and the Red Menace: Segregationists, Anticommunism, and Massive Resistance, 1945–1965* (Gainsville: University Press of Florida, 2004).

[48] *Brown v Board of Education of Topeka,* 347 US 483 (1954).

[49] Lewis, *supra* note 47 at 52.

[50] Katagiri, *supra* note 47 at 23.

[51] US, House Committee on Un-American Activities, The American Negro in the Communist Party (22 December 1954).

[52] Katagiri, *supra* note 47 at 23.

[53] Anthony B Newkirk, "'A Delicate Matter': The 1958 Special Education Committee Hearing" (2019) 78:3 Arkansas Historical Quarterly 274.

[54] Siegel, *supra* note 26 at 2119.

[55] Mohammed Elnaiem, "In the McCarthy Era, to Be Black Was to Be Red" JSTOR (13 November 2019) online: <daily.jstor.org/

thinkers, such as Paul Robeson, Alice Childress, and Lorraine Hansberry, were targeted by the FBI and put on watch lists as potential traitors to the nation for their sympathies towards socialist ideals, their community activism, and/or their association with Communists. Nor was the phenomenon of racial McCarthyism specifically confined to the rise of Senator Joseph McCarthy. In what she calls the "Longue Durée of McCarthyism," Charisse Burden-Stelly argues that the 1940 Alien Registration Act (the first peacetime sedition act in the United States) along with the 1950 Internal Security Act launched a "strong anti-Black and anti-communist hysteria" which "created the conditions for the persecution of thousands of progressives [and] launched an all-out attack on their civil rights."[56] Within the intellectual space, Burden-Stelly describes this branch of McCarthyism as one "which erases, silences, distorts, and/or discredits the intellectual production of African descendants deemed subversive, un-American, and threatening to national security for dedicating their lives to challenging these conjunctures."[57]

The historical pattern of racial McCarthyism as marking the convergence of anti-Black and anti-communist hysteria helps us understand how CRT became such a successful political boogeyman—the veritable *Red October*. Christopher Rufo himself is blatant in his admission of racial McCarthyist tactics. On 15 March 2021, Rufo published a tweet that acknowledged the anti-CRT campaign as one of political disinformation, stating that "[t]he goal is to have the public read something crazy in the newspaper and immediately think 'critical race theory.' We have decodified the term and will recodify it to annex the entire range of cultural constructions that are unpopular with Americans."[58]

Additionally, Rufo's initial "investigations" on CRT in the Federal government uses excerpts from mild diversity training materials that do not ground themselves in the systemic and historically

---

in-the-mccarthy-era-to-be-black-was-to-be-red/>.

[56] Charisse Burden-Stelly, "Claudia Jones, the Longue Durée of McCarthyism, and the Threat of US Fascism" (2019) 3:1 J Intersectionality 46 at 50.

[57] Charisse Burden-Stelly, "Modern U.S. Racial Capitalism" Monthly Review (1 July 2020) online: <monthlyreview.org/2020/07/01/modern-u-s-racial-capitalism/>.

[58] Christopher F Rufo, "The goal is to have the public read something crazy in the newspaper and immediately think "critical race theory."" (15 March 2021), online: <twitter.com/realchrisrufo/status/1371541044592996352?s=20>.

contingent analysis of race that is characteristic of CRT. Rather, examples of voluntary racial sensitivity training are caricatured as "anti-white indoctrination session[s] imposed upon federal employees by totalitarian bureaucrats."[59] It is clear that Rufo and many of the most vociferous anti-CRT critics do not understand CRT nor care to accurately represent it, and that is precisely the point—an intentional distortion to turn the idea "toxic" and to will this recodification into being "through writing and persuasion," to use Rufo's words.[60]

What we are left with is a sort of "Schrodinger's CRT" phenomenon. By vacating CRT of its original substantive content and filling the vacuum with a variety of right-wing anxieties, anti-CRT campaigners can take advantage of conflicting meanings encapsulated around the strategy. As a result, claims around CRT as a school of thought can be *simultaneously* real and false. CRT can be charged with promoting individualized racialized guilt[61] even when it does the opposite by looking at the systemic legacies and impacts of slavery and colonialism. It can be charged with creating racial hierarchy even when it is explicitly dedicated to dismantling it. It can mean something or nothing—it doesn't really matter as incoherence is a key element of this strategy.[62] This has created the conditions for a racialized disinformation campaign to

---

[59] Samuel Hoadley-Brill, "Chris Rufo's critical race theory reporting is filled with errors, and he doesn't seem to care" Flux (26 July 2021) online: <flux.community/samuel-hoadley-brill/2021/07/chris-rufo-obsessed-critical-race-theory-he-also-doesnt-understand-it/>.

[60] Christopher F Rufo, "Yes, I envisioned a strategy—turn the brand "critical race theory" toxic—and, despite having virtually no resources compared to my opponents, willed it into being through writing and persuasion." (24 May 2021) online: <twitter.com/realchrisrufo/status/1396961964190961665?s=20>

[61] Jonathan Butcher and Mike Gonzalez, "Feeling Guilty About Everything? Thank Critical Race Theory" (7 December 2020), The Heritage Foundation, online: <heritage.org/progressivism/commentary/feeling-guilty-about-everything-thank-critical-race-theory>.

[62] For instance, Rufo has asserted that CRT promotes "principles of segregationism, group-based guilt, and race essentialism – ugly concepts that should have been left behind a century ago," despite a key tenet of CRT being the social construction of race, which directly opposes race essentialism. Benjamin Wallace-Wells, "How a conservative activist invented the conflict over critical race theory" The New Yorker (18 June 2021) online: <newyorker.com/news/annals-of-inquiry/how-a-conservative-activist-invented-the-conflict-over-critical-race-theory>.

centre around opposition to an imaginary of CRT as its lynchpin.[63] However, part of the immense success of this campaign has also been due to its ability to feed into several deep-seeded contemporary political and economic anxieties.

White Nationalist Anxieties: Internal and External

The terminology of racial McCarthyism implies politicized hysteria that has both a racial and economic dimension. Within the anti-CRT rhetorical playbook, this has manifested as efforts to manufacture a direct intellectual genealogy between CRT and Marxism. I argue that this connection feeds on two sides of white nationalist anxieties: (1) a domestic anxiety around mass movements for Black liberation and racial justice; and (2) an international anxiety around the United States being challenged as the preeminent global superpower by a rising China.

On the domestic front, a 42-page report released by the Heritage Foundation in December 2020 attempts to advance the connection between CRT and Marxism as explicitly as possible. In addition to claiming that CRT has deep Marxist roots, the Heritage Report also claims to reveal how the Black Lives Matter movement uses CRT to justify "violent riots," how educators were integrating CRT into K-12 instruction, and how the Parkland mass shootings in 2018 could be traced to policies informed by CRT advocates.[64]

The Heritage Report surveys the origins of critical theory to the Frankfurt School in 1937 which, as being influenced by Marxist thought, is described as "an unremitting attack on Western institutions and norms [...] written at the height of Joseph Stalin's purges."[65] It then moves to the origins of critical legal theory (CLT) in 1977, which

---

[63] Tactics such as keyword squatting have been leveraged by right-wing media to increase the output of stories around "critical race theory" from essentially zero in May 2020 to over 900 stories a month by September 2020. See Collins-Dexter and Donovan, *supra* note 5.

[64] Jonathan Butcher and Mike Gonzalez, "Critical Race Theory, the New Intolerance, and Its Grip on America" (7 December 2020) The Heritage Foundation, Backgrounder No 3567, online: <heritage.org/sites/default/files/2020-12/BG3567.pdf> at 3-4 [Heritage Report].

[65] *Ibid.*

was influenced by the works of European Philosophers such as Marx, Weber, Horkheimer, Gramsci, and Foucault. The authors then position CLT's proclaimed opposition to "the hierarchical structures of modern society" as a smoking gun that reveals its dangerous Marxian tendencies.[66] The Heritage Report then finally takes on CRT, characterizing it as "a short step" from CLT.[67] The report conflates the use of CRT as a prism to analyze racial inequality in society with making "everything about race."[68] It also decries CRT's suspicion and critique of liberalism in the United States, particularly claims of legal objectivity, neutrality, and equality. The report goes on to critique CRT's framing of the collective impacts of systemic racism as undergirding identity politics which poses a threat to the liberal idea of the individual as the central agent in society.[69]

However, the simple linear genealogy presented by the Heritage Report is at odds with the significant tensions between CLT and CRT as well as CRT and Marxism. As elucidated by several of its co-founders, CRT was created in part as a critique to the reductionist tendencies of the "class not race" elements of CLT—who some CRT scholars characterized as "vulgar Marxists."[70] Indeed, one of the catalysts for the creation of CRT as a school of thought was the failure of CLT "to reflect the lived experience of people of color," a failure that came to a head in the mid-late 1980s.[71] These divergences appeared in a variety of areas including critique of rights discourse, the law's role in reflecting and (re)producing racial power, and the dominance of whiteness even in progressive-left spaces in the academy.[72] Conversely, some Marxists have argued that the use of concepts like white supremacy as descriptors of social hierarchy are damaging to radical, emancipatory movements as they alienate white workers from their Black (and other non-white) counterparts.[73]

---

[66] *Ibid* at 6.

[67] *Ibid* at 8.

[68] *Ibid*.

[69] *Ibid* at 12.

[70] Kimberlé Williams Crenshaw et al, "Introduction" in Kimberlé Williams Crenshaw et al, eds, *Critical Race Theory: The Key Writings That Formed the Movement* (New York: New Press, 1995) xiii at xxvi [CRT Introduction].

[71] *Ibid* at xxiii.

[72] *Ibid* at xxiii–xxiv.

[73] Sean Walton, "Why the Critical Race Theory Concept of 'White Supremacy' Should Not Be Dismissed by Neo-Marxists: Lessons from Contemporary Black Radicalism"

But even if we were to take the Heritage argument at its highest and assume that CRT comfortably sat as an extension of Marxist political-legal thought, another question emerges: "so what?" Why don't anti-CRT activists then go to the heart of the threat and agitate for the purging and censorship of Marxism and other leftist ideas outright? The fact that anti-CRT advocates have not pursued this route (a more direct anti-communist type of McCarthyism) hints at the continued and explosive salience of race in American society. Direct repression against leftist ideas and organizing in the aftermath of Occupy Wall Street, rising economic inequality, rising costs of living, neoliberal globalization, and significant popular anger against massive wealth accumulation by economic elites would alienate many across the political spectrum. Further, in large part due to the mass mobilizations after the police murder of George Floyd in May 2020, Black Lives Matter has become a majoritarian issue.[74] As a result, a modern McCarthyist campaign could not frame itself as opposing anti-racism, nor could it frame itself as opposing class struggle, but *could* frame itself as opposing CRT—thus explaining the massive investment of intellectual energy in connecting CRT to Marxist thought.

Furthermore, the racial justice uprisings of 2020 explicitly combined critiques of class relations with racialized police brutality and a historically materialist analysis of racial inequality in the United States. These simultaneous critiques of race and class serve as a major threat to white nationalism and the capitalist order in America in their ability to articulate a common ground among a variety of disenfranchised and marginalized groups.[75] The reaction from the anti-CRT campaign has therefore been to position CRT as animating the 2020 racial justice protests, which are framed as violent riots indicative of state subversion. As the Heritage Report opines: "[t]he year 2020, with its protests and riots—as well as the overwhelming acceptance by the media, professional sports, corporations, the academy, and virtually all power centers, that America is irredeemably racist and must overhaul its entire system—has demonstrated that CRT's teachings

---

(2020) 12:1 Power and Education 78.

[74] Steven Long and Justin McCarthy, "Two in Three Americans Support Racial Justice Protests" *Gallup* (28 July 2020) online: <news.gallup.com/poll/316106/two-three-americans-support-racial-justice-protests.aspx>.

[75] Siddhant Issar, "Listening to Black Lives Matter: Racial Capitalism and the Critique of Neoliberalism" (2021) 20 Contemporary Political Theory 48.

have moved beyond the ivory towers and ivy walls."[76] This claim that CRT's tenets are elitist seem particularly ironic given that free-market think tanks and action groups funded by billionaires Charles and David Koch have played a significant role in manufacturing anti-CRT outrage.[77]

On the international front, the salience of geopolitical anxiety towards the rise of China has helped fuel racial McCarthyist hysteria. Derrick Bell, the "intellectual godfather" of CRT,[78] argued in his famous essay on interest-convergence that the Supreme Court's 1954 decision to find racial segregation of schools unconstitutional could not be understood without the need "to provide immediate credibility to America's struggle with Communist countries to win the hearts and minds of emerging third world peoples."[79] One key takeaway from Bell's analysis was that the *Brown* decision was motivated by the political and economic concerns of white elites *both* at home and abroad. If domestic racial politics during the civil rights era was influenced by America's geopolitical rivalry with the Soviet Union, then contemporary domestic racial politics is being significantly influenced by geopolitical rivalry with the People's Republic of China.

Indeed, a key condition of possibility that has fuelled anti-CRT racial McCarthyism is growing anxiety in the United States. with respect to the rise of China as a geopolitical rival—predicted to surpass the United States as the largest economic superpower by 2028.[80] The domestic manufacturing of Red Scare through the rise of a facially-socialist China (socialist in form, state capitalist in substance)[81] has resulted in numerous geopolitical antagonisms which greatly intensified during the Trump presidency: a prolonged trade war,

---

[76] Heritage Report, *supra* note 64 at 13.

[77] Jasmine Banks, "The Radical Capitalist Behind the Critical Race Theory Furor" The Nation (13 August 2021) online: <thenation.com/article/politics/charles-koch-crt-backlash/>

[78] Richard Delgado and Jean Stefancic, "Living History Interview with Richard Delgado & Jean Stefancic" (2011) 19 Transnat'l L & Contemp Probs 221 at 225.

[79] Derrick A Bell, "Brown v Board of Education and the Interest-Convergence Dilemma" (1980) 93:3 Harv L Rev 518 at 524.

[80] Larry Elliott, "China to Overtake US as World's Biggest Economy by 2028, Report Predicts" *The Guardian* (26 December 2020) online: <theguardian.com/world/2020/dec/26/china-to-overtake-us-as-worlds-biggest-economy-by-2028-report-predicts>

[81] Eli Friedman, "Why China Is Capitalist" Spectre Journal (15 July 2020) online: <spectrejournal.com/why-china-is-capitalist/>.

naval buildup in the South China Sea, Magnitsky sanctions against key Chinese officials (prompting a set of reciprocal sanctions on US officials), and perhaps most devastatingly, the stoking of a racialized discourse against China and Chinese people as to blame for the catastrophic global COVID-19 pandemic.[82]

Canada has also been dragged into this escalating geopolitical rivalry. The Canadian government's 2018 detention of Huawei CFO Meng Wanzhou upon an extradition request from the United States based on enforcement of US economic sanctions on Iran sparked a diplomatic row resulting in the reciprocal detention and conviction of Canadians Michael Kovrig and Michael Spavor in China, as well as a massive deterioration in the bilateral China-Canada relationship.[83] The strategic scapegoating of Chinese people for the COVID-19 pandemic led to a staggering spike in anti-Asian racism in Canada, with community organizations documenting over 1,150 racist attacks in 2020 and the Vancouver police reporting a 717 percent increase in anti-Asian hate crimes between 2019 and 2020.[84]

As a result, a "New Cold War" narrative has been pushed by nationalists on both sides which has significantly strengthened the national security apparatuses in both China and the West. Former US Secretary of State Mike Pompeo has described the Communist Party of China (CPC) as an "existential threat" to America[85] while former Conservative Party of Canada leader Erin O'Toole has called the Chinese government a "grave threat" to Canada, underlining the need to oppose "the sharp edges of communism."[86]

---

[82] Tobita Chow, "The Democratic Platform on China Is a Failure of Imagination" The Nation (31 July 2020) online: <thenation.com/article/politics/democratic-platform-china/>.

[83] Lizzi C Lee, "What Will Happen in Huawei CFO Meng Wanzhou's Canada Extradition Case?" The Diplomat (21 August 2021) online: <thediplomat.com/2021/08/what-will-happen-in-huawei-cfo-meng-wanzhous-canada-extradition-case/>.

[84] Katie Nicholson, "Surveys Find More than 1,000 Self-Reported Incidents of Anti-Asian Racism Since Start of Pandemic: Report" CBC News (23 March 2021) online: <cbc.ca/news/canada/asian-racism-hate-canada-pandemic-1.5959788>.

[85] David Rutz, "Chinese Communist Party an 'Existential' Threat that Biden Must Confront: Pompeo" Fox News (19 January 2021) online: <foxnews.com/world/chinese-communist-party-existential-threat-biden-confront-pompeo>.

[86] John Paul Tasker, "As Conservatives Call for Crackdown, O'Toole Calls Chinese Influence a Grave 'Threat' to Canada" CBC News (17 November 2020) online: <cbc.ca/news/politics/otoole-china-greatest-threat-1.5804972>.

The anti-CRT campaign has also capitalized on this Chinese Red Scare by tying CRT to the fearful spectre of the chaotic political violence instigated by the Mao-era cultural revolution—rhetoric explicitly deployed in Trump's Mount Rushmore speech.[87] Certain right-wing Chinese-language media outlets, such as the Epoch Times, have provided an important platform for these arguments. The spread of this China-specific racial McCarthyist messaging resulted in organized opposition to California's proposed high school ethnic studies requirement: AB-101.[88] For instance, in April 2021 a group of Chinese American parents organized a rally in Los Angeles against AB-101, stating that they opposed "the inculcation of CRT" in schools and holding signs such as "AB101 = Hate Education" and "No Communist Culture Revolution in CA!!!"[89] The messaging from these organizing spaces follows rhetoric that conflates ethnic studies with CRT and teaching racial literacy with normalizing racial hatred.

Yet unlike the Cold War era in which Derrick Bell conceived of interest-convergence, the idea that this antagonism is one between communism and capitalism is not reflected by current reality. Indeed, the Communist Party of China (CPC) has long since moved China to a state-guided capitalist economy. Initiated by the Dengist reforms of the 1980s, this process has been characterized by China's integration into the WTO in 2001, massive layoffs of tens of millions of state-sector workers as part of privatization campaigns, criminalization of independent trade unions, and the mass proletarianization of migrant workers through dispossession of peasants and an internal passport system (*hukou*) that excludes rural migrants from labour protections and social services.[90]

---

[87] Similar rhetoric invoking Red Scare and the threat of international communism (specifically the experience of the Soviet Union and North Korea) was raised during the opposition to the Statement of Principles requirement for Ontario lawyers to reflect on their professional and human rights obligations pertaining to diversity. See Joshua Sealy-Harrington, "Twelve Angry (White) Men: The Constitutionality of the Statement of Principles" (2020) 51(1) Ottawa L Rev 195.

[88] US, AB 101, An act to amend Sections 51225.3 and 51226.7 of the Education Code, relating to pupil instruction, Reg Sess, Cal, 2021 (enacted).

[89] Linda Jiang, "Chinese Californians Urgently Protest Against Critical Race Theory" Epoch Times (Chinese) (27 April 2021) online: <epochtimes.com/b5/21/4/27/n12907966.htm?utm_source=dable&fbclid=IwAR2SrOJlGo7iVF_EHXD8-Zvtbv2XTGyrBstQz_8u9mlz3VcnfXNGy6BoYumM>.

[90] Friedman, *supra* note 81.

As Thomas Mullaney notes, growing inequality, the forces unleashed by Chinese state capitalism, and the rise of ethnic scapegoating through Han Chinese resentment has rolled back the ideals of socialist multiculturalism into a distinctly capitalist form of racialization.[91] Racial capitalism in China has found its most brutal manifestation in the Northwest frontier of Xinjiang, where U.S.-led "global war on terror" politics has been weaponized against Uyghurs and other non-Han Indigenous populations, whose bodies have been rendered as sites of venture capital policing and surveillance technologies[92] and systematically converted into a racialized surplus force through re-education camp-to-factory pipelines.[93] Crucially then, the anti-CRT campaign's use of China-specific Red Scare messaging is *not* about a clash of ideology, but rather the *manufacture* of such a clash in order to uphold racial capitalism globally.

Concluding Remarks: Transnational Racial McCarthyism and the Canadian Context

As of 31 December 2022, at least 28 states had adopted at least one anti-CRT measure at the state level. Of those 28 states, 16 had specifically enacted anti-CRT legislation which has weaponized the law to cripple racial and gender equity education, programming, and policy-making.[94] The rapid proliferation of this raft of speech-suppressive laws and its devastating impact on the teaching of anti-racist education and history surprised those who assumed that anti-CRT hysteria was a specifically Trumpian political boogeyman that would go away once President Biden rescinded EO 13950 in January 2021. As a result,

---

[91] Thomas S Mullaney, "How China Went from Celebrating Ethnic Diversity to Suppressing It" The Guardian (10 June 2021) online: <theguardian.com/commentisfree/2021/jun/10/china-celebrating-diversity-suppressing-xinjiang-communist-party>.

[92] Darren Byler, Spirit Breaking: Uyghur Dispossession, Culture Work and Terror Capitalism in a Chinese Global City (Doctor of Philosophy, University of Washington, 2018) at 328 [Unpublished].

[93] Laura T Murphy and Nyrola Elimä, "In Broad Daylight: Uyghur Forced Labour and Global Solar Supply Chains" (2021) online (PDF): <shu.ac.uk/-/media/home/research/helena-kennedy-centre/projects/pdfs/evidence-base/in-broad-daylight.pdf>.

[94] Alexander, et al, *supra* note 21 at 5.

the response from many progressives was initially to dismiss its threat as limited to diversity trainings in the government under Trump or to distance work and teaching on racial justice from CRT[95] — oblivious to the use of CRT as a Trojan horse for racial McCarthyism and its explosive potential to leverage law and state power to silence efforts to speak about and address systemic racism.

Fortunately, there have also been many organizations that identified the devastating threat to free speech and racial and gender justice that the anti-CRT repression campaign posed. The African American Policy Forum, led by CRT co-founder Kimberlé Crenshaw, mobilized the TruthBeTold campaign to track the impacts of EO 13950 and state-level copycat bans while the NAACP Legal Defense Fund and Lambda Legal both launched constitutional challenges against Trump's Executive Order.[96] The latter suit was eventually successful in winning a nationwide injunction on enforcement of sections 4 (federal contractors) and 5 (federal grant recipients) based on *prima facie* violations of the free speech clause of the First Amendment and the due process clause of the Fifth Amendment.[97] A similar coordinated legal response is expected as parties affected by the many state-level anti-CRT bans begin to step forward as plaintiffs.

While an in-depth doctrinal treatment of the constitutional issues surfaced by these challenges would be urgent and useful, they miss the more important issues of political economy which drive the mass adoption of these laws—many of which have been drafted in ways that are blatantly unconstitutional. Indeed, the chilling effect in education and academia goes well beyond CRT and, by virtue of the campaign's intentional vagueness and incoherence, effectively implicate all areas of critical inquiry and search for historical truth.

---

[95] See e.g. Joe Wojtas, "Stonington Says It Does Not Teach Critical Race Theory in Its Schools" The Day (10 August 2021) online: <yahoo.com/news/stonington-says-does-not-teach-040100685.html>.

[96] "NAACP Legal Defense Fund, National Urban League, National Fair Housing Alliance File Suit Against Trump Administration; African American Policy Forum Launches #TruthBeTold Campaign" (29 October 2020), online: <naacpldf.org/press-release/naacp-legal-defense-fund-national-urban-league-national-fair-housing-alliance-file-suit-against-trump-administration-african-american-policy-forum-launches-truthbetold-campaign/>.

[97] *Santa Cruz Lesbian and Gay Community Center et al v Trump et al*, Case No 20-cv-07741-BLF (ND Cal 2020) at 29–31.

In Canada, while related protests decrying anti-Black racism and demanding justice for the genocidal legacy of Indian Residential Schools have spread across the country, there have also been signs that conservatives are playing with the idea of using CRT as a Trojan horse to preclude the ability to discuss or address systemic racism. In addition to StopSOP's targeting of CRT and CRT scholars at the Law Society of Ontario, conservative journalists such as Tristin Hopper have taken a page from the Christopher Rufo playbook in presenting anti-racism training materials used at Global Affairs Canada as indicative that CRT is a dangerous ideology infiltrating the Canadian federal bureaucracy. Like Rufo on Fox News, Hopper's April 2021 investigation in the *National Post* takes significant liberties with explaining CRT, claiming the idea that "only white people can be racist" is a key tenet of CRT—an idea that is antithetical to CRT tenets.[98]

Similarly, anti-CRT advocates in Canada rallied behind the suicide of former Toronto District School Board principal Richard Bilkszto in July 2023, blaming his death on the apparent humiliation he felt when attending an anti-racism workshop. Bilkszto helped found the Toronto Chapter of Foundation Against Intolerance and Racism (FAIR), a key US-based anti-CRT lobbying group.[99] This chapter has organized specifically against Bill 67, the *Racial Equity in the Education System Act*, by arguing that racial equity and anti-racism training in fact will "further racism" and "runs the risk of inviting and affirming divisive ideological frameworks."[100]

In remarks to the Canadian Press following Bilkszto's death, the Bilkszto family's lawyer, Lisa Bildy—a key organizer of the StopSOP campaign—characterized diversity, education, and inclusion trainings as "woke struggle sessions," once again making a racial McCarthyist connection to the Cultural Revolution under Maoist

---

98 Tristin Hopper, "Only White People Can Be Racist: Inside Global Affairs' Anti-Racism Course Materials" The National Post (22 April 2021) online: <nationalpost.com/news/canada/only-white-people-can-be-racist-inside-global-affairs-anti-racism-course-materials>.

99 The Canadian Press, "Education Minister Orders Review into Allegations of TDSB Principal who Died by Suicide" CBC News (25 July 2023) online: <cbc.ca/news/canada/toronto/lecce-tdsb-principal-death-staff-review-1.6917432>.

100 FAIR Ontario, "FAIR Ontario's Comments on Bill 67" (last visited 25 august 2025), online: <https://www.fairforall.org/ontario/bill-67-racial-equity-in-the-education-system-act-2021/>.

China.[101] In response, Ontario Minister of Education Stephen Lecce ordered a formal review of the circumstances around Bilkszto's death in a process that a coalition of Black community organizations in the GTA has criticized as "an active campaign to villainize and undermine anti-racism work in this province."[102]

While anti-CRT hysteria has yet to gain the same mass traction north of the border, particularly in the form of speech-repressive legislation and policy which has swept through the U.S., many of the same conditions of possibility, from political backlash against mass mobilizations for racial justice to increased geopolitical antagonisms, exist in Canada as well. The geopolitical aspect of racial McCarthyism in the form of anti-Palestinian racism was in explosive display after Palestinian militant group Hamas launched a systematic attack into Israel on 7 October 2023, to which the Israeli government responded with mass and indiscriminate bombing of the Gaza Strip resulting in the forced displacement of over a million Gazans. As of August 2025, at least 1,100 people have been killed in Israel,[103] while at least 62,000 have been killed in Gaza.[104]

Activists, students, and scholars who have called attention to the historical and structural aspects of the Israeli-Palestinian conflict— particularly those surfaced ongoing legacies of settler colonialism, apartheid, land theft, and ethnic cleansing—have been subject to harassment and suppression including employment discipline, censorship, doxxing, and smearing. For instance, NYU Law student body president Ryna Workman had her job offer with Winston & Strawn publicly withdrawn after stating that Israel bore responsibility for the lives lost in the Hamas attack and affirming solidarity with the

---

[101] The Canadian Press, *supra* note 99.

[102] Brendan Kennedy, "Black Community Groups Say TDSB Principal's Suicide Is Being Used to 'Villainize and Undermine' Anti-Racism Training" *The Toronto Star* (2 August 2023) online: <thestar.com/news/gta/black-community-groups-say-tdsb-principal-s-suicide-is-being-used-to-villainize-and-undermine/article_744ad4b7-e325-5b1a-a7c6-717b69f7c330.html>.

[103] Belkis Wille, Robin Taylor & Devon Lum, "'I Can't Erase All the Blood from My Mind': Palestinian Armed Groups' October 7 Assault on Israel" (17 July 2024) online (Webpage): <hrw.org/report/2024/07/17/i-cant-erase-all-blood-my-mind/palestinian-armed-groups-october-7-assault-israel>.

[104] Al Jazeera, "Israeli attacks, forced starvation have killed 62,000 Palestinians in Gaza" *Al Jazeera* (18 August 2025), online: <aljazeera.com/news/2025/8/18/israeli-attacks-forced-starvation-have-killed-62000-palestinians-in-gaza>.

Palestinian resistance.[105] Harvard University students who signed letters expressing Palestinian solidarity had their names and faces plastered on a mobile billboard truck labelled "Harvard's Leading Anti-Semites."[106] In France, the Ministry of the Interior went as far as ordering a ban on pro-Palestinian rallies, citing concerns about disturbances to the public order.[107]

Canada has also seen a surge of censorship and repression for those criticizing Israeli settler occupation and its attendant abuses towards the Palestinian people.[108] This atmosphere of intimidation and censorship has in part been facilitated through the media.[109] On 13 October 2023, prominent labour and employment lawyer Howard Levitt wrote in the *Financial Post* that any "employee in a public-facing or managerial position who participated in any of Canada's Hamas-supporting 'hate fests' should similarly be fired for cause. And if any of them sue, I will personally act for their employers, pro bono."[110]

In Ontario, Sarah Jama, MPP for Hamilton Centre, was attacked for her public statement which called for an immediate ceasefire and an end to Israeli occupation, identifying the causes of the conflict in "violence and retaliation rooted in settler colonialism."[111] In response,

[105] Megan Tribe, "Winston Scraps NYU Student's Job Offer Over Israel Comments" Bloomberg Law (11 October 2023) online: <news.bloomberglaw.com/business-and-practice/winston-scraps-nyu-law-students-job-offer-over-israel-email>.

[106] Catherine Thorbecke, "Names and Faces of Harvard Students Linked to an Anti-Israel Statement Were Plastered on Mobile Billboards and Online Sites" CNN Business (12 October 2023) online: <cnn.com/2023/10/12/business/harvard-doxxing-truck-israel-hamas-statement>.

[107] Dalal Mawad and Eve Brennan, "France Bans All Pro-Palestinian Protests" CNN World (12 October 2023) online: <cnn.com/2023/10/12/europe/france-ban-pro-palestinian-intl/index.html>.

[108] Islamophobia Research Hub, Documenting the 'Palestine Exception': An Overview of Trends in Islamophobia, Anti-Palestinian, and Anti-Arab Racism in Canada in the Aftermath of October 7, 2023 (Toronto: Islamophobia Research Hub, 2025), online (PDF): <yorku.ca/laps/research/islamophobia/wp-content/uploads/sites/874/2025/09/documenting-the-palestine-exception-2025.pdf>.

[109] *When Genocide Wasn't News: How Canadian media covered up the destruction of Gaza*, ed by Martin Lukacs, Dania Majid & Jason Toney (Montréal: Breach Books, 2025).

[110] Howard Levitt. "If your Employer Expresses Sympathy for Hamas, Here Are your Options" The Financial Post (13 October 2023) online: <financialpost.com/fp-work/employer-sympathy-hamas>.

[111] Katherine DeClerq, "Doug Ford served cease-and-desist letter by NDP MPP Sarah Jama" CTV News (19 October 2023) online: <ctvnews.ca/toronto/article/doug-ford-served-cease-and-desist-letter-by-ndp-mpp-sarah-jama/>.

Conservative Ontario Premier Doug Ford issued a statement alleging that Jama had "a long and well-documented history of antisemitism" and "hateful views." Ford went further in characterizing Jama's statement as "publicly supporting the rape and murder of innocent Jewish people."[112] The Ford government also put forward a motion requesting that the House Speaker not recognize Jama in the Ontario Legislature until she retracts or deletes her statement. Jama issued a cease-and-desist letter to the Premier's Office, alleging legal defamation.[113] Jama was soon expelled from the Ontario New Democratic Party caucus for refusing to backtrack on her comments and supposedly having "contributed to unsafe work environments for staff."[114] In another case of workplace discipline, Dr. Ben Thomson, a nephrologist at Mackenzie Richmond Hill Hospital, was suspended from his job, threatened, and had his addressed shared online after he posted pro-Palestinian views on social media.[115]

Anti-racist educators in this context are left to grapple with a self-fulfilling prophecy: censorship of anti-racist education, activism, and programs only works in the context of an *impoverished understanding of racism*. A lack of racial and decolonial literacy leaves publics susceptible to ethnonational projects weaponizing race in service of protecting structures of social hierarchy in their specific racial microclimes. This is precisely *why* ethnonationalists deliberately seek to target, discredit, and villainize critical race theory, decolonial and postcolonial studies for delegitimization and censorship.[116]

The symbolic threat of the *Red October* continues to lurk right beneath the surface and holds enormous potential to unleash its repressive racial McCarthyist arsenal, particularly in reaction to times of racial and economic upheaval. Critical legal scholars ought to

---

[112] *Ibid.*

[113] *Ibid.*

[114] Samantha Beattie and Bobby Hristova, "Ontario NDP kicks Hamilton MPP Sarah Jama from caucus after controversial Gaza comments" (23 October 2023) CBC News, online: <cbc.ca/news/canada/hamilton/jama-ndp-caucus-1.7005056>.

[115] Brishti Basu, "Ontario Doctor Suspended, his Address Published After Pro-Palestinian Social Media Posts" CBC News (20 October 2023) online: <cbc.ca/news/canada/doctor-doxed-suspended-palestinian-posts-1.7001887>.

[116] Vincent Wong, "Nationalist Backlash to Antiracist Education: A Transnational Blueprint for Academic Unfreedom" in Nandini Ramanujam & Frédéric Mégret, eds, *Academic Freedom in a Plural World: Global Critical Perspectives* (Budapest; New York: Central European University Press, 2024) 115.

remain ever vigilant of this potential. At stake is our very ability as researchers, teachers, and students to interrogate and speak the truth about the role of law and legal institutions within the broader legacies of settler colonialism, white supremacy, and heteropatriarchy both at home in the Canadian nation-state and abroad.

CHAPTER B-5

The School Policing Origins of *R v Grant*

Lisa M Kelly[*]

Abstract

A generation of law students, lawyers, and judges are intimately familiar with the doctrinal holdings of the Supreme Court in *R v Grant* (2009). *Grant* clarified the framework for deciding when unlawfully obtained evidence should be excluded under section 24(2) of the *Charter* and provided guidance on the law of detention. Although the *Grant* decision has generated a rich body of empirical analysis and critical commentary, the fact that police surveilled, stopped, questioned, detained, and arrested Grant as part of a school policing operation has largely gone unnoticed. Abstracting the police patrol in *Grant* outside of this context disguises and mystifies the racial, class, and generational hierarchies that produced it. This chapter brings those dynamics to light. The story I trace here is one not only about the policing *of* schools and children. It is also crucially about the discursive role of policing *for* schools and children – calls to protect vulnerable young people from other dangerous youths – and what this powerfully authorizes in law and politics.

[*] I thank Ben Berger, Kim Brooks, Maria Dugas, Afroditi Giovanopoulou, Kyle Kirkup, Sonia Lawrence, Zinaida Miller, Palma Paciocco, Ashwini Vasanthakumar, and the anonymous reviewers for their insightful and generous feedback on earlier drafts.

Résumé

Une génération d'étudiant·e·s en droit, d'avocat·e·s et de juges est intimement familiarisée avec les conclusions doctrinales de la Cour suprême dans l'affaire *R c Grant* (2009). L'arrêt *Grant* a clarifié le cadre permettant de décider quand une preuve obtenue illégalement devrait être exclue en vertu de l'article 24(2) de la *Charte* et a fourni des orientations sur le droit de la détention. Bien que la décision *Grant* ait généré un grand nombre d'analyses empiriques et de commentaires critiques, le fait que la police ait surveillé, arrêté, interrogé, détenu et arrêté Grant dans le cadre d'une opération de maintien de l'ordre à l'école est largement passé inaperçu. L'effacement de la patrouille de police de *Grant* de ce contexte masque et mystifie les hiérarchies raciales, de classe et générationnelles qui en sont à l'origine. Cet essai met en lumière ces dynamiques. L'histoire que je retrace ici ne concerne pas seulement le maintien de l'ordre dans les écoles et auprès des enfants. Il s'agit aussi et surtout du rôle discursif du maintien de l'ordre dans les écoles et auprès des enfants - les appels à protéger les jeunes vulnérables contre d'autres jeunes dangereux - et de ce que cela autorise puissamment en droit et en politique.

Just after noon on November 17, 2003, Donnohue Grant, a Black teenager, was walking down a sidewalk in the Greenwood-Danforth area of Toronto. With temperatures hovering just above freezing, Grant was wearing a three-quarter length jacket. Walking northward, he noticed a car drive past with two men inside. The men would later claim that he had stared at them in an unusually intense way. Unbeknownst to Grant, the two men were undercover police officers; and, unbeknownst to them, he was carrying a gun.[1]

What transpired moments later gave rise to criminal charges against Grant, followed by a trial at which he was convicted of multiple weapons offences and sentenced to eighteen months in prison. Grant appealed his conviction and sentence to the Ontario Court of Appeal and later the Supreme Court of Canada. In 2009, the Supreme Court released its landmark decision in *R v Grant* in which it held that

Gregory Pike provided exceptional research assistance. I acknowledge the support of funding from the Social Sciences and Humanities Research Council in this work.
[1] My statement of the facts in this case is based on the original trial transcript and judicial opinions in *R v Grant*.

police had violated Grant's rights to be free from arbitrary detention and to be informed of his right to counsel upon detention.[2] The judges nevertheless held that the handgun evidence obtained in violation of the *Canadian Charter of Rights and Freedoms* had been properly admitted at trial.[3] The Court entered an acquittal on one weapons trafficking charge and upheld the remaining convictions.[4]

A generation of law students, lawyers, and judges are intimately familiar with the doctrinal holdings in *R v Grant*. *Grant* clarified the framework for deciding when unlawfully obtained evidence should be excluded under section 24(2) of the *Charter* and provided guidance on the law of detention.[5] As the Supreme Court had affirmed since *R v Therens*, a person may be found to have been psychologically detained in cases that fall short of physical detention.[6] Psychological detention occurs when a person is lawfully obliged to comply with a restrictive request or demand by police or when a reasonable person would have concluded that they had no choice but to comply.[7] Writing for the majority in *Grant*, Chief Justice McLachlin and Justice Charron held that reviewing courts should consider the "particular characteristics or circumstances" of the person facing detention to determine if psychological detention had occurred.[8] They provided a non-exhaustive list of factors that courts should consider when deciding whether

---

[2] *R v Grant*, 2009 SCC 32 [*Grant* SCC].

[3] *Ibid* at para 140.

[4] *Ibid* at para 149.

[5] See Benjamin Johnson, Richard Jochelson & Victoria Weir, "Exclusion of Evidence under Section 24(2) of the *Charter* Post-*Grant* in the Years 2014–2017: A Comprehensive Analysis of 600 Cases" (2019–2020) 67 Crim LQ 56 at 59; Justine Milne, "Exclusion of Evidence Trends Post *Grant*: Are Appeals Courts Deferring to Trial Judges? (2015) 19 Can Crim L Rev 373; Patrick McGuinty, "Section 24(2) of the *Charter*: Exploring the Role of Police Conduct in the *Grant* Analysis" (2018) 41 Man LJ 273; Richard Jochelson, Debao Huang & Melanie J Murchison, "Empiricizing Exclusionary Remedies - A Cross Canada Study of Exclusion under s 24(2) of the *Charter*, Five Years After *Grant*" (2016) 63: Issues 1 & 2 Crim LQ 206; Mike Madden, "Marshalling the Data: An Empirical Analysis of Canada's Section 24(2) Case Law in the Wake of *R v Grant*" (2011) 15:2 CCLR 229; Steven Penney & Moin Yahya, "Section 24(2) in the Trial Courts: An Empirical Analysis of the Legal and Non-Legal Determinants of Excluding Unconstitutionally Obtained Evidence in Canada" (2021) 58(3) Osgoode Hall Law J 509.

[6] *R v Therens*, 1985 SCC 29.

[7] See *R v Grant*, *supra* note 1 at paras 30, 44.

[8] *Ibid* at para 44.

an interaction with police constitutes detention.[9] They adopted a modi-fied objective standard: how might a reasonable person of similar "age, physical stature, minority status, [and] level of sophistication" have interpreted the interaction with police?[10] A decade later, in *R v Le*, the Court belatedly provided substantive content to this standard by tak-ing judicial notice of the ways that a history of racially discriminatory policing will influence the perceptions of Black, Indigenous and racial-ized youths and adults when interacting with police.[11]

In this chapter, I turn our gaze back on the police operation that fall day in 2003. Although the *Grant* decision has generated a rich body of empirical analysis and critical commentary, the fact that police surveilled, stopped, questioned, detained, and arrested Grant as part of a school policing operation has largely gone unnoticed.[12] Abstracting the police patrol in *Grant* outside of this context disguises

[9] *Ibid.*

[10] *Ibid.*

[11] *R v Le*, 2019 SCC 34.

[12] On the remedial analysis under s 24(2), See e.g. Kent Roach, "Determining the Seriousness of the Violation under Section 24(2) of the *Charter*" (2014) 61:2 Crim LQ 157; Nick Kaschuk, "Gauging Society's Interest in Adjudication on the Merits" (2015) 62:3 Crim LQ 384; David Porter & Brent Kettles, "The Significance of Police Misconduct in the Analysis of s 8 *Charter* Breaches and the Exclusion of Evidence under s 24(2) in *R v Grant, R v Harrison* and *R v Morelli*" (2012) 58:3–4 Crim LQ 510. For a brief discussion of the Supreme Court's treatment of the "community policing" argument, see Tim Quigley, "Was it Worth the Wait? The Supreme Court's New Approaches to Detention and Exclusion of Evidence" (2009) 66 CR-ART 88; Steven Penney & James Stribopoulos, "'Detention' under the *Charter* after *R v Grant* and *R v Suberu*" (2010) 51:2 SCLR 439; and Jonathan Dawe & Heather McArthur, "*Charter* Detention and the Exclusion of Evidence after *Grant, Harrison* and *Suberu*" (2010) 56:4 Crim LQ 376; Matthew Pearn, "Section 24(2): Does the Truth cost Too Much" (2011) 62 UNBLJ 147; Jennifer Woollcombe, "*Grant, Suberu,* and *Harrison*: Detention, the Right to Counsel and a New Analysis under Section 24(2): Some Practical Impacts" (2010) 51 SCLR 479. On the erasure of race and class in the Supreme Court's detention jurisprudence, see Benjamin L Berger, "Race and Erasure in *Mann*" (2004) 21 CR (6th) 58; David Tanovich, "The Further Erasure of Race in *Charter* Cases" 38 (2006) Criminal Reports 84; Amar Khoday, "Ending the Erasure?: Writing Race into the Story of Psychological Detentions – Examining *R v Le*" (2021) 100 SLCR (2d) 165; Elsa Kaka, "The Supreme Court of Canada's Justification of *Charter* Breaches and Its Effect on Black and Indigenous Communities" (2020): 43:5 Man LJ 117; Lewis Waring, "Detained on Sight: The Socioeconomic Aspect of Social Context in *R v Le*" (2021): 44:6 Man LJ 138.

and mystifies the racial, class, and generational hierarchies that produced it.[13] This chapter brings those dynamics to light.

In Part II, I revisit the moral panic around youth offending and school discipline in the United States and Canada in the 1990s and early 2000s. Part III provides a close reading of the police patrol and seven-minute interaction with Donnohue Grant that preceded his arrest. I show how "hot spot" policing converged with public trespass laws to subject certain schools and students to intense surveillance. Part IV examines the trial and appellate review of police conduct in this case. At trial, Judge Harris framed the police stop of Grant as both essential and trivial. In performing the crucial work of keeping schools safe, Judge Harris found that police had neither detained Grant nor violated any of his *Charter* rights. Both the Ontario Court of Appeal and the Supreme Court of Canada rejected this conclusion and held that police had psychologically detained Donnohue Grant. In reaching this conclusion, the appellate courts nevertheless legitimated a host of "neighbourhood policing" tactics that fall short of detention. This fits a pattern. While in the liberal legalist imaginary, courts and constitutional law stand as a bulwark against coercive state power, Canadian courts have in fact played a key role in facilitating and expanding police powers.[14] The story I trace here is one not only about the policing *of* schools and children. It is also crucially about the discursive role of policing *for* schools and children—calls to

---

[13] See Karl Marx, *Capital: A Critique of Political Economy*, ed by Friedrich Engels, translated by Ben Fowkes (London, U.K.: Penguin Books in association with New Left Review, 1990) vol 1, where Marx argues mainstream understandings of capitalism are mystified by and to the favour of dominant classes. For contemporary elaboration on Marx's theory of historical mystification, see Trevor Purvis & Alan Hunt, "Discourse, Ideology, Discourse, Ideology, Discourse, Ideology [...]" (1993) 44:3 The British J of Sociology 473; Tamás Tóth, "On The Discreet (C)harm of Ideology - The Mystification of Domination in Postmodern Global Capitalism" (2021): 16:2 J of Multicultural Discourses 155.

[14] See James Stribopolous, "In *Search* of Dialogue: The Supreme Court, Police Powers and the *Charter*" (2005) 31:1 Queen's LJ 1; Steve Coughlan, "*Charter* Protection against Unlawful Police Action: Less Black and White Than It Seems" (2012) 57 SCLR 205; Vanessa McDonnell, "Assessing the Impact of the Ancillary Powers Doctrine on Three Decades of *Charter* Jurisprudence" (2012) 57 SCLR 225; Richard Jochelson, David Ireland, Ryan Ziegler, Erika Brenner, & Kirsten Kramar, "Generation and Deployment of Common Law Police Powers by Canadian Courts and the Double-Edged *Charter*" (2020) 28 Critical Criminology 107.

protect vulnerable young people from other dangerous youths—and what this powerfully authorizes in law and politics.

Youth Predators and Zero Tolerance

In 1995, the American political scientist John J. DiIulio wrote a dystopian cover story for *The Weekly Standard* titled, "The Coming of the Super-Predators."[15] Then a professor at Princeton, DiIulio coined a term that captured and fuelled a racist and class-driven panic about young offending. Extrapolating from a study of Philadelphia's youth crime rate, DiIulio warned that thirty thousand young "murderers, rapists, and muggers" would be roaming America's streets within five years.[16] Trafficking in animalistic rhetoric that white supremacists had long used to dehumanize African Americans, DiIulio predicted that "as many as half of these juvenile super-predators could be young black males."[17] The myth gained prominence with the support of James Q. Wilson, DiIulio's dissertation advisor and intellectual architect of "broken windows policing."[18]

That DiIulio's ominous forecast never came to pass was beside the point. Apart from a brief increase in the youth crime rate in the mid-1990s, youth offending in the United States fell at the very time that the super-predator myth gained traction.[19] Lawmakers and

---

15 John DiIulio, "The Coming of the Super-Predators", *Washington Examiner* (27 November 1995), online: <https://www.washingtonexaminer.com/weekly-standard/the-coming-of-the-super-predators>.

16 *Ibid.*

17 John DiIulio, "My Black Crime Problem, and Ours" (1996) 6:2 City Journal 14, cited in Kristin Henning, *The Rage of Innocence: How America Criminalizes Black Youth* (New York: Pantheon Books, 2021) at 88.

18 Barry Krisberg. "Chapter 1. Juvenile Justice: Myths and Realities" in *Juvenile Justice and Delinquency*, 1st ed (Los Angeles, CA: SAGE Publications, 2018) at 3.

19 DiIulio later expressed regret and tried to "put the brakes" on his super-predator theory, which had by then "taken on a life of its own." While he continues to defend the quality of his research and denies direct responsibility for increased incarceration rates, DiIulio acknowledges his projections have since been disproven. See Elizabeth Becker, "As Ex-Theorist on Young 'Superpredators,' Bush Aide Has Regrets" *New York Times* (9 February 2001), online: <https://www.nytimes.com/2001/02/09/us/as-ex-theorist-on-young-superpredators-bush-aide-has-regrets.html>; see Office of Juvenile Justice and Delinquency Prevention, *Statistical Briefing Book: Juvenile Arrest Rate Trends* (Washington, D.C.: U.S. Department of Justice, 2017);

political leaders seized on the rhetoric to mobilize support for their carceral agendas. When then-First Lady Hillary Rodham Clinton spoke in 1996 in support of the federal crime bill that her husband had signed into law two years earlier, she warned of ties between juvenile offenders and organized crime. "We need to take these people on," she said. "They are often connected to big drug cartels; they are not just gangs of kids anymore. They are often the kinds of kids that are called super predators. No conscience, no empathy. We can talk about why they ended up that way, but first we have to bring them to heel."[20] Talk of bringing young people to heel, as one might a dog, disguised and legitimated the structural and individual violence inflicted on poor and Black children by libelling these children as threats to the social order.[21]

Fears about the primal tendencies of young people resonated north of the border. During this same period, Canadian media outlets and public figures expressed growing panic about youth violence and gang activity.[22] Newspaper headlines warned of a "generation ex" that might be permanently lost to violence and hopelessness; others used militaristic rhetoric to lament the violence that was "invad[ing] school playgrounds."[23] A shared feature of the young offender panic across North America was a view that youth sentences were too

Jeffrey A Butts, "Youth still leading violent crime drop: 1988–2018", (6 November 2019), online: John Jay College's Research and Evaluation Center <https://johnjayrec.nyc/2019/11/06/databits201901/>.

[20] Hillary Clinton, "Seven Principles of President Clinton's Campaign," Speech to Keene State College (Keene, NH, 1996), online: CSPAN, <https://www.c-span.org/program/public-affairs-event/hillary-clinton-campaign-speech/54206>.

[21] For a history of how white American childhood became synonymous with innocence from the mid-nineteenth century onward as popular culture constructed white children as innocent and vulnerable while excluding Black youth from these qualities, see Robin M Bernstein, *Racial Innocence: Performing American Childhood from Slavery to Civil Rights* (New York: New York University Press, 2011).

[22] See Canada, Department of Justice, *A Review of the Young Offenders Act and the Youth Justice System in Canada: Report of the Federal-Provincial Task Force on Youth Justice* (Ottawa: Department of Justice, 1996) [Review of YOA] at 14–19. Nicholas Bala, "What's Wrong With YOA Bashing? What's Wrong With the YOA? Recognizing the Limits of the Law" (1994) 36 Can J Criminology 247.

[23] Keri Sweetman, "When violence invades school playgrounds", *Ottawa Citizen*, June 15, 1991; Sandy Cameron, "Generation Ex: Losing our young people before our eyes", *Vancouver Sun*, November 20, 1992.

lenient, especially for those who committed violent crimes. [24] During the 1990s, all fifty U.S. states reformed their juvenile criminal laws with many making it easier to transfer minors to adult court.[25] In Canada, both Progressive Conservative and Liberal governments amended the *Youth Offenders Act* (*YOA*) in the 1990s to allow for more transfers of youths to adult courts and to impose longer youth sentences for murder.[26]

As in the United States, public perceptions of youth crime in Canada did not correspond with statistical or legal realities. While the rate of police-reported youth crime in Canada increased in the late 1980s and early 1990s, just as it did in the United States, it peaked in 1991 and by 2006 had fallen by 25% from the rate in 1991.[27] A Federal-Provincial committee review of the *YOA* in 1996 concluded: "Judgments of the youth justice system are often derived from sources that present inadequate information, that emphasize unrepresentative cases, or that refer to what occurs in the United States or elsewhere."[28] Media and cultural narratives circulating throughout North America stoked public fear and drove political responses.

These fears only intensified around schools. Even though Canada has never experienced the American scourge of continual school

---

[24] Nicholas Bala & Sanjeev Anand, *Youth Criminal Justice Law*, 3rd ed (Toronto: Irwin Law, 2012) at 16.

[25] Eric C Nystrom and David S Tanenhaus, "The Future of Digital Legal History: No Magic, No Silver Bullets," (2016) 56 Amer J Legal Hist 150; Eric C Nystrom & David S Tanenhaus, "Let's Change the Law": Arkansas and the Puzzle of Juvenile Justice Reform in the 1990s" (2016) 34 Law & Hist Rev 957 (2016).

[26] See also Nicholas Bala, "Dealing with Violent Young Offenders: Transfer to Adult Court and Bill C-58" (1990) 9 Can J Fam L 11; *An Act to Amend the Young Offenders Act and the Criminal Code*, SC 1992, c 11; *An Act to amend the Young Offenders Act and the Criminal Code*, SC 1995, c 19.

[27] Statistics Canada, *Youth Crime in Canada*, 2006 Catalogue No 85-002-X2008003 (Ottawa: Statistics Canada 2008) <https://publications.gc.ca/collections/collection_2018/jus/J4-58-2016-eng.pdf>. For debates amongst criminologists about changes in reporting and recording practices versus patterns of youth offending, see Peter J Carrington, "Has Youth Crime Increased? Comment on Corrado and Markwart" (1995) 37 Can J Crim 61 contrasted against Raymond Corrado & Alan Markwart, "A Response to Carrington (Has Violent Youth Crime Increased?)" (1995) 37 Can J Crim 74; Peter J Carrington, "Trends in Youth Crime in Canada 1977–1996" (1999) 41 Can J Crim 1; Anthony Doob & Jane B Sprott, "Is the 'quality' of youth violence becoming more serious?" (1998) 40 Can J Crim 185.

[28] Review of *YOA*, *supra* note 22 at 19.

shootings, school safety still came to dominate public debates over education in Canada in the 1980s and 1990s.[29] National media coverage of serious incidents of school-based violence sparked fears among families, police, lawmakers, and school officials. In 1993, Ontario's Royal Commission on Learning observed that "[t]he problem of violence in the schools has been raised at our hearings more than any other issue."[30] Proposed solutions ranged from the sartorial to the carceral. Calls for clear backpacks, lanyards, and school uniforms arose alongside demands for heightened surveillance, increased police presence in schools, and harsher criminal sentences for young offenders.[31]

Fears about student safety created political opportunities for fiscally conservative governments. In 2000, Progressive Conservative Premier Mike Harris swept into power in Ontario with a campaign promising "zero tolerance" for misconduct in public schools.[32] Channelling—and creating—"common sense" desires for safety in schools, the Harris government introduced the *Safe Schools Act* (*SSA*), which created new disciplinary infractions for students, increased the disciplinary power of teachers and principals, and mandated suspensions or expulsions for certain rule violations.[33] The *SSA* was introduced in 2001, just two years before Donnohue Grant was arrested as part of a "school safety" policing patrol.

Less than six months before Grant's arrest, lawyer Kenneth Bhattacharjee published a review of the *SSA* for the Ontario Human Rights Commission entitled "The Ontario *Safe Schools Act*: Discipline and Discrimination."[34] The Bhattacharjee report found

---

[29] See RD Gidney, *From Hope to Harris: The Reshaping of Ontario's Schools* (Toronto: University of Toronto Press, 1999) at 180–81.

[30] *Ibid* at 181.

[31] See "Security cameras touted for schools", *Toronto Star*, October 26, 1994; Frank Calleja, "Social skills training tackles violence in Peel classrooms", *Toronto Star*, July 20, 1995; Michelle Shephard, "Uniforms cool school hotheads", *Toronto Star*, February 6, 1999.

[32] See Richard Mackie, "Harris Cracks Down on Student Misconduct: Code Features Automatic Suspensions, Expulsions", *The Globe and Mail* (21 March 2000), online: <www.theglobeandmail.com/news/national/harris-cracks-down-on-student-misconduct/article1037991>.

[33] See *Safe Schools Act, 2000*, SO 2000, c 12, ss 309 (1)–(22) (mandatory expulsion), ss 306 (1)–(13) (mandatory suspension).

[34] Ken Bhattacharjee, *The Ontario Safe Schools Act: School Discipline and Discrimination*, (Ontario Human Rights Commission, 2003).

a strong perception in the Greater Toronto Area and other parts of Ontario, supported by some independent evidence, that the *SSA* and school board policies were being applied disproportionately against racialized students and students with disabilities. Many interviewees criticized zero tolerance policies for contributing to youth criminalization and the school-to-prison pipeline.[35] Several directors of community legal clinics reported that suspended or expelled students tended to hang out on streets or in malls during the school day, creating a "powerful excuse for police to stop them and question why they aren't in school [...] [thereby] escalat[ing] police supervision of racialized kids."[36] Exclusionary school discipline policies operated as a form of exile that could permanently alter a young person's life trajectory. More likely to drop out, more likely to use substances, more likely to run afoul of the criminal law, and more likely to be routinely profiled and policed, they were reduced to what social worker Akua Benjamin later called the "walking wounded."[37]

"Hot Spot" Schools

This public panic about deviant youths and their threat to schools produced and legitimized the policing operation that targeted Donnohue Grant near a so-called school crime "hot spot" in November 2003. "Hot spot" or "focused deterrence" policing proliferated across North America in the 1980s and 1990s onward as empirical and technological advances enabled police to trace "crime clusters" to street

---

[35] *Ibid* at 57–58. See also Abigail Tsionne Salole & Zakaria Abdulle, "Quick to Punish: An examination of the school to prison pipeline for marginalized youth" (2015) 72 Can Rev of Soc Policy 124.

[36] *Ibid*.

[37] See Ontario Human Rights Commission, *The Road to Health: A Final Report on School Safety*, vol 1 (Toronto: School Community Safety Advisory Panel, 2008) (Julian N Falconer). On the effects of school suspensions, see Thomas J Mowen, John J Brent and John H Bowman IV, "The Effect of School Discipline on Offending Across Time" (2020) 37(4) Justice Quarterly 739; Robert Balfanz, Vaughan Byrnes & Joanna Fox, "Sent Home and Put Off-Track: The Antecedents, Disproportionalities, and Consequences of Being Suspended in the Ninth Grade" (2014) 5:2 J of Applied Research on Children 1; Janet E Mosher, "Lessons in Access to Justice: Racialized Youths in Ontario's Safe Schools" (2008) 46:4 Osgoode Hall LJ 807.

blocks and even specific addresses.[38] Heralded as an evidence-based approach to policing that fit under the rubric of "community policing," this place-based approach was spurred on by the work of environmental criminologists who argued that focused police interventions could reduce total crime.[39] Using an efficiency and crime control rubric, proponents argued that police should focus resources on "micro-units of geography" to more effectively prevent crime.[40] In cities across North America, focused policing also relied on stop-and-frisk operations, street checks, and carding, overwhelmingly of young, racialized boys and men like Donnohue Grant.[41] Reporting by the *Toronto Star* showed that the Danforth-East York Zone where Grant was arrested was one of the top contact areas in Toronto for police stops and carding between 2003 and 2008.[42]

On the November day when Grant was stopped, three officers were patrolling the Danforth-East school zone after Toronto Police Division 55 had declared the area's high schools and surrounding neighbourhood a crime "hot spot." The demographic profiles of the target schools—St. Patrick's High School, Monarch Park Collegiate Institute, Danforth Technical Institute, Greenwood Secondary, and Eastern Commerce High School—suggests a significant number of the students being surveilled that day were racialized, immigrant, and from mixed and lower-income households.[43]

---

[38] See Anthony Braga, "The Crime Prevention Value of Hot Spot Policing" (2006) 18:3 Psicothema 630.

[39] See Anthony Braga, "Hot spots policing and crime prevention: A systematic review of randomized controlled trials" (2005) 1 J of Exper Crim 317 at 317–318; Lawrence Sherman & David Weisburd, "General deterrent effects of police patrol in crime 'hot spots': A randomized, controlled trial" (1995) 12:4 Justice Q 625; David Weisburd, Lorraine Green & Debra Ross, "Spatial Analysis of Crimes Committed in Street-Level Drug Markets" (1994) 27:1 Criminologie (Montréal) 49.

[40] David Weisburd & Cody W Telep, "Hot Spots Policing: What We Know and What We Need to Know" (2014) 30:2 J of Contemp Crim J 200 at 201.

[41] For a review of street checks generally, see Ontario, The Honourable Michael H Tulloch, *Report of the Independent Street Check Review* (Toronto: Queen's Printer for Ontario, 2018).

[42] "Toronto Star Analysis of Toronto Police Service Data - 2010 Advanced Findings", *Toronto Star* (2010), online: <www.thestar.com/content/dam/thestar/static_images/advancedfindings2010.pdf>.

[43] Toronto District School Board, "Greenwood SS Mission: Empowering Newcomer Students to Find Their Voice" online: <https://www.tdsb.on.ca/Find-your/Schools/schno/5579>.

Constable Justin Gomes, who had been with Toronto Police Services for two years, was on a "directed patrol" that day of these high schools where there had been recent reports of drug activity, assaults, and robberies. In uniform and driving a marked car, Constable Gomes' mandate was to "maintain high visibility" to deter crime during the lunch break. The two other officers deployed that day, Constables Philip Worrell and Ryan Forde, were from the Street Crime Unit and were in plain clothes driving an unmarked car. Their primary task was to visit the schools to identify anyone who should not be there—trespassers—"either non-students or students from another school." Constable Worrell testified at trial that police would attend the schools "normally on the property" to address what he called an "infiltration of students from other schools in that area" during lunch hour.[44] He looked for students he may not have recognized from prior visits or for young people not wearing their school uniform.

Trespass law converged with zero-tolerance suspension and expulsion policies to create an enforcement dragnet. One of the consequences of a suspension or expulsion is that the excluded student is deemed a trespasser if they try to visit their school while formally excluded. As Anthony Brown, former General Counsel for the Toronto District School Board explains, although "a student who is enrolled in a school should not be trespassed from it during school hours or school activities," they may be sanctioned for trespassing if they are suspended or expelled "and therefore have no business being there."[45] Zero tolerance suspension and expulsion policies created a slew of potential trespassers, providing yet another rationale for a police presence at schools. When approaching these young people, Constable Worrell testified that he would normally ask them questions including "whether they had anything they shouldn't have," the precise question Constable Gomes asked Donnohue Grant that day. The officers testified that their assignment was "to keep an eye out to see what was going on, with the hopes of keeping the environment for students safe."[46]

---

[44] *R v Grant*, 2004 CarswellOnt 8779 (Trial Transcript, vol 1 at 14 [Transcript vol 1]) at 53.

[45] Anthony F Brown, *Legal Handbook for Educators*, 6th ed (Toronto: Carswell, 2009) at 32.

[46] Transcript vol 1, *supra* note 44.

Keeping the environment safe for students meant deterring wrongdoing *and* promoting good relations with police. When asked at trial if the officers were dressed in plain clothes "so as not to alert the public to the fact you're police officers," Constable Worrell answered affirmatively. That was not the only reason. As Constable Worrell explained, part of the Street Crime Unit's mandate was to build rapport with students: "We want to have the rapport with them without the uniform, without that - just, you know, in kind of an easy-going capacity."[47] The import of their testimony was that students who "belonged" at a given school would recognize them as police officers, whereas interlopers would be caught off guard. The police worked undercover to surreptitiously detect trespassers, while also socializing known students to accept and even welcome a regular police presence at school.

At trial, Constables Worrell and Forde testified that as they drove past Grant that November day, his behaviour aroused their suspicion. According to police, just after 12:30 p.m., Grant was walking north on Greenwood Avenue. Constable Forde stated that Grant stared at them in an unusually intense way. "For us, being in an unmarked car, he was staring at us […]. He stared at us for a couple of seconds. I stared back. And as we were driving away he kept looking at us as we were driving off."[48] Although the stare of the police officers produced the encounter, it was Grant's stare that they interpellated as a sign of public danger.[49] Constable Forde further testified that in these few seconds he noticed Grant "fidgeting around."[50] Constable Worrell likewise testified that Grant had "fidgeted" with his coat and pants in a way that the officer found "just kind of a little bit, I guess, suspicious."[51] The two officers saw Constable Gomes pulled over on Greenwood Avenue, drove up alongside him, and suggested he "have a chat" with Grant.[52]

---

[47] *Ibid* at 32.

[48] *R v Grant*, 2004 CarswellOnt 8779 (Trial Transcript, vol 2 at 95 [Transcript vol 2]).

[49] For Marxist scholarship on interpellation, or the process by which culture and ideological values are internalized, see Louis Althusser, *On the Reproduction of Capitalism: Ideology and Ideological State Apparatuses*, translated by G M Goshgarian (London, UK: Verso, 2014); Frantz Fanon, *Black Skin, White Masks*, translated by Charles Lam Markmann (London, UK: Pluto Press, 1986).

[50] Transcript vol 2, *supra* note 48 at 95.

[51] Transcript vol 1, *supra* note 44 at 16.

[52] *Ibid* at 18.

Constable Gomes followed their advice. He pulled over, got out of his car, and then stood on the sidewalk directly in Donnohue Grant's path. According to Gomes, Grant put his head down and did not make eye contact. "What's going on?" asked Constable Gomes. "Not much. Just coming from my boy's house down at Greenwood and Gerrard," Grant replied.[53] The officer asked Grant for his name and address. According to Constable Gomes, Grant voluntarily produced an Ontario Health card. "[Y]our evidence is that you didn't actually ask him for identification, he just produced it, is that right?" defence counsel asked on cross-exam. "Yes, that's what I have in my notes, yes. He voluntarily gave me it."[54] Even if one accepts the veracity of this account, it suggests that this was hardly the first time Donnohue Grant had been stopped by police and questioned. Grant had learned the script for supposedly "non-coercive" police stops. When asked his name and address, he should provide an ID card.

At this stage, after Donnohue Grant allegedly adjusted his jacket one more time, Constable Gomes asked him to keep his hands in front of him.[55] Constables Forde and Worrell had now returned and parked at the side of the street. They approached Grant and Constable Gomes, identified themselves as police officers, and assumed positions obstructing Grant's way forward. Constable Gomes asked Grant if he had anything on him that he shouldn't. Grant admitted to having a "small bag of weed." When the officer asked if that was it, Grant lowered his head and said: "Yes, well, no." "Well, what is it that you have?" the officer asked. "I have a firearm," Grant replied. Upon this disclosure, the officers arrested Grant and informed him of his right to counsel.[56] They asked if he wanted to call a lawyer. He asked for his mother.

Judging Police

R v Grant proceeded through the courts as a race-neutral or, more accurately, race-evasive case.[57] At trial and on appeal, the central

---

[53] Transcript vol 2, *supra* note 48 at 70.

[54] *Ibid* at 70–71.

[55] *Ibid* at 72.

[56] Transcript vol 2, *supra* note 48 at 80–83.

[57] I draw the term "race-evasive" from Joshua Sealy-Harrington, "The *Charter* of Whites: Systemic Racism and Critical Race Equality in Canada" 39 (2023) Windsor

criminal procedure question was whether police had detained Grant prior to his arrest. The officers acknowledged at trial that they did not have legal grounds to detain Grant prior to his incriminating statements.[58] Defence counsel did not argue racial profiling at trial, and race, as David Tanovich has written, was "erased from the narrative presented to the court."[59] Justice Binnie in his concurring opinion was the sole reviewing judge at any level of court in *Grant* to discuss race and racism in police stops.[60] The Chief Justice and Justice Charron concluded for the majority, "the police conduct here, while not in conformity with the *Charter*, was not abusive. There was no suggestion that Donnohue Grant was the target of racial profiling or other discriminatory police practices."[61]

At trial, Judge Harris concluded that police had not detained Donnohue Grant prior to his arrest and had not violated his *Charter* rights. An express commitment to facilitating police work shaped his open-textured legal analysis. Citing another Ontario Court of Justice decision, Judge Harris wrote: "We do not expect the police to sit in their station houses waiting for those who commit offences to walk in and confess. We expect them to be out in the community and when suspicious events occur to make inquiries. The *Charter* is not a barrier to those inquiries."[62] The necessity of proactive policing surely gave police a "right to approach and speak to the accused."[63]

Central to Judge Harris's reasons was a menacing vision of the youth threat and gun panic in Toronto especially. Both the police in their testimony and the trial judge in his reasons referred to the recent assaults at the targeted schools as "swarmings"—a term used frequently by police, the media and criminologists in the 1990s, especially in Canadian cities.[64] In his reasons, the trial judge characterized the "directed patrol" as a protective response to these "disgusting

---

Yearbook of Access to Justice 544 at 544.

[58] *Ibid* at 74–75.

[59] David Tanovich, "The Further Erasure of Race in *Charter* Cases" 38 (2006) Criminal Reports 84.

[60] *Grant* SCC, *supra* note 2 at paras 154–155.

[61] *Ibid* at para 134.

[62] *R v Orellana*, [1999] OJ No 5746 at para 32, cited in *R v Grant*, 2004 CarswellOnt 8779 [*Grant* OCJ].

[63] *Grant* OCJ, *ibid*.

[64] Velmer S Burton, "Swarming" in Jeffrey Ian Ross, ed, *Encyclopedia of Street Crime in America*, (Los Angeles; London, U.K.: SAGE Publications, 2013) at 406.

activities."[65] Like the super-predator myth, this image of deviant youths "swarming" innocent students conjured an animalistic brutality that demanded and authorized police power. "I infer that the police were assigned to patrol and to protect the defenseless and vulnerable students who were being considered for or were being swarmed and robbed," the trial judge wrote, "not only of money, but perhaps even their clothing."[66] Calls to protect vulnerable young people from deviant predators powerfully authorized police power.

And, yet, even as the trial judge suggested a visible police presence served a protective function, he simultaneously downplayed its coercive significance. He described the "conversation" between Constable Gomes and Donnohue Grant as "no more than that, a conversation and an attempt to chit chat or make chit chat. Here again, I find it was all meant to check the temperature of the community."[67] Judge Harris accepted the Crown's submissions that Donnohue Grant could have walked away from police at any time. "He could have walked around the one police officer or the three police officers and could have kept going," the trial judge wrote. "All he had to do, in my view, is say, 'Excuse me.' To suggest for one moment that he couldn't or they wouldn't permit it is speculation."[68]

The Supreme Court of Canada rejected this view that a reasonable person with the same characteristics of Donnohue Grant would have believed he could simply walk away at any time. They found that while the order to "keep his hands in front of him" may not by itself indicate detention, viewed in context with what transpired afterward, it did in this case. They pointed to the fact that Grant was singled out for "particularized suspicion" and was asked questions to elicit incriminating information. The power imbalances in this "inherently intimidating" encounter were exacerbated "by Donnohue Grant's youth and inexperience."[69] They found that "a reasonable person in his position [...] would conclude that his or her right to choose how to act had been removed by the police, given their conduct."[70] Police had detained Donnohue Grant without lawful grounds to do so.

---

[65] *Grant* OCJ, *supra* note 62.

[66] *Ibid.*

[67] *Ibid.*

[68] *Ibid.*

[69] *Grant* SCC, *supra* note 2 at para 50.

[70] *Ibid.*

In finding an unlawful detention on these facts, the Court proceeded to legitimate police action that falls short of it. The majority did so by treating police interactions that do not meet the threshold for psychological or physical detention as socially valuable and necessary. This reasoning follows a pattern identified by Steven Coughlan in which courts "look for something the police have done which can be identified as 'wrong', and in the absence of finding any such thing concludes that the officers had the power to do what was done."[71] In this case, the Court looked for police conduct that was sufficiently coercive to constitute detention and then treated scenarios that did not meet this threshold as legitimate community policing. "Effective law enforcement is highly dependent on the cooperation of members of the public," Chief Justice McLachlin and Justice Charron wrote. "The police must be able to act in a manner that fosters this cooperation, not discourages it."[72] Although they conceded that the line between cooperation and coercion can blur, they nevertheless insisted on the distinction. Police coercion during active criminal investigations and arrests served as the contrast with supposedly non-coercive pedestrian stops. "[G]eneral inquiries by a patrolling officer present no threat to freedom of choice," the majority wrote.[73]

This reasoning masked the coercive power exercised by police during pedestrian stops and the profound alienation that can flow from them. As the Canadian Civil Liberties Association noted in its intervention in *Grant*, what occurred in this case was standard police practice in Toronto at the time: "approaching persons on the street, especially young persons and/or persons of colour, getting their names, doing a CPIC [Canadian Police Information Centre] search and then launching into aggressive questioning aimed at incrimination."[74] Some years after Donnohue Grant's unlawful detention, the *Toronto Star* reported that between 2008 and 2012, police filled out 1.8 million cards from such stops documenting the physical appearance, address, and contact information of those they stopped.[75]

---

[71] Coughlan, *supra* note 14 at 210.

[72] *Grant* SCC, *supra* note 2 at para 39.

[73] *Ibid* at para 41.

[74] *Grant* SCC (Factum of the Intervener Canadian Civil Liberties Association) at para 26.

[75] Jim Rankin and Patty Winsa, "As criticism piles up, so do police cards", *Toronto Star* (27 September 2013), online: <https://www.thestar.com/news/gta/knowntopolice2013/

This was intelligence gathering on a mass scale. Between 2008 and 2013, the Toronto Police Service conducted 2,123 street checks for every 1,000 Black people living in Toronto—approximately 2.1 stops for every Black person in the city. By contrast the street check rate for white people was 653.7 per 1,000.[76]

Intrusive policing of this sort all too easily produces what legal sociologist Monica Bell has called "legal estrangement"—a radical individual and collective exclusion that prevailing discourses of police "legitimacy" and "public confidence in the administration of justice" obscure.[77] For students out at lunch, for teenagers like Donnohue Grant walking from a friend's place, the sidewalk "is a public path to move about, to get from one place to another, and also a social space—probably the most available, accessible, and relatively nonrestrictive social space to meet, 'hang out,' and converse," notes education scholar Carl James.[78] This is why Robyn Maynard describes police profiling as "itself a form of violence, because it infringes on Black people's ability to move freely and without fear in public space."[79] For profiled individuals, one's very presence in the public sphere is policed.

This constant intrusion into the lives of Black and other marginalized community members was not prevented or even legally precluded by the rules of criminal procedure established in *Grant*. Rather, it fits a logic of regarding myriad police-community interactions as non-coercive and beneficial, without regard to the ways that police stops structurally exclude targeted groups from the public sphere.[80] The police stop in *Grant* was exceptional because the vast majority of street checks never result in a criminal charge, let alone a trial. The

---

2013/09/27/as_criticism_piles_up_so_do_the_police_cards.html>.

[76] Scot Wortley, Akwasi Owusu-Bempah, & Huibin Lin "Race and Criminal Justice: An Examination of Public Perceptions of, and Experiences with, The Criminal Justice System Among Residents of the Greater Toronto Area" (Toronto: Ryerson University Faculty of Law, 2021) at 17.

[77] Monica Bell, "Police Reform and the Dismantling of Legal Estrangement" (2017) 126 Yale L J 2054.

[78] Carl James, "'Up to No Good': Black on the Streets and Encountering Police" in Carl James, *Colour Matters: Essays on the Experiences, Education, and Pursuits of Black Youth* (Toronto: University of Toronto Press, 2021) at 227.

[79] Robyn Maynard, *Policing Black Lives: State Violence in Canada from Slavery to the Present* (Halifax: Fernwood Publishing, 2017) at 191.

[80] On legal estrangement flowing from police surveillance and subordination, see Bell, *supra* note 77.

alienation and cynicism that flow from them, with devastating effects on Black and other marginalized youth in terms of their ability to move in the world, and in terms of their self-perception, are not remedied or even registered by criminal courts. Those of us who study and teach *Grant* would do well to widen the frame to see how courts may authorize police power and police interactions that are unlikely to ever come before them for legal review or remedy.[81]

Conclusion

School safety is a vital human good. Anyone who has experienced or committed violence at school knows that an absence of safety undermines one's ability to act and learn. As political theorist Amia Srinivasan has argued in the context of gendered violence, the consequences of unsafety are existential as well as material. "The privation of safety doesn't just mean the exposure to forms of physical harm or even psychological harm; it also means the erosion of our sense of selves as agents in the world," Srinivasan writes.[82] The self-perception of students who experience and fear harm can be undermined at the very age it should be formed.

To insist on safety at school does not mean one must treat punishment and policing as its precursors. Too often in public discourse and academic research, policing has been treated as a necessary and preferred response to real concerns about crime and dangerousness, including in schools. Reading *Grant* alongside empirical literature that shows that environmental supports at school produce better outcomes than policing or surveillance allows us to analyze the policy preferences that often inform judicial decision-making in this area.[83]

---

[81] For a parallel critique of the narrow focus of social science of policing work on crime variables, to the exclusion of other community outcomes, see Monica Bell, "Next-Generation Policing Research: Three Propositions" (2021) 35:4 J of Economic Perspectives 29.

[82] Amia Srinivasan, "The Politics of Safety" *Financial Times* (13 August 2021) online: <https://www.ft.com/content/de097d02-3fa9-4041-ade2-d517af30818c>.

[83] See Denise C. Gottfredson et al, "Effects of School Resource Officers on School Crime and Responses to School Crime" (2020) 19 Crim & Public Policy 905; Benjamin W Fisher, Ethan M Higgins, and Emily M Homer, "School Crime and Punishment and the Implementation of Security Cameras Findings from a National Longitudinal Study" (2021) 38 Justice Q 22.

When officers approached Donnohue Grant as part of a school safety operation, they embodied the merging of what Louis Althusser theorized as the ideological state apparatus of public schooling and the repressive state apparatus of policing.[84] If schools function, in part, to train students in the rules of the governing social and economic order, police embody the state's ability to enforce those rules with violence.[85] Treating certain schools and specific student populations as dangerous "hot spots" requiring ongoing police presence produces winners and losers. Whereas some schools and communities experience the paired problems of being over-policed and under-protected, other more affluent and whiter districts enjoy responsive policing and relative safety. The problem of police reform, as Bell concludes, is not simply one of poverty or racism, but of "inequality in access to the machinery of the law."[86]

This inequality in access to the machinery of the law was on full display on December 22, 2004, as Donnohue Grant's mother, aunt, and sister sat in Courtroom 116 in Toronto's Old City Hall to hear Judge Harris sentence their loved one. In sentencing Grant, Judge Harris stated:

> I am obliged in this case to consider the fact that he is a youthful first offender. He was 18 when he was picked up. I am obliged to consider that. He has no prior record. I have also considered the fact that he does not do a darn thing in his life. There is no productivity whatsoever or so it appears on the day in relation to his life.
>
> So, he's not a big star by any stretch of the imagination, notwithstanding what his mother may feel and how he's breaking her heart and the hearts of some of his family.[87]

---

[84] See Louis Althusser, *Ideology and Ideological State Apparatuses*, (London, UK: Verso, 2014).

[85] On schools and education as different, though overlapping, processes, see Mwalimu J Shujaa, "Education and schooling: You can have one without the other" (1993) 27 Urban Education 328 at 330–331 (arguing that schooling is a "process *intended* to perpetuate and maintain the society's existing power relations and the institutional structures that support those arrangements" and contrasting this with "education" as a "process of transmitting from one generation to the next knowledge of the values, aesthetics, spiritual beliefs, and all things that give a particular cultural orientation its uniqueness").

[86] Bell, *supra* note 77 at 2115.

[87] *R v Grant*, 2004 CarswellOnt 8783 at paras 14–15.

At an age when life opens up for many, it had closed in on Donnohue Grant. Three days before Christmas, Judge Harris sentenced Grant to eighteen months in prison, with a reduction of six months for time already served.

The life trajectories of the four people who stood on that Toronto sidewalk in 2003 have diverged sharply since. The three officers who unlawfully detained Donnohue Grant have continued their careers with the Toronto Police Services and have all since advanced in rank. As of the time of writing, Justin Gomes is Detective, and Philip Worrell and Ryan Forde are Sergeants.

In 2016, Toronto Police issued an arrest warrant for Donnohue Grant in connection with an alleged assault and carjacking in North York. Police tweeted an image that appeared to be a recent mugshot— a practice that critics note can create a permanent visual association between a subject and criminal activity, regardless of guilt.[88] Wearing a dark blue hoodie, Grant appeared resigned beyond his thirty-one years of age; his forehead was furrowed; his shoulders were slightly slumped. Just as he allegedly looked down when police approached him that November day on a sidewalk thirteen years earlier, he did not make eye contact with the photographer.

---

[88] See Brooke Rink, "If a Picture is Worth a Thousand Words, Your Mugshot Will Cost You Much More: An Argument for Federal Regulation of Mugshots" (2020) 73 Fed Comms. L J 317; Olivia Solon, "Haunted by a mugshot: how predatory websites exploit the shame of arrest; Sites are collecting people's mugshots, then charging huge sums to remove them. Should Google be doing more to stop it?," *The Guardian* (June 12, 2018).

An Open Letter to Legal Workers: Imagining a World Beyond Civilian Oversight of Policing

Meenakshi Mannoe[*]

Abstract

This letter invites legal workers to challenge the efficacy of police reform and civilian oversight as responses to systemic police violence in so-called Canada. Informed by grassroots struggle, abolitionist study, frontline legal work, and the experiences of families directly impacted by fatal police violence, this letter argues that oversight agencies—whether civilian-led or government-controlled—legitimize and perpetuate the colonial policing narratives they purport to regulate. Specifically, this letter contends that police violence against Indigenous peoples is not an

[*] Thank you to Laura Holland, Kwitsel Tatel, Martha Martin, Claudette Beals-Clayton, Nhora Aust, Magín Payet Scudellari, Aisha Benslimane, and Joshua Sealy-Harrington who patiently worked with me to develop my ever-evolving analysis and this (love) letter to legal workers. This piece is foremost informed by the families of people killed by the police. These survivors of state violence are some of the most tenacious, dedicated, and extraordinary community organizers that we have the privilege to work alongside. Their fight against police violence is informed by the darkest moments in their lives. Nothing but gratitude for each mother who fights for a world where their baby's dreams can soar. May we build a world where every one of us is free from threats of violence.

aberration but a fundamental feature of Canada's ongoing colonial occupation of sovereign Indigenous homelands and critically examines how legal professionals are co-opted into systems that uphold dispossession, underscoring the complicity of institutions such as oversight agencies, municipal governments, and the broader legal framework in sustaining settler colonialism. Rejecting reformist approaches, this letter calls for a paradigm shift toward dismantling colonial legal orders and reimagining justice beyond the promises of institutional reform.

Résumé

Cette lettre invite les personnes qui œuvrent dans le monde juridique à remettre en question l'efficacité de la réforme policière et de la surveillance civile en tant que réponses à la violence systémique de la police dans ce qu'on appelle le Canada. S'appuyant sur les luttes communautaires, les études abolitionnistes, le travail juridique de terrain et les expériences des familles directement touchées par la violence policière mortelle, cette lettre soutient que les organismes de surveillance – qu'ils soient dirigés par des civils ou contrôlés par le gouvernement – légitiment et perpétuent les récits coloniaux sur la police qu'ils prétendent réguler. Plus précisément, cette lettre affirme que la violence policière envers les peuples autochtones n'est pas une anomalie, mais une caractéristique fondamentale de l'occupation coloniale continue des terres autochtones souveraines par le Canada. Elle examine de manière critique la manière dont les professionnels du droit sont cooptés par des systèmes qui soutiennent la dépossession, soulignant la complicité d'institutions telles que les organismes de surveillance, les gouvernements municipaux et le cadre juridique plus large dans le maintien du colonialisme de peuplement. Rejetant les approches réformistes, cette lettre appelle à un changement de paradigme visant à démanteler les ordres juridiques coloniaux et à réimaginer la justice au-delà des promesses de réformes institutionnelles.

This contribution to *Critical Conversations in Canadian Public Law* is built around imagining a world beyond the promises of police reform and civilian oversight as a means to stem police violence and murder. Informed by frontline legal work, organizing, and abolitionist study, this letter to the legal community challenges the notion of reform as a viable challenge to systemic and systematic police violence on occupied Indigenous lands.

Since July 2020, global actions against police violence have been sparked by police murders of Black and Indigenous people. As the 2020 George Floyd uprising inspired people to take the streets, there was concurrently sustained attention on the systems of policing that enforce colonial laws in so-called Canada.

In response, agencies such as the Canadian Association of Chiefs of Police quickly distinguished fundamental differences in North American policing models, citing how Canadian forces "focused their approach on community engagement and well-being, and proactive crime prevention."[1] While expressing sadness at the tragic death of George Floyd or Tyre Nichols,[2] Canadian police agencies are silent on the police murders of Jared Lowndes (Wet'suwet'en), Julian Jones (Tla-o-qui-aht), Regis Korchinski-Paquet (Afro-Indigenous), Chantel Moore (Tla-o-qui-aht), and far too many unnamed relations. When it comes to police-involved deaths in Canada, these forces often cite their need to comply with oversight agencies' investigations and rely on attrition, as families navigate deeply broken systems that amplify harm and violence, rather than upholding justice and dignity.

Abolition of the Prison Industrial Complex

Police executions clearly target Black and Indigenous people, as well as other people of colour, drug users, and psychiatrized community members. The rage at murder after murder has turned into demands focused on the resources available to police. A spectrum of political demands have arisen since the George Floyd uprisings of 2020, including calls to detask the police, defund the police, and abolish the police. This intense focus on policing resources is informed by an abolitionist ethos of non-reformist reforms that

---

[1] Canadian Association of Chiefs of Police, "CACP statement - The death of George Floyd in Minneapolis, Minnesota, USA" (10 June 2020), online: <vpd.ca/news/2020/06/15/cacp-statement-the-death-of-george-floyd-in-minneapolis-minnesota-usa/>.

[2] Vancouver Police Department, News Release, "Statement from Chief Adam Palmer on the tragic death of Tyre Nichols" (28 January 2023), online: <vpd.ca/news/2023/01/28/statement-from-chief-adam-palmer-on-the-tragic-death-of-tyre-nichols/>.

recognizes "the only way to diminish police violence is to reduce contact between the public and the police."[3] As Mariame Kaba states "efforts to solve police violence through liberal reforms like these have failed for nearly a century."[4]

Police murders are not an aberration from the norms of policing. The organizing and actions that began in 2020 stem from long-standing resistance to police, and their violence, at the behest of colonial and imperialist agents. Amidst broader conversations about reform and redress, questions about accountability inevitably surface. In recent years, mainstream work around police accountability has significantly shifted, from treating police as an institution capable of reform toward defunding, disarming, and dismantling policing. This includes advocacy that targets police budgets, as well as amplifying and bringing awareness to incidents of harm and death at the hands of police.

Liberal reforms in policing have been roundly critiqued by abolitionist organizers across the territories currently known as Canada and the United States. Charlotte Rosen contrasts liberal reform with conservative tough-on-crime politics, noting that "while less overt and sensational than conservatives' dog whistle and thinly-veiled racist law and order politics, proponents of liberal law and order helped sustain racial violence by ironically seeking to remove racial bias from law enforcement."[5] Liberal policing reforms are marked by a failure to address the structural features of policing, including the enforcement of colonial laws made on unceded and sovereign Indigenous territory, the rigid ordering of racial capitalism including anti-Black racism and white supremacy, the punishment of poverty, the eugenicist state-sanctioned disposability of disabled peoples, and the coercive power of heteropatriarchal power relations. Rather than seeking individual redress and retraining of staffers, prison

---

[3] Mariame Kaba, "Yes, We Literally Mean Abolish the Police," *The New York Times* (12 June 2000), online: <https://www.nytimes.com/2020/06/12/opinion/sunday/floyd-abolish-defund-police.html>.

[4] *Ibid.*

[5] Charlotte Rosen, "ABOLITION OR BUST: LIBERAL POLICE REFORM AS AN ENGINE OF CARCERAL VIOLENCE," *TransformHarm.org* (26 June 2020), online: <transformharm.org/abolition-or-bust-liberal-police-reform-as-an-engine-of-carceral-violence/>.

industrial complex (PIC) abolitionists recognize these features as inbuilt and essential to the ordering of police and prisons.

Critical Resistance, an abolitionist organization formed in 1997 defines the PIC as "the overlapping interests of government and industry that use surveillance, policing, and imprisonment as solutions to economic, social and political problems."[6] In tandem, Critical Resistance defines PIC abolition as "a political vision with the goal of eliminating imprisonment, policing, and surveillance and creating lasting alternatives to punishment and imprisonment."[7] This definition of the PIC clearly includes police forces, prisons, jails, and correctional centres.

Policing violence is intertwined with the violence of the settler, genocidal, apartheid state that is so-called Canada.

Contextualizing Canadian Police

The first national police force in Canada, the North-West Mounted Police was founded in 1873, and then grew into the Royal Canadian Mounted Police (RCMP).[8] Prior to its formation, the British Columbia Provincial Police was formed in 1858,[9] to police the Colony of British Columbia—sovereign territory governed by Indigenous Nations who have never ceded, sold, or otherwise surrendered their land. The role of police in enforcing the violent, colonial occupations of the territories currently known as Canada and the United States is undeniable.

Independent scholar Mike Gouldhawke states, "[c]onventional Canadian mythology maintains that the RCMP was created to protect Indigenous people from marauding Americans at Cypress Hills. But even this whitewashed story underlines the force's role in expanding and maintaining the borders of Canada while facilitating the

---

[6] Critical Resistance, "WHAT IS THE PIC? WHAT IS ABOLITION?", online <critical resistance.org/mission-vision/not-so-common-language/>.

[7] *Ibid.*

[8] Mike Gouldhawke, "A Condensed History of Canada's Colonial Cops", online (2020) <thenewinquiry.com/a-condensed-history-of-canadas-colonial-cops/>.

[9] Frederick John Hatch, *The British Columbia police, 1858-1871*, online (Master of Arts, University of British Columbia, 1955) at 3-4, online: <open.library.ubc.ca/soa/cIRcle/collections/ubctheses/831/items/1.0106820>.

development of infrastructure such as the Canadian Pacific Railway across Indigenous lands by whatever means necessary, from forcibly relocating Indigenous people to breaking workers' strikes."[10] Gouldhawke details the military and police response to the self-governance infrastructure of the Red River Métis throughout the late 1800s.[11] Historian Sean Carleton has similarly noted that Canadian police and military units have a long-standing role in suppressing Indigenous resistance and clearing a path for capitalist accumulation by colonial dispossession.[12]

Despite what police, governments, and colonial courts might like us to believe—this land is not Canada. This land is governed by an illegal occupation. Oral histories of the Wet'suwet'en and Gitxsan Nations, relied on in the 1997 Delgamuukw/Gisday'wa court case, affirm this uninterrupted relationship to hereditary land. In *Delgamuukw*, the Supreme Court of Canada found that "lands subject to aboriginal title cannot be put to such uses as may be irreconcilable with the nature of the occupation of that land and the relationship that the particular group has had with the land which together have given rise to aboriginal title in the first place."[13] As Dr. Karla Tait (Wet'suwet'en) and Anne Spice (Tlingit, Kwanlin Dün First Nation) have noted, *Anuk Nu'at'en (Wet'suwet'en law)* pre-dates Canadian and provincial law.[14]

Police Violence is a Canadian Staple

Killing Indigenous people in the interest of a colonial government is also older than Canada itself.

While there is not reliable information on the first person killed by the police in Canada, early executions of Indigenous leaders exemplify the racist violence that Canada is built upon. In 1864,

---

[10] Gouldhawke, *supra* note 8.

[11] *Ibid.*

[12] Sean Carleton, "Putting the RCMP raid on the Wet'suwet'en in historical perspective," *The Toronto Star* (11 February 2020), online: <thestar.com/opinion/contributors/2020/02/11/putting-the-rcmp-raid-on-the-wetsuweten-in-historical-perspective.html>.

[13] *Delgamuukw v British Columbia*, 1997 CanLII 302 (SCC) at para 128.

[14] Karla Tait and Anne Spice, "An Injunction Against the Unist'ot'en Camp: An embodiment of healing faces eviction," *Yellowhead Institute* (12 December 2018), online: <yellowheadinstitute.org/2018/12/12/an-injunction-against-the-unistoten-camp/>.

Tŝilhqot'in leaders Klatsassin, Piell, Tellot, Tahpit, and Chessus were executed after being sentenced to death by Judge Matthew Baillie Begbie.[15] The following year, a sixth Tŝilhqot'in leader, Ahan, was executed.[16] Years of colonial violence led to these executions: between June 1862 and January 1863, it is estimated that over 70 percent of the Tŝilhqot'in died of smallpox.[17] Following that, settlers targeted the Tŝilhqot'in through disrespect, abuse, starvation, economic exploitation, and threats of biological warfare.[18] The hostile behaviour of European settlers led to the Tŝilhqot'in War of 1864, wherein "warriors effectively removed all settlers from their lands, forcibly and by death if warnings went unheeded."[19] One hundred and fifty years after executing six Tŝilhqot'in leaders, the provincial and federal governments apologized for the wrongful trial and hanging of the Chiefs, and they were exonerated by the Province of B.C. on 23 October 2014.

Indigenous people in Canada are more than ten times more likely to have been fatally shot by a police officer in Canada.[20] Tracking (In) Justice, a research project dedicated to transparent data on deaths in custody across Canada, seeks to track numbers, to develop a better understanding on issues related to policing, use of force, discrimination, and the criminal justice system in Canada. The project further notes that project data must be situated in the context of "contemporary and historical context of policing, discrimination and colonialism."[21]

As Sherene Razack describes in *Dying from Improvement: Inquests and Inquiries into Indigenous Deaths in Custody*, systematic state violence against Indigenous people deploys benevolent concern in inquiries and inquests that erase the violence of ongoing settler colonialism

[15] Gord Hill and Sean Carleton, "The Tsilhqot'in War of 1864," *Graphic History Collective*, online <graphichistorycollective.com/project/poster-14-tsilhqotin-war-of-1864>.

[16] *Ibid.*

[17] Tŝilhqot'in National Government, *The Chilcotin War and Lhats'as?in Memorial Day*, online: <https://tsilhqotin.ca/our-nation/heritage/>.

[18] *Ibid.*

[19] *Ibid.*

[20] Ryan Flanagan, "Why are Indigenous people in Canada so much more likely to be shot and killed by police?" *CTV News* (19 June 2020) online: <ctvnews.ca/canada/why-are-indigenous-people-in-canada-so-much-more-likely-to-be-shot-and-killed-by-police-1.4989864?cache=%3FclipId%3D64268>.

[21] The Tracking Injustice Project, "Understanding the Data: Historical and Contemporary Context of Policing, Colonialism and Discrimination" *Tracking Injustice* (10 February 2023), online: <trackinginjustice.ca/analysis-policing-colonialism-and-discrimination/>.

and occupation of sovereign land.[22] Similarly, critical criminologist Jeff Shantz has noted "every time the police murder another person, they justify the belief that criminalized populations deserve death. No amount of oversight or reform will ever untether the police from their role as protectors of a capitalist and colonial state."[23]

Mapping Police "Oversight"

Reliance on oversight as the primary mechanism to address police violence and murder neglects the limitations of seeking justice, while Indigenous people continue to live under occupation. Even on a granular level, oversight agencies often mimic policing agencies and employ former police officers as staff.[24]

In B.C., police and prison agencies are subject to varying, uneven levels of oversight—including civilian oversight. Several agencies form the backbone of police oversight here, specifically: the Office of the Police Complaint Commissioner (OPCC), Independent Investigations Office (IIO), Commission for Public Complaints Against the RCMP, B.C. Coroners Service, and the Policing and Security Branch. The Police Complaint Commissioner oversees and monitors complaints and investigations involving municipal police and is responsible for the administration of discipline and proceedings under the *Police Act*.[25] The IIO is a civilian-led agency responsible for conducting criminal investigations into incidents of death or serious physical harm that may have been the result of the actions or inactions of a police officer, whether on or off duty.[26]

While currently headed by a civilian lawyer, Prabhu Rajan, the OPCC has also been led by a former high-ranking police officer—

---

[22] Sherene Razack, *Dying from Improvement: Inquests and Inquiries into Indigenous Deaths in Custody* (Toronto: University of Toronto Press, 2015).

[23] Jeff Shantz, "Accountable to Themselves Alone: On Police Killings" *The Anarchist Library* (2018) online: <theanarchistlibrary.org/library/jeff-shantz-accountable-to-themselves-alone-on-police-killings>.

[24] Independent Investigations Office of BC, "How many IIO Investigators are former police officers?", (last visited 25 August 2025) online: <iiobc.ca/faqs/how-many-iio-investigators-are-former-police-officers-3/>.

[25] *Police Act*, RSBC 1996, c 367, ss 47, 51.02.

[26] Independent Investigations Office of BC, "About the IIO", (last visited 25 August 2025) online: <iiobc.ca/>.

Clayton Pecknold, who served as OPCC Commissioner from 2019-2024 and previously served as deputy police chief in the Saanich Police Department. And while B.C.'s Policing and Security Branch is currently run by a civilian, it has previously been led by RCMP officers, including Wayne Rideout and Brenda Butterworth-Carr.[27] Meanwhile, the IIO has faced ongoing criticism for its hiring of former police officers to act as "independent" investigators; at least half of B.C.'s IIO investigators are former police officers.[28] Notably, many leaders within systems of police oversight have pronounced legal backgrounds; however, this training typically refers to education and training in the colonial legal orders that have been imposed on sovereign Indigenous Nations across so-called Canada.

The OPCC mission statement states that its office "promotes accountable policing within our communities and enhances public confidence in law enforcement through impartial, transparent civilian oversight."[29] Similarly, both the IIO and its Chief Civilian Director share goals "to serve the people of B.C. in a manner that inspires confidence in the organization and police accountability." Unsurprisingly, given the tone and tenor of leadership, civilian inquiries into the deaths of Indigenous people in police custody have failed to abate or end violence. Accountability for institutions should not be limited to conducting empty investigations; it should lead to effective change which in many cases means abolishing those institutions. As long as policing still exists, these oversight bodies demonstrate their inability to enact any meaningful change that benefits Indigenous, Black and otherwise racialized, colonized, and oppressed peoples.

Civilian oversight agencies like the OPCC and IIO lack both the jurisdiction and interest in making fundamental changes to policing. Furthermore, calls for expansion of civilian oversight, as part of calls to defund and dismantle police fail to grapple with the vested

---

[27] Paul Willcocks, "A Former Mountie Will Set the Police Budget for Vancouver. That's Wrong," *The Tyee* (16 March 2021) online: <thetyee.ca/Analysis/2021/03/16/Former-Mountie-Sets-Vancouver-Police-Budget/>; "Director of police services for B.C. announces resignation," *CBC News* (17 December 2020), online: <cbc.ca/news/canada/british-columbia/bc-brenda-butterworth-carr-resigns-1.5845002>.

[28] Independent Investigations Office of BC, *supra* note 24.

[29] Office of the Police Complaint Commissioner, (last visited 25 August 2025) online:

interests that these institutions hold. It is unsurprising, therefore, that the everyday understanding of the PIC does not conventionally include police oversight bodies, including civilian oversight bodies. As one examines the makeup of these organizations, however, their innate relationship to the PIC becomes clear.

Fomenting Resistance to Reform

In 2020, Critical Resistance produced an informative resource "Reformist reforms vs. abolitionist steps in policing," illustrating the difference between expanding the reach of policing and chipping away at the power and impact of police. Regarding Civilian Review/Oversight Boards, Critical Resistance determined that these institutions did not reduce police funding, challenge the notion that police increase safety, reduce police tools/tactics/technology, or the scale of policing. Critical Resistance determined that civilian review/oversight "further entrenches policing as a legitimate, reformable system, with a 'community' mandate. Some boards, tasked with overseeing them, become structurally invested in their existence."[30]

Ultimately, police oversight agencies—civilian or government-controlled—simply legitimate policing narratives. None of these agencies is willing to acknowledge that police have no jurisdiction, and neither do the overseers that enable their violence. In reality, police violence against Indigenous people is part of the continued colonial occupation of Canada. As Sto:lo Matriarch Kwitsel Tatel often remarks—the federal policy of Indians has never changed from "kill an Indian."

Reforming policing through the expansion of civilian oversight will not bring justice to survivors of police violence, or family members in the wake of a police murder. Of note—there is no consistent legal aid funding available to families as they navigate the aftermath of a police killing. Instead, they must suddenly rely on family resources, mutual aid, and piecemeal donations. In B.C., there is no

---

[30] Critical Resistance, "Reformist reforms vs abolitionist steps in policing" (14 May 2020) online: <criticalresistance.org/resources/reformist-reforms-vs-abolitionist-steps-in-policing/>.

funding for survivors or next of kin to access independent legal advice, counsel, advocacy, emotional, or financial support.

The depth of fundraising that families must undertake is unimaginable. Instead of a cohesive funding structure, people rely on GoFundMe campaigns and social media callouts in order to make ends meet, while dealing with the gravity of police murders. On top of financial insecurity and housing precarity, families are fighting an uphill battle with oversight agencies that manage survivors far more effectively than they end police violence.

There is no clear appeal process for the outcome of IIO investigations. There is also no oversight of the IIO's Chief Civilian Director's final investigation findings.

Responding to Unthinkable Violence

While families navigate the unending horror of police murder, they also seek resistance and recognition in areas beyond colonial courtrooms. This includes organizing marches, rallies, teach-ins, and contributing to international and local organizing efforts to end police violence—and policing as an institution. Mothers who grieve murdered children spend their evenings and weekends feeding the people, an act of care and mutual aid.

In 2022 and 2023, the art exhibit, "Honour Their Names" was organized by Alunaye Laura Holland, a Wet'suwet'en woman from the Laksilyu Clan, from Tsee K'al K'e yex (House on a Flat Rock). Her relationship to police violence is personal, intergenerational, and arguably a birthright conferred upon all Indigenous women forced to live under colonial occupation.

On 8 July 2021, Holland's son Jared Leigh Lowndes, known to loved ones as Jay, was executed by the Campbell River RCMP. While centering Holland's lived experience, Honour Their Names also highlighted the names of Indigenous people shot and killed by the police across Canada, including: John Joseph "JJ" Harper (Wasagamack Indian Band)—killed by Winnipeg Police in March 1988;[31] and Anthony

---

[31] Government of Manitoba, Aboriginal Justice Implementation Commission, *The Death of John Joseph Harper*, vol III (Manitoba: Statutory Publications Office, 2001).

"Dudley" George (Kettle and Stony Point First Nation)—killed by Ontario Provincial Police (OPP) on 5 September 1995.[32]

More than just names, the stories and spirits of people killed by police are brought into our imagination, each and every time they are recited or depicted. We are also reminded of the promises made in the wake of their unjust deaths. Harper's murder was investigated by the Public Inquiry into the Administration of Justice and Aboriginal People, and the Manitoba Aboriginal Justice Implementation Commission issued its final report in 1991.[33] Following the OPP murder of George, an inquiry was held, and the *Ipperwash Inquiry Report* was published over a decade later, with 100 recommendations.[34]

In the case of Lowndes, as of February 2024, the B.C. Prosecution Service is still determining whether or not their agency will proceed with charges against at least three police officers identified in the 2021 killing of Lowndes.[35] B.C. prosecutors' charge assessment guidelines include consideration of whether or not prosecution is in the "public interest."[36] The notion of a fair and objective assessment of public interest erases how systemic racism and colonial ideologies define law, order, and justice.

Continuing Toward Abolition

The current framework for addressing police murders in Canada has no serious chance of ending fatal violence or use of force. Instead, the agencies that are tasked with accountability and oversight lack the

---

[32] Union of Ontario Indians, "Ipperwash: Tragedy to Reconciliation" (2008) at 6, online (PDF): <anishinabek.ca/wp-content/uploads/2016/06/Ipperwash-booklet-final.pdf>.

[33] *Ibid.*

[34] Sidney B Linden (Commissioner), *The Ipperwash Inquiry Report* (31 May 2007), online: <ontario.ca/page/ipperwash-inquiry-report>.

[35] Independent Investigations Office of BC, "IIO Has Submitted Report to Crown Counsel for Consideration of Charges Regarding the Death of One Man in Campbell River in July 2021 (2021-179)" (27 October 2023), online: <iiobc.ca/media/iio-has-submitted-report-to-crown-counsel-for-consideration-of-charges-regarding-the-death-of-one-man-in-campbell-river-in-july-2021-2021-179/>.

[36] BC Prosecution Service, "Overview of the Adult Justice System" (last modified 11 October 2019), online: <gov.bc.ca/gov/content/justice/criminal-justice/bc-prosecution-service/criminal-court-process/adult>.

ability to produce policy change. Instead, their mandate relies on public trust in police.

Disarming, defunding, and dismantling the police charts a path away from illegal systems of violence that have grown roots in so-called Canada. While this chapter focuses on police murder, other police violations have been normalized. This includes the policing of poverty and displacement of unhoused community members from public space (including parks), the targeting of drug users, and constant violations of Indigenous land. In recent years, of course, police trespassing on the Wet'suweten Yintah has become normalized. Spokespeople for the Gidimt'en Checkpoint, controlling access to Cas Yikh House territory,[37] have documented extensive RCMP harassment.[38]

Rather than attempting to hire more non-police at the IIO, or hire more racialized staffers at the OPCC, redirecting funds away from policing would protect Indigenous community members as a short-term solution because the current modes of resource creation, extraction, and distribution are inherently colonial in this racial capitalist settler colony and worldwide.

How Can Legal Workers Support?

I invite legal workers—including legal assistants, paralegals, lawyers, and other people with expertise in colonial legal systems—to consider how their skills and knowledge can be used to betray the prison industrial complex. Legal workers, and lawyers in particular, hold immense privilege when communicating with agents of the state, including police. Their power can be particularly effective in the immediate aftermath of a crisis. This includes the moments that follow arrest, brutality, or murder. Their power, however, must be leveraged in partnership with the communities directly affected by harm and organizers who support them. Expertise does not mean authority. I invite legal workers to consider how they can humbly work in partnership with PIC abolitionists, rather than replicate the

---

[37] Gidimt'en Checkoint, "ALL OUT FOR WEDZIN KWA" (last visited 26 August 2025) online:

[38] Gidimt'en Access Point, "RCMP Harassment at 44 km," (6 June 2022), online (video): <youtube.com/watch?v=WkxCr8LWeWI>.

same colonial standards that position lawyers above all other knowledge holders.

Occasionally, legal workers will approach families and organizers assuming that their issues arise from a lack of understanding or awareness of police brutality and murder. The reality, however, is that the communities most impacted by these injustices have a lifetime of navigating criminalization, often intergenerationally. They have lessons to teach us—and we can learn to work as accomplices to their efforts.

Legal workers must also recognize that their education and skillset are designed for cooptation. I've seen this firsthand—in the rise of community lawyers to attorneys general[39] or the hiring of advocates within agencies like the IIO. Legal workers may assume that the problem with institutions such as the municipal, provincial, and federal government, or oversight agencies, is that there are not enough "good" people working within them. I don't believe that is the problem: these institutions and agencies are flawed and fail people by design. So-called Canada is built on the premise of dispossessing Indigenous people from their lands, laws, and systems of self-governance. The use of police violence undergirds the illegal occupation we call Canada. Colonial legal orders authorize this occupation. There is no reforming this racist system!

As Coast Salish, Nuu-Chah-Nulth, and Snuneymuxw Matriarch Xhopakelxhit observes, "Creating a culture of resistance and support requires us all to know what our strong suits and talents are and to cultivate them, so they benefit the cause in a manner that is respectful and meaningful."[40]

---

[39] See for example "David Eby promises swift, decisive action on homelessness if he becomes B.C. premier," *CBC News* (17 August 2022) online: <cbc.ca/news/canada/british-columbia/david-eby-stephen-quinn-interview-homelessness-housing-1.655322>; Charlie Smith, "Attorney General Niki Sharma charts a journey to justice in B.C. regardless of one's race or gender" *Pancouver* (2 September 2023) online: <pancouver.ca/attorney-general-niki-sharma-charts-a-journey-to-justice-in-b-c-regardless-of-ones-race-or-gender/>.

[40] Xhopakelxhit, *Everyone Calls Themselves an Ally Until it Is Time to Do Some Real Ally Shit*, (Portland, OR: Microcosm Publishing, 2015) at 6, available online (PDF): <indigenousaction.org/wp-content/uploads/simple-file-list/ancestral_pride_zine.pdf>.

Indigenous People Killed by Canadian Police in 2020
Attachie Ashoona – Feb 26 – RCMP (Kinngait, Nunavut)
Eishia Hudson – April 8 – Winnipeg Police Service (Manitoba)
J. C. – April 9 – Winnipeg Police Service (Manitoba)
Kevin Stewart Andrews – April 18 – Winnipeg Police Service (Manitoba)
Everett Riley Patrick – April 12 – RCMP (Prince George, B.C.)
Abraham Natanine – May 5 – RCMP (Clyde River, Nunavut)
Regis Korchinkski Paquet – May 27 – Toronto Police Service
Chantel Moore – June 4 – Edmundston Police Force (New Brunswick)
Rodney Levi – June 12 – RCMP (Sunny Corner, New Brunswick)
Marty Powder – September 18 – Edmonton Police Service (Alberta)

Indigenous People Killed by Canadian Police in 2021
Julian Jones – February 27 – RCMP (Tofino, B.C.)
Braden Herman – May 11 – RCMP (Prince Albert, Saskatchewan)
Lionel Ernest Grey – June 17 – RCMP (High Prairie, Alberta)
Jared Lowndes – July 8 – RCMP (Campbell River, B.C.)
David Baker – August 31 – RCMP (Quesnel, B.C.)
Dillon Macdonald – December 14 – RCMP (Montreal Lake Cree Nation, Saskatchewan)
Randal Waylon Matthew Gladue – December 31, 2021 – Edmonton Police Service (Edmonton, Alberta)

Indigenous People Killed by Canadian Police in 2022
James Hanna – February 23 – Edmonton Police Service (Edmonton, Alberta)
Trent Byron Angus – February 26 – RCMP (Waseca, Saskatchewan)
Jimmie Johannesson – April 8 – RCMP (Surrey, B.C.)
Kerry (Kyriakos) Flanders – April 27 – Vancouver Police Department (Vancouver, B.C.)
Rojun Alphonse – July 10 – RCMP (Williams Lake, B.C.)
Christopher Amyotte, Leaping Frog Man – August 22 – Vancouver Police Department (Vancouver, B.C.)
Nathan Leather – December 25 – RCMP (Strathmore, Alberta)

Indigenous People Killed by Canadian Police in 2023

John Gardiner (Daigneault) – January 16 – Prince Albert Police Service (Prince Albert, Saskatchewan)

Wesley Wanuch – February 4 – RCMP (Cold Lake First Nation, Alberta)

Erin Norman "Chug" – April 4 – RCMP (Surrey, B.C.)

Derek Deon – April 13 – RCMP (Red Deer, Alberta)

Boden Umpherville – April 26 – Prince Albert Police Service (Prince Albert, Saskatchewan)

Levon Boyce Jackson Fox – May 29 – Calgary Police Service (Calgary, Alberta)

Indigenous People Killed by Canadian Police in 2024

James Wood – January 27 – Winnipeg Police Service (Winnipeg, Manitoba)

Jack Piché – August 29 – RCMP (Buffalo Narrows, Saskatchewan)

Hoss Lightning–Saddleback – August 30 – RCMP (Wetaskiwin, Alberta)

Tammy Bateman – September 2 – Winnipeg Police Service (Winnipeg, Manitoba)

Jason West – September 6 – Windsor Police Service (Windsor, Ontario)

Steven "Iggy" Dedam – September 6 – RCMP (Elsipogtog First Nation, New Brunswick)

Daniel Knife – September 8 – RCMP (Ahtahkakoop Cree Nation, Saskatchewan)

Jon Wells – September 17 – Calgary Police Service (Calgary, Alberta)

We only know a few of the names of people killed by police and prisons.

We will never stop fighting for a world free of this violence.

SECTION C

BOUNDARIES AND BORDERS OF PUBLIC LAW

The Xenophobic Gap in the *Charter's* Equality Guarantee

Y Y Brandon Chen

Abstract

Despite the equality guarantee in the *Canadian Charter of Rights and Freedoms*, xenophobic laws and government decisions persist in Canada. A review of relevant cases, including a line of lower court decisions grappling with the constitutionality of migrants' exclusion from publicly funded health care, shows Canadian courts have significantly limited the anti-xenophobic potential of the *Charter's* equality protection. Courts have regularly dismissed non-citizens' *Charter* equality claims by finding either that they suffer no differential treatment when compared with citizens, or that the differential treatment at issue is not based on a prohibited ground of discrimination. Consequently, *Charter* claims aiming to counter xenophobia rarely advance to the stage of equality analysis where discriminatory effects of the impugned differential treatment are scrutinized. To the extent that this case law contradicts the *Charter* equality jurisprudence more broadly, it suggests the possibility of a xenophobic bias within the Canadian judiciary.

Résumé

Malgré la garantie d'égalité inscrite dans la *Charte canadienne des droits et libertés*, des lois et décisions gouvernementales xénophobes persistent au Canada. Un examen des décisions pertinentes, y compris une série de décisions d'instances inférieures sur la constitutionnalité de l'exclusion des personnes migrantes des soins de santé financés par des fonds publics, révèle que les tribunaux canadiens ont considérablement limité le potentiel anti-xénophobe de la protection d'égalité de la *Charte*. Les tribunaux ont régulièrement rejeté les revendications d'égalité des non-citoyen·ne·s en vertu de la *Charte* en concluant soit qu'ils ne subissent aucun traitement différentiel par rapport aux citoyen·ne·s, soit que le traitement différentiel en question ne repose pas sur un motif interdit de discrimination. Par conséquent, les revendications fondées sur la *Charte* visant à contrer la xénophobie atteignent rarement le stade de l'analyse de l'égalité, où les effets discriminatoires du traitement différentiel contesté sont examinés. Dans la mesure où cette jurisprudence contredit l'interprétation plus large de l'égalité dans la *Charte*, elle suggère la possibilité d'un biais xénophobe au sein de la magistrature canadienne.

Xenophobia denotes the rejection, exclusion, and vilification of individuals who are perceived as foreign due to "intense dislike or fear of strangers or people from other countries."[1] Despite the fundamental role that immigration has played in Canada's nation building, the country is no stranger to xenophobia. Measures such as head taxes imposed on Chinese immigrants and the continuous journey requirement designed to thwart immigration from South Asia illustrate the long shadow that xenophobia has cast on Canadian policies historically.[2] Equally, xenophobia was evident in Canada's exclusion of African American immigrants in the early twentieth century because they supposedly "do not readily take to [its] climate,"[3] as well as that of European Jewish refugees before and during the Second

---

[1] International Labour Office, International Organization for Migration & Office of the United Nations High Commissioner for Human Rights, *International Migration, Racism, Discrimination and Xenophobia* (Geneva: United Nations, 2001) at 2.

[2] Ninette Kelley & Michael Trebilcock, *The Making of the Mosaic: A History of Canadian Immigration Policy*, 2nd ed (Toronto: University of Toronto Press, 2010) at 15.

[3] *Ibid* at 157.

World War because "[n]one [...] is too many."[4] Today, Canadian society remains replete with xenophobic portrayals of non-citizens as threats, burdens, and adversaries of "Canadian values."[5] These discourses have animated laws that, among others, bar the admission of certain would-be immigrants with disabilities,[6] disqualify family-sponsored immigrants from social assistance, sometimes for as long as 20 years,[7] and consign migrants to precarious legal statuses with limited pathways to permanent residence.[8]

One may expect the constitutional guarantee of equality rights in the *Canadian Charter of Rights and Freedoms* to function as a shield against xenophobic laws and government decisions. Section 15(1) of the *Charter* promises that "[e]very individual is equal before and under the law and has the right to the equal protection and equal benefit of the law without discrimination and, in particular, without discrimination based on race, national or ethnic origin, colour, religion, sex, age or mental or physical disability."[9] A *prima facie* breach of this promise is found when a two-step test is met. First, *Charter* claimants must demonstrate that they have been treated differently by the impugned law or government action based on at least one of the prohibited grounds of discrimination enumerated in section 15(1) or grounds that are considered analogous. Then, pursuant to the current iteration of the test, claimants must prove that such a distinction "perpetuates, reinforces or exacerbates disadvantage" that they face as members of an equity-seeking group.[10]

Ever since its first encounter with section 15(1) of the *Charter*, the Supreme Court of Canada has recognized non-citizen status as a

---

[4] Irving Abella & Harold Troper, *None Is Too Many: Canada and the Jews of Europe, 1933–1948* (Toronto: University of Toronto Press, 2012) at xix.

[5] Donald Galloway, "Immigration, Xenophobia and Equality Rights" (2019) 42:1 Dal LJ 17 at 19.

[6] Constance MacIntosh, "Medical Inadmissibility, and Physically and Mentally Disabled Would-be Immigrants: Canada's Story Continues" (2019) 42:1 Dal LJ 125.

[7] Xiaobei Chen & Sherry Xiaohan Thorpe, "Temporary Families? The Parent and Grandparent Sponsorship Program and the Neoliberal Regime of Immigration Governance in Canada" (2015) 1:1 Migration, Mobility & Displacement 67.

[8] Y Y Brandon Chen, "The Future of Precarious Status Migrants' Right to Health Care in Canada" (2017) 54:3 Alta L Rev 649.

[9] *Canadian Charter of Rights and Freedoms*, s 15, Part I of the *Constitution Act, 1982*, being Schedule B to the *Canada Act 1982* (U.K.), 1982, c 11 [*Charter*].

[10] *Fraser v Canada (AG)*, 2020 SCC 28 at para 50 [*Fraser*].

prohibited ground of discrimination, analogous to those characteristics listed in the section.[11] In *Andrews v Law Society of British Columbia*, a majority of the Supreme Court struck down a provision in British Columbia's *Barristers and Solicitors Act* that restricted admission to the practice of law to Canadian citizens.[12] Justice McIntyre held that the promise of equality found under section 15(1) of the *Charter* "appl[ies] to all persons whether citizens or not," and to exclude an entire group of people from legal practice solely based on their non-citizen status, without accounting for individual merits such as educational and professional qualifications, was discriminatory.[13] Both he and Justice Wilson described non-citizens as a "discrete and insular minority" whose concerns ought to attract constitutional review because, without a right to vote, their interests are prone to be overlooked.[14] Justice La Forest went a step further and asserted that "[b]y and large, the use in legislation of citizenship as a basis for distinguishing between persons [...] harbours the potential for undermining the essential or underlying values of a free and democratic society."[15]

Notwithstanding this initial victory, section 15(1) *Charter* jurisprudence since *Andrews* has left much to be desired in terms of the equality guarantee's potential as a tool to counter xenophobic laws and government actions.[16] Indeed, to date, *Andrews* remains the only decision in which the Supreme Court of Canada strikes down a statute for having violated non-citizens' *Charter* equality rights.[17] A particular problem facing non-citizen equality claimants has been the difficulty in passing the

---

[11] *Andrews v Law Society of British Columbia*, [1989] 1 SCR 143, 1989 CarswellBC 701 [*Andrews*].

[12] *Ibid.*

[13] *Ibid* at 183.

[14] *Ibid* at 152, 183.

[15] *Ibid* at 196–197.

[16] See generally Catherine Dauvergne, "How the *Charter* Has Failed Non-citizens in Canada: Reviewing Thirty Years of Supreme Court of Canada Jurisprudence" (2013) 58:3 McGill LJ 663.

[17] To the best of the author's knowledge, there have been four section 15(1) cases since *Andrews* in which the Supreme Court decided on the merits of discrimination claims against non-citizens: *Chiarelli v Canada (Minister of Employment and Immigration)*, [1992] 1 SCR 711, 1992 CarswellNat 18 [*Chiarelli*]; *Vancouver Society of Immigrant and Visible Minority Women v MNR*, [1998] 1 SCR 10, 1999 CarswellNat 19; *Lavoie v Canada*, 2002 SCC 23; and *Charkaoui v Canada (Citizenship and Immigration)*, 2007 SCC 9 [*Charkaoui*]. In *Chiarelli*, *Vancouver Society* and *Charkaoui*, the Court found no section 15(1) *Charter* infringements. In *Lavoie*, a majority of the Court held that while the impugned statutory

first step of the section 15(1) test. As I shall demonstrate, Canadian courts have regularly dismissed non-citizens' *Charter* equality claims by finding either that they suffer no differential treatment when compared with citizens, or that the differential treatment at issue is not based on a prohibited ground of discrimination. Consequently, relatively little attention has been paid by courts under section 15(1) to the harmful effects of what non-citizens allege as xenophobic laws or government actions.

In this chapter, I highlight three developments in case law that contribute to the hurdles facing non-citizen equality claimants in meeting the first part of the section 15(1) test. I begin by considering a pair of decisions from the Supreme Court of Canada that point to the guarantee of Canadian citizens' mobility rights alone under section 6(1) of the *Charter* as justification for rejecting non-citizens' equality rights claims. These cases suggest that at least in some circumstances, a successful section 15(1) *Charter* challenge cannot rest on a comparison between Canadian citizens and non-citizens, thus reducing the availability of the *Charter* as a recourse against xenophobia.

Next, I show that even when a citizenship-based equality claim is not deemed to have been precluded by section 6 of the *Charter*, non-citizens have had limited success convincing courts that the differential treatment they experience is based on their lack of Canadian citizenship. Contrary to the approach to other grounds of discrimination prohibited by section 15(1), courts have narrowly interpreted citizenship-based discrimination as capturing only laws and government actions that treat all non-citizens less favourably than citizens. This enables laws and government actions that disadvantage a subset of non-citizens to evade section 15(1) scrutiny from the perspective of citizenship status.

In the penultimate section of this chapter, I further demonstrate that when non-citizens try to root their claims of discrimination on the ground of "immigration status" instead of citizenship, perhaps hoping to circumvent unfavourable precedents associated with a citizenship-based approach, courts have refused to acknowledge immigration status as a *Charter* protected ground. Immigration status has been repeatedly described by courts as a mutable personal characteristic unlike most other enumerated and analogous grounds found under section 15(1), and as such there is apparently no *Charter* protection against distinctions

---

provision infringed section 15(1), the infringement was "demonstrably justified in a free and democratic society" and therefore saved by section 1 of the *Charter*.

created by law on that basis. To conclude, I argue that these three impedi-ments to non-citizens' successful section 15(1) *Charter* challenges pare down the equality guarantee's protection of non-citizens so much so that it offers no meaningful remedy against xenophobia. Moreover, to the extent that these difficulties facing non-citizens are above and beyond those already experienced by equality rights claimants in general, they reveal a xenophobic bias within the Canadian judiciary itself.

Before embarking on my analysis, a comment concerning termi-nology is warranted. The word "migrants" has been imparted various meanings on different occasions. At times, it refers to people who volun-tarily move to another country, in contrast to refugees and asylum seek-ers who must migrate to escape persecution or armed conflict.[18] Other times, it is used as an umbrella term to denote all people who have changed their country of residence either permanently (e.g., immigrants) or temporarily (e.g., migrant workers and international students), includ-ing refugees and asylum seekers.[19] Strictly out of convenience, it is this latter meaning of "migrants" that I use in this chapter. Even when broadly defined in this way, "migrants" and "non-citizens" are not syn-onyms. While migrants make up a significant portion thereof, non-citi-zens in Canada also include stateless individuals born in the country,[20] as well as tourists who visit Canada for short-term purposes rather than to change their country of residence.[21] The use of these two terms in dif-ferent parts of this chapter is intended to reflect this distinction.

Charter Mobility Rights as a Shield Against Citizenship-Based Equality Claims

One obstacle to non-citizens' success under section 15(1) concerns the interplay between *Charter*-guaranteed equality rights and mobility

---

[18] See e.g. Adrian Edwards, "UNHCR Viewpoint: 'Refugee' or 'Migrant'—Which Is Right?" (11 July 2016), online: *UNHCR* <unhcr.org/news/latest/2016/7/55dfoe556/unhcr-viewpoint-refugee-migrant-right.html>.

[19] See e.g. *Recommendations on Statistics of International Migration: Revision 1*, Statistics Paper Series M, No 58, Rev 1 (New York: United Nations, 1998), at para 32 [*Statistics of Migration*].

[20] See generally Canadian Centre on Statelessness, "Statelessness in Canada" online: <www.statelessness.ca/canada.html>.

[21] See generally *Statistics of Migration, supra* note 19.

rights. Section 6(1) of the *Charter* stipulates that "[e]very citizen of Canada has the right to enter, remain in and leave Canada."[22] The fact that this constitutional protection of mobility rights is exclusively conferred on Canadian citizens has been used to justify the dismissal of non-citizens' equality rights claims in leading authorities. Of the four section 15(1) cases since *Andrews* in which claims of discrimination against non-citizens are denied by the Supreme Court of Canada,[23] two rest on this line of reasoning.

In its 1992 decision in *Canada (Minister of Employment and Immigration) v Chiarelli*, the Supreme Court dismissed a constitutional challenge to a legislative scheme that required permanent residents to be deported following conviction for a serious criminal offence in Canada.[24] With respect to section 15(1), Chiarelli submitted that the impugned law discriminated against permanent residents because Canadian citizens convicted of the same offence were allowed to remain in the country. The Supreme Court rejected this claim in a short paragraph, holding that the distinction between Canadian citizens and non-citizens in the deportation context is provided for by section 6(1) of the *Charter* and therefore does not constitute discrimination under section 15(1).[25]

The same reasoning was adopted by the Supreme Court 15 years later in *Charkaoui v Canada (Immigration and Citizenship)* to reject a section 15(1) challenge to the security certificate regime created by the *Immigration and Refugee Protection Act*.[26] The regime at that time permitted the federal government to issue a certificate of inadmissibility, based on evidence that it was entitled to not disclose, against non-citizens who it reasonably believed to be a danger to national security. Once deemed inadmissible, these non-citizens were subject to removal from Canada and could be detained for an indeterminate amount of time while awaiting deportation. Although aspects of the certificate regime were ultimately struck down by the Supreme Court for having breached other sections of the *Charter*, the regime in its entirety was found compliant with section 15(1). In another terse judgment, the Court reiterated the guarantee of citizens' mobility rights

---

[22] *Charter, supra* note 9, s 6(1).

[23] See *supra* note 17.

[24] *Chiarelli, supra* note 17.

[25] *Ibid* at 715.

[26] *Charkaoui, supra* note 17.

under section 6(1) and held that a deportation scheme imposed on non-citizens alone would not contravene the *Charter*'s equality protection. And since the security certificate regime as it was applied to the *Charter* claimants in this case was not in the Court's view "unhinged from the state's purpose of deportation," it did not result in discrimination even if the pre-removal detention had been lengthy.[27]

The precedents set by these two cases have the effects of immunizing differential treatment between citizens and non-citizens from section 15(1) scrutiny when such differentiation relates to the immigration process. In both *Chiarelli* and *Charkaoui*, section 6(1) is presented by the Supreme Court as the full answer to non-citizens' equality rights claims, thus eliminating the need for it to consider the actual effects of the citizenship-based distinction at issue on non-citizens. As Donald Galloway points out, the Court "is not here cataloguing all the factors that are required to show that a distinction *is* discriminatory. Instead, [it] is identifying a preliminary finding that must be made before the inquiry can continue."[28] Indeed, as seen, the Court makes it clear in *Charkaoui* that section 6(1) categorically renders a fulsome section 15(1) review unnecessary so long as the differential treatment being asserted by non-citizens *vis-à-vis* Canadian citizens serves "the state's purpose of deportation."[29]

Catherine Dauvergne has made a similar observation. She notes that the Supreme Court's resort to section 6(1) in these cases effectively blocks non-citizens from alleging discrimination by comparing themselves with Canadian citizens, if the impugned law or government action concerns one's right to enter, remain in or leave Canada. At the same time, the Court has arguably stretched the content of such mobility rights, going so far as to extend the reach of section 6(1) in *Charkaoui* to pre-deportation detention where deportation is not imminent. Together, these two moves allow section 6(1) to function akin to a shield capable of deflecting any *Charter* equality rights challenge to immigration rules and procedures, broadly defined, whenever such challenge turns on differential treatment between Canadian citizens and non-citizens.[30]

---

[27] *Ibid* at para 131.
[28] *Supra* note 5 at 27 [emphasis in original].
[29] *Charkaoui, supra* note 17 at para 131.
[30] *Supra* note 16.

The availability of section 6(1) as a shield against non-citizens' *Charter* equality claims undercuts the seemingly promising legacy of *Andrews*. It turns out that for those seeking to challenge citizenship-based discrimination, the precedential value of *Andrews* is largely confined to cases where the impugned law or government action falls clearly outside the immigration realm. When a citizenship-based distinction is tied to an immigration-related government objective, it is for all intents and purposes protected from a section 15(1) inquiry, no matter that it may have the effect of further disadvantaging non-citizens and fuelling xenophobic stereotypes, such as linking migrants to criminality and terrorism.[31] This purpose-focused approach contradicts the Supreme Court's own pronouncement that a section 15(1) analysis should centre on the impact of the impugned law or government action.[32] Moreover, by emphasizing the difference between citizens and non-citizens in the immigration context, it resurrects a formal understanding of equality already rejected by the Supreme Court, which proposes "things that are alike should be treated alike, while things that are unalike should be treated unalike in proportion to their unlikeness."[33]

Admittedly, contestation of xenophobic laws or government actions under section 15(1) need not be couched exclusively in terms of citizenship status. As Justice La Forest remarked in *Andrews*, "[d]iscrimination on the basis of nationality has from early times been an inseparable companion of discrimination on the basis of race and national or ethnic origin."[34] This intersectionality suggests that a section 15(1) *Charter* challenge based on other prohibited grounds such as race and national or ethnic origin may represent a viable litigation strategy against xenophobia in some situations. More importantly, a *Charter* equality claim of this sort can in theory bypass the citizenship-based shield stemming from section 6(1).

---

[31] For discussions on the stereotype of migrants as security threats, see e.g. Idil Atak & François Crépeau, "National Security, Terrorism and the Securitization of Migration" in Vincent Chetail & Céline Bauloz, eds, *Research Handbook on International Law and Migration* (Cheltenham, UK: Edward Elgar, 2014) 93.

[32] See e.g. *Withler v Canada (AG)*, 2011 SCC 12 at para 39, where the Court stated, "[t]he focus of the inquiry is on the actual impact of the impugned law, taking full account of social, political, economic and historical factors concerning the group" [*Withler*]. See also Galloway, *supra* note 5.

[33] *Andrews*, *supra* note 11 at 166.

[34] *Ibid* at 195.

Indeed, some migrants have had notable successes overturning xenophobic government policies, including those governing the immigration process, by framing their equality claims in terms of national origin. The successful *Charter* challenges to the federal government's policy on designated countries of origin offer an example. The now repealed policy aimed at deterring unfounded asylum claims by placing a range of disadvantages on asylum seekers from a list of countries that were considered "safe." Among other things, these asylum seekers were entitled to a narrower set of publicly funded health care services relative to those from elsewhere, and they were barred from appealing a negative refugee determination decision.[35] In *Canadian Doctors for Refugee Care v Canada (Attorney General)*, the Federal Court struck down the aspect of the policy that provided lesser health care entitlement to asylum seekers from designated countries as discriminatory on the basis of national origin.[36] The Court reasoned that the impugned policy "perpetuates the stereotypical view that [asylum seekers from designated countries] are cheats and queue-jumpers, that their refugee claims are 'bogus', and that they have come to Canada to abuse the generosity of Canadians."[37] A year later, for substantially the same reasons, the Federal Court in *YZ v Canada (Citizenship and Immigration)* also found the denial of a right of appeal to asylum seekers from designated countries to be a breach of section 15(1).[38]

Despite favourable case law, equality claims based on national origin only provide a partial solution for challenging xenophobic laws and government actions. They offer no relief when non-citizens with one legal status are treated differently from those with another status, irrespective of where they come from originally. Moreover, as Galloway laments, the triumphs in *Canadian Doctors* and *YZ* rest on the Federal Court's accentuation of how the impugned law stereotyped asylum seekers from designated countries, whereas the same prejudicial stereotypes are in fact commonly inflicted on all asylum

---

[35] Immigration, Refugees and Citizenship Canada, News Release, "Canada Ends the Designated Country of Origin Practice" (17 May 2019), online: www.canada.ca/en/immigration-refugees-citizenship/news/2019/05/canada-ends-the-designated-country-of-origin-practice.html>.

[36] 2014 FC 651 [*Canadian Doctors*].

[37] *Ibid* at para 13.

[38] 2015 FC 892.

seekers.[39] In other words, confining the purview of the discrimination inquiry to national origin risks overstating the dissimilarities among victims of xenophobia, when "we should instead recognize that it [was] because [nationals of particular countries] were part of the larger group of non-citizens that they were treated with disdain and disrespect."[40] These concerns underscore the need to make citizenship-based *Charter* equality challenges available as a tool in the struggle against xenophobia. The Supreme Court's section 15(1) jurisprudence on citizenship-based distinctions, which yields much ground to the *Charter*'s mobility rights guarantee, falls short in this regard.

Narrow Interpretation of Citizenship-Based Distinctions

Outside the immigration domain, section 6(1) has posed less of a hurdle to non-citizens who seek to advance a *Charter* equality claim on the basis of citizenship status. Instead, the main problems encountered by non-citizen section 15(1) claimants in this context concern courts' unwillingness to broadly interpret what constitutes citizenship-based distinctions, as well as to recognize immigration status as a prohibited ground of discrimination akin to citizenship status. I discuss the former in this section and the latter in the next. To illustrate both points, I turn my gaze to a handful of section 15(1) *Charter* challenges launched by migrants opposing their exclusion from publicly funded health care. To the best of my knowledge, these cases, along with *Canadian Doctors* mentioned above, represent all the reported judicial decisions on section 15(1) involving migrants' demand for greater health care coverage. The fact that non-citizens were only partially victorious in one of these cases, namely *Canadian Doctors*, by framing their claims on the ground of national origin, epitomizes the obstacles non-citizens face when drawing on the *Charter*'s equality rights protection to counter xenophobia.

My case law review begins with the 1998 decision in *Clarken v Ontario (Health Insurance Plan)*[41] and the 2001 decision of the Ontario Court of Appeal in *Irshad (Litigation guardian of) v Ontario (Ministry of*

---

[39] *Supra* note 5 at 46.
[40] *Ibid* at 47.
[41] (1998), 79 ACWS (3d) 1064 [*Clarken*].

Health).[42] Both cases emerged against the backdrop of Ontario's health care reform in 1994. At that time, Ontario was experiencing financial troubles after years of recession and escalating debts, so it decided to tighten eligibility for its health care program as a way to control public spending.[43] Pursuant to changes made to the province's regulations under the *Health Insurance Act*, to qualify for the Ontario Health Insurance Plan (OHIP), a person must not only establish ordinary residence in Ontario as before, but also demonstrate possession of either Canadian citizenship or certain immigration statuses.[44] This had the effect of excluding international students, asylum seekers, and some holders of temporary resident permits from OHIP coverage. For people who remained OHIP-eligible, many faced a new waiting period such that health care coverage only started after three months of residence in the province.[45] In addition, most spouses and dependent children of OHIP beneficiaries no longer qualified for health care coverage by association. They instead had to establish OHIP eligibility independently, meaning that they may not be entitled to health care if they do not possess the necessary citizenship or immigration status.[46]

In *Clarken*, a group of international students and their dependents who lost their OHIP coverage sought to reverse these legislative changes. They contended that the amended OHIP eligibility rules breached section 15(1) of the *Charter* by discriminating against them on the basis of their lack of Canadian citizenship and their immigration status. Ontario's Divisional Court dismissed both claims, finding that the first step of the section 15(1) test had not been satisfied. The Court's ruling with respect to immigration status in this case will be discussed later on. Concerning the citizenship-based claim, the Court held:

> Although it is true that generally all foreign students will be citizens of other countries and not citizens of Canada, this is not the basis for the distinction made to the OHIP coverage. Rather, it is

---

[42] (2001), 55 OR (3d) 43 (Ont CA), rev'g in part (1999), 85 ACWS (3d) 801 (Ont Ct J [Gen Div]), leave to appeal to SCC refused, 28571 (13 September 2001) [*Irshad*].

[43] *Ibid* at para 24.

[44] *Ibid* at para 36.

[45] *Ibid* at paras 60–63.

[46] *Ibid* at paras 69–70.

a residency requirement which also applies certain limitations to students from other provinces who are Canadian citizens: these students are also barred from receiving OHIP coverage until after a period of residence of 3 months in the province.[47]

To paraphrase the Court, the OHIP reform did not neatly draw a line along citizenship status. In particular, some Canadian citizens saw their OHIP coverage narrowed as well due to the newly introduced three-month waiting period.

What the Court neglected to note was that while this waiting period applied to all individuals moving to Ontario, for non-citizens, it was accompanied by other policy changes that, together, imposed a greater burden on their establishment of health care eligibility. Had the claimants in *Clarken* maintained their OHIP eligibility, they still would have had to meet the waiting requirement if they ever needed to re-establish their ordinary residence in the province. Additionally, when Canadian citizens move to Ontario from other parts of the country, they typically have public health insurance from their previous province or territory of residence as a backstop during the three-month wait.[48] The same option is not available to non-citizens moving to Ontario from another country. The Court's reference to the waiting period, therefore, amounted to nothing more than smoke and mirrors that obscured the substance of the equality claim at issue: namely, the amended OHIP eligibility criteria disproportionately affected non-citizens, as exemplified by the complete disentitlement of ordinarily resident international students and their dependents.

Despite this, according to the Divisional Court, any distinction created by the 1994 OHIP reform lay between Ontario residents and non-residents: whereas residents would continue to be entitled to health insurance coverage, non-residents would not.[49] And this residency-based differential treatment was constitutionally permitted.[50] Section 6(3) of the *Charter* specifically contemplates the possibility for citizens' and permanent residents' inter-provincial mobility rights to be encumbered by "any laws providing for reasonable residency requirements as a qualification for the receipt of publicly provided

---

[47] *Clarken, supra* note 41 at para 48.
[48] *Irshad, supra* note 42 at para 145.
[49] *Clarken, supra* note 41 at para 54.
[50] *Ibid* at para 53.

social services."[51] The Court gathered that if citizens and permanent residents do not have a constitutional right to be free from "reasonable residency requirements," non-citizens who lack permanent residence must not, either. And seeing as non-residents in Ontario, albeit uninsured, could theoretically still access emergency care, the Court ruled that OHIP's residency-based eligibility rules were reasonable.[52]

The way that the Divisional Court interpreted the interplay between sections 6(3) and 15(1) of the *Charter* arguably cedes too much discretion to the provinces in their design of social programs. Seemingly, so long as entitlement to social benefits such as health care is tied to residency, provinces can freely define what constitutes residency, however discriminatory it may be, including, as in the case of OHIP, narrowly construing residents as people who hold certain citizenship or immigration statuses. Any section 15(1) inquiry into the definition of residency is apparently forestalled by the permission of residency requirements under section 6(3). As such, for a time, *Clarken* functioned as an equivalent to *Chiarelli* and *Charkaoui* outside the immigration context, as it immunized potentially xenophobic social policies from section 15(1) scrutiny. The decision from the Ontario Court of Justice in *Irshad* offered a case in point.

Irshad involved a section 15(1) *Charter* challenge against the 1994 OHIP reform launched by a different group of migrants, who either lost their OHIP coverage due to the new citizenship and immigration status requirement, or incurred health care costs during the three-month wait. The trial judge, citing *Clarken*, dismissed the case on the ground that section 6(3) of the *Charter* protected reasonable residency requirements from being challenged under section 15(1). In fact, Justice Dilks doubled down on *Clarken* and held that people who were not Canadian citizens or permanent residents lacked a *Charter* right to even "insist that residency requirements affecting them be reasonable."[53] Presumably, had constitutional drafters intended for these non-citizens to be so entitled, they would not have specified citizens and permanent residents in the relevant part of section 6 of the *Charter*. It followed that if residency requirements attached to social services gave rise to any discrimination against these non-citizens,

---

[51] *Charter, supra* note 9, s 6(3).
[52] *Clarken, supra* note 41 at para 54.
[53] *Irshad, supra* note 42 at para 93.

the discrimination was "clearly recognized and tolerated by the *Charter* itself."[54]

On appeal, Justice Dilks' ruling concerning section 6 of the *Charter* was partially reversed. The Court of Appeal for Ontario accepted that non-citizens who are not permanent residents of Canada cannot challenge a residency requirement under section 6(3) by arguing that the requirement is unreasonable.[55] However, section 6(3) does not shelter residency requirements from section 15(1) review as the two sections supposedly serve different objectives. The appellate court explained: "A residency requirement as a prerequisite to access to a publicly funded social service may be reasonable in the sense that it does not unduly limit mobility rights but it may still be discriminatory either in its purpose or its effect."[56] Put another way, whereas section 6(3) guards against residency requirements that are unduly onerous, such as imposing a waiting period that is too lengthy, section 15(1) ensures residency requirements do not differentiate between people in a discriminatory manner. Therefore, non-citizens who are not permanent residents are not per se prevented from availing themselves of the *Charter*'s equality guarantee when looking to challenge xenophobic, residency-based laws.

Be that as it may, the Court of Appeal in *Irshad* ultimately rejected the migrants' equality claims. It found neither OHIP's eligibility criteria nor the three-month waiting period distinguished ordinary residents of Ontario pursuant to citizenship status. With respect to the former, the Court stressed that "[m]any non-citizens are eligible for OHIP under the definition of resident," and as such, "Canadian citizenship is but one of many criteria which [...] make [a] person eligible for OHIP."[57] Concerning the alleged disparate impact of the three-month wait, the Court similarly held that "Canadian citizens may or may not have been covered by a health care plan of another province," while awaiting the start of their OHIP coverage, and conversely, non-citizens may be free from the adverse effects of the waiting period if they moved to Ontario from another province where they were publicly insured.[58]

---

54 *Ibid.*

55 *Ibid* at para 95.

56 *Ibid* at para 96.

57 *Ibid* at para 125.

58 *Ibid* at para 148.

Much like the Divisional Court's reasoning in *Clarken*, the Court of Appeal was troubled by the imperfect line drawing between Canadian citizens and non-citizens under the amended OHIP. Because the new OHIP rules did not leave *all* citizens unscathed or disadvantage *all* non-citizens alike, any differential treatment they imposed apparently could not be based on citizenship status. No consideration was given to the possibility that the differential treatment between citizens and non-citizens could have been a matter of degree, rather than the binary of citizens having all attendant rights and non-citizens having none at all.

Such a narrow construction of what counts as a citizenship-based distinction under section 15(1) raises both practical and doctrinal problems. Practically, the insistence that a citizenship-based distinction draws a clean line between Canadian citizens and non-citizens in order to be recognizable under section 15(1) severely diminishes the potential of the *Charter*'s equality rights guarantee as a tool against xenophobia. In modern liberal democracies such as Canada, rarely do policies delineate rights and responsibilities along citizenship status, except in the political sphere. As William Rogers Brubaker discerns: "For most purposes, the crucial status is residence, not citizenship: more particularly the status of 'privileged,' 'established,' or 'permanent' resident, which confers an ordinarily nonrevocable right of residence as well as a wide range of civil and socioeconomic rights."[59] For example, Canada's immigration system is predominantly premised on the distinction between citizens and permanent residents on the one hand, and so-called "foreign nationals" on the other.[60] In regard to health care entitlement, permanent residents too are treated virtually akin to citizens.[61] Indeed, the bulk of xenophobic policies in Canada today operates by constraining non-citizens' access to pathways toward permanent residence.[62] Given this policy landscape, to borrow

---

[59] William Rogers Brubaker, "Membership Without Citizenship: The Economic and Social Rights of Noncitizens" in William Rogers Brubaker, ed, *Immigration and the Politics of Citizenship in Europe and North America* (Washington, DC: University Press of America, 1989) 145 at 147. See also Saskia Sassen, *Losing Control? Sovereignty in the Age of Globalization* (New York: Columbia University Press, 1996).

[60] *Immigration and Refugee Protection Act*, SC 2001, c 27, s 2(1), sub verbo "foreign national".

[61] Chen, *supra* note 8 at 655.

[62] Chen, *supra* note 8.

Chief Justice Dickson's remark in a different context, "[i]f a finding of discrimination required that every individual in the affected group [i.e., non-citizens] be treated identically, legislative protection against [xenophobic] discrimination would be of little or no value."[63]

What is more, the demand that an impugned citizenship-based distinction precisely divides Canadian citizens and everyone else is inconsistent with how courts have approached other prohibited grounds of discrimination. The Supreme Court of Canada has repeatedly acknowledged the heterogeneity that may exist within an equity-seeking group, as well as the possibility that such heterogeneity may lead to different members of the group being treated differently.[64] "Partial discrimination," the Supreme Court cautions, is "no less discriminatory than those in which all members of a protected group are affected."[65] What matters is whether, on balance, the impugned law or government action affects members of a protected group more than it affects others. As such, a corporation's group insurance policy that excluded pregnant women, as opposed to all women, from disability benefits was found by the Supreme Court to constitute sex-based discrimination.[66] Likewise, a workers' compensation scheme that provided reduced benefits to injured workers who developed chronic pain, relative to those suffering from other types of injuries, was ruled discriminatory on the ground of disability.[67] It should follow that a distinction ought to be considered citizenship-based even if it adversely affects a subset of, rather than all, non-citizens. There is no apparent doctrinal reason why a more stringent test should be adopted under section 15(1) when assessing whether a differential treatment is based on citizenship status versus other prohibited grounds of discrimination.

Rejection of "Immigration Status" as an Analogous Ground

As an alternative strategy, and perhaps conscious of the difficulties with establishing citizenship-based distinctions under section 15(1),

---

[63] *Janzen v Platy Enterprises Ltd*, [1989] 1 SCR 1252 at 1288–1289, 1989 CarswellMan 158.

[64] *Fraser, supra* note 10 at para 75.

[65] *Ibid* at para 72.

[66] *Brooks v Canada Safeway Ltd*, [1989] 1 SCR 1219, 1989 CarswellMan 160.

[67] *Nova Scotia (Workers' Compensation Board) v Martin*, 2003 SCC 54.

some non-citizens have sought to challenge xenophobic laws by formulating their *Charter* equality claims in terms of immigration status. They argue that immigration status qualifies as an analogous ground under section 15(1), and therefore any distinction based on this ground that perpetuates, reinforces or exacerbates migrants' disadvantage is *prima facie* prohibited. Canadian courts, however, have so far remained largely unsympathetic to this pivot, adopting an arguably xenophobic posture of their own in the process. The case of *Toussaint v Canada (Attorney General)* is illustrative of this dynamic.[68]

Following the 1994 OHIP reform, which deprived asylum seekers in Ontario of publicly funded health care coverage, Canada introduced the Interim Federal Health Program (IFHP) with a view to bridge the coverage gap. Over time, the IFHP was expanded to also provide health care benefits to refugees, victims of human trafficking, and non-citizens in immigration detention.[69] The fact that the IFHP does not cover the health care costs of other migrants with humanitarian needs, such as those who are undocumented, was challenged in *Toussaint*. Regarding equality rights, the claimant initially argued that the government's refusal to grant her IFHP coverage was discrimination against non-citizens.[70] This argument was summarily dismissed by the Federal Court, consistent with the strict interpretation of citizenship-based distinction in cases like *Clarken* and *Irshad*, above. Justice Zinn explained that the claimant was excluded from the IFHP "because of her illegal status in Canada," and this was a legislative distinction based on immigration, rather than citizenship, status.[71] However, because Toussaint did not make any argument in relation to immigration status, her section 15(1) claim failed.[72]

Taking her cue from Justice Zinn, Toussaint modified her equality claim on appeal and argued that the IFHP's eligibility rules unfairly distinguished between foreign nationals based on the as yet

---

[68] 2011 FCA 213, leave to appeal to SCC refused, 34446 (26 September 2011) [*Toussaint FCA*].

[69] Ruby Dhand & Robert Diab, "Canada's Refugee Health Law and Policy from a Comparative, Constitutional, and Human Rights Perspective" (2015) 1:1 Can J Comparative & Contemporary L 351.

[70] *Toussaint v Canada (AG)*, 2010 FC 810 at para 79 [*Toussaint FC*].

[71] *Ibid* at para 81.

[72] *Ibid* at para 82.

unrecognized analogous ground of "immigration status."[73] The Federal Court of Appeal responded by holding that immigration status does not constitute a prohibited ground of discrimination that is analogous to the enumerated characteristics in section 15(1).

Since the Supreme Court's 1999 decision in *Corbiere v Canada (Minister of Indian and Northern Affairs)*, the determination of whether a personal characteristic amounts to an analogous ground under section 15 has followed an immutability test.[74] According to the majority in *Corbiere*, analogous grounds, like their enumerated counterparts, represent "constant markers of suspect decision making or potential discrimination."[75] What sets them apart from other personal traits is that they are "immutable or changeable only at unacceptable cost to personal identity."[76] With respect to the second type of traits, which the Supreme Court describes as "constructively immutable," it is further explained that their immutability stems from the fact that "the government has no legitimate interest in expecting us to change to receive equal treatment under the law."[77]

In *Toussaint*, the Federal Court of Appeal found immigration status to be neither actually immutable nor constructively so.[78] Focusing on Toussaint's status as an undocumented person, the appellate court reasoned that not only was immigration status changeable as a matter of fact, but also in this case, the government had "a real, valid and justified interest" in expecting such a status change, to ensure that all those in Canada have the legal right to be present.[79]

This ruling echoed the conclusion reached by Ontario courts previously in *Clarken* and *Irshad*. Besides citizenship-based arguments, the claimants in those cases submitted that the impugned OHIP policies also violated their *Charter* equality rights on the basis of immigration status. Both Ontario's Divisional Court and its Court of Appeal declined to recognize immigration status as an analogous ground under section 15(1) due to the supposed mutability of the status.[80] Specifically, in

---

[73] *Toussaint FCA, supra* note 68 at para 98.

[74] [1999] 2 SCR 203, 1999 CarswellNat 663.

[75] *Ibid* at para 8.

[76] *Ibid* at para 13.

[77] *Ibid.*

[78] *Toussaint FCA, supra* note 68 at para 99.

[79] *Ibid.*

[80] *Clarken, supra* note 41 at para 52; *Irshad, supra* note 42 at para 136.

Irshad, the appellate court rationalized its finding by observing that four of the five claimants who were temporary residents in Canada at the start of this case indeed changed their immigration status in the course of the litigation by gaining permanent residence.[81] There was, however, no analysis of the difficulties or costs that these claimants incurred to achieve their status change, and if these costs might have crossed the line of acceptability to render immigration status constructively immutable. Furthermore, the characterization of immigration status as alterable trivialized the Court's own remarks about the fifth temporary resident claimant in this case. For this claimant to become a permanent resident, the Court acknowledged, he would have to either successfully overturn the immigration officer's inadmissibility finding against him, or appeal to the immigration minister for a status change.[82] Successful outcomes from either option were far from guaranteed.

After *Toussaint*, the question of whether immigration status should be accepted as an analogous ground resurfaced in *Canadian Doctors*. The *Charter* claimants in that case, in addition to arguing discrimination based on national origin, contended that all asylum seekers regardless of where they were originally from were treated less favourably than Canadian citizens with respect to the breadth of public health care coverage they received. This distinction, they argued, was discrimination based on immigration status. The Federal Court cited both *Toussaint* and *Irshad* and held that it was bound to follow these precedents to find immigration status unqualified as an analogous ground.[83]

The judiciary's rejection of immigration status as an analogous ground of discrimination is problematic on multiple levels. I agree with Galloway's assessment that characterizing immigration status as mutable "runs counter to common experience."[84] For many migrants, the process of changing one's legal status is complex, laborious, and taxing.[85] While some have found it useful to retain third

---

[81] *Irshad, supra* note 42 at para 136.

[82] *Ibid.*

[83] *Canadian Doctors, supra* note 36 at paras 861–70.

[84] *Supra* note 5 at 46.

[85] See e.g. Delphine Nakache & Leann Dixon-Perera, "Temporary or Transitional? Migrant Workers' Experience with Permanent Residence in Canada" (2015) 55 IRPP Study 1; Robert Falconer, "Slow, Subjective and Stressful: A Guide to Canada's Asylum System" (2019) 12:24 School Public Policy Publications 1.

parties to help them maneuver the immigration system, not everyone can afford such services.[86] Time and resources aside, changing immigration status for undocumented migrants like Toussaint further demands that they accept a very real risk of detection and deportation, thus jeopardizing their lives in Canada.[87] Even after enduring all this, the success of one's application for status change still depends on government approval. Given these barriers, any suggestion that immigration status is mutable appears disingenuous.

Moreover, not recognizing immigration status as a prohibited ground of discrimination sits in tension with the Supreme Court's reasoning in *Andrews*. For one thing, citizenship status is technically no less mutable than immigration status, and yet it is accepted as an analogous ground under section 15(1).[88] For another, as much as non-citizens are "relatively powerless politically, and whose interests are likely to be compromised by legislative decisions,"[89] so too are migrants. In fact, Justice Zinn acknowledged this in *Toussaint* by opining that "[i]t may be fair to say that illegal migrants lack political power, are frequently disadvantaged, and are incredibly vulnerable to abuse."[90] These considerations, says the Supreme Court in *Corbiere*, remain relevant to the analogous grounds inquiry insofar as they are encapsulated in the immutability test.[91] The various courts' narrow focus on whether immigration status can actually be altered, therefore, superficially applies the immutability test as it misses the broader circumstances that shape migrants' options and decision-making.[92]

---

[86] Vic Satzewich, "Lawyers, Immigration Consultants and the 33 Year Jurisdictional War" (2021) 58:2 Can Rev Sociology 186.

[87] Jean McDonald, "Migrant Illegality, Nation-Building, and the Politics of Regularization in Canada" (2009) 26:2 Refuge 65.

[88] Similarly, marital status and the decision made by Indian band members to live on or off their reserves are strictly speaking changeable. Nevertheless, both characteristics have been recognized by the Supreme Court of Canada as analogous grounds under section 15. See *Miron v Trudel*, [1995] 2 SCR 418, 1995 CarswellOnt 93; *Corbiere, supra* note 74.

[89] *Andrews, supra* note 11 at 195.

[90] *Toussaint FC, supra* note 70, n 3.

[91] *Supra* note 74 at para 13.

[92] For further discussion about the flaws of applying a narrow immutability test to determine analogous grounds, see Joshua Sealy-Harrington, "Assessing Analogous Grounds: The Doctrinal and Normative Superiority of a Multi-Variable Approach" (2013) 10 JL & Equal 37.

By extension, labelling immigration status a mutable trait amounts to victim blaming. The upshot of this message is effectively that migrants are being treated differently by the impugned law or government actions because of certain choices they have made; had they chosen more wisely, their status would have been different, and they could have enjoyed equal protection and benefit of the law like others. The Federal Court of Appeal made this point clear in *Toussaint* when it decried that "most fundamentally, the appellant by her own conduct [...] has endangered her life and health. The appellant entered Canada as a visitor. She remained in Canada for many years, illegally. Had she acted legally and obtained legal immigration status in Canada, she would have been entitled to [health care] coverage."[93] Such blame-shifting ignores the Canadian immigration system's well-documented favouritism toward migrants who are deemed economically productive and self-reliant, which often reinforces existing racist, sexist, ableist, and classist biases.[94] For those less favoured, like Toussaint, a Black woman from the Global South, irregular migration is as much a calculated decision—albeit one made in the context of a global economy that disadvantages less developed countries—as it is an outcome of immigration laws and policies designed to exclude and marginalize them.[95] Thus, to downplay one's immigration status as a personal choice is to miss the *modus operandi* of systemic inequality wherein, as Sonia Lawrence explains, "[a]ny number of structural conditions push people towards their choices, with the result that certain choices may be made more often by people with particular 'personal characteristics'."[96]

---

[93] *Toussaint FCA, supra* note 68 at para 72.

[94] See e.g. Alexandra Dobrowolsky, "The Intended and Unintended Effects of a New Immigration Strategy: Insights From Nova Scotia's Provincial Nominee Program" (2011) 87:1 Studies in Political Economy 109; Sedef Arat-Koc, "Neo-liberalism, State Restructuring and Immigration: Changes in Canadian Policies in the 1990s" (1999) 34:2 J Can Studies 31.

[95] Basia D Ellis, "The Production of Irregular Migration in Canada" (2015) 47:2 Can Ethnic Studies 93.

[96] "Choice, Equality and Tales of Racial Discrimination: Reading the Supreme Court on Section 15" in Sheila McIntyre & Sanda Rodgers, eds, *Diminishing Returns: Inequality and the Canadian Charter of Rights and Freedoms* (Markham, ON: LexisNexis Butterworth, 2006) 115 at 124. For a further critique of the various ways that the concept of choice has been used to stymie *Charter* equality claims, see Diana Majury, "Women Are Themselves to Blame: Choice as a Justification for Unequal

Conclusion

The idea of citizenship as binary, consisting of citizens with all the attendant rights and non-citizens with no such rights at all, is frequently disputed.[97] It takes only a quick look at our daily lives to confirm the presence of a sizeable number of "denizens" in liberal democracies like Canada, who are made partial members of society and enjoy some of the rights typically associated with citizenship.[98] Likewise, the notion that migrants, especially those without a secure immigration status, can readily alter their legal standing is seriously contested in the literature, which brings to light "the legal production of illegality and precariousness [that] leads to a diverse array of marginalizing legal statuses, which can change over time and place, and operate unevenly across differentially racialized bodies and groups."[99] However, Canadian courts have so far remained blind to these complex realities, often subscribing to a dichotomous construction of citizenship and overstating non-citizens' control over their immigration status.

In this chapter, I set out to illustrate this legal fiction and its implications for non-citizens who turn to the *Charter*'s equality guarantee for protection against xenophobic laws. By problematizing judicial reasoning in a number of section 15(1) cases where non-citizen claimants failed to even get past the first step of the relevant legal test, I show that whatever promise *Andrews* might have held about the ability of section 15(1) to stamp out xenophobia has been gradually chipped away by the Supreme Court itself as well as by lower courts. Adopting an expansive interpretation of the *Charter*'s guarantee of Canadian citizens' mobility rights, while simultaneously denying the possibility of non-citizens having similar rights, the Supreme Court has effectively shielded all laws and government actions pertaining to immigration from citizenship-based section 15(1) challenges. Outside

---

Treatment" in Fay Faraday, Margaret Denike & M Kate Stephenson, eds, *Making Equality Rights Real: Securing Substantive Equality under the Charter* (Toronto: Irwin Law, 2006) 209.

[97] See e.g. Linda Bosniak, "Universal Citizenship and the Problem of Alienage" (2000) 94:3 Nw UL Rev 963.

[98] Brubaker, *supra* note 59 at 161.

[99] Luin Goldring, Carolina Berinstein & Judith K Bernhard, "Institutionalizing Precarious Migratory Status in Canada" (2009) 13:3 Citizenship Studies 239 at 245.

the immigration setting, the availability of section 15(1) to counter citizenship-based discrimination has also been limited to the rare instances where impugned laws or government actions draw a bright line between Canadian citizens and all others, as exemplified by the impugned statute in *Andrews*. Moreover, when non-citizens switch tactics and launch *Charter* equality claims based on immigration status, they have had minimal success due to the judiciary's fanciful characterization of immigration status as a mutable trait.[100]

This lineage of cases sits uneasily with the Supreme Court's broader *Charter* equality jurisprudence, which emphasizes the need to adopt a substantive, contextual analysis "grounded in the actual situation of the [claimant] group and the potential of the impugned law to worsen their situation."[101] What is worse, aspects of these cases turn the *Charter*'s equality guarantee on its head by rationalizing the xenophobic effects of law as a consequence of personal choice, the discriminatory institutions that contribute to such choices be damned. To date, no satisfactory explanation has been provided by courts for why such an anemic approach to equality ought to be adopted when assessing section 15(1) claims that are grounded in citizenship or immigration status. This opens the door for one to question whether the judiciary's own xenophobic bias may be at play. If so, then correcting judicial xenophobia will be crucial to reversing the troubling precedents discussed in this chapter and allowing the real potential of section 15(1) to be unleashed as a protection for non-citizens.

---

[100] The only case known to the author in which immigration status is expressly recognized as an analogous ground is *Jaballah (Re)*, 2006 FC 115. In that case, the Federal Court found the lesser procedural safeguard accorded to foreign nationals detained under a security certificate relative to what was provided to permanent residents in the same situation constituted a section 15(1) breach on the ground of immigration status.

[101] *Withler, supra* note 32 at para 37.

Disruptive Choices: Agency, Religious Freedom, and Veiling Muslim Women in Canadian Constitutional Law

*Ashleigh Keall**

Abstract

Choice is a central virtue in constitutional law's protection for religious freedom. It is also ever-present in dominant discursive constructions of veiling Muslim women. This chapter critically analyzes the concept of choice and its influence on the judicial treatment of Muslim women's veiling practices within Canadian constitutional law, with a focus on the freedom of religion guarantee under s 2(a) of the *Canadian Charter of Rights and Freedoms*. It draws on an alternative feminist account of agency to complicate the simple binary of coercion and resistance that marks veiling debates and demonstrates the mismatch between these more complex characterizations of veiling practices and the choice-based framing of religious freedom claims by Canadian courts. It argues that the prevailing assumptions and structures of religious freedom doctrine in Canadian law risk

---

* I would like to thank the anonymous peer reviewers and the editors and contributors of this collection for their useful feedback, all of which served to improve the chapter. Special thanks to Lorna Amor for the writing retreat in which this chapter took shape.

underserving Muslim women who veil, whether their practice is framed in the language of obligation or of choice.

Résumé

Le choix est une vertu centrale dans la protection de la liberté de religion par le droit constitutionnel. Il est également omniprésent dans les constructions discursives dominantes concernant les femmes musulmanes portant le voile. Ce chapitre analyse de manière critique le concept de choix et son influence sur le traitement judiciaire des pratiques de port du voile des femmes musulmanes dans le cadre du droit constitutionnel canadien, en se concentrant sur la garantie de liberté de religion prévue à l'article 2(a) de la *Charte canadienne des droits et libertés*. S'appuyant sur une perspective féministe alternative de l'agence, il remet en question le simple binôme coercition/résistance qui marque les débats sur le port du voile et met en évidence le décalage entre ces caractérisations plus complexes des pratiques de voile et l'encadrement basé sur le choix des revendications en matière de liberté de religion par les tribunaux canadiens. Il soutient que les hypothèses et structures prédominantes de la doctrine sur la liberté de religion dans le droit canadien risquent de mal servir les femmes musulmanes portant le voile, que leur pratique soit formulée dans le langage de l'obligation ou du choix.

In December 2021, Grade 3 teacher Fatemeh Anvari was reassigned to a non-teaching post at Chelsea Elementary School because she wore a hijab (headscarf) in the classroom. Her well-publicized dismissal[1] was a result of the school enforcing what is popularly known as Bill 21, the legislation in force in Quebec that prohibits public employees in certain positions of authority from wearing religious

---

[1] See e.g. Kimberley Molina, "Quebec teacher removed from classroom for wearing hijab under law banning religious symbols", *CBC News* (9 December 2021), online: <https://www.cbc.ca/news/canada/ottawa/fatemeh-anvari-removed-from-grade-three-classroom-1.6278381>; Leyland Cecco, "Outrage as Quebec teacher removed from classroom for wearing hijab", *Guardian* (13 December 2021), online: <https://www.theguardian.com/world/2021/dec/13/canada-quebec-teacher-removed-classroom-hijab>.

symbols or clothing in the workplace.[2] Thus far the province's attempt
to shield the statute from constitutional challenge by invoking section
33 of the *Constitution Act, 1982* (the "notwithstanding clause")[3] has
proven largely successful[4] and, at the time of writing, the Act remains
in force despite its discriminatory impact on religious adherents, particularly Muslim women.

In press coverage of Anvari's reassignment, Pascal Bérubé—
member of the National Assembly of Quebec and then Parti Québecois
critic for secularism—defended the decision by explaining that
Anvari chose this path for herself. He stated that "[t]he reason why
this teacher doesn't have a job [...] is because she doesn't respect the
law."[5] For Bérubé, a teacher like Anvari "has a choice to make: her job
or religion." Anvari simply made the wrong choice: "[s]he tried to
make a statement wearing a hijab."[6]

In these comments, Bérubé reverted to a familiar theme in the
treatment of religious freedom, reducing complex questions of religious belonging and expression to the simple metric of choice.
However, his statements reflect an emaciated, decontextualized conception of choice. A person's decision to wear religious clothing may
be shaped by a wide range of factors, including one's social relationships, cultural ties, religious commitments, and political convictions.
Bérubé, like so many before him, ignores this context and instead
uses the discourse of choice to justify the attribution of blame and

---

[2] *Loi sur la laïcité de l'État*, LQ 2019, c 12. As one reviewer insightfully noted, there is a
risk in defaulting to the popular term for this legislation which refers to it as a Bill
rather than an Act. Potential confusion over whether the legislation is in force (it is)
may understate its effects on vulnerable communities. However, I have chosen to
retain the term "Bill 21" for the sake of consistency with academic, legal, and
political commentary on the Act.

[3] *The Constitution Act, 1982*, Schedule B to the *Canada Act 1982* (UK), 1982, c 11, s 33
[*Charter*].

[4] See e.g. *Organisation mondiale sikhe du Canada c Procureur général du Québec*, 2024
QCCA 254 (legislation upheld in full, save the s 8 requirement of members of
Quebec's National Assembly to exercise their functions with their faces uncovered,
which violates s 3 of the *Charter*); *Hak c Procureure générale du Québec*, 2019 QCCA 2145
(dismissal of appeal against decision refusing interlocutory injunction; application
for leave to appeal to the Supreme Court of Canada denied on 9 April 2020).

[5] Sabrina Jonas, "Quebec politicians divided, federal MPs outraged after teacher removed
for wearing hijab", *CBC News* (10 December 2021), online: <https://www.cbc.ca/news/
canada/montreal/federal-politicians-react-removal-quebec-teacher-hijab-1.6280719>.

[6] *Ibid*.

legal culpability to Anvari. This is a classic illustration of the "choice talk" that marks public debates and responses to contentious social issues, through which the actor is construed as either a fully autonomous chooser deserving of blame or censure for her bad choices, or a vulnerable victim in need of state protection.[7]

This chapter considers some of the difficulties posed by "choice talk" in Canadian constitutional law's treatment of religious freedom. While Canadian courts routinely justify freedom of religion on the grounds of the autonomy interest it protects, the discourse of choice is simultaneously used to undermine religious freedom claims. I examine this issue through the lens of Muslim veiling, drawing on an alternative feminist account of agency to complicate the simplistic binary of coercion/resistance that underpins popular understandings of veiling and to critique the narrative of choice that finds such favour under section 2(a) of the *Canadian Charter of Rights and Freedoms*, the constitutional provision that protects freedom of conscience and religion.[8] I argue that this dichotomous portrayal of veiling Muslim women, overlaid with the treatment of religious practices as either obligatory or voluntary (never both), underserves veiling Muslim women who may find themselves before Canadian courts.

Feminist Encounters with the Obligation/Choice Paradigm

The language of choice permeates contemporary representations of Muslim veiling.[9] It underpins the tired dichotomy one sees in public debates over a woman's right to veil: between the freely choosing, autonomous subject on the one hand and the imperiled, coerced woman forced to veil by domineering male relatives, an oppressive state, or patriarchal religious doctrine on the other. Politicians, scholars, and judges continually reinforce this distinction, predicating legal protection for women who wear a veil on the condition that they belong in the former, and not the latter, category. In a House of Lords

---

[7] Lisa Kerr, "Choice Talk" (2016) 28 CJWL 676; Angela Campbell, *Sister Wives, Surrogates and Sex Workers: Outlaws by Choice?* (London, UK: Routledge, 2013).

[8] *Charter, supra* note 3.

[9] I use the term "veiling" broadly to include head coverings (*hijab*) as well as face veils such as the *niqab*, sacrificing specificity for the sake of brevity. Where the distinction is relevant, it is noted in the text.

judgment (in the United Kingdom) on school uniform accommodations, for instance, (then) Baroness Hale emphasized in concurring reasons that the law will protect a woman's right to veil "[b]ut it must be the woman's choice, not something imposed upon her by others."[10]

The reflexiveness with which the question of coercion is raised in veiling disputes suggests that there is something inherently suspect about a woman wearing a veil. Indeed, while the agency of religious women in general is often questioned,[11] this scrutiny is heightened for Muslim women.[12] Veiling is often taken to signify the abdication of autonomy and the subordination of women. Muslim girls and women are deemed vulnerable to "cultural compulsion," a trope repeatedly called upon to justify the French ban on headscarves in schools[13] and its ban on face veils in the public sphere. Sometimes framed as a feminist response, this view holds multiculturalism to the fire in a race for gender equality.[14] The pervasive stereotype of the "imperiled Muslim woman"[15] plays out in the Canadian context as

---

[10] *R (on the application of Begum) v Headteacher and Governors of Denbigh High School*, [2006] UKHL 15 at para 95.

[11] Lori Beaman, *Defining Harm: Religious Freedom and the Limits of the Law* (Vancouver: University of British Columbia Press, 2008) at 100–139.

[12] Lila Abu-Lughod writes of the stubbornness with which people outside the Muslim world assume that women who veil are coerced in Abu-Lughod, *Do Muslim Women Need Saving?* (London, UK: Harvard University Press, 2013) at 17.

[13] Joan Wallach Scott, *The Politics of the Veil* (Princeton: Princeton University Press, 2007) at 127; see 124–131 more generally.

[14] For the definitive, largely discredited articulation of this view, see Susan Moller Okin, "Is Multiculturalism Bad for Women?" in Joshua Cohen et al, eds, *Is Multiculturalism Bad for Women?* (Princeton: Princeton University Press, 1999) 7. For critique see e.g. Leti Volpp, "Feminism versus Multiculturalism" (2001) 101 Colum L Rev 1181; Vrinda Narain, "Critical Multiculturalism" in Beverley Baines, Daphne Barak-Erez & Tsvi Kahana, eds, *Feminist Constitutionalism: Global Perspectives* (Cambridge: Cambridge University Press, 2012) 377 at 381–384.

[15] On Sherene Razack's account, the imperiled Muslim woman is joined by two other tropes: the dangerous Muslim man and the civilized white Westerner: Razack, *Casting Out: The Eviction of Muslims from Western Law and Politics* (Toronto: University of Toronto Press, 2008). Building on Razack's work, Jennifer Selby, Amélie Barras and Lori Beaman identify the following figures as "discursive constructions that haunt late modern imaginaries": the terrorist, the imperiled Muslim woman, the Enlightened Muslim Man, the Foreigner, the Good Citizen, and the Pious Muslim: in Selby, Barras & Beaman, *Beyond Accommodation: Everyday Narratives of Muslim Canadians* (Vancouver: University of British Columbia Press, 2018) at 26, 24–59 more generally.

well, as seen in public debates around faith-based arbitration and Shari'a law in Ontario, and the accommodation of Muslim dress and practices in Quebec.[16]

Perhaps it is in response to the negative power of this stereotype that so many women describe and defend their own veiling practices as freely chosen. In her analysis of interviews conducted with niqab-wearing women in Ontario and Quebec, scholar Natasha Bakht notes that all respondents emphasized the lack of coercion involved in their decision to veil; all framed it as a matter of choice.[17] This explicit invocation of the language of autonomy and choice is a common refrain in qualitative studies of women who veil.[18] It also dovetails with the contemporary, postcolonial feminist response to veiling which views it as a form of resistance, whether to religious, state, or patriarchal authority; to western colonialism; to Islamophobia; or to societal expectations of women. Here the discourse of choice is empowering, the act of veiling inherently bound to an emancipatory project.[19] Veiling allows women to claim greater freedoms and to participate in the public sphere without cutting familial ties or violating their sincere religious beliefs. Homa Hoodfar, for instance, refers to veiling in this sense as an instrumental or "adaptive strategy" that allows women to navigate freely between two worlds.[20] Less the "mobile prison" claimed by critics of veiling, this response imagines the veil instead as a "mobile home"—a form of liberation that bridges one's belonging in a moral or familial community and one's greater participation in the social world.[21]

---

[16] See e.g. Razack, *ibid*; Natasha Bakht, "Religious Arbitration: Protecting Women by Protecting Them from Religion" (2007) 19 CJWL 119.

[17] Natasha Bakht, *In Your Face: Law, Justice, and Niqab-Wearing Women in Canada* (Toronto: Delve Books, 2020) at 23.

[18] See e.g. Scott, *supra* note 13 at 126; Eva Brems, ed, *The Experiences of Face Veil Wearers in Europe and the Law* (Cambridge: Cambridge University Press, 2014): see chapters in Part 1 for the repeated assertion by respondents that they freely chose to veil.

[19] Sirma Bilge, "Beyond Subordination vs. Resistance: An Intersectional Approach to the Agency of Veiled Muslim Women" (2010) 31 Journal of Intercultural Studies 9 at 18–21; Saba Mahmood, *Politics of Piety: The Islamic Revival and the Feminist Subject* (Princeton: Princeton University Press, 2005) at 6–10.

[20] Homa Hoodfar, "More than Clothing: Veiling as an Adaptive Strategy" in Sajida Sultana Alvi, Homa Hoodfar & Sheila McDonough, eds, *The Muslim Veil in North America: Issues and Debates* (Toronto: Women's Press, 2003) 3, 17–35.

[21] Abu-Lughod, *supra* note 12 at 36.

Though the understanding of veiling as resistance provides an important and politically useful response to mainstream depictions of Muslim women as non-agentic victims, it is an incomplete response to the choice/coercion binary described above. For one, it leaves the binary undisturbed, with those veiling women cast as autonomous choosers still attracting blame or censure for their choice to veil. Angela Campbell documents how blame for bad choices is heaped upon women engaged in socially contested activities such as sex work, surrogacy, and polygamy.[22] It is no different in the case of veiling, particularly as legal and political assessments of veiling occur against a backdrop of the prevailing "clash of civilizations" narrative, in which Muslim religiosity is painted as the antithesis to the West—with Muslims as pre-modern, patriarchal, and guided by backward traditions or culture, held up against Western values of gender equality, democracy, and human rights: i.e., modernity.[23] In this script, veiling is taken to symbolize the dangerous prioritizing of religion over state and the rejection of western, liberal values. It is viewed as a product of excess. In a literal sense, Muslim women are simply *wearing too much clothing*; figuratively, the veil represents an overabundance of religiosity, a sense of going too far in asserting oneself as religious.[24]

Lori Beaman has skilfully analyzed how Canadian courts regulate religious freedom through the discursive construction of the "reasonable" religious claimant.[25] Religious claimants are deemed unreasonable through notions of excess or fanaticism, a depiction more likely to attach to claimants from minority religious traditions.[26] Excess is thus indexed to choice and blame as well, in that it is one's *choice* to be "unreasonable" or excessive in one's religiosity that attracts suspicion. Drawing on the work of Vincent Geisser, Talal Asad explains how the symbol of the veil in French media reports is seen to pose an even graver threat to the state when it is characterized as a product of choice; veiled women's "voluntary servitude" becomes

---

[22] Campbell, *supra* note 7.

[23] See e.g. Razack, *supra* note 15 at 88–91; Selby, Barras & Beaman, *supra* note 15 at 24–62.

[24] Hence the suggestion by the European Court of Human Rights that the veil has an inherent proselytizing effect: see e.g. *Dahlab v Switzerland*, [2001] ECHR 449 at 463.

[25] Beaman, *supra* note 11.

[26] *Ibid* at 70–71.

a sign of fanatical (and thus intolerable) religious commitment.[27] In this narrative, Muslim women who have freely chosen to veil may not be considered hapless victims of their culture but instead are blamed for an unreasonable exercise of their agency.

A second problem with the coercion/choice binary is that it is an incomplete and inaccurate reflection of women's varied motivations for veiling. Certainly, some women do experience veiling as a form of dominance, others as a form of (feminist) resistance. But much is left out of this conceptual frame, which strips religious practices like veiling of their complexity and context. Empirical work in this area has highlighted women's multiple, intersecting reasons for veiling, such as the preservation of modesty, the cultivation of virtue, community belonging, physical or emotional comfort, defiance of western imperialism and/or secular modernity, self-expression, nostalgia, self-protection, dignity, and religious piety.[28] I would like to draw attention to piety in particular, which the above-cited authors found was typically the primary motivation for women's veiling practices. The quest for piety is interesting as it reveals the limitations of the choice binary and the mismatch between women's experiences of veiling and the protection that law is prepared to offer.

These limitations are brought to life in the work of anthropologists Saba Mahmood and Mayanthi Fernando, who describe the experiences of Muslim women "for whom choice may not be the ultimate litmus test of a worthy life."[29] Mahmood's landmark book *Politics of Piety* offers an alternative feminist account of Muslim women's agency that is rooted in neither subordination nor resistance to dominant norms.[30] The book focuses on a group of Egyptian women involved in Cairo's mosque movement (itself part of the wider Islamic Revival) who led small congregations of women in sharing religious teachings and learning to cultivate Islamic virtues together. Through detailed

---

27 Talal Asad, "French Secularism and the 'Islamic Veil Affair'" (2006) Hedgehog Review 93 at 104–05. See also Hussein Ali Agrama, "Religious Freedom and the Bind of Suspicion in Contemporary Secularity" in Winnifred Fallers Sullivan et al, eds, *Politics of Religious Freedom* (Chicago: University of Chicago Press, 2015) 301 at 305–06.

28 See e.g. Scott, *supra* note 13 at 135–140; Bakht, *supra* note 17 at 18–26; Brems, *supra* note 18; Leila Ahmed, *A Quiet Revolution: The Veil's Resurgence, from the Middle East to America* (New Haven: Yale University Press, 2011) at 207–213.

29 Abu-Lughod, *supra* note 12 at 18.

30 Mahmood, *supra* note 19.

interviews conducted over several years, Mahmood found that these women were successfully creating space for themselves in a male-dominated religious world on terms that largely accepted their subordination to male authority. They did not set out to disrupt systems of male domination (although that may have been the effect) or to resist dominant religious norms.[31] Rather, they aimed to become better Muslims—to cultivate virtue and piety through submission to religious duty. They believed that one learned to be a "good Muslim" by inhabiting religious norms through rigorous behavioural practices such as ritual prayer, fasting, and veiling.[32] Much like a budding piano virtuoso who submits to a punishing regime of daily practice,[33] many of the women Mahmood met believed they had to perform the duties and rigours of physical devotion by (for instance) veiling in order to realize their true, pious selves.[34] The formation of the self through habituated learning thus provides a different way of understanding the agency of veiling Muslim women that does not replicate the domination/resistance paradigm.[35]

Mayanthi Fernando's more recent research on French Muslim women who veil builds on Mahmood's observations by taking seriously women's desires to constitute themselves as ethical, religious subjects through their submission to external rules.[36] The women in her study started their journey toward greater religious piety by deferring to authoritative religious texts and teachings which persuaded them of the obligation to veil. The ritualistic practice of veiling then allowed them to cultivate the discipline needed to become "properly pious" Muslims.[37] And yet, quite literally schooled in the values of French republicanism, as Fernando notes, they also embraced the language of personal autonomy and choice. They emphasized that veiling was a way for them to live their own lives as individual religious agents.[38] The practice of veiling was *at the same time* choice

---

[31] *Ibid* at 14–15.

[32] *Ibid* at 44–56.

[33] *Ibid* at 29.

[34] *Ibid* at 120–152.

[35] *Ibid* at 153–188.

[36] Mayanthi Fernando, "Reconfiguring Freedom: Muslim Piety and the Limits of Secular Law and Public Discourse in France" (2010) 37 American Ethnologist 19.

[37] *Ibid* at 25; see 24–26 more generally.

[38] *Ibid* at 23–24.

and obligation: it required their "learning to undertake willingly what is necessary," until the "desire to perform what are in fact duties flows naturally from within the self."[39] The choice they faced was whether to abide by duty, but the goal was to transform the practice from duty to desire. Their experience of veiling collapses the choice/compulsion binary by tethering the very notion of individual autonomy to their submission to religious authority.

Importantly, Fernando goes on to examine how prevailing secular, legal norms could not comprehend the veil in this way. At the time of the furious debates over the ban on headscarves in schools in the mid-2000s, French legal discourse essentially reduced freedom of religious conscience to the freedom to choose one's religious beliefs. Forced to frame their arguments in the language of choice, the essence of what was really at stake for them was lost.[40] The conflation of choice and duty in these women's experiences landed them in "a no-man's-land of discursive and legal unintelligibility."[41]

Muslim Veiling and the Courts: Choice Under Fire?

In an insightful article on choice in women's constitutional religious freedom claims,[42] Jonnette Watson Hamilton and Jennifer Koshan cite portions of an interview with one of the few women to raise the issue of niqab-wearing before a Canadian court. Zunera Ishaq, a Pakistan-born permanent resident of Canada who wore a niqab, took the federal government to court in January 2014 over a policy denying citizenship certificates to anyone reciting the citizenship oath in a public ceremony with her face covered. Ishaq was successful at the Federal Court and the government's appeal was dismissed.[43] Her *Charter* right to religious freedom was not considered by either court, as the decisions hinged on the conflict between the policy and the

---

[39] *Ibid* at 25.

[40] *Ibid* at 28–30. See also Mayanthi Fernando, *The Republic Unsettled: Muslim French and the Contradictions of Secularism* (London, U.K.: Duke University Press, 2014) at 145–163.

[41] Fernando, *supra* note 36 at 30.

[42] Watson Hamilton & Koshan, "The Role of Choice in Women's Freedom of Religion Claims in Canada" (2017) 36 Religious Studies and Theology 171.

[43] *Ishaq v Canada (Citizenship and Immigration)*, 2015 FC 156, aff'd 2015 FCA 194.

regulations under which it was enacted. However, Ishaq's case marked an important moment in Canada's political history and revealed some interesting truths about the nation's willingness to countenance religious or racial difference.[44]

With that background in mind, let us return to the interview. In it she speaks of her veiling practice on terms much like Fernando's subjects: she describes it as both choice ("it was my personal choice [...] nobody has ever forced me") and duty ("it is a religious duty of mine to cover my face in public at all times").[45] Koshan and Watson Hamilton note in passing that her words convey a form of religious practice that transcends the "usual dichotomy" between choice and obligation.[46] In their conclusion, they remark that the language of choice will not capture the experiences of many women who veil out of a sense of religious duty, for whom it is a way of "constitut[ing] themselves as ethical subjects."[47] They suggest that it might, therefore, be more advantageous for religious claimants to characterize their veil-wearing as a matter of duty or obligation, rather than choice.

In this section I consider these observations in more detail and in light of the theoretical perspectives outlined in the preceding section. I argue that Canadian religious freedom doctrine is not well equipped to deal with claims such as Ishaq's. The doctrine under s. 2(a) of the *Charter* is shot through with the language of choice: freedom from religious coercion and freedom to make religious choices sit at the apex of the constitutional right. The claims of Muslim women who veil will be understood within a conceptual frame that sets choice in opposition to obligation or duty. However, I am less sanguine than Watson Hamilton and Koshan about cloaking these claims in the language of obligation. I maintain that veiling Muslim women, so often beset by rocks and hard places in the rhetorical spaces they occupy, face obstacles in both instances. As such, they are wildly underserved by the prevailing method and structure of religious freedom doctrine in Canadian law.

---

[44] See e.g. Sherene Razack, "A Site/Sight We Cannot Bear: The Racial/Spatial Politics of Banning the Muslim Woman's Niqab" (2018) 30 CJWL 169.

[45] "Zunera Ishaq, who challenged ban on niqab, takes citizenship oath wearing it", *CBC News* (5 October 2015), online: <https://www.cbc.ca/news/politics/zunera-ishaq-niqab-ban-citizenship-oath-1.3257762>.

[46] Watson Hamilton & Koshan, *supra* note 42 at 174.

[47] *Ibid* at 183.

"At the heart" of it: Religious Freedom and the Discourse of Choice

I begin with a quick review of the doctrinal structure of religious freedom claims under the *Charter*. Section 2(a) breaches are judged according to the two-part test laid out by the Supreme Court of Canada in *Syndicat Northcrest v Amselem*.[48] First, a claimant must establish that she holds a sincere belief or practice that has a nexus with religion. This standard is subjective and hinges on sincerity: it does not matter on the face of it whether the religious practice in question forms part of an established belief system or whether it is mandated by one's religion. It is sufficient that the person honestly wishes to perform that act as a function of her faith or believes it will foster her connection to the divine.[49] Notably for our purposes, the provision protects "both obligatory as well as voluntary expressions of faith."[50] Second, a claimant must show that the state has interfered with her ability to act in accordance with her beliefs in a more than trivial or insubstantial manner.[51] If a s. 2(a) breach is made out, then the analysis shifts to s. 1 of the *Charter*—and indeed, the bulk of the analysis in religious freedom cases typically occurs under s. 1. Here the court will assess whether the limit on the right is reasonable and demonstrably justified by applying the familiar *Oakes* criteria, which ask whether the limiting measure is rationally connected to the government's pressing and substantial objective, minimally impairing of the right, and proportionate in its effects.[52]

Although these doctrinal tests do not explicitly use the language of choice, notions of individual autonomy and choice are central to the analysis. Indeed, Benjamin Berger notes that whether the claimant was free to make religious choices often serves as the "ultimate diagnostic" of whether the limit on the right is sufficiently serious to ground a violation.[53] From its very first iteration of the scope and import of s. 2(a) of the *Charter* in *R v Big M Drug Mart*,[54] the Supreme

---

[48]   2004 SCC 47 [*Amselem*].

[49]   *Ibid* at paras 40–56; *Multani v Commission scolaire Marguerite-Bougeoys*, 2006 SCC 6 at para 34 [*Multani*].

[50]   *Amselem, supra* note 48 at para 47. Also worth noting is the distinction between the two; religious practices are *either* voluntary *or* obligatory.

[51]   *Amselem, ibid*; *Multani, supra* note 49 at para 34.

[52]   [1986] 1 SCR 103, 26 DLR (4th) 200.

[53]   Benjamin Berger, *Law's Religion: Religious Difference and the Claims of Constitutionalism* (Toronto: University of Toronto Press, 2015) at 82.

[54]   [1985] 1 SCR 295, 18 DLR (4th) 321 [*Big M*].

Court has consistently held that religious freedom "revolves around the notion of personal choice"[55] and that the ability to exercise a meaningful choice in matters of religion "lies at the heart" of the right.[56] Writing for the majority in *Amselem*, for instance, Justice Iacobucci justified the Court's subjective understanding of religious freedom by explaining that it reflects the importance of individual self-definition, autonomy, and choice, "elements which undergird the right."[57] He affirmed that the emphasis of the s. 2(a) inquiry "is on personal choice of religious beliefs."[58]

This is unsurprising. It reflects law's culture of liberalism by which religion is understood in Canadian law.[59] Broadly speaking, liberal thinkers largely defend law's protection of religious freedom on the grounds of individual autonomy. Individuals are considered the authors of their own life who need the freedom to choose from a range of options regarding religion or belief.[60] Chief Justice Dickson nailed the Court's understanding of s. 2(a) to this plank when he wrote in *Big M* that:

> Freedom can primarily be characterized by the absence of coercion or constraint. If a person is compelled by the state or the will of another to a course of action or inaction which he would not otherwise have chosen, he is not acting of his own volition and he cannot be said to be truly free. One of the major purposes of the *Charter* is to protect, within reason, from compulsion or restraint.[61]

---

[55] *Amselem, supra* note 48 at para 40.

[56] *Alberta v Hutterian Brethren of Wilson Colony*, 2009 SCC 37 at para 99 [*Hutterian Brethren*]; see also paras 88–94.

[57] *Amselem, supra* note 48 at para 42. See also para 48, where Justice Iacobucci writes that the alternative, objective approach to religious freedom requiring the claimant to "show some sort of objective religious obligation, requirement or precept to invoke freedom of religion [...]. *would be inconsistent with the underlying purposes and principles of the freedom emphasizing personal choice* as set out by Dickson C J in *Big M* and *Edwards Books*" (emphasis added).

[58] *Amselem, ibid* at para 43.

[59] Berger, *supra* note 53.

[60] For a review of how autonomy rationales underpin the right to religious freedom in the liberal tradition see Carolyn Evans, *Freedom of Religion Under the European Convention on Human Rights* (Oxford: Oxford University Press 2001) at 29–32.

[61] *Big M, supra* note 54 at para 95 (emphasis added).

This broad commitment to the ideal of non-coercion plays out in two ways under s. 2(a). First, it serves a protective function: courts will uphold religious freedom complaints under s. 2(a) on the grounds that a person's autonomy or ability to make free choices was impaired.[62] The impugned coercive effect could be direct or indirect; both are considered serious constitutional defects. In *Amselem*, for instance, a Supreme Court majority held that Orthodox Jewish condominium residents could not be forbidden from building temporary succahs on their balconies despite the availability of other options for celebrating the religious holiday of *Succot*, such as a communal succah on the building grounds or—the nuclear option—moving elsewhere.[63] The majority's conclusion that the residents "did not have a real choice" in the matter meant the prohibition could not stand; it was not consistent with the majority's characterization of religious freedom as "a function of personal autonomy and choice."[64]

Equally, however, the discourse of non-coercion or choice under s. 2(a) can serve to *undermine* rights claims by justifying state incursions on religious freedom. The paradigmatic case to this effect is *Alberta v Hutterian Brethren of Wilson Colony*, concerning the s. 2(a) claim by members of a Hutterite colony who objected to the requirement of a photograph on provincial drivers' licences.[65] Though they considered it sinful to be photographed, they needed continued access to the highways to sustain their communal, agrarian lifestyle rooted in religious tradition. A Supreme Court majority rejected this claim, repeatedly stressing the lack of religious coercion imposed upon the claimants. Unlike the claimants in *Amselem*, the colony members were not considered sufficiently "deprived of a meaningful choice to follow or not to follow the edicts of their religion."[66] They could, for instance, hire drivers or arrange commercial transport to ferry their produce to markets and thereby maintain their traditional way of life.[67] Having

---

[62] See e.g. Berger, *supra* note 53 at 80–91.

[63] *Amselem, supra* note 48.

[64] *Ibid* at para 42. See also *Multani, supra* note 49; *R v Edwards Books and Art Ltd*, [1986] 2 SCR 713, 35 DLR (4th) 1 (s 2(a) violations upheld where coercive impact of state action identified).

[65] *Hutterian Brethren, supra* note 56.

[66] *Ibid* at para 98.

[67] *Ibid* at paras 96–99, 104.

found that the legislation did not sufficiently impinge on the colony members' liberty to make religious choices, described by Chief Justice McLachlin as "[t]he most fundamental" of the constitutional values,[68] the majority held that the limit on their right to religious freedom was justified under s. 1.

Veiling as Obligation

Religious freedom claims will be understood by courts from within this dominant frame, in which choice is a paramount value. However, it must be recalled that s. 2(a) protects both obligatory and voluntary religious practices.[69] This creates an interesting tension with potential implications for veiling Muslim women. Where will their veiling practice be deemed to fall on the binary between obligation and choice? And how might that characterization serve them under existing constitutional doctrine, particularly when overlaid upon the pervasive and damning depiction of veiling Muslim women as either victims of coercion or (blameworthy) free agents?

Understood as an obligatory practice, veiling should be expected to fall reasonably comfortably within the parameters of the *Charter* right to religious freedom. In *Multani v Commission scolaire Marguerite-Bourgeoys*, for instance, the Supreme Court upheld the s. 2(a) claim of a young orthodox Sikh student who had been prevented from wearing a kirpan to school.[70] Both the claimant and the Court understood the practice as one clearly required by the tenets of his religion.[71] This did not appear to trouble the Court; indeed, *Multani* might be characterized as the Court's most expansive s. 2(a) judgment to date. Judicial protection for religious practices that involve submission to religious authority is also in line with the Court's subjective, "hands-off" approach to s. 2(a) and its reluctance to inquire into the veracity of the claimant's beliefs beyond the threshold question of sincerity.

However, the tenor of the Court's repeated pronouncements on choice and freedom from coercion strains somewhat against a conception of religious practices as obligatory or mandated by one's faith. Recall Chief Justice Dickson's statement that "[o]ne of the major purposes of the *Charter* is to protect, within reason, from compulsion or

---

[68] *Ibid* at para 88.
[69] *Amselem, supra* note 48 at para 47.
[70] *Multani, supra* note 49.
[71] *Ibid* at paras 36–40.

restraint."[72] If religious freedom is indeed aimed at protecting autonomy *viz.* the individual freedom to make choices, then practices seen as "conformist" or "mandatory" might be thought to lie further from the core of the s. 2(a) guarantee.[73] As Kathryn Chan notes, the Court's endorsement in *Amselem* of John Stuart Mill's statement that "the only freedom which deserves the name, is that of pursuing our own good in our way" makes it "hard to escape the conclusion that pursuing God's good in God's way is a lesser choice."[74] Justice Rowe made this point more recently, concurring in *Law Society of British Columbia v Trinity Western University*, when he described the character of religious freedom as "noncoercive" and "its antithesis [as] coerced conformity."[75]

A Muslim woman who veils out of a sense of religious duty or compulsion may find herself on even bumpier terrain. The suggestion that she might be veiling as a religious requirement risks raising the spectre of the imperiled Muslim woman, forced to "hide herself" by some combination of patriarchal religious code or dangerous, coercive male relations. This risk is even greater in the case of a face covering (niqab), which unlike the hijab seems to provoke a near-hysterical clamour to ban it or remove it from the public sphere, to "free" the women within.[76] These prevailing conceptions of the niqab make for a smoother elision of religious obligation and religious coercion; religious duty shades into other, more nefarious forms of compulsion. Her agency discounted by the assumption that she is veiling on another's orders, the veiled Muslim woman becomes a figure whose

---

[72] *Big M, supra* note 54 at para 95.

[73] See e.g. Kathryn Chan, "The Duelling Narratives of Religious Freedom: A Comment on *Syndicat Northcrest v. Amselem*" (2005) 43 Alta L Rev 451 at 456.

[74] *Ibid* at 464.

[75] 2018 SCC 32 at para 213 [*Trinity Western*].

[76] See e.g. Bakht, *supra* note 17 at 6–7, 38; Razack, *supra* note 44. Bakht observes that even well-informed, liberal academics and feminists purport to "'draw the line' at the niqab" (6). As an academic with a stated interest in religious freedom, I cannot count the number of times I have told someone of my research area and been immediately confronted with an angry tirade condemning the niqab. Of course, it is also easy to overstate public antagonism to the niqab; see, for instance, the many activists opposing Quebec's efforts to ban religious symbols in the public sphere: Fathima Cader, "Made You Look: Niqabs, the Muslim Canadian Congress, and *R v NS*" (2013) 31 Windsor Y B Access Just 67 at 83. For a review of legislative attempts in Canada to restrict the wearing of niqabs see Bakht, *supra* note 17 at 124–132.

rights are harder to square with prevailing s. 2(a) doctrine and theory. Not only are such forms of compulsion or coercion considered anti-thetical to the *Charter*, but they are also easily characterized as "un-Canadian," as threats to secular state values and projects.

This framing can be found in the only Supreme Court decision on face veiling, *R v NS*.[77] The case was brought by a sexual assault complainant who was ordered to remove her niqab while testifying in court. The majority reasons, penned by Chief Justice McLachlin, introduced an analytical framework to be used by judges in deciding whether a witness should be permitted to testify in a niqab, which balances the witness's religious freedom rights against the fair trial rights of the accused.[78] In separate reasons, Justice LeBel (joined by Justice Rothstein) advocated a clear rule forbidding trial witnesses from testifying in niqabs, while Justice Abella, dissenting, held that they must always be permitted to do so provided the witness's identity is not in issue.

For present purposes, I wish to draw attention to the Court's characterization of the practice of face veiling as either obligatory or freely chosen. Notably, the majority was not terribly concerned with whether face veiling was a mandatory or voluntary religious practice. Although Chief Justice McLachlin typically referred to NS as believing she was "required" to cover her face,[79] at other times she described the practice in terms of NS's subjective "desire" or "wish" to veil.[80] In fact, when describing how a court might judge the deleterious effects to the witness of being required to remove the niqab, the majority stated: "The value of adherence does not depend on whether a religious practice is a voluntary expression of faith or a mandatory obligation under religious doctrine."[81]

Justice LeBel, however, stated at the outset of his concurring reasons that "the complainant says that her Islamic faith requires her to wear a full-face veil, the niqab, in public, in court."[82] Unlike the majority justices, who vaguely attributed the source of NS's obligation to

---

[77] 2012 SCC 72 [*NS*].

[78] The question was remitted to the preliminary inquiry judge who, in applying the *NS* framework, denied NS the right to testify in a niqab.

[79] *NS, supra* note 77 at paras 1, 4, 11, 14.

[80] *Ibid* at paras 3, 11, 13, 29.

[81] *Ibid* at para 36.

[82] *Ibid* at para 60.

her "religious beliefs,"[83] Justice LeBel clearly pinpointed its source as "the Islamic faith." It is interesting—though hardly conclusive—that the precision with which NS's religious practice was characterized as a duty to obey religious authority is followed by a highly uncompromising position on niqab-wearing as something fundamentally at odds with Canadian values. Justice LeBel prefaces his reasons with reference to "the tension and changes caused by the rapid evolution of contemporary Canadian society and [...] the growing presence in Canada of new cultures, religions, traditions and social practices."[84] The concurrence repeatedly positions niqab-wearing in opposition to Canadian traditions and "common values" like openness, communication, religious neutrality, democracy, and the rule of law.[85] Here, obligatory face veiling has become a placeholder for an overly aggressive form of religiosity, one saddled by "traditional" forms of religious authority that cannot hold up against the supposed virtues of the secular state with all its liberality, openness, and freedom.[86]

However, conceptions of veiling as mandatory need not lead one down the path hewn by the concurrence in NS, nor is it inevitable that they will be conflated with dangerous religious coercion. Consider the dissenting reasons of Justice Abella in the same case: she too characterized the veil as a mandatory religious practice.[87] And yet she showed sensitivity to the wider political, historic, and gendered context of the case and refrained from casting the practice of face veiling as a threat to Canadian values. Though Justice Abella's reasons remain rooted in the narrative of choice, such as by describing the crux of NS's dilemma as the stark choice she was forced to make between adhering to her religious beliefs and seeking justice for her alleged sexual assault,[88] they demonstrate the possibility of a more nuanced judicial treatment of veiling.

---

[83] For example: "N.S. testified that her religious belief required her to wear a niqab" (*ibid* at para 4); "[...] a witness whose sincerely held religious belief requires her to wear a niqab" (*ibid* at para 1).

[84] *Ibid* at para 59; see Cader, *supra* note 76 at 88–90.

[85] *NS*, *supra* note 77 at paras 59–61, 69–75.

[86] See Cader, *supra* note 76 at 81 for how the Muslim Canadian Congress characterized niqabs in its intervener factum as "excessively religious and oppressive."

[87] *NS*, *supra* note 77 at paras 81, 93-95.

[88] *Ibid* at paras 93-95.

Veiling as Choice

An additional problem that may arise for veiling Muslim women who find themselves before the courts is that if their veiling is framed instead as a subjective choice, its restriction could be considered less serious and thus less likely to breach s. 2(a) of the *Charter*.[89] For instance, the respondent government had implied before the Federal Court in *Ishaq* that the optionality of the claimant's veiling practice meant that there was simply too little at stake for the claimant if she were forced to remove her niqab.[90] Drawing a telling comparison between Islam and Christianity, the government argued, in the Court's words, that "wearing the niqab is just a personal choice, not a basic sacrament."[91] Choice, the fundamental value underpinning religious freedom, becomes weaponized in a quest to deny *Charter* protection.

The seriousness of the violation is an issue that arises under both sections 2(a) and 1 of the *Charter*. Recall that under s. 2(a), a claimant must prove that her sincere belief in a religious practice or belief was interfered with in a more than trivial manner.[92] Interference is established on an objective basis. There is little guidance for courts on how to conduct this inquiry and, in fact, few cases falter on the question of interference alone.[93] However, it does appear harder for claimants to make out non-trivial interference if their religious practice is not considered obligatory but is, as the government said of Ishaq's veiling, "just a personal choice."[94] Despite Justice Iacobucci's repeated assurances in *Amselem* that s. 2(a) equally protects practices that are required by religious precept and those that "subjectively engender a personal

---

[89] See also Watson Hamilton and Koshan, *supra* note 42 at 180–181.

[90] The government's argument that the interference with Ishaq's religious beliefs was trivial appeared to be influenced by the lack of any objective, religious precept mandating veiling. In its summary of the government's triviality argument, the Court states that, "[a]ccording to the Respondent, the Applicant has asserted nothing more than a subjective belief that her freedom of religion would be interfered with if she uncovered her face [...]" (*Ishaq, supra* note 43 at para 34).

[91] *Ibid* at para 38. As the Court did not consider it necessary to examine the *Charter* arguments, it made no pronouncement on this line of reasoning.

[92] *Amselem, supra* note 48; *Multani, supra* note 49.

[93] On the nature of the interference inquiry see: Howard Kislowicz, "*Loyola High School v Attorney General of Quebec*: On Non-Triviality and the *Charter* Value of Religious Freedom" (2015) 71 SCLR (2d) 331.

[94] *Ishaq, supra* note 43 at para 38.

connection with the divine," he still had a far easier time concluding that the harm to the claimant who felt under a religious *duty* to dwell in his own succah constituted a non-trivial interference, compared to the claimants who simply *preferred* to do so.[95] This issue arises again under s. 1, where a court is asked to consider and weigh the deleterious effects of the limiting measure. Again, limitations on a religious practice that is framed as a mere preference as opposed to an actual or perceived religious obligation are generally considered less serious, and thus easier to justify.

The Supreme Court's decision in *Trinity Western*[96] is instructive on this point. The case considered whether the provincial Law Society was justified in refusing accreditation of a law school at a private, religious university because it required its students and staff to abide by the terms of a mandatory covenant forbidding sexual intimacy between same-sex partners. The majority judges held that the impact of non-accreditation on the claimants' religious freedom was minimal, largely because the religious practice at issue was optional.[97] The covenant was "not absolutely required for the religious practice."[98] Likewise, studying together in a community of like-minded adherents abiding by a common code of conduct was merely "preferred (rather than necessary) for their spiritual growth."[99] The claimants simply wished to study "in their *optimal* religious learning environment"[100] and had "much less at stake" than claimants in prior s. 2(a) cases.[101] The majority concluded by noting, somewhat sarcastically, that "denying

---

[95] Whereas the interference was "evident" for the first claimant, the others had to provide evidence of harm sufficient to establish non-trivial interference: *Amselem, supra* note 48 at paras 74–77. See also *Cham Shan Temple v Director, Ministry of the Environment*, [2015] OERTD No 9: although the proposed windfarm might have some noise impact on the pilgrimage route in a Buddhist meditation centre, the claimants' religion did not require them to follow that particular route, nor did it oblige them to meditate in a noise-free environment (at paras 587–592).

[96] *Trinity Western, supra* note 75.

[97] *Ibid* at para 87.

[98] *Ibid*.

[99] *Ibid* at para 88.

[100] *Ibid* at para 87 (emphasis in original).

[101] *Ibid* at para 90; see paras 85–90 more generally.

someone an option they would merely appreciate certainly falls short of 'forced apostasy.'"[102]

"Forced apostasy" was a reference to the Court's majority judgment in *Hutterian Brethren*, where Chief Justice McLachlin explained in her analysis of the limit's deleterious effects:

> There is no magic barometer to measure the seriousness of a particular limit on a religious practice. [...] Some aspects of a religion, like prayers and the basic sacraments, may be so sacred that any significant limit verges on forced apostasy. Other practices may be optional or a matter of personal choice. Between these two extremes lies a vast array of beliefs and practices, more important to some adherents than to others.[103]

The implication here is that restrictions on practices which arise from personal choice will be less serious and will carry less weight in the proportionality inquiry. Indeed, in *NS*, Chief Justice McLachlin again suggested that the "strength" of the claimant's conviction was relevant to the balancing exercise.[104] The weightiness of a religious freedom claim based on mere choice will of course depend on what other rights and interests are at play in the proportionality analysis. In *NS*, the religious obligation to veil faltered against the accused's fair trial rights. If the niqab had instead been framed as a function of personal choice, like the practice in *Trinity Western*, it seems highly likely that on the question of "strength" it would have fared even more poorly.

The vulnerability of religious freedom claims based on choice may be even more acute when those choices are not in line with dominant norms and practices. Legal discourse often blames people who engage in socially contested activities like sex work and polygamy for

---

[102] *Ibid* at para 90. Chief Justice McLachlin disagreed with this characterization in her concurring reasons at paras 128-132, though she did concede that "optional practices which allow the individual to *stay true to his or her religious practices* by adopting a different course, may reduce the degree of impairment of the right" (para 132, emphasis in original).

[103] *Hutterian Brethren, supra* note 56 at para 89.

[104] *NS, supra* note 77 at para 13. In contrast, Justice Abella questioned the relevance of the strength of one's beliefs and noted the difficulty of assessing it, given "the highly subjective and imprecise nature of the freedom of religion analysis" (at para 89).

their ostensibly poor decisions, using choice as a "vector of responsi-bility" that points directly to the actors themselves.[105] This serves to justify the imposition of legal restrictions, leaving injustices intact and entrenching systemic inequalities.[106] As noted, the rhetoric of choice is often used to undermine rights claims, serving as a recur-ring motif across Canadian constitutional law subjects.[107] The harm suffered by a rights-bearer is attributed to her suspect choices, "her unwise exercise of her own judicially protected liberty."[108] The suspi-cion and blame that attaches to the figure of the veiling Muslim woman, particularly she who wears a niqab, exacerbates the problem. One can almost hear the unspoken question in the margin of the cases: why can't she just remove her veil in order to play the game of Canadian justice (or, why can't she just choose differently)? Indeed, the government spoke this concern aloud in *Ishaq*, wondering why "a citizenship ceremony, which happens once in a lifetime, is not one of those rare instances where it is absolutely necessary for the Applicant to remove her *niqab*."[109] The harm to the claimant thus minimized and carefully redirected to rest on the woman's own shoulders, the state remains free to assert its own vision of "Canadian-ness" that leaves only the narrowest of margins for veiling Muslim women to exercise their freedom.

Conclusion

This leaves veiling Muslim women in a difficult position. If their claim is understood as a voluntary or "optional" expression of their

---

[105] Campbell, *supra* note 7 at 191; see also Watson Hamilton & Koshan, *supra* note 42 at 181–182.

[106] Campbell, *ibid*; Sonia Lawrence, "Choice, Equality, and Tales of Racial Discrimination: Reading the Supreme Court on Section 15" (2006) 33 SCLR (2d) 115 at 132.

[107] See e.g. Lawrence, *ibid*; Diana Majury, "Women are Themselves to Blame: Choice as a Justification for Unequal Treatment" in Fay Faraday, Margaret Denike & Kate Stephenson, eds, *Making Equality Rights Real: Securing Substantive Equality under the Charter* (Toronto: Irwin Law, 2009) 209; Mary Jane Mossman, "Choice and Commitments for Women: Challenging the Supreme Court of Canada in the Context of Social Assistance" (2004) 42 Osgoode Hall LJ 615; Campbell, *supra* note 7; Kerr, *supra* note 7.

[108] Lawrence, *supra* note 106 at 116.

[109] *Ishaq, supra* note 43 at para 38.

faith, then its restriction may be considered less serious and the attendant harm attributed not to the limiting measure but to the claimant herself, for having willfully exceeded the bounds of "reasonable" dress. Conversely, claims that are seen as an obligatory practice required by one's religion may elicit fears of religious compulsion or coercion stemming from pervasive myths of the "imperiled Muslim woman." This strains against the traditional, liberal conception of individual autonomy as freedom to choose that underpins religious freedom. Veiling Muslim women are damned if they choose, and damned if they don't.

Admittedly, there are few Canadian veiling cases against which to test this critique, fewer still that engage in a full s. 2(a) *Charter* analysis.[110] We have also seen that the false dichotomy will not always dictate the outcome of a veiling case; despite the rhetoric of the concurrence, the outcome in *NS* was arguably not overtly affected by the choice/obligation binary. Indeed, judges are certainly capable of adopting a nuanced understanding of veiling practices and of engaging with section 2(a) doctrine in a critical and contextual fashion. However, bright line distinctions between voluntary and obligatory religious practices and rigid caricatures of freely choosing or coerced Muslim women do great disservice to all rights claimants. Berger explains that law systematically cuts away at or "renders" religion into a shape that fits within law's normative commitments and practices, leaving behind an "experiential residue [...] on the cutting room floor."[111] In the case of Muslim veiling, the detritus is substantial. As one reviewer helpfully pointed out, this mismatch may also have broader impacts on the shape of *Charter* litigation in this area. Law's flattening of human experience can direct the types of *Charter* arguments that lawyers make on behalf of Muslim women. More complex characterizations of the claimant's religious beliefs or practices are compromised in favour of a formalist, categorial approach that fits

---

[110] Recall that *Ishaq, ibid* was not a *Charter* case, and that the substantive analysis of s 2(a) of the *Charter* in Bill 21 cases (see *supra* note 5) is limited by the Act's invocation of s 33 of the *Charter*.

[111] Berger explains that although law purports not to make comprehensive claims about religion, its power and authority mean that "[...] law's understanding of religion quickly becomes the only game in town" (*supra* note 53 at 103). Referencing Robert Cover, "Nomos and Narrative" (1983) 97 Harv L Rev 4, he writes that "the very nature of law is that it kills other normative arrangements and interpretations" (at 103).

neatly within existing doctrine but at the cost of a more fulsome, intersectional approach to *Charter* rights.

Alternative feminist accounts of agency, such as Mahmood's and Fernando's, may help to fill in some of the gaps in law's understanding of veiling. At the very least, their accounts serve as a reminder that different conceptions of agency and choice are possible. It falls to judges to adopt, as per Berger's counsel, a posture of humility which acknowledges "that the constitutional rule of law is always in competition with other cultures, other compelling and rich ways of generating meaning and giving structure to experience."[112] Recognition of these other ontological stories is a recognition of the messiness of human experience and the limits of law. Importantly, it also makes space for a feminist ideal of freedom, one in which Muslim women are not ascribed a rigid identity on the basis of their clothing but, rather, are afforded the right to be multi-faceted, complicated authors of their own lives.[113]

The conclusions reached in this chapter also point to the need to continue pursuing avenues for resolving disputes over religious diversity outside of the formal adjudicative process. In their incisive study of the everyday lives of Muslim Canadians, for instance, authors Jennifer Selby, Amélie Barras and Lori Beaman propose moving away from more formalized, legalistic responses to managing religious difference toward approaches rooted in negotiation and communication.[114] Likewise, writing of religious belonging in public schools, scholar Dia Dabby explains that internal, school-based decision-making processes are often the best fora for dealing with such conflicts as they provide both the space for deeper reflection and participation by the parties and the scope for decisions that better promote inclusive, substantive equality.[115] This reasoning chimes with the problems I discuss in this chapter about the pervasive oversimplification of Muslim women's veiling practices when overlaid upon the doctrinal

---

[112] Berger, *ibid* at 172.

[113] See e.g. Lola Olufemi, *Feminism, Interrupted: Disrupting Power* (London, UK: Pluto Press, 2020) at 71 who writes, "If feminism means freedom, it means the right to self-determination and the right to be multi-dimensional, disorganised and even incoherent."

[114] Selby, Barras & Beaman, *supra* note 15.

[115] Dia Dabby, *Religious Diversity in Canadian Public Schools: Rethinking the Role of Law* (Vancouver: University of British Columbia Press, 2022).

approach to religious freedom under the *Charter* that privileges choice as a central virtue of s. 2(a).

Canadians cannot afford to be complacent about law's treatment of veiling Muslim women. It was not long ago that a gunman stormed a Montreal mosque and murdered six worshippers; even less time has passed since a man purposefully drove his car into a Muslim family in London, Ontario, killing all four. Meanwhile, protests continue in Quebec over provincial legislation banning certain public sector workers from wearing religious symbols in the workplace, after years of legislative attempts to shore up a tenuous form of *laïcité* that amounts to state-sponsored discrimination against racialized religious minorities. There is much to be proud of in the Canadian legal tradition, but much work still to be done.

Pour une application de la Charte fondée sur les droits de l'enfant

Mona Paré

Résumé

Ce chapitre explore la question de l'enfant en tant que sujet de droit public dans le cadre de l'application de la *Charte canadienne des droits et libertés*. Bien que la *Charte* garantisse des droits à « chacun », la situation particulière des enfants, en tant qu'individus dépendants de leurs parents ou tuteurs/tutrices, pose des défis quant à la conception de leur relation avec l'État. Le chapitre examine dans quelle mesure les droits protégés par la *Charte* peuvent être considérés comme des droits de l'enfant, en prenant en compte leur reconnaissance quasi universelle dans la *Convention relative aux droits de l'enfant*. À travers une analyse de la jurisprudence, le chapitre propose une interprétation critique et constructive de la protection des droits de la personne pour les enfants, tout en soulignant les limitations actuelles et les opportunités d'adaptation pour mieux garantir leurs droits au Canada.

Abstract

This chapter explores the question of the child as a subject of public law within the framework of the *Canadian Charter of Rights and Freedoms*. Although the *Charter* guarantees rights to "everyone," the situation of children, as individuals dependent on their parents or guardians, poses challenges regarding the conception of their relationship with the State. The chapter examines the extent to which the rights protected by the *Charter* can be considered children's rights, taking into account their near-universal recognition in the *Convention on the Rights of the Child*. Through an analysis of jurisprudence, the chapter offers a critical and constructive interpretation of human rights protection for children, while highlighting current limitations and opportunities for adaptation to better safeguard their rights in Canada.

Les enfants sont sujets de droit[1]. La protection des droits de la personne est un domaine dans lequel la relation entre les sujets de droit et l'État est facile à concevoir. Dans cette branche du droit, l'État doit garantir la jouissance des droits à tous sans discrimination. Ainsi, la personne a une relation avec l'État dans laquelle elle est protégée d'abus dont l'État, ses démembrements, organes ou représentants seraient à l'origine. De plus, cette relation demande non seulement une absence de violation de droits, mais aussi une protection active de l'individu par l'État. Au Canada, les droits de la personne reçoivent la reconnaissance juridique la plus élevée dans la *Charte canadienne des droits et libertés (Charte)*[2], faisant partie du droit constitutionnel canadien. Des droits sont aussi protégés par les lois fédérales, provinciales et territoriales qui garantissent le traitement sans discrimination[3].

Les enfants sont sujets des droits protégés par ces instruments de droit interne. En effet, la *Charte* garantit des droits à « chacun » dans plusieurs de ses dispositions. Toutefois, la position de l'enfant comme individu dépendant de ses parents ou tuteurs légaux en fait un sujet inhabituel de droit public, et on conçoit mal la relation entre l'enfant et l'État sans des adaptations. On peut ainsi se demander si on peut considérer les droits protégés dans la *Charte* comme des droits de l'enfant. Une étude de la jurisprudence s'avère nécessaire afin

---

[1] Par enfant, nous faisons référence à toute personne mineure, âgée de moins de 18 ans.

[2] *Charte canadienne des droits et libertés*, art 7, partie I de la *Loi constitutionnelle de 1982*, constituant l'annexe B de *la Loi de 1982 sur le Canada* (R-U), 1982, c 11 [*Charte*].

[3] Il est à noter que la *Charte des droits et libertés de la personne*, RLRQ c C-12 du Québec inclut plusieurs droits en plus du droit à la non-discrimination.

d'examiner l'étendue de l'application de la Charte aux enfants et d'en analyser le contenu en ce qui concerne les droits de l'enfant qui ont reçu une reconnaissance quasi universelle au niveau international du fait de leur insertion dans la *Convention relative aux droits de l'enfant* (CDE), ratifiée par le Canada[4].

Afin de porter un regard critique sur l'enfant comme sujet de droit public dans le cadre de l'application de la *Charte*, nous allons aborder la protection des droits de la personne qu'accorde la *Charte* et l'impact des limitations de cette protection sur les enfants. Nous allons également examiner la jurisprudence dans une approche critique et constructive afin d'ouvrir la voie à une interprétation de la *Charte* fondée sur les droits de l'enfant.

La protection limitée des droits de la personne au Canada

Ce qu'on appelle les droits et libertés au Canada, ce sont les droits de la personne qui sont juridiquement garantis par la législation interne, et notamment au niveau constitutionnel et quasi constitutionnel. Dans la *Charte*, ces droits sont qualifiés de droits civils et politiques au niveau international, mais classés en faisant ressortir les valeurs canadiennes : les libertés fondamentales, les droits démocratiques, la liberté de circulation, les garanties juridiques, le droit à l'égalité et les droits linguistiques. Ces droits incluent des droits protégés notamment par le *Pacte international relatif aux droits civils et politiques* (PIDCP), tels que le droit à la liberté de religion, d'expression, de réunion et d'association, le droit de vote, le droit à la vie, et les droits en cas de détention et d'arrestation.

Le Canada est aussi tenu de respecter ses engagements internationaux en matière de droits de la personne[5]. En effet, le Canada a ratifié sept des neuf traités principaux des droits de la personne des

---

[4] 20 novembre 1989, RTNU, vol 1577. La CDE est l'instrument international des droits de la personne le plus ratifié ; même les États-Unis ont signifié leur acceptation de ce traité par leur signature. Voir Nations Unies, *Collection des Traités, Convention relative aux droits de l'enfant*, en ligne : <treaties.un.org>.

[5] Tel que reconnu à maintes reprises dans la jurisprudence de la Cour suprême du Canada. Pour une affirmation récente de la valeur contraignante des traités ratifiés par le Canada, voir *Québec (Procureure générale) c 9147-0732 Québec inc*, 2020 CSC 32 (CanLII) aux paras 32 et 39, [2020] 3 RCS 426.

Nations Unies[6]. Parmi ceux-là figurent le PIDCP et le *Pacte international relatif aux droits économiques, sociaux et culturels*. Ce dernier reconnaît des droits tels que le droit au travail, le droit à la santé, le droit à l'éducation et le droit à la sécurité sociale. Tous ces différents types de droits, qu'ils entrent dans la catégorie des droits civils et politiques ou des droits économiques, sociaux et culturels, se retrouvent également dans la plupart des conventions plus spécialisées auxquelles le Canada est partie, telles que la *Convention sur l'élimination de toutes les formes de discrimination à l'égard des femmes*, la CDE et la *Convention relative aux droits des personnes handicapées*[7]. Au regard de ces traités, on peut soutenir que le Canada a une vision étroite des droits de la personne à l'interne, puisque les droits protégés n'incluent pas l'ensemble des droits de la personne découlant de la *Déclaration universelle des droits de l'homme* (DUDH), qui est à la base de toutes les conventions dans ce domaine[8]. Cela ne signifie pas que le Canada ne met pas en œuvre les conventions qu'il a ratifiées, puisque des mesures législatives, politiques et autres sont prises pour assurer l'accès à l'éducation, aux soins de santé et aux conditions de travail adéquates, mais ces accès et conditions ne sont pas reconnus comme des droits fondamentaux en droit interne.

Une autre limite de la protection des droits accordée au Canada touche spécifiquement aux enfants. Bien qu'on puisse reconnaître les enfants comme des sujets de la plupart des dispositions de la *Charte* et au moins de celles qui font référence à « chacun » ou « tous »[9], un

---

[6] Les conventions que le Canada n'a pas ratifiées sont la *Convention internationale sur la protection des droits de tous les travailleurs migrants et des membres de leur famille* et la *Convention internationale pour la protection de toutes les personnes contre les disparitions forcées*.

[7] L'exception est la *Convention contre la torture et autres peines ou traitement cruels, inhumains ou dégradants*, qui porte sur un droit spécifique plutôt qu'un groupe de personnes.

[8] La DUDH et les deux pactes sont considérés comme la *Charte internationale des droits de l'homme*.

[9] Par opposition à « citoyen ». L'application de cette notion aux enfants est controversée. Selon la définition reliée à la nationalité, les enfants sont bien entendu citoyenn·e·s. Mais selon la notion reliée aux droits et devoirs démocratiques, les enfants ne sont pas citoyen·ne·s, puisqu'ils n'obtiennent le droit de vote qu'à l'âge de 18 ans. Dans cette acception, les enfants sont des citoyenn·e·s en devenir. Toutefois, de nombreuses chercheuses et chercheurs en sociologie s'intéressent à la citoyenneté des enfants, reconnaissant ces derniers en tant qu'actrices et acteurs sociaux. Dans ce contexte, on peut distinguer entre la citoyenneté substantive, qui se définit par des pratiques

examen de la jurisprudence révèle que ses articles trouvent rarement une application directe aux enfants. D'évidence les enfants n'ont pas la même capacité juridique que les adultes et ils ont besoin de l'intervention d'un tuteur pour faire valoir leurs droits devant les tribunaux. On pourrait donc s'attendre à ce que les parents introduisent des recours au nom de leurs enfants afin de défendre leurs droits. Toutefois, cela se fait très peu, car proportionnellement, il y a une sous-représentation des recours introduits au nom d'enfants par rapport à ceux qui concernent la violation des droits des adultes. Plusieurs questions se posent alors. Est-ce parce que les droits de la *Charte* ne concernent pas les enfants ? Est-ce qu'ils ne leur sont pas adaptés ? Dans les faits, l'enfant se retrouve-t-il rarement dans une situation où il fait face à l'État et où ses droits risquent d'être bafoués ? Ou est-ce parce que les parents n'introduisent que des recours qui les intéressent plutôt que d'examiner la situation du point de vue de leur enfant qui n'a pas accès aux tribunaux ? Il est probable que les réponses à toutes ces questions apportent des pistes de solution.

Afin d'évaluer l'applicabilité concrète des droits de la *Charte* aux enfants, nous procéderons à une comparaison de ces droits avec ceux garantis dans la CDE. Ensuite, nous discuterons de leur application lorsque les tribunaux examinent une affaire qui concerne un enfant. Nous nous limiterons à la jurisprudence de la Cour suprême du Canada (CSC) à des fins d'illustration de nos propos.

Droits de la personne et droits de l'enfant

Lorsque nous comparons les droits universellement reconnus avec ceux de la Charte, notre première constatation a trait à l'observation que nous avons faite quant au champ limité des droits de la personne au Canada. En effet, la CDE contient des droits des deux grandes catégories de droits de la personne. Parmi ceux qui semblent particulièrement importants pour les enfants, on trouve le droit à l'éducation et le droit à la santé. Ces droits n'ont pas d'équivalent dans la *Charte*. Il y a également, dans la CDE, des droits qui concernent plus particulièrement les enfants ou qui ont été adaptés pour eux, ainsi que

---

d'appartenance sociale et politique, et la citoyenneté formelle ou légale, qui se définit par le droit de vote. Voir Stéphanie Gaudet, « Introduction : citoyenneté des enfants et des adolescents », (2018) 80 Lien soc & Politiques 4.

des principes d'application de ces droits. L'article 3 contient le principe de la considération de l'intérêt de l'enfant dans toutes les décisions à son sujet. Ce principe ne se trouve pas dans la *Charte*, mais on en a maintes fois discuté dans la jurisprudence canadienne, y compris dans des domaines du droit public[10]. D'autres droits qui s'appliquent particulièrement à l'enfant sont, entre autres, le droit à l'identité (nom, nationalité, relations familiales), le droit à la protection de l'enfant séparé de son milieu familial, ainsi que le droit à la protection contre les mauvais traitements. Plusieurs de ces droits sont inclus dans la *Charte*, particulièrement aux articles 7 et 12, selon l'interprétation faite des notions clés dans ces dispositions.

Les droits de la CDE qui trouvent leur équivalent explicite dans la *Charte* sont les libertés classiques, telles que les libertés de religion, d'expression, de réunion et d'association. Des droits fondamentaux comme le droit à la vie et les droits des personnes face au système judiciaire existent également dans les deux instruments. Examinons certains de ces droits, particulièrement le droit à la vie, qui est un droit fondamental de la personne.

Charte, article 7 :

> Chacun a droit à la vie, à la liberté et à la sécurité de sa personne ; il ne peut être porté atteinte à ce droit qu'en conformité avec les principes de justice fondamentale.

CDE, article 6 :

> 1. Les États parties reconnaissent que tout enfant a un droit inhérent à la vie.
> 2. Les États parties assurent dans toute la mesure possible la survie et le développement de l'enfant.

L'article 7 de la *Charte* contient trois droits : la vie, la liberté et la sécurité de sa personne. Il est limité non seulement par l'article premier de la *Charte*, qui prévoit la possibilité pour les droits d'être restreints de manière raisonnable et justifiée dans le cadre d'une société libre et démocratique, mais aussi par le concept du principe de justice

---

[10] Particulièrement dans le domaine du droit de l'immigration et des droits des réfugiés. Voir par exemple *Baker c Canada (Ministre de la Citoyenneté et de l'Immigration)*, 1999 CSC 699 (CanLII), [1999] 2 RCS 817 [*Baker*] et *Kanthasamy c Canada (Citoyenneté et Immigration)*, 2015 CSC 61 (CanLII), [2015] 3 RCS 909.

fondamentale. Ainsi, le droit à la vie n'est pas violé si son atteinte est en conformité avec les principes de justice fondamentale, définis dans la jurisprudence[11]. Une autre limite découle de l'inclusion de l'article 7 dans la section sur les « garanties juridiques », puisque les droits qui y sont énumérés ont été interprétés de manière assez limitative[12].

Dans la CDE, au contraire, comme dans les autres traités internationaux, le droit à la vie est interprété de manière large, et ce droit inclut des obligations positives à la charge des États[13]. Cette vision est renforcée dans la CDE puisque le droit à la vie est suivi des obligations en lien avec la survie et le développement de l'enfant, qui, contrairement au droit à la vie, ne sont pas des droits absolus, mais que les États doivent assurer dans la mesure du possible. Par exemple, le Comité des droits de l'enfant, organe des Nations Unies chargé de la mise en œuvre de la CDE, demande aux États ce qu'ils font pour prévenir le suicide des enfants[14].

Dans la CDE, les droits qui équivaudraient aux droits à la liberté et à la sécurité de sa personne dans la *Charte* ne se trouvent pas à l'article 6, mais plutôt à l'article 37. Ce dernier inclut le droit de l'enfant de ne pas être soumis à la torture ou à des peines ou traitements cruels, inhumains ou dégradants, à la peine capitale, à l'emprisonnement à vie sans possibilité de libération ; de même que l'interdiction de la privation de liberté illégale ou arbitraire, la privation de liberté devant être une mesure de dernier ressort et d'une durée aussi brève que possible ; ainsi que le traitement avec

---

[11] En ce qui a trait aux principes s'appliquant particulièrement aux enfants, la CSC a jugé que le principe de l'intérêt supérieur de l'enfant ne faisait pas partie des principes de justice fondamentale : *Canadian Foundation for Children, Youth and the Law c Canada (Procureur général)*, 2004 CSC 4 (CanLII), [2004] 1 RCS 76 [*Canadian Foundation*]. mais elle a jugé que la présomption de culpabilité moins élevée des adolescents en était un : *R c DB*, 2008 CSC 25 (CanLII), [2008] 2 RCS 3 [*DB*].

[12] Voir notamment *Gosselin c. Québec (Procureur général)*, 2002 CSC 84 (CanLII) au para 77, [2002] 4 RCS 429.

[13] Pour l'interprétation actuelle du droit à la vie dans le système international de protection des droits, voir Comité des droits de l'homme, *Observation générale no 36 sur le droit à la vie (art 6)*, Doc NU CCPR/C/GC/36, 2019-9-3 (3 septembre 2019).

[14] Comité des droits de l'enfant, *Directives spécifiques à l'instrument concernant la forme et le contenu des rapports périodiques que les États parties doivent soumettre en application du paragraphe 1b) de l'article 44 de la Convention relative aux droits de l'enfant*, Doc NU CRC/C/58/Rev 3, 2015 au para 26.

humanité et avec respect de l'enfant privé de liberté, pour une question de dignité, en tenant compte des besoins liés à son âge. Comme nous allons voir, c'est en effet dans le domaine du droit pénal que les droits de la personne de l'enfant sont le plus souvent examinés, dans la jurisprudence de la CSC, et que les droits de la CDE trouvent leur équivalent dans les droits fondamentaux des enfants au Canada.

L'application de la Charte aux enfants : survol de la jurisprudence

Depuis l'arrêt *Baker* de 1999[15], considéré comme le point de départ de l'utilisation de la CDE par les tribunaux aux fins d'interprétation de la loi et 2023, on compte, moins de 10 cas de jurisprudence de la CSC qui traitent de l'application de la *Charte* aux enfants[16], comparativement à plus de 500 du côté des adultes. Des cas repérés, trois ont trait à la justice pénale pour les adolescents et un s'avère un recours en contestation de la constitutionnalité d'une disposition de droit interne par un organisme communautaire. Nous n'avons relevé que trois affaires, traitées depuis 1999, qui concernent directement des enfants qui, avec l'aide de leur tuteur, intentent un recours demandant la reconnaissance de la violation de leurs droits constitutionnels. Ce sont l'affaire

---

[15] *Supra* note 10.

[16] Les arrêts : *Canadian Foundation for Children, Youth and the Law, supra* note 11 ; *Auton (Tutrice à l'instance de) c Colombie-Britannique (Procureur général)*, 2004 CSC 78 (CanLII), [2004] 3 RCS 657 ; *Multani c Commission scolaire Marguerite-Bourgeoys*, 2006 CSC 6 (CanLII), [2006] 1 RCS 256 ; *R c B* 2008 CSC *DB, supra* note 11, [2008] 2 RCS 3 ; *AC c Manitoba (Directeur des services à l'enfant et à la famille)*, 2009 CSC 30 (CanLII), [2009] 2 RCS 181 [AC] [2009] 2 RCS 181 ; *R c KJM, 2019 CSC 55 (CanLII)*, [2019] 4 RCS 39, et *R c C P, R c CP*, 2021 CSC 19 (CanLII), [2021] 1 RCS 679. Il faudrait compter aussi les arrêts dans l'affaire *Khadr*, puisqu'Omar Khadr avait 16 ans au moment des faits, même si la Cour ne considère pratiquement pas son statut de mineur, mentionnant seulement qu'il était adolescent dans *Canada (Premier ministre) c Khadr*, 2010 CSC 3 (CanLII) aux paras 24, 25 et 30, [2010] 1 RCS 44 [Khadr] aux paras 24, 25 et 30. Nous ne comptons pas les causes (peu nombreuses, également) qui concernent l'application à un enfant du droit à la non-discrimination reconnu dans les lois provinciales, puisque notre contribution se limite aux droits de la *Charte* canadienne. Nous n'incluons pas non plus les recours intentés par des parents dans le cas de revendications linguistiques en matière d'instruction, puisqu'il s'agit de droits accordés aux parents (art 23 de la *Charte*).

Auton, relative à l'application des articles 7 et 15 de la *Charte* dans le contexte d'un recours pour obtenir le financement d'une thérapie pour traiter l'autisme, l'affaire *Multani*, concernant la liberté de religion d'un élève sikh à l'école au regard du paragraphe 2a) de la *Charte*, et l'affaire *AC* portant sur le consentement aux soins de santé d'une adolescente au regard des articles 7 et 15 de la *Charte*[17]. Il s'agit donc de trois cas répartis sur une période de plus de 20 ans.

La rareté des cas de la *Charte* concernant les enfants ne signifie pas cependant que leurs droits ne sont pas discutés du tout. En effet, on fait référence à la CDE et à des principes des droits de l'enfant comme l'intérêt supérieur de l'enfant (ISE) dans des causes dissociées de la *Charte* canadienne. Certains cas ont trait à la *Loi sur l'immigration et la protection des réfugiés*, puisque, depuis l'arrêt *Baker*, on doit considérer l'ISE dans les décisions d'ordre humanitaire. De plus, il y a des jugements dans lesquels on a considéré les droits des enfants de manière incidente ou indirecte. On peut noter l'affaire *R c Sharpe*, dans laquelle la Cour suprême a confirmé que la protection des enfants justifiait des restrictions à la liberté d'expression[18]. D'autres jugements concernent des familles, où l'affaire est examinée du point de vue des droits des parents, dont l'un est demandeur, alors que les droits de l'enfant sont aussi mentionnés (en droit familial ou de protection de l'enfance)[19]. Ainsi, les droits de l'enfant, et parfois plus particulièrement la CDE, sont mentionnés dans plusieurs jugements, mais peu concernent l'examen d'une violation de droit fondamental d'enfant. Cela crée une distinction entre droits de l'enfant et droits de la personne, alors que les droits de l'enfant sont des droits de la personne adaptés aux enfants[20].

---

[17] *Ibid.*

[18] *R c Sharpe*, 2001 CSC 2 (CanLII), [2001] 1 RCS 45.

[19] Par exemple, *Bureau de l'avocat des enfants c Balev*, 2018 CSC 16 (CanLII), [2018] 1 RCS 398 ; *Office des services à l'enfant et à la famille de Winnipeg c KLW*, 2000 CSC 48 (CanLII), [2000] 2 RCS 519. Cette catégorie inclut des jugements antérieurs à *Baker*, tels que *Young c Young*, 1993 CanLII 34 (CSC), [1993] 4 RCS 3 et B (R) c *Children's Aid Society of Metropolitan Toronto*, 1995 CanLII 115 (CSC), [1995] 1 RCS 315

[20] Voir Michael Freeman, « Children's Rights as Human Rights: Reading the UNCRC », dans Jens Qvortrup, William A Corsaro et Michael-Sebastian Honig, dir, *The Palgrave Handbook of Childhood Studies*, New York, Palgrave Macmillan, 2009, 377-393 ; Anne McGillivray, « Why Children Do Have Equal Rights: In Reply to Laura Purdy » (1994) 2 Intl J Child Rts 243 ; Mona Paré, « Children's Rights Are Human Rights and Why Canadian Implementation Lags Behind » (2017) 4:1 Canadian

Les principes d'application fondés sur les droits de l'enfant

Nonobstant le petit nombre de jugements au sujet de l'application des droits de la *Charte* aux enfants, on note différentes occasions manquées pour l'application d'une approche fondée sur les droits de l'enfant dans la jurisprudence qui concerne les enfants. D'abord, la CSC se réfère à la CDE surtout dans une approche protectrice et non pour faire valoir l'ensemble des principes des droits de l'enfant. Ensuite, le principe de l'ISE n'est pas appliqué de manière rigoureuse et systématique dans les branches de droit concernant l'enfant. Finalement, les références à la CDE sont souvent manquantes, alors qu'elles auraient pu aider à renforcer les liens entre les droits de l'enfant et les droits de la personne reconnus en droit interne.

Premièrement, en examinant la jurisprudence, on note que la majorité des jugements se référant à la CDE le font pour affirmer ou réitérer la vulnérabilité inhérente des enfants et leur besoin de protection. Cette approche fait partie des droits de l'enfant, mais ne reflète pas l'entièreté de ces droits et doit être balancée avec d'autres considérations. En fait, la CSC ne traite pas de tous les principes des droits de l'enfant de manière égale. Les principes des droits de l'enfant, à des fins d'application de la CDE, sont la non-discrimination, l'ISE, la vie, la survie et le développement de l'enfant, ainsi que le respect de l'opinion de l'enfant[21]. Le principe de l'ISE est souvent présent dans la jurisprudence. On peut l'associer au droit à la vie, à la survie et au développement de l'enfant pour renforcer la notion de protection de l'enfant, car c'est souvent dans cette optique qu'on l'applique[22]. Le

---

Journal of Children's Rights / Revue canadienne des droits des enfants 24, en ligne : https://doi.org/10.22215/cjcr.v4i1.1163

[21] Comité des droits de l'enfant, *Directives générales concernant la forme et le contenu des rapports initiaux*, Doc NU CRC/C/5, 1991 au para 13. Sur l'application de ces principes au Canada, voir notamment Mona Paré, « La mise en œuvre de la Convention relative aux droits de l'enfant : une question de principes », dans Le Tribunal des droits de la personne et le Barreau du Québec, dir, *Race, femme, enfant, handicap : les conventions internationales et le droit interne à la lumière des enjeux pratiques du droit à l'égalité*, Cowansville, Éditions Yvon Blais, 1990 aux pp 391–427.

[22] Voir Mona Paré, « Les droits (de la personne) de l'enfant : regard sur les notions de vulnérabilité et d'égalité dans la jurisprudence de la juge Abella », dans *L'honorable Rosalie Silberman Abella : une vie d'avant-garde*, Toronto, Irwin Law dans Vanessa MacDonnell, Stephen Bindman & Gerald Chan (eds.), *Justice Rosalie Silberman Abella : A Life of Firsts*, University of Toronto Press, 2025 aux pp 299-314.

droit à la vie et au développement de l'enfant n'est pas reconnu comme un principe en soi au Canada, mais il est englobé dans le concept du droit de l'enfant à sa protection et à la reconnaissance de sa vulnérabilité. La Cour suprême s'y réfère même sans lien avec une loi quelconque[23]. La protection de l'enfant agit donc comme un principe autonome qui regroupe certains principes de la CDE.

Le droit à la non-discrimination et à l'égalité et le droit de l'enfant d'être entendu sur toute question le concernant sont des principes qui favorisent l'agentivité de l'enfant et encouragent son autonomisation. Le principe de non-discrimination, avec son pendant, l'égalité, est reconnu aux enfants au Canada, mais relativement peu de causes en traitent[24]. Quant au principe du respect de l'opinion de l'enfant, il se trouve rarement dans les jugements concernant les enfants. L'affaire *AC* est une exception, puisque la Cour y analyse le concept d'autonomie de l'enfant en profondeur, mais aboutit tout de même à une décision favorisant plutôt la protection[25]. A.C., une adolescente, témoin de Jéhovah, contestait la constitutionnalité d'une loi sur la base de laquelle une ordonnance de transfusion sanguine avait été rendue contre ses souhaits. Selon la Cour, l'ISE, sur lequel se fondait la disposition législative contestée, doit être interprété en considérant les valeurs opposées de l'autonomie et de la protection de l'enfant. Pour une adolescente « manifestement mature à exercer un jugement autonome », il faut comprendre que le respect de sa capacité est « par définition dans son intérêt[26]. » Ainsi, plus l'enfant est capable de démontrer sa maturité, plus il est certain que son intérêt supérieur et son opinion vont coïncider. En fin de compte, la Cour affirme la constitutionnalité de la disposition législative sur la base de cette interprétation, mais elle n'applique pas son analyse à la situation spécifique d'A.C., qui est déboutée de sa demande.

Deuxièmement, le principe de l'ISE, bien que souvent présent, l'est particulièrement dans certains contextes, alors qu'en tant que

---

[23] Voir par exemple *AB c Bragg Communications Inc*, 2012 CSC 46 (CanLII), [2012] 2 RCS 567, concernant la protection de la vie privée d'une adolescente.

[24] Voir respectivement un jugement où la discrimination a été reconnue et un autre où l'allégation a été rejetée : *Moore c Colombie-Britannique (Éducation)*, 2012 CSC 61 (CanLII), [2012] 3 RCS 360 ; *Ward c Québec (Commission des droits de la personne et des droits de la jeunesse)*, 2021 CSC 43 (CanLII), [2021] 3 RCS 176

[25] *Supra* note 16.

[26] *Ibid* aux paras 80-84.

principe s'appliquant aux droits de l'enfant, il devrait être considéré dans tous les cas de prise de décision ayant trait aux enfants. L'ISE est très présent dans la jurisprudence en matière de droit familial, domaine où on l'a introduit et inséré dans la législation. Comme mentionné précédemment, il est aujourd'hui aussi présent dans les cas concernant le droit de l'immigration et les droits des réfugiés, mais seulement en lien avec les décisions liées aux considérations d'ordre humanitaire. Curieusement, alors que la *Charte* est surtout appliquée aux enfants dans le système de justice pénale pour adolescents et que les références à la CDE sont fréquentes dans ce cas, le principe de l'ISE est toujours absent de ces jugements. Vu la nature floue du principe, il serait intéressant de le développer dans les domaines où il n'a pas été défini. L'ISE devrait être traité avec moins de suspicion dans les domaines se distinguant du droit familial et du droit de l'immigration. L'affaire *Canadian Foundation* montre que le principe est sujet à différentes approches quant à son application. Il s'agissait d'une contestation de la constitutionnalité de l'article 43 du *Code criminel*, qui offre une défense aux parents qui utilisent la force contre leur enfant. La demande faisait valoir que cette disposition était notamment contraire à l'article 7 de la *Charte*, puisqu'elle ne respecterait pas l'ISE en tant que principe de justice fondamentale relié aux enfants. Selon la Cour, l'ISE ne peut être un tel principe, puisque l'issue de son application varie selon le contexte et qu'il peut concurrencer d'autres intérêts[27]. Pourtant, l'ISE est clair en tant que principe procédural, à la lumière des travaux du Comité des droits de l'enfant de l'ONU[28]. L'envisager ainsi signifie qu'il doive toujours être examiné dans les décisions, incluant le développement de politiques et de lois, concernant les enfants. Ceci n'empêche pas de reconnaître que les éléments à considérer pour définir l'ISE peuvent varier d'un domaine et d'un cas à un autre[29]. En fait, il est même recommandé de développer des listes de facteurs par secteur[30]. Ainsi, dans le domaine criminel, il faudrait examiner

---

[27] *Supra* note 11 aux paras 10-11.

[28] Comité des droits de l'enfant, *Observation générale n° 14 sur le droit de l'enfant à ce que son intérêt supérieur soit une considération primordiale*, Doc NU, CRC/C/GC/14, 2013.

[29] Mona Paré, « L'intérêt supérieur de l'enfant : la recherche de convergences parmi les approches divergentes », dans Simon Lapierre et Alexandra Vincent, dir, *Le meilleur intérêt de l'enfant victime de violence conjugale : enjeux et réponses sociojudiciaires*, Québec, Presses de l'Université du Québec, 2022 aux pp 33-48.

[30] *Canadian Foundation*, note 11 au para 50.

l'incidence de certaines règles sur l'ISE, qu'elles concernent l'enfant comme victime ou comme auteur d'infractions. Parmi ces éléments, on pourrait inclure la sécurité de l'enfant, sa santé, ses relations familiales et sa réhabilitation.

Troisièmement, la CDE n'est pas utilisée dans l'interprétation de la *Charte* de manière constante. Parfois, il n'y a qu'une simple référence, sans que la CDE serve véritablement d'instrument d'interprétation, et d'autres fois, la convention n'est même pas mentionnée, alors que l'équivalent du droit de la *Charte* examiné existe dans la CDE. L'affaire *Multani* est un exemple d'application directe de la *Charte* à un enfant, dont on a violé le droit à la liberté de religion. La CDE reconnaissant aussi le droit de l'enfant à la liberté de religion, il aurait été utile de renforcer ce droit en tant que droit de l'enfant avec une référence à son article 14. De même, dans l'affaire *Auton*, aucune référence n'a été faite à la CDE alors que celle-ci contient le droit à la non-discrimination et à l'égalité ainsi qu'un article sur les droits des enfants handicapés[31]. L'article 23 de la CDE contenant plusieurs dispositions sur les formes d'aide et de services qui devraient être fournis aux enfants handicapés aurait pu appuyer une interprétation plus large de la notion de « service essentiel » nécessaire pour garantir l'égalité pour ce groupe d'enfants. L'affaire *K.J.M.*, traitant de l'application aux adolescents des délais maximaux déterminés pour les procès pénaux pour adultes, ne fait nulle mention des droits procéduraux des enfants prévus à l'article 40 de la CDE[32]. L'utilisation de la CDE dans l'analyse aurait permis d'examiner la situation du point de vue des enfants et d'éviter ainsi une approche formelle à l'application du droit de l'enfant, ceci en vue d'obtenir un jugement dans un délai raisonnable. De manière plus flagrante, dans l'affaire *Khadr*, la CSC effleure à peine la notion d'intérêt de l'enfant sans pour autant reconnaître expressément que les droits de l'enfant de l'adolescent de 16 ans devaient s'appliquer en l'espèce[33]. Si la Cour avait développé le principe de l'ISE, elle aurait dû procéder à un examen de la situation du jeune citoyen canadien, détenu au camp de Guantánamo et interrogé par les agents du Service canadien du renseignement de sécurité, à l'époque des faits (en 2003). Elle aurait aussi dû tenir compte

---

[31] Articles 2 et 23. Voir aussi : Comité des droits de l'enfant, Observation générale N° 9, *Le droit des enfants handicapés*, Doc NU CRC/C/GC/9 (17 novembre 2007).

[32] Contrairement au jugement dissident de la juge Abella.

[33] *Khadr*, *supra* note 16. Ceci, contrairement au jugement de la Cour d'appel fédérale : *Canada (Premier ministre) c Khadr*, 2009 CAF 246 (CanLII), [2010] 1 RCF 73 au para 53.

des conséquences des décisions prises sur l'avenir de l'enfant[34]. Une telle analyse aurait pu influencer la décision de la Cour quant à la réparation, qui a pris la forme d'une simple déclaration de la Cour, alors que Khadr demandait son rapatriement[35].

Conclusion

Les droits de l'enfant font partie des droits de la personne, et les enfants doivent pouvoir jouir de la protection de leurs droits comme tout autre sujet de droit canadien. Étant donné que la CDE n'a pas été incorporée en droit interne et que le Canada considère que ses lois permettent de respecter ses engagements internationaux, nous devons considérer que la *Charte* offre une protection au moins égale à celle de la convention[36]. On s'attendrait alors à ce que l'application de la *Charte* comme expression des droits de l'enfant au Canada se manifeste dans la jurisprudence. La pratique est pourtant tout autre, avec un recours rare à la *Charte* pour protéger les droits des enfants et une interprétation de la *Charte* qui n'est pas souvent en phase avec la CDE.

Afin de promouvoir une application de la *Charte* fondée sur les droits de l'enfant, il faudrait des références plus constantes et plus substantielles à la CDE, incluant ses principes et articles pertinents à la cause. Ceci aiderait à démontrer que les droits constitutionnels des enfants sont conformes aux obligations internationales du Canada et interprétés de manière à prendre en compte la spécificité des enfants. Sans cette prise en compte, ne risque-t-on pas de tomber dans l'adultisme et la discrimination envers les enfants ? Finalement, il ne faut pas oublier que la protection égale de la loi est aussi une question d'accès à la justice. La relation entre l'enfant et l'État doit se traduire par de réelles possibilités d'entendre des causes provenant d'enfants et de remédier aux violations de leurs droits.

---

[34] Voir notamment *Baker*, *supra* note 10 au para 71.

[35] Voir Paré, *supra* note 21 aux pp 425-426.

[36] Voir la position du gouvernement dans le rapport initial présenté au Comité des droits de l'enfant : Doc. NU CRC/C/11/Add.3, 1994.

Critical Disability Theory and Public Law in Canada: The Case of *Longueépée v University of Waterloo*

*Ravi Malhotra**

Abstract

Structural barriers in Canadian society severely impact people with disabilities, restricting their access to employment, public spaces, technology, and transportation. These obstacles, compounded during the COVID 19 crisis, lead to high levels of poverty, unemployment, and isolation for many. Neoliberal policies, which prioritize market stability and corporate profitability, exacerbate these challenges by reducing state support for vulnerable populations. Critical disability theory offers a framework to reimagine a society where people with disabilities can thrive. This chapter explores the development of this theory, particularly the social model of disablement, and incorporates insights from Cornelius Castoriadis' concept of social imaginary significations. By analyzing the *Longueépée v University of Waterloo* case, the chapter demonstrates how public law can better support people with disabilities and highlights the importance of reparative readings of legal texts to promote inclusion and equality.

---

* Thanks to the editors for inviting me to contribute this chapter and the peer reviewer for valuable insights. All errors remain my responsibility.

Résumé

Les obstacles structurels dans la société canadienne ont un impact profond sur les personnes en situation de handicap, limitant leur accès à l'emploi, aux espaces publics, à la technologie et aux transports. Ces obstacles, aggravés pendant la crise de la COVID-19, entraînent des niveaux élevés de pauvreté, de chômage et d'isolement pour de nombreuses personnes. Les politiques néolibérales, qui privilégient la stabilité des marchés et la rentabilité des entreprises, exacerbent ces défis en réduisant le soutien de l'État pour les populations vulnérables. La théorie critique du handicap offre un cadre pour réimaginer une société où les personnes en situation de handicap peuvent s'épanouir. Ce chapitre explore le développement de cette théorie, en particulier le modèle social du handicap, et intègre les idées de Cornelius Castoriadis sur les significations imaginaires sociales. À travers l'analyse de l'affaire *Longueépée c Université de Waterloo*, le chapitre démontre comment le droit public peut mieux soutenir les personnes en situation de handicap et souligne l'importance de lectures réparatrices des textes juridiques pour promouvoir l'inclusion et l'égalité.

Structural barriers for people with disabilities permeate Canadian society. From inaccessible architecture that blocks the dreams and aspirations of mobility-impaired people in work and play to information technology that produces data, web sites, and apps that are not readily usable by blind and visually impaired individuals to transportation systems that are not designed for people with all manner of disabilities, disabled people[1] face tremendous obstacles in their daily life. The consequences are dire: high rates of poverty and unemployment for people with disabilities, exclusion from public facilities and isolation from mainstream society. Many of these barriers have been compounded during the COVID-19 crisis. Indeed, few other identity groups are composed of members who are mostly outside the labour market, living in deep poverty, and experiencing daily barriers to access transportation and housing. The restructuring of the neoliberal state to focus on ensuring corporate profitability and stable market conditions for investors creates a particularly inhospitable environment, featuring a permanent state of austerity and cutbacks to

[1] I use the terms "disabled people" and "people with disabilities" interchangeably.

the welfare state, for inclusion and equality for disabled people.[2] As Bretton-Purdy, Kapcynzki and Grewal observe, neoliberalism may be characterized as "a demand for deregulation, austerity, and an attempt to assimilate government to something more like a market—but it never was as simple as a demand for 'free markets.'"[3] Rather, they suggest that it was a demand to protect the market from democratic demands for redistribution.

Critical disability theory offers a way of reimagining a world that is inclusive of disabled people, enabling us to flourish in our daily lives. For public law scholars, that means reconsidering how existing case law, statutes and procedure have marginalized disabled people and how public law might do better to achieve equality for disabled people. In so doing, I articulate what Danish Sheikh has identified as a reparative reading of the jurisprudence. He argues that "read[ing] a text for the possibility of repair, is to read a text to see the resources it can offer us."[4] In this chapter, I illustrate the importance of critical disability theory and how it can empower disabled people as follows. To begin, I offer an overview of critical disability theory, tracing its origins in the work of theorists of the social model of disablement such as Michael Oliver and Colin Barnes. I also suggest how critical disability theory might be fruitfully supplemented by engagement with the radical French philosopher Cornelius Castoriadis and his concept of social imaginary significations.[5] Social imaginary significations enable us to reimagine how we think about the world and identify the governing myths in a particular society. In the third section, I shift gears by providing an overview of a recent decision of the Ontario Court of Appeal, *Longueépée v University of Waterloo*,[6] a

---

[2] See e.g. Jedediah Britton-Purdy, Amy Kapcynzki & David Singh Grewal, "How Law Made Neoliberalism" *Boston Review* (22 February 2021) available online at http://bostonreview.net/law-justice/jedediah-britton-purdy-amy-kapczynski-david-singh-grewal-how-law-made-neoliberalism.

[3] *Ibid.*

[4] Danish Sheikh, "Staging Repair" (2021) 25 Law Text Culture 144 at 146. I thank an anonymous peer reviewer for suggesting I incorporate Sheikh's analysis.

[5] For leading works by Castoriadis, see Cornelius Castoriadis, *The Imaginary Institution of Society*, trans Kathleen Blamey (Cambridge: Polity Press, 1987) [Castoriadis, *Imaginary*]; Cornelius Castoriadis, *World in Fragments; Writings on Politics, Society, Psychoanalysis and the Imagination,* trans and ed David Ames Curtis (Stanford, California: Stanford University Press, 1997) [Castoriadis, *World*].

[6] 2020 ONCA 830 (CanLII).

judicial review of a human rights tribunal decision in the context of post-secondary education. the fourth section, I offer an analysis of the case through the prism of critical disability theory. In the final section, I offer some brief concluding remarks.

An Overview of Critical Disability Theory

The principal animating concept that lies at the heart of critical disability theory is the social model of disablement. The social model of disablement stands for the proposition that it is structural barriers that impede the lives of disabled people. As Colin Barnes and Geof Mercer have noted, it seeks to challenge the social exclusion and oppression of disabled people in order to achieve dignity and independent living.[7] The focus is consequently on eliminating barriers that handicap disabled people, rather than eliminating physiological impairments. These barriers may take the form of physical obstacles such as a staircase that does not allow entry or egress for a wheelchair user. Or they may take the form of pernicious attitudes which result in exclusion and marginalization of disabled people. The social model focuses on eliminating barriers, be they physical or attitudinal, rather than altering the disabled person's body through surgery or physiotherapy, sometimes known as the individual or medical model of disablement.[8] One of the earliest formulations of the social model was made by the British organization of disability rights advocates, the Union of the Physically Impaired Against Segregation (UPIAS) in 1976. Popularized by Mike Oliver and Colin Barnes and building on work by Finkelstein and Hunt, it was a materialist conception of disablement that insightfully distinguished between impairment, the focus of medical and rehabilitation professionals, and disability, which may only be redressed through the transformation of society.[9] The social model

---

[7] Colin Barnes & Geof Mercer, "Understanding Impairment and Disability: toward an International Perspective" in Colin Barnes & Geof Mercer, eds, *The Social Model of Disability and the Majority World* (Leeds: The Disability Press, 2005), 1 at 1.

[8] Mike Oliver, "The Individual and Social Model of Disability" (23 July 1990), available online: https://disability-studies.leeds.ac.uk/wp-content/uploads/sites/40/library/Oliver-in-soc-dis.pdf.

[9] Due to space constraints, this is inevitably a stylized account and largely omits the development of poststructuralist theories of disablement more commonly taught in the

gradually gained acceptance by mainstream British disability organizations such as the British Council of Disabled People in the 1980s and spread internationally through Disabled Peoples' International to gain influence in Canada and the United States.[10] While the social model has understandably been critiqued as not paying sufficient attention to concerns of intersectionality including the experiences of racialized disabled people, disabled women and girls, and LGBTQIA+ people who identify as disabled,[11] it remains a powerful prism that shines a light on challenging barriers while placing the empowerment of disabled people at the centre of its political priorities.

Too often, disabled people have been regarded as objects of pity or applauded as "supercrips" who overcame their otherwise tragic and pitiful impairments through bravery and personal courage.[12] Despite the growth of disability history and biographies of disabled people that seek to render the lives of disabled people in a more nuanced, complicated way and understand how ableism shaped the choices of disabled people, these demeaning and stereotypical tropes remain with us, damaging the well-being and dignity of disabled people.[13] In that context, the social model had a dramatic impact in transforming the consciousness of many disabled people to become self-aware of

United States, particularly in the humanities. For a representative work, see Alison Kafer, *Feminist, Queer, Crip* (Bloomington, Indiana: Indiana University Press, 2013).

[10] Carol Thomas, *Sociologies of Disability and Illness: Contested Ideas in Disability Studies and Medical Sociology* (New York: Palgrave Macmillan, 2007) at 57-58. While the American and British versions of the social model are not identical, the social model of disablement might be regarded globally as an example of policy diffusion. For a remarkable study of this in the context of disability supports for independent living, see generally Georgia van Toorn, *The New Political Economy of Disability: Transnational Networks and Individualised Funding in the Age of Neoliberalism* (London, U.K.: Routledge, 2021) (examining policy diffusion of disability supports in England, Scotland and Australia).

[11] See e.g. Alexis Buettgen et al, *Understanding the Intersectional Forms of Discrimination Impacting Persons with Disabilities* (Winnipeg: Canadian Centre on Disability Studies, 2018), available online at http://www.disabilitystudies.ca/assets/ccds-int-dis--151110-final-report-en-full.pdf

[12] Kim E Nielsen, "The Perils and Promises of Disability Biography" in Michael Rembick, Catherine Kudlick & Kim E Nielsen, eds, *The Oxford Handbook of Disability History* (Oxford: Oxford University Press, 2018) 21 at 21–22.

[13] *Ibid.* For a recent biography of a disabled political activist, see Ravi Malhotra & Benjamin Isitt, *Able to Lead: Disablement, Radicalism and the Political Life of E.T. Kingsley* (Vancouver: University of British Columbia Press, 2021).

how disability was a political problem that required a political solution invoking the language of liberation, rights, and equality.

One illustration of how the social model may be operationalized to illustrate the marginalization of disabled people is testimonial injustice. Scully defines testimonial injustice as "what happens when prejudice against a group results in its members being given less credibility than they would otherwise have."[14] An example might be ignorant perceptions by university or college instructors that requests for academic accommodations are unwarranted attempts to game the system or beliefs that recipients of disability benefit programs, such as the Ontario Disability Support Program, are simply fraudsters who are faking their disabilities to avoid work. A second category that Scully identifies is hermeneutical injustice. This refers to situations where the specialized knowledge that disabled people develop about their own experiences is not recognized by society due to structural prejudice.[15] While this can apply to many identity groups, an example in the disability community is the very specialized knowledge that wheelchair users acquire about how wheelchairs are funded, what the best models are, and even how one can adapt one's attire to dress fashionably while using a wheelchair. Students with disabilities are often the most knowledgeable with respect to which assistive educational technology products work best for their situation. Most people, including those committed to social justice, have no knowledge of these questions as the expertise is not regarded as valuable. In the fourth section, the salience of these concepts will be elaborated.

In the legal context, disability rights have been instantiated by the prohibition of disability discrimination in provincial and federal human rights legislation and a duty to accommodate disabled people up to the point of undue hardship, although interestingly only after disability rights advocates protested their exclusion in the 1980s.[16] Similarly, section 15 of the *Charter of Rights and Freedoms* prohibits

---

[14] Jackie Leach Scully, "Epistemic Exclusion, Injustice, and Disability" in Adam Cureton & David T Wasserman, eds, *The Oxford Handbook of Philosophy and Disability* (Oxford: University Press, 2020) 297 at 300. Scully relies on the work of Fricker to develop her theory.

[15] *Ibid* at 302.

[16] See e.g. *Ontario Human Rights Code*, RSO 1990 c H 19.

discrimination on the basis of disability.[17] More recently, several provinces including Ontario, British Columbia, Manitoba, and Nova Scotia have adopted accessibility legislation that sets out specific standards for covered organizations to meet.[18] The tools of critical disability theory allow lawyers and advocates to consider how statutes can be crafted and interpreted in a manner that empowers disabled people.

It is also important for public law students and scholars to bear in mind that law is simply one possible way of achieving some of the goals of the social model. The literature on the limitations of law as a tool for social transformation is voluminous.[19] For our purposes, it is critical to remember that victories through litigation are necessarily partial, fragile, and imperfect. They are always susceptible to subsequent reversal by the legislature, reluctant enforcement by overburdened and underfunded administrative tribunals or even simply being ignored by relevant policy actors.

Melding aspects of classical Marxism with psychoanalysis, work by the renowned Greek-French philosopher Cornelius Castoriadis points to the necessity of constructing social imaginary significations that can challenge the ideological myths of a given society.[20] Social imaginary significations are Castoriadis' attempt to construct a social theory that transcends functionalism and structuralism. Kavoulakos observes that Castoriadis regards functionalism as reducing the existence and functions of institutions to the functions they perform in society. Similarly, structuralism according to Castoriadis fails to comprehend the symbolic

---

[17] *Canadian Charter of Rights and Freedoms*, Part I of the *Constitution Act, 1982*, being Schedule B to the *Canada Act 1982* (U.K.), 1982, c 11, s 15.

[18] See e.g. Accessibility for Ontarians with Disabilities Act, SO 2005 (AODA). While many provinces have such legislation, they typically have little to no enforcement mechanisms. For a critique of the AODA in the education context, see Michelle Flaherty & Alain Roussy, "A Failed Game Changer: Post-Secondary Education and the *Accessibility for Ontarians with Disabilities Act*" (2014) 24:1 Education LJ 1 at 1–23.

[19] See e.g. Byron Sheldrick, *Perils and Possibilities: Social Activism and the Law* (Halifax: Fernwood, 2004); Orly Lobel, "The Paradox of Extralegal Activism: Critical Legal Consciousness and Transformative Politics" (2007) 120 Harv L Rev 937.

[20] Castoriadis, *Imaginary, supra* note 5. For a scholarly overview of Castoriadis' framework see generally Suzi Adams, *Castoriadis' Ontology: Being and Creation* (New York: Fordham University Press, 2011). Castoriadis, a genuine polymath who was a professional economist, philosopher and psychoanalyst, is perhaps best noted as one of the leading members of the legendary Socialisme ou Barbarie group in France that anticipated many of the upheavals that rocked French public life after the May 1968 General Strike.

elements of society by reducing the world on the basis of a binary logic of oppositions.[21] This opens the door to recognizing the creative nature of symbolic systems. Social imaginary significations help to regulate social relations in a given polity and pose big philosophical questions, such as what is the main underlying purpose of a society?[22]

Perhaps one of the most common and pernicious social imaginary significations in Western capitalist societies is the market, the notion that people ought to be valued by their contribution to producing surplus value in capitalist society. Disabled people are inevitably seen as disposable burdens in such a framework and this trend has only accelerated as neoliberalism dominates contemporary policy debates and is a configuration in the very makeup of institutional structures including post-secondary institutions. I suggest Castoriadis' work can also be used to construct new social imaginary significations about disabled life which value individuals for their inherent talents and contributions, rather than their value in market terms.[23] Similarly, higher education, a theme of this chapter, is increasingly constructed as a tool to produce skilled employees with defined and marketable credentials, rather than producing knowledge for its own sake. A Castoriadan vision can and does work in tandem with carefully crafted litigation strategies. Advocates for social justice do not have to choose between law or politics. We can do both. I illustrate the importance of such an approach in the fourth section of this chapter but first provide an account of the case, an illustration of discrimination in higher education, under discussion in the third section.

Longueépée v University of Waterloo

Roch Longueépée applied for admission to the Faculty of Arts program at the University of Waterloo in July 2013. He had obtained his

---

[21] Konstantinos Kavoulakos, "Cornelius Castoriadis on Social Imaginary and Truth" (2006) 12 *Ariadne* 201 at 202–203.

[22] *Ibid* at 203.

[23] See Castoriadis, *Imaginary, supra* note 5 at 139-46. I develop these ideas at greater length in Ravi Malhotra, "The Legal Politics of Marta Russell: A Castoriadan Reading" in Ravi Malhotra, ed, *Disability Politics in a Global Economy: Essays in Honour of Marta Russell* (London, U.K.: Routledge, 2016) 3 at 3–23.

GED assessment, a high school equivalency, in 1999 and later that year enrolled as a student at Dalhousie University but dropped out after a year due to poor grades. Longueépée was a survivor of institutional child abuse and had experienced physical, psychological, and sexual trauma. He had a moderate traumatic brain injury and experienced post-traumatic stress disorder (PTSD). However, he was unaware that he had these conditions during his time at Dalhousie and received no accommodations during his studies.[24] He chose to apply to Waterloo because of its proximity to family and social and medical support networks. At the time of his application, he informed the Registrar's office of his traumatic brain injury and how his impairment had impacted his grades during his previous studies. He also submitted records of his volunteer work and references. Longueépée was told that the class was full. However, the Registrar's office nevertheless collected his grades and medical documentation to determine his eligibility.[25] After reviewing his application, the Admissions Committee determined that his grades were too poor, falling well below Waterloo's 65 percent cutoff, and consequently recommended that he apply elsewhere.[26]

In the fall of 2013, Longueépée filed a human rights complaint with the Human Rights Tribunal of Ontario (HRTO) alleging that Waterloo discriminated against him on the basis of disability in violation of the *Human Rights Code*. He argued that the Admissions Committee's 65 percent standard for admission was discriminatory as it did not take into account the fact that his previous academic performance reflected work he completed with no academic accommodations. Furthermore, he argued that Waterloo had failed to consult the university's Accessibility Services and failed to consider his potential to study part-time.[27] The HRTO completely rejected Longueépée's arguments. It noted that the duty to accommodate persons with disabilities contained both procedural and substantive components. It held that Waterloo accommodated him by considering his application outside the regular process because of his extenuating circumstances. The

---

[24] *Longueépée v University of Waterloo*, 2019 ONSC 5465 at paras 7–8 (CanLII)

[25] *Ibid* at paras 8–10.

[26] *Longueépée v University of Waterloo*, 2017 HRTO 575 at para 49. Athabasca, Ryerson Continuing Education and Guelph Open Learning were suggested as appropriate choices.

[27] *Ibid* at para 40.

HRTO held that Waterloo could not be expected to deem Longueépée a successful candidate simply because another university had failed to accommodate his disabilities 13 years earlier.[28] It further held that there was no evidence that the involvement of Accessibility Services in the admission process would have changed the committee's decision. In the end, the HRTO concluded that Waterloo was entitled to rely on Longueépée's past academic performance.[29] As the learned Vice Chair Jennifer Scott expressed it, "[t]he difficulty is that in an academic setting, the ability to succeed is measured by grades: there is no other measure to evaluate success." [30]

On reconsideration, Vice Chair Scott upheld her earlier decision. She held that it was simply not possible for one university to assess the accommodations provided by another university by consulting accessibility services in the context of an admissions application.[31] The decision is a striking example of a social imaginary signification, academic standards, having such weight in the mind of the adjudicator that adaptation is simply inconceivable. To fully challenge this thinking requires, as Castoriadis would argue, for a social imaginary signification that reimagines the purpose of universities as an institution for more than credentialing students for the workplace. It would entail rethinking why we require educated citizens and why that is important for a democratic polity. It requires rethinking the very purpose of post-secondary institutions as a prerequisite for fostering democratic citizenship to assist members of society to engage in self-improvement and acquiring knowledge to make a better world.

The Divisional Court quashed the HRTO's decision and reconsideration decisions. Justice Mew for the Court held that the question of admission must be remitted back to the Admissions Committee to freshly evaluate the case.[32] The Divisional Court set out the Supreme Court of Canada's three-part test from *Grismer* to demonstrate that a *bona fide* occupational requirement, such as Waterloo's admissions cutoff standard, complied with human rights jurisprudence. First, the responding party must demonstrate that it adopted the standard for a purpose or goal that is rationally connected to the function being

---

[28] *Ibid* at para 42, 49.

[29] *Ibid* at paras 44–49.

[30] *Ibid* at para 51.

[31] *Longueépéee v University of Waterloo*, 2017 HRTO 1698.

[32] *Longueépée, supra* note 24 at para 63.

performed. Second, it must demonstrate that it adopted the standard in good faith, in the belief that it is necessary for the fulfillment of the purpose of the goal. Third, the standard is reasonably necessary to accomplish its purpose or goal, as the respondent cannot accommodate individuals with the characteristics of the applicant without incurring undue hardship.[33] The Court found that while the first two factors were met, Waterloo failed to meet the third branch of the test. The Court found that Waterloo acknowledged that the earlier marks earned by Longueépée at Dalhousie were tainted by discrimination and yet it provided no mechanism to assess his competency apart from these poor grades. It also did not claim that to accommodate the applicant would constitute undue hardship and presented no evidence on this defence.[34] Consequently, the Court quashed the decision of the HRTO. In applying the *Grismer* test in such a robust manner, the Court was open to new ways of thinking about what matters in educational achievement. It embodied an openness to applying the creativity that Castoriadis argued was so important in crafting and proposing new social imaginary significations to develop new legal principles.

On appeal to the Court of Appeal, the majority of the Court of Appeal, in a decision by Justice van Rensburg, substantially upheld the decision of the Divisional Court and dismissed Waterloo's appeal. Justice van Rensburg concluded that the Vice Chair had failed to properly analyze the third branch of the *Grismer* test. The majority concluded that Waterloo could not simultaneously disregard other criteria of assessment beyond grading while accepting the applicant's Dalhousie grades which it knew were obtained without appropriate accommodations for his disability.[35] As well, the majority concluded that the Vice Chair implicitly decided that Waterloo would experience undue hardship if it had to modify its admission policy to accommodate individuals with brain injuries who had a record of unaccommodated grades. This was not appropriate because Waterloo failed to make an undue hardship argument before the Tribunal and did not marshal any evidence as to the impact of altering its admission

---

[33] *British Columbia (Superintendent of Motor Vehicles) v British Columbia (Council of Human Rights)*, 1999 CanLII 646 (SCC) at para 20 [*Grismer*].

[34] *Longueépée, supra* note 24 at paras 56–58.

[35] *Longueépée v University of Waterloo*, 2020 ONCA 830 at para 84.

process.[36] Consequently, the decision of the Divisional Court was upheld. However, the Court of Appeal held that the decision should be remitted to the HRTO rather than Waterloo's Admissions Committee because in light of the Supreme Court of Canada's decision in *Canada (Minister of Citizenship and Immigration) v Vavilov*,[37] it was better to allow the HRTO to craft an appropriate remedy.[38] In a short concurrence, Justice Lauwers agreed with the reasons of Justice van Rensburg in the case at bar but interestingly chose to write separately in order to state his concern that university autonomy and academic freedom was a strong normative value that warranted protection.[39]

Critical Disability Theory in Action

What would a critical disability theory analysis of the *Longueépée* matter look like? At first glance, the decision seems like a resounding victory for inclusion and equality for disabled people. The decision incrementally expands the opportunities for applicants with disabilities seeking enrolment in post-secondary institutions to challenge rigid and inflexible admission policies. This is likely welcome news for many students with learning disabilities and brain injuries, particularly mature students who may have in years past completed some post-secondary education without appropriate or indeed any accommodations in place. Indeed, it likely will be relevant for students with a variety of impairments, including blind and deaf students who completed their studies when appropriate assistive technology was less widely available or accepted and when some disabled students may have attended segregated institutions. As post-secondary institutions are frequently large impersonal bureaucracies, the decision is a promising first step, although at this time of writing, the HRTO has yet to release a decision in light of the Ontario Court of Appeal's reasons.

---

[36] *Ibid* at paras 85–86.
[37] 2019 SCC 65. In the interests of space, I have omitted commentary of the Court of Appeal's analysis of questions of the appropriate standard of review. However, nothing significant turns on that analysis.
[38] *Longueépée, supra* note 35 at paras 89–94.
[39] *Ibid* at paras 97–106.

However, it seems likely that the specific facts and the institutional processes at play in the case drove the outcome. Waterloo undertook a rather unusual litigation strategy and did not call any evidence with respect to undue hardship. Had it done so, it is not clear that the Court of Appeal would have reached the same decision. Indeed, all decision-makers were clear that they intend to accord significant deference to internal university decisions in a typical case in the future and expect they will by and large be insulated from judicial review. This is particularly apparent in the concurrence by Justice Lauwers. That suggests that Scully's notion of testimonial and hermeneutical injustice is likely relevant.[40] Many faculty perceive disability accommodations in academia as infringements on academic integrity, a canonical example of testimonial injustice and an illustration of how public law jurisprudence is clarified through critical disability theory.[41] Furthermore, people with brain injuries are the experts regarding the best strategies for them to learn and retain information. Their insights for appropriate accommodations are invaluable in order to develop learning strategies that are effective and appropriate. This font of knowledge is unfortunately too often devalued and dismissed as the voices of pedagogical experts are privileged. Much of university education retains a cookie-cutter approach in which disabled students are expected to fit rather than universal design principles that are inclusive of the learning needs of all students.

Ultimately, critical disability theory requires that one go beyond an individualized approach of providing accommodations as an exception to a rule. While the Court of Appeal in *Longueépée* is open to a more robust admission process, it is still one contingent on the provision of extensive documentation approval by medical authorities to bypass an admission system predicated on compulsory ablebodiedness.[42] This places an enormous onus on the disabled student

---

[40] See *supra* notes 14–15 and accompanying text.

[41] See e.g. Teri Hibbs & Dianne Pothier, "Post-secondary Education and Disabled Students: Mining a Level Playing Field or Playing in a Mine Field" in Dianne Pothier & Richard F Devlin, eds, *Critical Disability Theory: Essays in Philosophy, Politics, Policy and Law* (Vancouver University of British Columbia Press, 2006) 195 at 200.

[42] *Ibid* at 195–222. See also Leyton Schnellert et al, "Enacting Equity in Higher Education Through Critical Disability Studies: A Critical Community Self-Study" (2019) 39:2 Disability Stud Q, available online at https://dsq-sds.org/article/

to acquire documentation from approved gatekeepers, assemble materials, and eloquently articulate their accommodation needs as exceptions to a standard rule. The institutional process in play reinscribes a social imaginary signification that values conformity to traditional and arbitrary admission standards. This approach is inconsistent with the principles of the duty to accommodate as set out by the Supreme Court of Canada in *Meiorin*[43] which is rooted in the idea that standards that are discriminatory are to be modified. Post-secondary education should not be crafted as a human rights-free zone of exception.

Beyond that, Castoriadis assists us in thinking about the larger purposes of post-secondary education and indeed the larger purposes of our society itself. Castoriadis asks us to think about the representations that capture our popular imagination, the social imaginary significations about who we are as a people and what are our dreams and aspirations for a better life.[44] The commodification of education is now so widespread that it often does not elicit questions or even notice from the general public. While there are without a doubt important accommodation battles to be fought for inclusion of disabled students in professional schools such as, *inter alia*, law schools, and medical schools,[45] it is imperative that one bear in mind that the case at bar concerned admission to an undergraduate program. Castoriadis helps us to understand that the Greek concept of paideia or education concerns public education to improve the citizenry as was a feature of life in Ancient Greece.[46] In other words, a

---

view/6150; Cynthia Bruce & M Lynn Aylward, "Accommodating Disability at University" (2021) 41:2 Disability Stud Q, available online at https://dsq-sds.org/article/view/6973/5942.

43 *British Columbia (Public Service Employee Relations Commission) v BCGSEU*, [1999] 3 SCR 3, 1999 CarswellBC 1907 [*Meiorin*].

44 Castoriadis, *Imaginary, supra* note 5 at 139–46.

45 The literature on disability accommodation in law schools goes as far back as M David Lepofsky, "Disabled Persons and Canadian Law Schools: The Right to the Equal Benefit of the Law School" (1991) 36(2) McGill LJ 636. For disability accommodation for medical students in the American context, see Michael McKee et al, "Medical Schools' Willingness to Accommodate Medical Students with Sensory and Physical Disabilities: Ethical Foundations of a Functional Challenge to 'Organic' Technical Standards" (2016) 18(10) AMA J Ethics 993 at 993–1002.

46 Cornelius Castoriadis, "The Greek and the Modern Political Imaginary" in Castoriadis, *World, supra* note 5, 84 at 95.

new social imaginary signification of education entails an under-standing that education is about self-improvement of a citizen to assist in making a better world. The marketization of post-secondary education has occluded this original goal of post-secondary educa-tion with constantly increasing tuition, research funding geared toward serving the needs of the market including through the priori-tization of public-private partnerships, and greatly diminished public funding.[47]

When one takes this broader perspective, accommodation issues seem to be of less salience because the very purpose of education shifts from scores on a set rubric to genuine learning for self-under-standing and reshaping the world. Given such a wide-ranging onto-logical vision, why would an applicant's high school grades be salient for her potential contribution to society as a citizen to pursue wisdom as its own end? Do minimum grade cutoffs for any student serve any valid purpose beyond neoliberal branding for a particular institu-tion? Castoriadis' legacy enables a richer understanding of critical disability theory and a richer vision of a public education that works for all students. And that is only a first step toward building what Castoriadis styles an autonomous world where people are free to fol-low their aspirations, unbound by the pressures of a market society that requires most to work long hours at modest pay, conditions that inevitably exclude disabled people from the labour market and a decent life.

Conclusion

Public law scholars and students alike need critical disability theory to help build a world of accessibility and inclusion. Recent scholar-ship has marked a shift from a focus on disability accommodation to placing disability justice at the centre. This paradigm shift reflects the embodiment of the values of universal design and transforming stan-dards so that structures and rules are inclusive of disabled people. The Ontario Court of Appeal decision in *Longueépée v University of Waterloo* marks a small step forward in university admission standards.

---

[47] Bob Rigas & Renée Kuchapski, "'Strengthening' Ontario Universities: A Neoliberal Reconstruction of Higher Education" (2016) 180 Can J Ed Adm & Pol'y 47.

Moving forward there is no need to choose between a legal approach and a political approach. We must do both: crafting effective legal strategies while remaining cognizant of the big picture goals. To that end, the creative and challenging work of Cornelius Castoriadis enriches both the day-to-day work of public law advocates and our understanding of the social model of disablement. It is incumbent on public law scholars committed to equality for disabled people to ensure that we continue to build a world of accessibility and inclusion for all.

Critical Perspectives in Canadian Tax Law

*Samuel Singer and Allison Christians**

Abstract

The purpose of this chapter is to spotlight the role of critical tax law scholarship in Canada. We argue that critical perspectives are essential to identifying inequities in Canadian tax law, from the most specific tax rules to the core structure of tax regimes. We begin by focusing on the contribution of critical perspectives in analyzing specific tax rules, using examples of tax relief for trans medical expenses and the exemption of menstruation products from taxation. We then focus on the importance of critical perspectives in the analysis of tax law regimes and show how critical legal scholars reveal the colonialism reflected in Canada's tax relationships with First Nations and with other states. We demonstrate that a core challenge for critical tax law scholars is to navigate the

* Many thanks to the editors of this volume Karen Drake, Kyle Kirkup, Anne Levesque, Jena McGill and Joshua Sealy-Harrington, and to our anonymous peer reviewers, as well as Monica Cheng, Sylvia Rich, and Vanessa MacDonnell for their comments, and to Khadija Ahmed, Gabriella Brown, Emily Halliday, and Garima Karia for their excellent research assistance. This article draws on research supported by the Social Sciences and Humanities Research Council.

disparity that arises between harmful tax policy choices that prompt reform and those which meet silence. We conclude that a major contribution of critical tax law scholarship in Canada to date has been to demonstrate that tax law cannot be exclusively delegated to technical experts but requires broad and inclusive policy attention.

Résumé

Ce chapitre vise à mettre en lumière le rôle de la recherche critique en droit fiscal au Canada. Nous soutenons que les perspectives critiques sont essentielles pour identifier les inégalités dans le droit fiscal canadien, qu'il s'agisse des règles fiscales spécifiques ou de la structure fondamentale des régimes fiscaux. Nous commençons par examiner la contribution des perspectives critiques dans l'analyse de règles fiscales spécifiques, en prenant comme exemples les allégements fiscaux pour les dépenses médicales liées à la transition de genre et l'exemption des produits menstruels de la taxe de vente. Nous nous concentrons ensuite sur l'importance des perspectives critiques dans l'analyse des régimes fiscaux, en montrant comment les expert·e·s en droit critique révèlent le colonialisme reflété dans les relations fiscales du Canada avec les Premières Nations et avec d'autres États. Nous démontrons qu'un défi central pour les chercheurs et chercheuses critiques en droit fiscal est de naviguer entre les choix de politiques fiscales néfastes qui suscitent une réforme et les personnes qui restent dans le silence. En conclusion, nous affirmons qu'une contribution majeure de la recherche critique en droit fiscal au Canada réside dans la démonstration que le droit fiscal ne peut être exclusivement délégué à des expert·e·s techniques, mais nécessite une attention politique large et inclusive.

Tax law is our government's largest socio-economic policy instrument. All taxpayers in Canada are personally impacted by decisions about who is taxed, what is taxed, and at what rate. Yet tax law is often perceived as an objective and technical field, reserved for those who specialize in economics or are good at math. Critical tax scholars reject this premise, arguing that presenting tax law as a technical discourse "den[ies] the normative content of tax law and policy" and "reproduce[s] social and economic inequalities."[1] They draw from feminist legal scholarship, critical race theory, Indigenous legal studies, queer legal studies, critical disability studies, and trans legal scholarship to explore the role of tax laws and tax systems in creating or maintaining socio-economic inequity.[2]

In this chapter, we argue that critical perspectives are essential to identifying inequities in Canadian tax law, from the most specific tax rules to the core structure of tax regimes. Using two key Canadian tax topics, we demonstrate how critical tax scholars help reveal bias and inequity in tax law.

Our first topic focuses on the contribution of critical perspectives in analyzing tax rules. We show how critical legal scholars and grassroots advocates have identified inequities in the tax treatment of two types of health expenses: tax relief for trans medical expenses and the exemption of menstruation products from sales tax. Our second topic focuses on the importance of critical perspectives in the analysis of tax law regimes. Critical legal scholars and grassroots advocates seek to identify large-scale economic injustices perpetuated by a complex tax legal order that involves sovereign nations within Canada, on the one hand, and foreign states on the other.

From a broader perspective, our study also reveals one of the core challenges for critical tax law scholarship, namely understanding and navigating the disparity that arises between harmful tax policy choices that attract public attention and prompt reform, and those that meet silence due to lack of understanding, indifference, or both. We conclude that a major contribution of critical tax law scholarship in Canada to date has been to demonstrate that tax law cannot be exclusively delegated to technical experts but requires broad and inclusive policy attention.

---

[1] Lisa Philipps, "Discursive Deficits: A Feminist Perspective on the Power of Technical Knowledge in Fiscal Law and Policy" (1996) 11:1 CJLS 141.

[2] See e.g. Anthony Infanti & Bridget Crawford, *Critical Tax Theory: An Introduction* (Cambridge, U.K.: Cambridge University Press, 2009); Kim Brooks, "Inter-Nation Equity: The Development of an Important but Underappreciated International Tax Value" in John G Head & Richard Krever, eds, *Tax Reform in the 21st Century: A Volume in Memory of Richard Musgrave* (Netherlands: Kluwer Law International, 2009) 471; Kim Brooks et al, eds, *Challenging Gender Inequality in Tax Policymaking: Comparative Perspectives*, 1st ed (London, U.K.: Hart Publishing, 2011).

Critical Study of Tax Rules

Every tax law system requires defining categories, which often entails including or excluding items from taxation or deduction. As in any other area of law, this kind of regulatory line-drawing is at its heart an ongoing dialogue between lawmakers, on the one hand, and taxpayers and their advisors on the other. The government, with ongoing feedback from interest groups and other policy observers across the political spectrum, seeks to create tax laws that achieve various socio-economic goals. At the same time, taxpayers, often aided by advisors, receive the law and engage in activities that test its resilience. Line drawing in tax emerges and evolves recursively through policymaking and implementation, iteratively reflecting changes in a host of law-making, law-implementing, and legal interpretation factors.[3] These factors include judicial interpretation, economic theory, social and cultural dynamics, and perhaps most importantly, politics.[4]

Regulatory line-drawing always poses difficult definitional choices and is therefore susceptible to broad critique across the legal discipline, and tax law is no exception. Virtually every aspect of the tax system can be characterized as an imperfect achievement of stated goals and in need of some reform or another. Tax law scholarship often aims to critique specific tax rules for being over- or under-inclusive or both, and often proposes doctrinal reforms. Critical tax law scholarship incorporates and adds to these common critiques by demonstrating how purportedly neutral tax regimes perpetuate inequities in practice.

A foundational aspect of line-drawing in income tax systems involves distinguishing between the kinds of outlays that ought to be deductible in computing taxable income and those that ought not to be, usually because they are personal consumption choices. As a practical matter, the line between these categories requires vigilance to protect the tax base, but it also serves a normative function in that

---

[3] See e.g. Terence C Halliday & Bruce G Carruthers, "The Recursivity of Law: Global Norm Making and National Lawmaking in the Globalization of Corporate Insolvency Regimes" (2007) 112:4 Am J Soc 1135.

[4] For a discussion of the key actors, norms, and processes involved in the recursive cycle of tax law making in the context of a global economy, see Allison Christians, "Historic, Comparative and Evolutionary Analysis of Tax Systems" in Misabel de Abreu Machado Derzi, ed, *Separation of Powers and Tax System Effectiveness* (Brazil: Del Ray Press, 2010) 287.

it ensures a justifiable allocation of tax obligations among those with greater and lesser ability to pay. The determination of eligibility for tax deductions has accordingly been a major theme for critical tax scholarship over many decades, in Canada and around the world.[5]

Challenges in line-drawing commonly arise for such items as work attire, skills training and certification, work-related travel and entertainment, childcare expenses, and health expenses. These categories have given rise to attention by critical legal scholars,[6] with childcare expenses a popular focus owing to its conventional connection to the perpetuation of unequal gender relations. For example, the Supreme Court of Canada decision in *Symes v Canada*[7] prompted critical tax law scholars to investigate the denial of full deductibility for childcare costs as business expenses as a systemic curtailment of work and wealth opportunities along gender, race, and class lines.[8] Health expenses provide a particularly vivid example of the difficult policy choices involved in the line between deductible and non-deductible expenses and taxable vs. non-taxable income, as discussed below.

Tax Relief for Medical Expenses

In the Canadian income tax system, taxpayers may obtain tax relief for eligible medical expenses, on the theory that such expenses diminish a taxpayer's ability to pay.[9] Similar tax relief is available in

---

[5] See e.g. Brooks et al, *supra* note 2.

[6] Claire F L Young, "(In)Visible Inequalities: Women, Tax and Poverty" (1995) 27:1 Ottawa L Rev 99; Claire F L Young, "It's All in the Family- Child Support, Tax, and *Thibaudeau*" (1995) 6:4 Const Forum Const 107; Kathleen A Lahey, "Women, Substantive Equality, and Fiscal Policy: Gender-Based Analysis of Taxes, Benefits, and Budgets" (2010) 22:1 CJWL 27; Samuel Singer, "Marginalizing Trans Medical Expenses: Line-Drawing Exercises in Tax" (2013) 31:2 Windsor YB Access Just 209; Audrey Macklin, "*Symes v MNR*: Where Sex Meets Class" (1992) 5:2 CJWL 498; Faye L Woodman, "Women and Children in the Economy: Reflections from the Income Tax System" (1998) 47 UNBLJ 311; Faye L Woodman, "A Child Care Expenses Deduction, Tax Reform and the *Charter*: Some Modest Proposals" (1990) 8:2 Can J Fam L 371.

[7] [1993] 4 SCR 695, 110 DLR (4th) 470.

[8] Faye Woodman, "The *Charter* and the Taxation of Women" (1990) 22:3 Ottawa L Rev 625; Woodman, "A Child Care Expenses Deduction," *supra* note 6; Macklin, *supra* note 6; Claire F L Young, "Child Care - A Taxing Issue?" (1994) 39 McGill LJ 539; Lahey, *supra* note 6.

[9] *Income Tax Act*, RSC 1985, c 1 (5th Supp), s 118(2); for commentary see David G Duff, "Disability and the Income Tax" (2000) 45:4 McGill LJ 79 at 814.

the United States and many other countries.[10] Canada has a public health care system, so the potential expenses at stake are those not covered by the public health system, or by supplemental private health insurance, if available. When governments provide tax relief for medical expenses, they are choosing to subsidize health care beyond that which the public system provides, within limitations. The Canadian approach is to explicitly list relief-eligible medical expenses by type, creating a narrow regulatory framework.[11]

Critical tax law scholars seek to understand the reasons why some medical expenses are eligible for tax relief, and some are left out, and whether these policy decisions were influenced by budgetary constraints, lobbying, or discriminatory reasons. Both the United States and Canada exclude cosmetic medical expenses from tax relief, for example. Trans medical expenses risk being mischaracterized as cosmetic and not medical due to a decision-makers' bias. In the United States, in *O'Donnabhain v Commissioner*, a trans woman appealed the IRS's decision to deny tax relief for her trans medical expenses on the basis that they were cosmetic.[12] The U.S. Tax Court found that her sex reassignment surgery and hormone expenses qualified, but not her breast augmentation. A body of critical tax scholarship critically analyzes the IRS's position and the U.S. Tax Court decision.[13]

---

[10] See e.g. *Internal Revenue Code*, IRC § 213; Revenue Irish Tax and Customs, "Health Expenses", (15 December 2021) online: <https://www.revenue.ie/en/personal-tax-credits-reliefs-and-exemptions/health-and-age/health-expenses/index.aspx>; NALOG.NL, "Reimbursement of Treatment Costs", (27 November 2019) online: <https://www.nalog.nl/en/baza-znanij/chastnym-licam/vozmeshhenie-rasxodov-na-lechenie/>.

[11] See Canada Revenue Agency, "Lines 33099 and 33199 – Eligible medical expenses you can claim on your tax return", online: <https://www.canada.ca/en/revenue-agency/services/tax/individuals/topics/about-your-tax-return/tax-return/completing-a-tax-return/deductions-credits-expenses/lines-33099-33199-eligible-medical-expenses-you-claim-on-your-tax-return.html#wb-auto-4>.

[12] *O'Donnabhain v Commissioner*, 134 TC no 4 (2010).

[13] See e.g. Max V Camp, "*O'Donnabhain v Commissioner*: Treatment Costs for Gender Identity Disorder Are Tax-Deductible Medical Expenses" (2011) 20 Law & Sexuality 133; Anthony C Infanti, "Dissecting *O'Donnabhain*" (2010) 126 Tax Notes 1403; Alesdair H Ittelson, "Trapped in the Wrong Phraseology: *O'Donnabhain v Commissioner* - Consequences for Federal Tax Policy and the Transgender Community" (2011) 26:2 Berkeley J Gender L & Just 356; Tamar E Lusztig, "Deducting the Cost of Sex Reassignment Surgery: How *O'Donnabhain v Commissioner* Can Help Us Make Sense of the Medical Expense Deduction" (2011) 3:1 Colum J Tax L 86; Singer, "Marginalizing Trans Medical Expenses", *supra* note 6.

Bias can influence the line-drawing exercises of the decision-makers charged with deciding the tax claims of marginalized people. Samuel Singer writes about how trans medical expenses have been subject to more rigid requirements than other medical expenses under Canadian tax law, because decision-makers are influenced by social stigma.[14] Similarly, Tamara Larre writes, in the context of tax case law about the disability tax credit, that "judges' attitudes, perceptions, and beliefs concerning disability are often not in line with those expressed in contemporary disability literature" and "reflected stereotypical views of persons with disabilities."[15]

Taxation of Menstruation Products

Looking beyond the income tax, a corollary to the medical expense categorization exercise can be seen in the "pink tax" movement.[16] This is a social movement led not by tax experts or scholars, but by non-specialists. The Pink Tax activists devised the moniker to refer to "the practice of charging women more than men for the same products and services."[17] The taxation of menstrual products (such as under a goods and services tax), which is assumed to raise the price on such products to consumers, has been criticized as a more literal form of pink taxation. For example, in the American context, Brenda J. Crawford and Emily Gold Waldman argue that sales taxes on menstruation products amount to unconstitutional gender discrimination, since condoms and medications for erectile dysfunction are not taxed.[18] A grassroots movement against the "tampon tax" led to the Canadian government's removal of Canada's federal goods and services tax (GST) on menstruation products in 2015.[19]

The push for an exemption on the taxation of menstruation products is not universally endorsed by critical tax law scholars. Rita

---

[14] Singer, "Marginalizing Trans Medical Expenses", *supra* note 6.

[15] Tamara Larre, "The Disability Tax Credit: Exploring Attitudes, Perceptions, and Beliefs about Disability" (2018) 29 J L & Soc Pol'y 92.

[16] Bridget J Crawford, "Pink Tax and Other Tropes" (2022) 34:1 Yale J L & Feminism 88.

[17] Canadian Labour Institute for Social and Economic Fairness, "Pink Tax: Women Pay High Price Just for Being Female", (6 October 2018), online: <http://www.canadianlabourinstitute.org/story/pink-tax>.

[18] Bridget J Crawford, & Emily Gold Waldman, "The Unconstitutional Tampon Tax" (2019) 53:1 U Rich L Rev 339.

[19] Haydn Watters, "Tampon Tax will end July 1", *CBC News* (28 May 2015), online: <https://www.cbc.ca/news/politics/tampon-tax-will-end-july-1-1.3091533>.

de la Feria declares the tax exemption of menstruation products "bad policy" because the savings are not passed on to consumers.[20] Miranda Stewart calls the focus on the exemption of menstruation products a "distraction" and urges a broader perspective on the tax system and its role in funding public services that benefit women.[21] There are also alternative policy choices outside of the tax realm, such as treating menstruation products as public goods. In 2019, British Columbia implemented a program to provide menstruation products without cost to students in the province's public schools.[22] Other provincial governments have followed this strategy and made broader commitments to address "period poverty."[23]

By illuminating the disparate impacts of seemingly objective tax rules and bringing alternative policy solutions to the foreground, critical tax law scholars open up public debate about the hidden costs and benefits of otherwise obscure tax policy choices. Critical tax law studies help show how exclusion is reflected and reinforced in the application of technical tax provisions, such as those providing tax relief for medical expenses and those providing sales tax exemption for certain personal products and not others. Sometimes, critical tax law scholarship seeks to illuminate ways to address such inequity issues in the tax law alone, such as by proposing changes to the design or administration of a tax provision—for example, to explicitly provide for tax relief for trans medical expenses, or to remove tax on menstruation products. Other times, critical tax law scholars seek to draw attention to

---

[20] Rita de la Feria, "Why We Should All Worry About the Abolition of the Tampon Tax", *Oxford University Centre for Business Taxation* (8 March 2021) online: <https://oxfordtax.sbs.ox.ac.uk/article/tampon-tax> (stating that studies overwhelmingly show that sales tax exemptions are not passed on to consumers as price reductions, and that even a modest price reduction would work to the benefit of richer consumers as much or more than poorer ones, since high income households consume more than lower income households, even in the case of essential items).

[21] Miranda Stewart quoted in Jessica Irvine, "Why you should keep paying the tampon tax", *The Sydney Morning Herald* (18 June 2018), online: <https://www.smh.com.au/politics/federal/why-you-should-keep-paying-the-tampon-tax-20180618-p4zm81.html>.

[22] Canadian Press, "B.C. spending $750K to expand access to free menstrual products", *CBC News* (27 May 2022), online: <https://www.cbc.ca/news/canada/british-columbia/free-menstrual-products-in-bc-1.6468643>.

[23] *Ibid.*

public policy choices outside of the tax law that could be used to address inequality issues, such as publicly funded access to menstruation products.

Whether examining the practical implications of a specific tax rule or the tax system as a whole, one of the challenges for critical tax law scholars is that it is seemingly easy for policymakers to hide socially harmful policy choices within highly complex and technical rule-based regulatory regimes, and then it is difficult for scholars to tell the hidden stories of inequity in a way that the public can grasp, let alone object to and seek change. Scholars typically face difficulty in convincing the public to invest their time and effort in understanding the tax law system even at a superficial level. The success of the pink tax movement is exemplary in this regard: because the inequity surrounding essential products is inherently personal to so many individuals, social movements successfully compelled lawmakers to redefine the relevant categories.

Critical Study of Tax Regimes

The barriers to understanding and effectively conveying inequity are higher when it is not one single tax rule but the interaction of abstract principles and technical rules across legal regimes that produces the grounds where inequity is sown. The way that national tax systems interact with each other should be subject to the same critical legal analysis as any domestic tax policy choice. Critical perspectives are key to analyzing modern tax regimes, as they demonstrate how Canadian tax regimes continue to reflect the racialized and colonial legacies of Canada's tax relationships with other nations, including both First Nations and foreign states.

Tax Relationships with Indigenous People

Critical tax law scholarship about Indigenous tax issues examines the inequities perpetuated by limited access to the tax exemption under the *Indian Act*,[24] the depiction of Indigenous people's tax relationship with Canada in the public realm, and the impact of these depictions on tax law reforms.

---

[24] *Indian Act*, RSC 1985, c I-5, s 87.

Canada's federal *Indian Act* contains a tax exemption for Indigenous people with status as "Indians" under that legislation, following historical colonial traditions that continue to feature offensive and often incoherent designations, categorizations, assumptions, and ambiguities.[25] Critical tax scholars take up the call of Indigenous scholars and advocates to debunk colonial and racist myths about the extent to which Indigenous people pay taxes in Canada.[26] For example, Cheyenne Neszo examined the negative and harmful stereotypes that are furthered by public discourse that greatly exaggerates the reach of income tax exemptions.[27] Martha O'Brien examined the tax treatment of investment income in the context of the exemption under the *Indian Act* and found an "apparent prejudice in the cases against independent business and investment activity sources of income" with the courts requiring that these activities "benefit the reserve community rather than the individual Indian, and that they preserve traditional Indian culture," which she described as "patronizing and discriminatory."[28]

Similarly, Bradley Bryan examined the purpose of federal exemptions for specified "public bodies," which exempt institutions that are "performing a function of government" from federal income taxes.[29] Bryan showed that even though the Canada Revenue Agency first started applying the public exemption to First Nations governments in the early 1980s, persistent legal ambiguities surrounding the

---

[25] *Ibid.* The exemption is reflected in the *Income Tax Act* at s 81(1)(a) ("There shall not be included in computing the income of a taxpayer for a taxation year [...] an amount that is declared to be exempt from income tax by any other enactment of Parliament, other than an amount received or receivable by an individual that is exempt by virtue of a provision contained in a tax convention or agreement with another country that has the force of law in Canada").

[26] See e.g. Chelsea Vowel, "Indigenous Writes: A Guide to First Nations, Métis, & Inuit Issues in Canada" (Winnipeg: Highwater Press, 2016); Wab Kinew, "STROMBO: SOAP BOX: Wab Kinew", *George Stroumboulopoulos Tonight on CBC* (January 10, 2012), online (video): <https://youtu.be/GlkuRCXdu5A>.

[27] Cheyenne Neszo, "The Section 87 Tax Exemption as a Tax Expenditure" (2020) 4:1 Lakehead LJ 50.

[28] Martha O'Brien, "Income Tax, Investment Income, and the *Indian Act*: Getting Back on Track" (2002) 50:5 Can Tax J 1570 at 1588.

[29] Bradley Bryan, "Indigenous Peoples, Legal Bodies, and Personhood: Navigating the 'Public Body' Exemption with Private Law Hybrid Entities" (2020) 6 Can J Comp & Contemp L 58.

criteria hampered many First Nations governments from accessing these exemptions in practice.

Indigenous tax issues are "one of the frontlines in Indigenous legal battles asserting treaty and sovereignty rights."[30] Critical tax scholarship about Indigenous tax issues helps demonstrate that Canada's relationship with First Nations continues to be negotiated through tax law. Though not always viewed in parallel, Canada's fiscal relationships with other states are similarly subject to continuous negotiation, and they similarly reflect colonial assumptions and divisions.

Tax Relationships With Foreign States

Perhaps the best-developed area of study about international tax law involves the critical analysis of income tax treaties, which are agreements among nations regarding the sharing of taxing powers and tax-relevant information between them.[31] Treaty-making is a main subject of critical legal attention because colonized nations, especially those in Sub-Saharan Africa, were historically excluded—and in many cases continue to be excluded—from the treaty networks of wealthy nations, as these nations prioritized fiscal coordination among themselves.[32] To this exclusion is added the historical exclusion of these same nations from the inter-governmental institutions

---

[30] Samuel Singer and Monica Cheng, "Directors' Liability in Canadian Tax Law: Critically Analyzing the Due Diligence Standard" (2022) 55:3 UBC L Rev 713.

[31] Nations started entering into income tax treaties at the beginning of the 20th century, after the geo-politically dominant countries began to view uncoordinated income taxation as a barrier to economic prosperity. The key experts of the day devised bilateral treaty templates (referred to as "Model Conventions") to which nations variously adhered according to their unique bargaining positions. See e.g. Sunita Jogarajan, *Double Taxation and the League of Nations* (Cambridge, U.K.: Cambridge University Press, 2018).

[32] Karen B Brown, "Missing Africa: Should U.S. International Tax Rules Accommodate Investments in Developing Countries" (2021-22) 23:1 U Pa J Intl L 45; Miranda Stewart, "Global Trajectories of Tax Reform: The Discourse of Tax Reform in Developing and Transition Countries" (2003) 44:1 Harv Intl LJ 139; Allison Christians, "Tax Treaties for Investment and Aid to Sub-Saharan Africa" in Karl P Sauvant & Lisa E Sachs, eds, *The Effect of Treaties on Foreign Direct Investment: Bilateral Investment Treaties, Double Taxation Treaties, and Investment Flows* (London, U.K.: Oxford University Press, 2009); Allison Christians, "Global Trends and Constraints on Tax Policy in the Least Developed Countries" (2009) 40 UBC L Rev 2; Karen B Brown, "Tax Incentives in Sub-Saharan Africa" (2021) 48:4 Pepp L Rev 995.

set up to facilitate cross-border coordination, a factor that continues to impact international tax relations to the present.[33]

The critical tax scholarship in this area focuses on fairness among nations, often referred to as inter-nation equity following the work of U.S. economists Peggy and Richard Musgrave, which established how seemingly neutral source and residence-based taxing powers produce disparate wealth-sharing among nations when capital flows are unequal.[34] For example, several scholars have shown that reciprocal treaty terms that may appear neutral have had disparate impacts for low-income, colonized, and formerly colonized nations.[35] Others have focused on the gendered, racialized, and imperialist

---

[33] See Irma Johanna Mosquera Valderrama, "Legitimacy and the Making of International Tax Law: The Challenges of Multilateralism" (2015) 7:3 World Tax J 343; Ricardo Garcia Antón, "The 21st Century Multilateralism in International Taxation: The Emperor's New Clothes?" (2016) 8:2 World Tax J 147; Peter Essers, "International Tax Justice Between Machiavelli and Habermas" in Bruno Peeters, Hans Gribnau & Joe Badisco, eds, *Building Trust in Taxation* (Cambridge, U.K.: Cambridge Univ Press, 2017) 235; Sissie Fung, "The Questionable Legitimacy of the OECD/G20 BEPS Project" (2017) 10:2 Erasmus L Rev 76; Allison Christians & Laurens van Apeldoorn, "The OECD Inclusive Framework" (2018) 72:4/5 Bull Intl Tax'n 1; Irma Johanna Mosquera Valderrama, "Output Legitimacy Deficits and the Inclusive Framework of the OECD/G20 Base Erosion and Profit Shifting Initiative" (2019) 72:3 Bull Intl Tax'n 160; Tarcísio Diniz Magalhães, "The OECD Multilateral instrument: Challenge or Opportunity of Multilateralism" in Joanna Wheeler, ed, *The Aftermath of BEPS* (Amsterdam, The Netherlands: IBFD, 2020) 161; Linda Brosens & Jasper Bossuyt, "Legitimacy in International Tax Law-Making: Can the OECD Remain the Guardian of Open Tax Norms?" (2020) 12:2 World Tax J 313; Shu-Yi Oei, "World Tax Policy in the World Tax Policy? An Event History Analysis of OECD/ G20 BEPS Inclusive Framework Membership" (2022) 47 Yale J Intl L 199; Yariv Brauner, "Serenity Now! The (Not So) Inclusive Framework and the Multilateral Instrument" (2022) 25:2 Fla Tax Rev 489.

[34] Peggy B Musgrave & Richard A Musgrave, "Inter-Nation Equity" in Richard M Bird & John G Head eds, *Modern Fiscal Issues: Essays in Honour of Carl S Shoup* (Toronto: Univ of Toronto Press, 1972) 63 at 72–73; Brooks, "Inter-Nation Equity", *supra* note 2; Anthony C Infanti, "Internation Equity and Human Development" in Yariv Brauner & Miranda Steward eds, *Tax, Law and Development* (Boston, MA: Edward Elgar, 2013) 209; Nancy H Kaufman, "Fairness and the Taxation of International Income" (1988) 29:2 Law & Pol'y Intl Bus 145; Ivan Ozai, "Inter-Nation Equity Revisited" (2020) 12:1 Colum J Tax L 58; Adam H. Rosenzweig, "International Vertical Equity" (2021) 52:2 Loy U Chi LJ 471.

[35] Tsilly Dagan, "The Tax Treaties Myth" (2000) 32 NYUJ Intl L & Pol 939; Lyne Latulippe, "The Expansion of the Bilateral Tax Treaty Network in the 1990s: The OECD's Role in International Tax Coordination" (2012) 27:4 Aust Tax Forum 851; Kim Brooks, "The

aspects of treaty terms,[36] information exchange standards,[37] and intergovernmental tax institutions and administrative processes.[38]

Critical legal scholarship continues to evolve in this area as nations continue to seek multilateral agreement regarding minimum taxes on multinational groups. These efforts are prompting increased

Troubling Role of Tax Treaties" in Geerten MM Michielse & Victor Thuronyi, eds, *Tax Design Issues Worldwide* (The Netherlands: Kluwer Law International, 2015) 159.

[36] Kim Brooks, "Global Distributive Justice: The Potential for a Feminist Analysis of International Tax Revenue Allocation" (2009) 21:2 CJWL 267; Sérgio André Rocha, "International Fiscal Imperialism and the 'Principle' of the Permanent Establishment" (2014) 68:2 Bull Intl Tax'n 83; Martin Hearson, "When Do Developing Countries Negotiate Away Their Corporate Tax Base?" (2018) 30:2 J Intl Dev 233; Oladiwura Ayeyemi Eyitayo-Oyesode, "Source-Based Taxing Rights from the OECD to the UN Model Conventions: Unraveling Efforts and an Argument for Reform" (2020) 13:1 L & Dev Rev 193; Martin Hearson, *Imposing Standards: The North-South Dimension of Global Tax Politics* (New York: Cornell University Press, 2021).

[37] Karen B Brown, "Harmful Tax Competition: The OECD View" (1999) 32:2 Geo Wash J Intl L & Econ 311; Alexander Townsend Jr, "Global Schoolyard Bully: The Organisation for Economic Co-Operation and Development's Coercive Efforts to Control Tax Competition" (2001) 25 Fordham Intl LJ 215; Vaughn E James, "21st Century Pirates of the Caribbean: How the Organization for Economic Cooperation and Development Robbed Fourteen CARICOM Countries of Their Tax and Economic Sovereignty" (2002) 34:1 U Miami Inter-Am L Rev 1; Sunita Jogarajan & Miranda Stewart, "Harmful Tax Competition: Defeat or Victory?" (2007) 22:1 Austr Tax Forum 3; Craig M Boise & Andrew P Morriss, "Change, Dependency, and Regime Plasticity in Offshore Financial Intermediation: The Saga of the Netherlands Antilles" (2009) 45:2 Tex Intl LJ 377; Allison Christians, "Sovereignty, Taxation and Social Contract" (2009) 18:1 Minn J Intl L 99; Diane Ring, "Democracy, Sovereignty and Tax Competition: The Role of Tax Sovereignty in Shaping Tax Cooperation" (2009) 9:1 Fla Tax Rev 555; Adam H Rosenzweig, "Why Are There Tax Havens?" (2010) 52:3 Wm & Mary L Rev 923; Andrew P Morriss & Lotta Moberg, "Cartelizing Taxes: Understanding the OECD's Campaign against Harmful Tax Competition" (2012) 4:1 Colum J Tax L 1; Lukas Hakelberg, *The Hypocritical Hegemon: How the United States Shapes Global Rules against Tax Evasion and Avoidance* (New York: Cornell University Press, 2020); Steven A Dean & Attiya Waris, "Ten Truths about Tax Havens: Inclusion and the 'Liberia' Problem" (2021) 70:7 Emory LJ 1657.

[38] Allison Christians, "How Nations Share" (2012) 87:4 Ind LJ 1407; Allison Christians, "BEPS and the New International Tax Order" (2016) 6 BYU L Rev 1603; Sérgio André Rocha, "The Other Side of BEPS: 'Imperial Taxation' and 'International Tax Imperialism'" in Sérgio André Rocha & Allison Christians, eds, *Tax Sovereignty in the BEPS Era* (The Netherlands: Kluwer Law International, 2017) 179; Tarcísio Diniz Magalhães, "What is Really Wrong With Global Tax Governance and How to Properly Fix It" (2018) 10:4 World Tax J 499; Ivan Ozai, "Institutional and Structural Legitimacy Deficits in the International Tax Regime" (2020) 12:1 World Tax J 53.

critical legal focus on both the standards and the standard-setters of international taxation.[39]

Conclusion

Tax law shapes socio-economic relationships, whether between individuals or entities or across societies. The content and impact of tax rules and tax regimes should therefore be central in scholarship and public discourse surrounding the role law plays in shaping our lives. Feminist legal scholarship, critical race theory, Indigenous legal studies, queer legal studies, critical disability studies, and trans legal scholarship have made the case for the central role of critical perspectives in legal analysis. Critical perspectives are essential to informing public debate by revealing and confronting the disparate and harmful impacts of tax rules and regimes.

Critical legal analysis of tax rules demonstrates how line-drawing can reflect and maintain inequities within societies, and how tax policy is central in public policy debates about the role of the state. Critical legal analysis of tax law regimes demonstrates how governments' tax relationships with First Nations and other states reflect and maintain inequities across societies. These two core areas of critical tax studies reveal that tax policy choices sometimes inspire public attention and legal reform, as in the case of the Pink Tax movement, while others continue unabated, as in the ongoing inequities in terms of tax cooperation among nations.

Critical tax law scholarship in Canada is key to making tax policy choices personal to experts and non-experts alike. It reveals the

---

[39] Irene Burges & Irma Mosquera, "Corporate Taxation and BEPS: A Fair Slice for Developing Countries?" (2017) 10:1 Erasmus L Rev 29; Allison Christians & Laurens van Apeldoorn, "Taxing Income Where Value is Created" (2018) 22:1 Fla Tax Rev 1; Allison Christians & Tarcísio Diniz Magalhães, "A New Global Deal for the Digital Age" (2019) 67:4 Can Tax J 1154; Ivan Ozai, "Two Accounts of International Tax Justice" (2020) 33:2 Can JL & Jur 317; Okanga Ogbu Okanga & Lyla Latif, "Effective Taxation in Africa: Systemic Vulnerability through Inclusive Tax Governance" (2021) 2 AfJIEL 100; Tarcísio Diniz Magalhães & Ivan Ozai, "A Different Unified Approach to Global Tax Policy: Addressing the Challenges of Underdevelopment" (2021) 4:1 Nordic J L & Soc 1; Martin Hearson, Rasmus Christensen & Tovony Randriamanalina, "Developing Influence: The Power of 'the Rest' in Global Tax Governance" (2022) 30:3 Rev Int'l Pol Econ 841.

subjective decision-making that has become embedded in traditional norms and assumptions and demonstrates the case for reform. Critical tax studies show that even obscure tax rules and complex tax regimes should not be shaped solely through discussion among experts but deserve broad-based, inclusive policy attention.

Biographies

Editors

Jena McGill is Associate Professor at the University of Ottawa, Faculty of Law. She holds a JD from the University of Ottawa, Faculty of Law and graduate degrees from the Norman Paterson School of International Affairs at Carleton University and Yale Law School. Prior to joining the University of Ottawa, Jena served as law clerk to Justice Louise Charron at the Supreme Court of Canada and worked at the United Nations International Law Commission in Geneva, Switzerland. McGill researches in the areas of Canadian constitutional law; gender and sexuality; women, peace and security in international law; intersectional feminist legal theory; and legal technology as a vehicle to promote access to justice. Her work on section 15 of the *Canadian Charter of Rights and Freedoms* has been cited by the Supreme Court of Canada and in 2021 she was co-recipient of the Martin Felsky Award for Excellence in Canadian Open Legal Commentary for her article (co-authored with Amy Salyzyn), "Judging by Numbers: How will judicial analytics impact the justice system and its stakeholders?" McGill is a three-time recipient of the University of Ottawa Common Law Student Society's Teaching Award.

Karen Drake is a member of the Wabigoon Lake Ojibway Nation and an Associate Professor at Osgoode Hall Law School at York University. She researches and teaches in the areas of Canadian law as it affects Indigenous peoples, Anishinaabe constitutionalism, Indigenous pedagogy within legal education, property law, and dispute resolution including civil procedure and Indigenous dispute resolution. She works with Anishinaabe nations to renew Anishinaabe laws in a way that is grounded in Anishinaabe lifeways and effective today. Before joining Osgoode, Drake completed a clerkship with the Ontario Court of Appeal and served as a part-time judicial law clerk with the Federal Court. She is a member of the legal advisory panel for RAVEN and previously served as a commissioner of the Ontario Human Rights Commission, on the Board of Directors of the Indigenous Bar Association, and on the Board of Directors of the Human Rights Legal Support Centre.

Kyle Kirkup is Associate Professor at the University of Ottawa Faculty of Law (Common Law Section). He has written widely on topics including the criminalization of HIV non-disclosure, human rights law, queer legal theory, and the legal regulation of sex work. After serving as a law clerk to the Honourable Madam Justice Louise Charron at the Supreme Court of Canada, Kirkup completed graduate studies at Yale Law School and the University of Toronto, where he studied as a Trudeau Foundation Scholar. His recent work has appeared in journals including the *University of Toronto Law Journal*, the *Canadian Journal of Law and Society*, and the *Dalhousie Law Journal*. Kirkup has appeared before the House of Commons Standing Committee on Justice and Human Rights as an expert witness on the criminalization of HIV non-disclosure and sex work. He has also appeared before the Standing Senate Committee on Human Rights as an expert witness on human rights in Canada's federal prisons.

Anne Levesque est professeure agrégée au Programme de common law français de l'Université d'Ottawa où elle a obtenu son diplôme en droit en 2007. Elle obtient une maîtrise en droit international de la personne de l'Université d'Oxford en 2016 où elle étudie grâce au généreux soutien de la Fondation Alma & Baxter Ricard. Sa recherche et ses publications portent sur les droits de la personne et les litiges d'intérêt public. Anne est admise au Barreau de l'Ontario en 2008 et fait valoir les droits de ses clients devant plusieurs tribunaux administratifs, des tribunaux de toutes les instances du Canada, dont la Cour suprême du Canada, et des organes conventionnels internationaux et régionaux en droits de la personne. Elle est une des avocates qui représente bénévolement la Société de soutien à l'enfance et à la famille des Premières Nations du Canada dans sa plainte de droits de la personne menant à une victoire historique en 2016 qui affirme le droit à l'égalité de plus de 165 000 enfants autochtones. Elle est titulaire de la Chaire Gordon F. Henderson sur les droits de la personne du Centre de recherche et d'enseignement sur les droits de la personne (CREDP) à l'Université d'Ottawa.

Joshua Sealy-Harrington is a passionate teacher, scholar, and advocate. As Associate Professor and Chair of Equality Law at the University of Windsor, Faculty of Law, Sealy-Harrington teaches constitutional law, equality rights, and critical legal theory. Before Windsor Law, he was an Assistant Professor at the Lincoln Alexander School of Law where he was voted "Professor of the Year" by the student body and awarded "Person of the Year" by the faculty association for his steadfast defence of Black, Palestinian, and academic freedom. As a doctoral candidate at Columbia Law School, Sealy-Harrington drew on critical race theory to explore the ways in which law mediates social hierarchy, with a particular focus on the promise and limitations of "identity" rhetoric in legal discourse and advocacy concerning Black and Palestinian solidarity/resistance. As counsel at Power Law, Sealy-Harrington uses criminal and constitutional law to advance the interests of marginalized communities. Most of his practice involves pro and low bono work promoting human rights and social justice, both in Canada and abroad. He has litigation experience before all levels of court, including as lead counsel before the Supreme Court of Canada, where he previously clerked for two years.

Contributors

Y. Y. Brandon Chen is Associate Professor at the University of Ottawa's Faculty of Law, Common Law Section. He holds Doctor of Juridical Science, Master of Social Work, and Juris Doctor degrees from the University of Toronto. A licensed lawyer in Ontario, he specializes in constitutional law, health law, and immigration and refugee law. His current research leverages socio-legal and action research methodologies to identify and examine injustices at the intersection of international migration and health. His published work has touched on such topics as migrants' health and rights, social determinants of health, border control of infectious diseases, and medical tourism. He was co-counsel for the Charter Committee on Poverty Issues, the Canadian Health Coalition, the FCJ Refugee Centre, and the Madhu Verma Migrant Justice Centre in their joint intervention in *Toussaint v Canada (Attorney General).*

Allison Christians is the H. Heward Stikeman Chair in the Law of Taxation at McGill University Faculty of Law where she teaches and writes on national, comparative, and international tax law and policy. She focuses especially on the relationship between taxation and economic development, the role of government and non-government institutions and actors in the creation of tax policy norms, and the intersection of taxation and human rights. She has written numerous scholarly articles, essays, and book chapters, as well as essays, columns, and articles in professional journals and has been named one of the "Global Tax 50" most influential individuals in international taxation. Recent research focuses on evolving international norms of tax cooperation and competition; the relationship between tax and sustainable development; the impact of technology on tax policy, and evolving conceptions of rights in taxation. She also engages on topics of tax law and policy via her website www.allisonchristians.com, and on Instagram as @profchristians.

Gordon Christie is Professor at the Peter A. Allard School of Law at the University of British Columbia. His research work has been nearly entirely directed toward Canadian Aboriginal law, and ways the contemporary legal scholar can theorize this law and its imposition on Indigenous peoples of Canada. He is Inuvialuit.

Lorena Sekwan Fontaine (BA, LLB, LLM, PhD) is Cree and Anishnaabe, and a member of the Sagkeeng First Nation in Manitoba. She is the Department Head of Indigenous Studies at the University of Manitoba and the author of *Creating Constitutional Space for First Nations' Language Rights in Education*. She has published extensively on Indigenous language rights, the legacy of residential schools, and cultural genocide. Her work on the legacy of residential schools was featured in the CBC documentary Undoing Linguicide. She also served as an expert witness to Canada's Standing Senate Committee on Aboriginal Peoples, providing insights on the *Indigenous Languages Act*. Fontaine co-organized an educational forum with the United States Holocaust Memorial Museum in Washington, DC. More recently, she co-organized "Mass Violence and Its Lasting Impact on Indigenous Peoples" at the University of Southern California, in partnership with the USC Center for Advanced Genocide Research. She has served on various national committees, including as an Equality Rights Panel member for the Court Challenges Program of Canada, a

National Steering Committee Member for the National Association of Women and the Law, and a board member for the Women's Legal Education and Action Fund. Fontaine received a Canada Fulbright Research Chair at San Diego State University, where she explored Indigenous cultural memory and language repatriation. She is also a recipient of the Queen Elizabeth II's Platinum Jubilee Medal for her community service.

Véronique Fortin est professeure et vice-doyenne à l'apprentissage expérientiel et aux relations avec la collectivité à la Faculté de droit de l'Université de Sherbrooke. Elle détient un doctorat en Criminologie, Droit et Société de University of California, Irvine. Elle s'intéresse aux différents modes de contrôle des populations marginalisées et ses recherches portent notamment sur la judiciarisation de l'itinérance, le contrôle de l'espace public, le concept de décriminalisation et les mesures punitives à l'aide sociale. Elle privilégie une approche empirique, le plus souvent ethnographique, pour ses recherches.

Ashleigh Keall is Assistant Professor at the University of Sussex, UK, where she teaches land law, public law, Canadian constitutional law, and Aboriginal law. Her research focuses on religious freedom and its intersections with theories of harm, equality, feminist legal theory, and constitutionalism. Before joining the University of Sussex, Keall completed a PhD in Law at University College London (UCL) in 2020 with a dissertation on conceptions of harm in the Canadian constitutional adjudication of religious freedom. She was supported in her postdoctoral research by a Modern Law Review Early Career Fellowship and in her PhD by a Canadian Social Sciences and Humanities Research Council Doctoral Fellowship, a Modern Law Review Scholarship, and a UCL Faculty of Laws Research Scholarship. Throughout her doctoral studies Keall as taught courses in Land Law and Equity & Trusts at UCL and Property Law at the London School of Economics, and co-founded and ran the UCL Laws Feminist Book Club. Prior to joining academia, she worked as a research assistant in the Public Law team at the Law Commission of England and Wales and served as judicial law clerk to Justice Louis LeBel at the Supreme Court of Canada. Keall holds an LLB from the University of British Columbia and a BA in Psychology and English Literature from the University of Ottawa. She is a non-practising member of the Law Society of Ontario and lives in London, UK, with her partner and kids, where she enjoys singing in a community choir.

Lisa M. Kelly is Associate Professor at Queen's University, Faculty of Law where she teaches criminal law, criminal procedure, evidence, and sexual and reproductive justice. Before joining Queen's Law, Kelly completed a postdoctoral fellowship at Columbia Law School and the Center for Reproductive Rights in New York City. She previously clerked at the Supreme Court of Canada for Justice Marshall E. Rothstein. Kelly holds law degrees from the University of Toronto and Harvard Law School. Kelly has published in the areas of family law, legal theory, sexual and reproductive health law, and youth criminal justice. She is the co-author, with Sanjeev Anand and Nicholas Bala, of the *Youth Criminal Justice Law*. In 2018, she received the Stanley M. Corbett Award for Teaching Excellence at Queen's Law.

Lisa Kerr, JD (UBC), LLM, JSD (New York University) is Associate Professor at Queen's University, where she is the Director of the Criminal Law Group and teaches courses on criminal law, evidence, sentencing and prison law. She clerked at the British Columbia Court of Appeal and was previously staff lawyer at Prisoners' Legal Services. She has worked on public interest litigation with Pivot Legal Society and served on the board of the British Columbia Civil Liberties Association. She supports the strategic litigation work of the Queen's Prison Law Clinic.

The Honourable Harry S. LaForme is an Anishinabe of the Mississaugas of the Credit First Nation, Ontario. He was born and raised on his reserve where some of his family continues to reside and remains active in First Nation's leadership. He graduated from Osgoode Hall Law School in 1977 and was called to the Ontario Bar in 1979. He articled with Osler, Hoskin and Harcourt; joined the law firm as an associate, and shortly thereafter commenced private practice in Indigenous law focused on Constitutional and *Charter* issues. He has appeared before each level of Canadian court, travelled extensively throughout Canada, and represented Canadian Indigenous interests in Geneva, in Switzerland, New Zealand and the British Parliament. He served as: Co-chair, Independent National Chiefs Task Force on Native Land Claims; Chief Commissioner, Indian Commission of Ontario; Chair, Royal Commission on Aboriginal Land Claims; and taught, and taught Rights of Indigenous Peoples at Osgoode Hall Law School. In January 1994 he was appointed a judge of the Superior Court of Justice, Ontario – then, one of three Indigenous judges ever appointed to this level of trial court in Canada. In November 2004, he was appointed a judge of the Ontario Court of Appeal. He is the first Indigenous judge appointed to an appellate court in Canada's history. He retired from the judiciary in October 2018. In December 2018 he commenced a position as Senior Counsel with Olthuis Kleer Townshend, LLP. LaForme has been honoured with the National Aboriginal Achievement Award in Law & Justice; a Talking stick carved by Git'san artist Chuck (Ya'Ya) Heit; a bursary in his name for Indigenous first-year law students at the University of Windsor Faculty of Law; and honorary Doctor of Law degrees from York University; University of Windsor, University of Toronto; the Law Society of Upper Canada; and an honorary Doctorate of Education, Nipissing University. LaForme is an Officer of the Order of Canada. LaForme has published numerous articles on issues related to Indigenous law and justice and human rights. He speaks frequently on Indigenous issues, Indigenous law, constitutional law, and civil, equality, and human rights.

Ravi Malhotra is Full Professor at the Faculty of Law, Common Law Section at the University of Ottawa and served as Vice-Dean of Graduate Studies. A graduate of Harvard Law School, he has worked on disability rights for many years. He is the author or editor of three books with Benjamin Isitt on disability history: *Able to Lead*, *Class Warrior* and *Disabling Barriers*. He also edited an anthology devoted to the legacy of a disability rights advocate, Marta Russell. For many years, he was a member of the Human Rights Committee of the Council of Canadians with Disabilities.

Meenakshi Mannoe (she/her/hers) is an abolitionist organizer living on the unceded territories of the xʷməθkʷəy̓əm, səlilwətał and S̱ḵwx̱wú7mesh Nations (aka Vancouver BC). She belongs to several local groups that resist the carceral colonial structures that constitute so-called Canada.

Mona Paré est professeure titulaire à la Faculté de droit, Section de droit civil, à l'Université d'Ottawa. Elle dirige le Laboratoire de recherche interdisciplinaire sur les droits de l'enfant (LRIDE) dont elle est co-fondatrice. Ses recherches et son enseignement se concentrent sur les droits de l'enfant et le droit international des droits de la personne. Elle s'intéresse particulièrement à la participation des enfants et les approches basées sur les droits de l'enfant dans différents domaines, incluant la justice et l'éducation. Elle dirige présentement un projet de recherche sur les enfants défenseurs des droits qui concerne l'accès des enfants à la justice.

Dayna Nadine Scott is a Professor at Osgoode Hall Law School and the Faculty of Environmental and Urban Change at York University. She held a York University Research Chair in Environmental Law and Justice in the Green Economy from 2018-2023. She is currently co-Principal Investigator with Heidi Kiiwetinepinesiik Stark of a SSHRC-funded Partnership Grant titled, *Infrastructure Beyond Extractivism.*

Samuel Singer is an Associate Professor at the Faculty of Law at the University of Ottawa. His research interests in tax law focus on tax administration and dispute resolution, the regulation of non-profits and charities, and critical tax theory. Recent articles focused on topics including non-profit and charity law reform, tax remission orders, evidentiary privilege for tax professionals, a critical analysis of directors' liability cases in tax law, and the tax treatment of trans medical expenses. He articled with the National Judicial Institute, clerked at the Tax Court of Canada, and practised as a tax lawyer with Stikeman Elliott LLP in Montreal. He went on to establish his own law practice, working in tax law, charity and non-profit law, and trans law. He is a member of both the Québec and Ontario Bars. Singer is also a scholar and advocate on trans legal issues. His article, "Trans Rights Are Not Just Human Rights: Legal Strategies for Trans Justice," was awarded the Canadian Law and Society Association English Article Prize in 2021 and cited by the Supreme Court of Canada in *Hansman v Neufeld*, 2023 SCC 14. Other contributions include a chapter on trans competent lawyering, reports on the history of trans rights in Canada, and an article on preventing misgendering in Canadian courts. He worked at a trans-advocacy group before law school, and later served as the supervisor of a trans-legal clinic in Montreal. In 2022, Singer received the Canadian Bar Association's Sexual Orientation and Gender Identity (SOGIC) Hero Award.

Kerry Sloan is a citizen and long-time board (governing council) member of the Metis Nation of Greater Victoria. She has family ties to Red River and Saskatchewan Metis communities, and to Metis people living in Syilx and Secwepemc territories in the southern BC interior. Sloan is an Assistant Professor and past Junior Boulton Fellow at

McGill University's Faculty of Law. She was a SSHRC postdoctoral fellow at the University of Saskatchewan College of Law, where she worked on a project on Metis spiritualities and law. She completed her PhD in Law and Society at the University of Victoria, and her undergraduate law degree at the University of Calgary. After graduating from law school, Sloan practised Aboriginal law and general litigation in Alberta. Her current research focuses on Metis law and legal issues, including Metis critical legal theory, Metis legal history, and Metis law and the arts.

João Velloso is Associate Professor in the French Common Law Program and the Civil Law Section of the Faculty of Law at the University of Ottawa, where he is currently serving as Vice-Dean of Graduate Studies. He works in the areas of criminal law and sentencing, immigration law, criminology, and socio-legal studies with a focus on the judicialization of social problems and the governance of security through the intersections between criminal law and administrative law. His research deals with the penalization of protesters and migrants, access to justice in detention, and the regulation of cannabis. Velloso coordinates the Working Group Judicialization of Social Problems of the International Sociological Association's Research Committee on Sociology of Law, and participates in various research networks, such as: Access to Law and Access to Justice, Observatory on Profiling, Prison Transparency Project, Canadian Partnership for International Justice, Observatory on Violence, Criminalization & Democracy in Latin America, Ottawa Hub for Harm Reduction Network, and Coalition for Academic Freedom in the Americas.

Reakash Walters is a lawyer and doctoral student at Berkeley School of Law. She is also a Research Fellow at Harvard Law School's Institute to End Mass Incarceration. Her research focuses on institutional design, alternative legal frameworks, and the criminalization of Black friendship and kinship. Her doctoral research is supported by funding from the Social Sciences and Humanities Research Council and a full Robbins JSD Fellowship. Walters completed her Master of Laws at Columbia University as a Fulbright Scholar and Davis Polk Fellow with High Honors and completed her JD *cum laude* at the University of Ottawa. She also served as law clerk to Justice Sheilah Martin at the Supreme Court of Canada. Before graduate school, she practised as a criminal defence lawyer at a prestigious criminal law firm in Toronto, Ontario. She has appeared before all levels of court, including before the Supreme Court of Canada in *R v Beaver*, 2022 SCC 54. Walters serves on the board of the Women's Legal Education and Action Fund (LEAF) and the Canadian Law and Society Association (CLSA).

Vincent Wong is Assistant Professor at the University of Windsor Faculty of Law and PhD Candidate at Osgoode Hall Law School, where he researches racial capitalism and status-excluded communities in Canada. He currently serves on the board of the Community Justice Collective (Tkaranto). Prior to academia, he was a Staff Lawyer at the Chinese and Southeast Asian Legal Clinic and Research Associate at the International Human Rights Program and the African American Policy Forum.

www.ingramcontent.com/pod-product-compliance
Lightning Source LLC
Chambersburg PA
CBHW061232220326
41599CB00028B/5405